Date Due

| | | | |
|---|---|---|---|
| | | | |
| | | | |
| | | | |
| | | | |
| | | | |
| | | | |
| | | | |
| | | | |
| | | | |
| | | | |

# Storm Water
# Pollution Control

# Storm Water Pollution Control

## Industry and Construction NPDES Compliance

## Roy D. Dodson, P.E.

*Dodson & Associates, Inc.,*
*Houston, Texas*

McGraw-Hill, Inc.

New York   San Francisco   Washington, D.C.   Auckland   Bogotá
Caracas   Lisbon   London   Madrid   Mexico City   Milan
Montreal   New Delhi   San Juan   Singapore
Sydney   Tokyo   Toronto

**Library of Congress Cataloging-in-Publication Data**

Dodson, Roy D.
   Storm water pollution control : industry and construction NPDES
compliance / Roy D. Dodson.
     p.    cm.
   Includes bibliographical references and index.
   ISBN 0-07-017334-6
   1. Factory and trade waste—Management.   2. Runoff—Management.
   3. Water—Pollution—Law and legislation—United States.  I. Title.
   TD897.5.D64   1995
   363.73'946'0973—dc20                          94-41861
                                                     CIP

1 2 3 4 5 6 7 8 9 0   DOC/DOC   9 0 0 9 8 7 6 5

ISBN 0-07-017334-6

*The sponsoring editor for this book was Larry Hager, the editing
supervisor was Joseph Bertuna, and the production supervisor was
Suzanne W. Babeuf. It was set in Century Schoolbook by McGraw-Hill's
Professional Book Group composition unit.*

*Printed and bound by R. R. Donnelley & Sons Company.*

This book is printed on acid-free paper.

*I am pleased to dedicate this book to my family:
to my wife, Pam; my children, Bradley and Alana;
and my mother, Vivian E. Dodson. God has blessed me
greatly through each of them.*

# Contents

# Illustrations and Tables

# Preface

This book will help you understand and comply with the Environmental Protection Agency (EPA) and state requirements for National Pollutant Discharge Elimination System (NPDES) storm water discharge permits.

Beginning in October 1992, most industrial facilities and construction projects in the United States have been required to obtain permits to discharge storm water according to the provisions of NPDES. This requirement affects hundreds of thousands of industrial sites and construction projects.

There has been tremendous confusion about the requirements of the NPDES program for storm water permits. Construction contractors, engineers, project owners, and industry representatives have all desperately attempted to obtain reliable information on how to comply with NPDES permit requirements and avoid penalties of up to $25,000 per day. This book provides that information.

**Why I wrote this book**

I began to write this book because of my company's work on a large number of permit applications and storm water pollution prevention plans (SWPPPs) for industrial and construction clients. The American Society of Civil Engineers (ASCE) also asked me to present a series of continuing education seminars on NPDES storm water permit compliance. As I presented these seminars across the United States, I gathered additional materials for this book.

Incidentally, you will notice that I use the term *storm water* rather than *stormwater* in this book. The EPA uses *storm water* in accordance with the conventions adopted by the U.S. Government Printing Office. Because of the extensive quotations from EPA documents in this book, it seems appropriate to maintain terminology which is consistent with the EPA.

## How to use this book

Everyone who reads this book should read the first three chapters, which provide the background of the NPDES storm water program. In order for you to do the best job in complying with a federal government program, it is important to understand the legal and regulatory background of the program.

Chapters 4 through 8 deal with industrial storm water discharges. If you are interested only in construction activities, you may skip these chapters.

Chapters 9 through 13 deal with construction storm water discharges. If you are interested only in other industrial activities, you may skip these chapters. However, note that obtaining an industrial storm water discharge permit does not allow you to discharge storm water from construction activities at the industrial facility. You may be required to obtain a separate construction storm water discharge permit. Therefore, these chapters may be important to you at some point in the future.

The majority of this book deals with the EPA requirements under the NPDES program. However, in most states, NPDES permits are actually administered by state agencies. Requirements vary somewhat from one state to another. Therefore, Chap. 14 discusses the individual requirements for each state and highlights those areas in which state requirements differ from EPA requirements. Refer to Chap. 14 for specific information for the state(s) where you work.

Four appendixes are included with this book. Appendixes A and B contain the full text of the EPA general permits for industrial storm water discharges and for construction storm water discharges. The last two contain examples of storm water pollution prevention plans for industrial and construction sites.

## Acknowledgments

Many people have contributed to the development and completion of this book, including our supportive group of clients, representatives of the EPA and state agencies, and those who participated in our ASCE-sponsored continuing education seminars. I want to particularly acknowledge the efforts of Kevin Weiss of the EPA Permits Division in Washington, who reviewed a portion of the book in draft form. Mostly, I want to acknowledge my coworkers at Dodson & Associates, Inc., who helped check facts, tracked down information, prepared exhibits and other materials, and generally "covered for me" while I took the time to write this book. However, I wish to emphasize that any errors or omissions in this book are entirely my responsibility.

*Roy D. Dodson*

# Storm Water
# Pollution Control

Chapter

# 1

# EPA Storm Water Regulations

The Environmental Protection Agency (EPA) regulations on storm water discharges affect thousands of industrial facilities and municipalities in the United States. In complying with these rules, industrial plant managers, industry executives, municipal employees, engineering consultants, and construction contractors may be exposed to EPA water quality requirements for the first time. Often, they do not have a strong background in the legal or regulatory issues related to water pollution control in the United States. Acronyms such as CWA, RCRA, CERCLA, SARA, and CFR may be meaningless and confusing to these readers.

This chapter will provide a brief background in the environmental laws and regulations of the United States which pertain to water pollution, particularly storm water discharges. This should make it much easier to understand and apply the more technical information presented in the remainder of the book.

This is the first of three consecutive chapters which provide basic information intended to be of interest to all readers. Chapters 4 through 8 provide information specific to those interested in industrial discharges. Chapters 9 through 13 provide information related to construction storm water discharges only. Chapter 14 provides additional information on specific state requirements.

## Legal Basis for the National Storm Water Program

The Environmental Protection Agency developed the *National Storm Water Program* (NSWP) in response to legislation passed by Congress.

The most important item of legislation was the *Federal Clean Water Act of 1972* (Public Law 92-500), which established the *National Pollutant Discharge Elimination System* (NPDES). The Clean Water Act (CWA) has been amended several times. One important set of amendments was the *Water Quality Act of 1987* (Public Law 100-4) that established a phased approach for storm water discharge regulation in the United States. Section 1068 of the *Intermodal Surface Transportation Efficiency Act of 1991* (Public Law 102-240) clarified the application of the NSWP to small municipal entities.

## Other Related Environmental Legislation

The NSWP also includes references to several other important items of environmental legislation, most of which have to do with hazardous wastes or toxic materials. These include the following:

- *RCRA,* the Resource Conservation and Recovery Act of 1976 (Public Law 94-580), requires a regulatory system for the generation, treatment, storage, and disposal of hazardous wastes.

- *CERCLA,* the Comprehensive Environmental Response, Compensation, and Liability Act of 1980 (Public Law 96-510), establishes a program to mitigate releases of hazardous waste from inactive hazardous waste sites that endanger public health and the environment.

- *SARA,* the Superfund Amendments and Reauthorization Act of 1986 (Public Law 99-499), amended CERCLA.

- *EPCRA,* the Emergency Planning and Community Right-to-Know Act of 1986, is another name for Title III of SARA. Title III was created as a freestanding law establishing requirements for federal, state, and local governments and industry regarding emergency planning and reporting on hazardous and toxic chemicals. Storm water discharge permits issued under the National Storm Water Program generally have special requirements for chemicals covered by Title III of SARA.

- *SMCRA,* the Surface Mining Control and Reclamation Act of 1977.

## Importance of the Clean Water Act

The Clean Water Act (CWA) has set the direction of water pollution control in the United States since 1972. It is based on the following principles [Kovalic, 1987].

1. *Waters of the United States:*   No one has a right to pollute the navigable waters of the United States.[1] Anyone wishing to discharge pollutants must obtain a permit to do so.

2. *Discharge permits:*   Permits shall limit the composition of a discharge and the concentrations of the pollutants in it. Anyone violating the conditions of a permit is subject to fines and imprisonment.

3. *Technology-based controls:*   Some permit conditions require specified levels of control based on a consideration of technology and cost, regardless of the receiving water's ability to purify itself naturally. In other words, some levels of control are always presumed to be worth their cost.

4. *Water-quality-based controls:*   Any limits or control higher than the minimum federal requirements must be based on the receiving water quality. The only way to impose higher standards than those required under the CWA is to demonstrate that continued protection of the receiving water demands such limits.

Title IV of the CWA gives the EPA the authority and responsibility to issue discharge permits to every point source (discussed in Chap. 3) discharger in the country. Section 402 of the CWA describes the permit system. As of about 1991, the EPA and authorized NPDES states had issued almost 50,000 NPDES permits for industrial process discharges and 16,000 NPDES permits for *publicly owned treatment works* (POTWs). As impressive as these numbers are, they are insignificant in comparison to the hundreds of thousands of facilities that discharge storm water.

Technology-based requirements represent the minimum level of control that must be imposed by an NPDES permit. Two technology-based requirements are appropriate for existing storm water discharges associated with industrial activity:

1. *Best conventional* (pollutant control) *technology* (BCT)

2. *Best available technology* (BAT) economically achievable

The BCT standard applies to the control of conventional pollutants, while the BAT standard applies to the control of all toxic pollutants and all pollutants which are neither toxic nor conventional pollutants. Both requirements are consistent with the third principle of the CWA listed above.

---

[1]The term *waters of the United States* has a very broad definition, as explained in Chap. 3.

In addition to technology-based controls, NPDES permits must include any conditions more stringent than technology-based controls necessary to meet state water quality standards. Water-quality-based requirements are established under this provision on a case-by-case basis. State water quality standards represent the mechanism by which the fourth principle of the Clean Water Act (discussed earlier) is enacted.

The Clean Water Act also contains many other provisions that are beyond the scope of this book, including a huge grant/loan program for the construction of municipal sewage treatment works. Section 404 of the CWA restricts the discharge of fill material into waters of the United States, including wetlands.

### Storm water discharge controls under the Clean Water Act

The Clean Water Act originally required control of all storm water discharges. However, the appropriate means of regulating storm water point sources within the National Pollutant Discharge Elimination System (NPDES) program has been a matter of serious concern since implementation of the NPDES program in 1972.

In 1973, the EPA issued its first storm water regulations. In making these regulations, the EPA admitted that storm water discharges fell within the definition of a point source. However, the EPA believed that pollution from storm water discharges was not easily controlled by the traditional, end-of-pipe controls that are the basis of the NPDES program for process discharges and discharges from publicly owned treatment works. The EPA was also intimidated by the task of issuing individual NPDES permits for the hundreds of thousands of storm water point sources in the United States. Therefore, the first storm water regulations required permits only for particular storm water discharges identified as significant contributors of pollution [38 FR 13530 (May 22, 1973)].

The Natural Resources Defense Council (NRDC) brought suit in the U.S. district court for the District of Columbia, challenging the EPA's authority to selectively exempt categories of point sources from permit requirements [*NRDC v. Train,* 396 F. Supp. 1393 (D.D.C. 1975), *aff'd. NRDC v. Costle,* 568 F. 2d 1369 (D.C. Cir. 1977)]. In response to the NRDC suits, a U.S. district court ruled in 1975 that every municipal storm water outfall (a pipe or other conduit that empties into surface waters) must have a permit [*NRDC v. EPA,* 396 F. Supp. 1386, 7 ER Cases 1881 (D.D.C. 1975)]. The district court also ruled that the EPA could not exempt discharges identified as point sources from regulation under the NPDES permit program.

The district court also ruled that a more complete permit program than the one proposed by the EPA could still be manageable. The court recognized two alternatives for reducing the permit workload:

1. Discretion to define what constitutes a point source
2. Discretion to use certain administrative devices, such as general permits, to help manage the workload. The court recognized that the EPA has wide latitude to rank categories and subcategories of point sources of different importance and treat them differently within a permit program, so long as they were all subject to basic permit requirements.

After the district court decision was appealed, the court of appeals recognized that section 402 provides the agency with flexibility in determining the appropriate scope and form of an NPDES permit. For example, permits may regulate industry practices to lessen point source pollution problems. As a result, the court suggested using area or general permits. In certain cases, it may be appropriate for the EPA to require a permittee simply to monitor and report effluent levels [568 F. 2d 1369, 1679 (1977)].

In 1984, the EPA again published permit application requirements and deadlines for storm water discharges. However, these regulations were never implemented. The regulations were in litigation when Congress enacted the Water Quality Act (WQA) on February 4, 1987, which directly specified a new national strategy for storm water control.

Despite the lack of a comprehensive permitting program for all storm water discharges prior to the passage of the WQA of 1987, permitting efforts nonetheless proceeded in some areas. Between 1974 and 1982, the EPA promulgated effluent limitations guidelines for storm water discharges from nine categories of industrial discharges:

1. Cement manufacturing (40 CFR part 411)
2. Feedlots (40 CFR part 412)
3. Fertilizer manufacturing (40 CFR part 418)
4. Petroleum refining (40 CFR part 419)
5. Phosphate manufacturing (40 CFR part 422)
6. Steam electric power generation (40 CFR part 423)
7. Coal mining (40 CFR part 434)
8. Ore mining and dressing (40 CFR part 440)
9. Asphalt emulsion (40 CFR part 441)

Before 1987, permitting efforts for storm water discharges focused on industrial facilities subject to these effluent limitations guidelines. In addition, some EPA regions and states with authorized state NPDES programs wrote permits for storm water discharges from other industrial facilities. For example, in some states and regions, storm water discharges from industrial facilities are often addressed when NPDES permits for process wastewaters of a facility are reissued.

## Water Quality Act of 1987

Congress periodically "reauthorizes" the Clean Water Act. These reauthorizations are generally accompanied by various amendments. In 1987, Congress passed a set of amendments to the Clean Water Act. The 1987 amendments to the CWA are commonly called the *Water Quality Act of 1987*. There are several provisions to this act, including one that established the National Storm Water Program. A two-phase storm water program was established, incorporating a prioritized approach to storm water.

### Phase I of the National Storm Water Program

Phase I of the NSWP provides for regulation of the following categories of storm water discharges:

1. *Discharges permitted before February 4, 1987:*  As noted previously, nine categories of industrial facilities already had NPDES permits for storm water. Congress made sure that these storm water discharges would continue to require permit coverage.

2. *Discharges associated with industrial activity (including construction activity):*  This category includes hundreds of thousands of facilities located in every state and territory. This book deals primarily with the permit requirements for this group.

3. *Discharges from large municipal separate storm sewer systems (MS4s):* A municipal separate storm sewer system is designed to carry storm water discharges only (not combined with sanitary sewage). A municipal separate storm sewer system includes "municipal streets, catch basins, curbs, gutters, ditches, man-made channels, or storm drains that discharge into the waters of the United States" [55 FR 47989 (Nov. 16, 1990)]. An MS4 that serves an urban population of 250,000 or more is considered large.

4. *Discharges from medium MS4s:*  A medium[2] MS4 is one that serves an urban population of 100,000 to 250,000.

---

[2]Large and medium MS4s are listed separately because the Water Quality Act of 1987 specified different permit application and compliance dates for each.

5.  *Discharges which the director of the NPDES program designates as contributing to a violation of a water quality standard or as a significant contributor of pollutants to the waters of the United States:* This is a general category which was included so that the EPA or state director, after proper study and notification, could require permitting of discharges other than those listed above.

It is necessary to contact individual states or EPA regional representatives to obtain the current list of regulated municipalities.

## Phase II of the National Storm Water Program

The Water Quality Act of 1987 directed the EPA, in consultation with the states, to conduct two studies on storm water discharges not regulated under phase I. The first study is to determine, to the maximum extent practicable, the nature and extent of pollutants in such discharges. The second study is for the purpose of establishing procedures and methods to control storm water discharges as necessary to mitigate impacts on water quality. Based on the two studies, the EPA, in consultation with state and local officials, is required to issue regulations which designate additional storm water discharges to be regulated to protect water quality and to establish a comprehensive program to regulate such designated sources.

Phase II was originally scheduled to begin October 1, 1992. However, because of delays in implementing phase I and delays in completing the required studies for phase II, the EPA did not begin phase II on schedule.

Current information indicates that phase II of the NSWP is likely to be an extension of the phase I approach. The requirement for permitting discharges from MS4s is likely to be extended to small municipalities serving an urban population of 50,000 or more and urbanized areas with a population density of 1000 people per square mile. In addition, some commercial businesses that handle industrial-type materials are likely to be required to obtain permits. Gas stations are a prime example.

## NPDES Storm Water Regulations

When Congress passes a bill and it becomes law through Presidential signature or congressional override, it represents only the beginning of a long process which must take place before the program intended by Congress is fully implemented.

After an item of legislation becomes law, the Government Printing Office incorporates the new law into the *United States Code* (U.S.C.), which codifies (categorizes and compiles) all federal legislation. For example, the Clean Water Act and its amendments are codified beginning at 33 U.S.C. 1251. The printed text of the *United States Code* is updated periodically (about once every 6 to 8 years). Each July, a CD-ROM version of the *United States Code* is released by the Government Printing Office.

In connection with new legislation, Congress generally specifies which government agency or department will be responsible for developing and implementing regulations to carry out the legislation. The CWA requires the Environmental Protection Agency to develop and implement regulations under the NPDES program.

The process of developing proposed regulations involves several internal steps within the EPA and coordination with the Office of Management and Budget (OMB). These steps are intended to ensure that the full intent of the congressional legislation is carried out through the regulations and that the resulting rules are as clear and fair as possible, with a minimum adverse impact on the economy.

### The *Federal Register*

After the process of preliminary rule making is complete, the EPA publishes the proposed regulation in the *Federal Register,* which is printed every weekday by the Government Printing Office. It contains items published by federal government agencies, including proposed regulations, final regulations, and notices or announcements. The *Federal Register* is usually cited by using the volume number and page number. Each volume represents a separate year. For example, volume 55 represents calendar year 1990. Pages are numbered consecutively throughout the year. In this book, the date of the issue containing the citation is added for easier reference. For example, an item that begins on page 47989 of volume 55 of the *Federal Register* is cited as 55 FR 47989 (Nov. 16, 1990).

Proposed regulations generally have four parts:

1. *Preliminary material,* including the agency name, a summary of the rule, and information on submitting comments.

2. The *preamble,* which provides the background, authorization, and reasoning behind the proposed rule. It can be very useful to review the preamble thoroughly.

3. The *proposed regulation* itself.

4. *Appendixes,* such as application forms, figures, maps, and other supportive material.

A proposed regulation does not have any regulatory standing; it is intended to provide information and give the public an opportunity to comment. It is not binding. After comments have been received on the proposed regulation, the EPA may modify the proposed rule according to the comments.

The EPA also publishes final rules in the *Federal Register*. These have the force and effect of law. Final rules have the same four parts as proposed rules. However, the preamble of a final rule generally contains the EPA's response to comments received on the proposed rule. Instead of stating and responding to each comment individually, the EPA often groups the comments into categories and prints responses to the comments within each category.

In relation to final regulations, the EPA also issues permits for particular types of discharges. A permit which covers an entire class of discharges is called a *general permit*. The EPA publishes announcements of general permits in the *Federal Register,* in order to provide public notice of the general permit.

The EPA has published numerous proposed rules in connection with the NPDES storm water program. The EPA has also published announcements of some general permits in the *Federal Register*. These permits are applicable only in those states in which EPA is directly responsible for issuing permits. (The role of the states in NPDES storm water permitting is described later in this chapter.) However, they also serve as a model for general permits issued by the states.

The *Federal Register* is available by subscription from the Government Printing Office. In addition, it is available on-line through various computer research services.

### Code of Federal Regulations

Each July 1, all final rules enacted within the previous year are collected in the *Code of Federal Regulations* (CFR). The CFR is divided into "titles" according to subject matter. Most EPA regulations are codified in 40 CFR.

Each CFR title is divided into various sections. The baseline regulations relating to the NPDES program are printed in 40 CFR 122, and the specific requirements for storm water discharge permits are printed in 40 CFR 122.26. However, the EPA general permits themselves are not printed in the CFR.

Each volume of the *Code of Federal Regulations* is available for purchase directly from the Government Printing Office or from U.S. government book stores.

### Role of the court systems in environmental regulations

As indicated by the earlier discussion of district court and appeals court rulings related to storm water permitting, the process of environmental rule making is often strongly affected by litigation. Environmental and industry groups often file suit to challenge proposed or final EPA rules. For example, the Natural Resources Defense Council (NRDC), an environmental organization, filed suit soon after the EPA published the proposed rules for the National Storm Water Program in November 1990, challenging several aspects of the program as being inadequate. Another suit by the American Mining Congress, an industry organization, also challenged the regulations, but for different reasons.

At times, these suits end in settlements which result in revisions to proposed or final EPA rules. Other cases result in court judgments which may uphold the EPA regulations or which may conclude that the EPA regulations must be revised to better reflect the intent of the original legislation.

### Role of the states in NPDES permitting

The Clean Water Act allows states to request EPA authorization to administer the NPDES program within their borders. The EPA must approve a state's request to operate the permit program once the EPA determines that the state has adequate legal authorities, procedures, and the ability to administer the program. The EPA is also obligated to adopt standard requirements for state NPDES programs, including guidelines on monitoring, reporting, enforcement, personnel, and funding, and to develop uniform national forms for use by both the EPA and approved states. At all times following authorization, state NPDES programs must be consistent with minimum federal requirements, although the programs may always be more stringent.

The 1987 Water Quality Act encouraged state control of NPDES permitting even more by allowing a state to assume the responsibility of only a portion of the NPDES program. At present, 39 states have chosen to assume storm water permitting authority. These are called *authorized states*. Within these states, all permit submittals are made to the state agency which administers and enforces the storm water program within the state. Additional nonauthorized states may gain permitting authority.

In nonauthorized states, the appropriate EPA regional office is responsible for permitting and permit enforcement. Currently 17 states and territories do not have NPDES permit authority: Alaska, American Samoa, Arizona, District of Columbia, Florida, Guam, Idaho, Louisiana, Maine, New Hampshire, New Mexico, Oklahoma, Puerto

Rico, South Dakota, Texas, and the Trust Territories of the Northern Mariana Islands.

The EPA requests that authorized states prepare and periodically update state storm water permitting plans. For nonauthorized states, the EPA prepares the state storm water permitting plans. The plans include the following sections:

1. *Municipal separate storm sewer systems:*   A list of municipal separate storm sewer systems serving a population of 100,000 or more within the state, a summary of the estimated pollutant loadings for each system, the status of the permits, and an outline of the major components of municipal storm water management programs, including any innovative approaches.

2. *Discharges associated with industrial activity:*   The status of the baseline general permits, a list of categories of industrial facilities being considered for industry-specific permits, a description of the procedures used to identify discharges appropriate for individual permits, and a description of how municipal system permits control pollutants in storm water discharges associated with industrial activity.

3. *Water quality standards:*   A list of receiving waters where regulated storm water discharges contribute to a violation of a water quality standard, a description of the procedures used to identify these waters, and a plan to evaluate improvements to water quality resulting from controlling storm water discharges.

4. *Unregulated storm water discharges:*   A list of receiving waters where unregulated storm water discharges contribute to a violation of a water quality standard or significantly contribute pollutants to the waters of the United States and a description of the procedures used to identify these waters. These unregulated discharges may be considered for designation under section 402(p)(2)(E) of the CWA as needing a permit.

## References

Government Printing Office: *Federal Register,* Office of the Federal Register, National Archives and Records Administration, Washington.
———: *United States Code,* Washington, 1988.
———: *Code of Federal Regulations,* Office of the Federal Register, National Archives and Records Administration, Washington, July 1, 1992.
Kovalic, Joan M.: *The Clean Water Act of 1987,* Water Environment Federation (formerly Water Pollution Control Federation), Alexandria, VA, 1987.

# 2

# Enforcement and Compliance with Storm Water Regulations

As stated in Chap. 1, the National Pollutant Discharge Elimination System (NPDES) permit requirement for storm water discharges is required by the Clean Water Act of 1972, as amended by the Water Quality Act of 1987. The Clean Water Act provides severe penalties for those who fail to obtain permit coverage for discharges and for those who do not comply with the terms and conditions of an NPDES permit. This chapter gives some practical advice on dealing with EPA enforcement actions.

This is the second of three consecutive chapters providing basic information for all dischargers.

## Agency Enforcement of the Clean Water Act

Section 309 of the Clean Water Act gives to the EPA or states broad enforcement authority. In an authorized state (one with NPDES permitting authority), the EPA notifies the state whenever a violation comes to its attention. In authorized states, the state government has the same enforcement authority as the EPA has in nonauthorized states. If the state fails to take appropriate action within 30 days, the EPA is empowered to commence enforcement action itself [Stimson et al., 1993]. In nonauthorized states, the EPA regional offices are the primary enforcement agencies.

Violations may include actions that are inconsistent with provisions of the law itself or actions that are inconsistent with conditions of permits issued by the EPA or states under the act. Violations may include discharges to U.S. waters and discharges to sewer systems. Violations of record keeping, reporting, and inspection requirements are included.

The Clean Water Act gives to the EPA three broad categories of enforcement authority:

1. *Administrative* authority to issue compliance orders and levy civil penalties for alleged violators of any of the law or permit requirements.

2. *Civil* authority, to cooperate with the U.S. Department of Justice to file a civil action in federal district court for appropriate relief, including temporary or permanent injunctions. The court may also impose civil penalties.

3. *Criminal* authority to prosecute, along with the Department of Justice, three classes of criminal violations: negligent, knowing, and knowing endangerment. Making a false statement is also prosecuted as a criminal offense.

The law also provides for citizen suits to enforce the provisions of the Clean Water Act, as described later in this chapter.

### Administrative enforcement actions

The EPA's administrative compliance orders are designed simply to halt the violations without court involvement. In addition to compliance orders, administrative penalties may be levied.

Class I penalties are limited to $10,000 per violation or $25,000 total. To impose a class I penalty, the EPA must issue a written notification to the violator. The violator has 30 days to request a hearing before an administrative law judge. Hearings for class I penalties are relatively informal [Adams and Jensen, 1987].

Class II penalties may be up to $10,000 per day with a $125,000 maximum. The EPA must also provide written notification, and alleged violators are entitled to a formal administrative hearing that must conform with section 554 of title 5, *United States Code.* Class II hearings are similar to courtroom proceedings.

Administrative hearings generally result in the issuance of an administrative order. The EPA must provide public notice of the order and receive public comments on the order. The administrative order may include specific compliance requirements for the violator, such as schedules of compliance and the physical details of the compliance activities. These compliance activities may take the place of the fines or may be additional requirements.

Administrative orders may be appealed within the EPA. These appeals are ultimately decided by a three-person panel appointed by the EPA administrator in Washington.

Within 30 days of the issuance of an administrative order, the violator can petition the federal court system to review the administrative order. For class I penalties, the order is reviewed by a federal district court. For class II penalties, the order is reviewed by a federal court of appeals. Any person who submitted a comment on the proposed administrative order (during the public comment period) also has the right to request a federal court review of the administrative order. This could include an environmental group that feels that stronger compliance activities or penalties are required.

### Civil enforcement actions

In addition to administrative penalties, the CWA allows the EPA to file civil court cases to enforce the law and administer penalties to violators. Parties that violate the law or permit conditions are subject to court-imposed civil penalties of up to $25,000 per day of violation. These penalties can accrue indefinitely (until the violation is corrected), with no maximum limit. Each day that a violation occurs is considered to be a separate violation for the purpose of computing maximum penalties.

Civil court actions may be initiated without any administrative orders being issued. To successfully prosecute a civil court action, the EPA must show only that the law, the applicable EPA regulations, or the terms and conditions of an NPDES permit are being violated. The EPA does not have to prove malice or negligence on the part of the violator. The EPA may seek temporary or permanent injunctions in addition to fines, or it may seek court-ordered compliance actions and schedules.

If the violator is a municipality, the state will be named as a defendant as well. The state may be liable for penalties that cannot be paid by the municipality.

### Determining the actual amount of penalties

The sections above indicate what the *maximum* fine should be for a violation of the CWA. These maximum fines can be quite high. For example, a fine of $25,000 per day will accrue at a rate of about $750,000 per month or over $9 million per year. Given that the EPA often does not seek enforcement action until a violation has continued for 90 days or more, the potential fine is often $2 million or more before the violator begins to discuss the problem with the EPA.

Simply because the law allows huge penalties does not mean that such penalties are justified in a particular case. The law also requires the EPA (or a civil court) to "take into account the nature, circumstances, extent and gravity of the violation, or violations..." [40 CFR 34.400(g)]. This means that it may be worthwhile for an alleged violator to perform background investigations on the receiving water affected by the violation. For example, if the receiving water has had a history of water quality problems unrelated to the violations presently alleged, then this information is pertinent to the determination of penalties. All past water quality studies, monitoring data, and records of other discharge permits into the same receiving water may be useful in performing such background investigations.

The law also requires the EPA and the courts to consider the violator's "...ability to pay, any prior history of such violations, the degree of culpability, economic benefit or savings (if any) resulting from the violation..." when determining the amount of any penalties [40 CFR 34.400(g)]. In practice, EPA investigators often go through an extensive fact-finding investigation in the process of setting the amount of penalties. EPA enforcement officials may request extensive cost data from alleged violators, including the cost of various alternatives for preventing the violation. The EPA will often persistently question every such cost estimate, seeking to make sure that every element of the cost has been accounted for, such as engineering, operational costs, and interest on capital investments. The reason for this intense interest in cost accounting is simple: Every dollar that the violator would have spent to prevent the violation represents an "economic benefit or savings" that justifies a higher penalty.

*The EPA's job is to make sure that it is always cheaper to spend money to prevent a violation than it is to simply violate the law and then pay the resulting penalty.* This removes the economic benefit of violating the law. Obviously, when an alleged violator is responding to questions from the EPA, it is important not to overestimate costs of compliance. It may be worthwhile to invest considerable effort to determine what would have been the lowest-cost alternative for avoiding a violation. If a low-cost alternative can be identified and proved, then the amount of penalties payable for past violations may be reduced accordingly [Jensen and Price, 1986].

### Criminal enforcement actions

The most serious violations of the Clean Water Act involve criminal penalties, all of which would be imposed by federal courts. Criminal cases are prosecuted by the Department of Justice, after referral from the EPA. Criminal penalties may be invoked for negligent violations, knowing violations, knowing endangerment, or making false statements.

These criminal penalties can include jail sentences as well as fines. If the violator is a corporation, the corporation may be fined while the persons holding responsible positions within the corporation may face fines and/or imprisonment. The persons prosecuted may include not only those with hands-on compliance responsibilities but also those who manage or supervise such activities.

*Negligent violations* are punishable by a fine of not less than $2500 and not more than $25,000 per day of violation and by imprisonment for not more than 1 year. Fines and prison sentences may be twice as high for repeat offenses.

*Knowing violations* carry penalties of $5000 to $50,000 per day of violation and up to 3 years' imprisonment. Again, courts may double these penalties for repeat violations.

*Knowing endangerment* occurs when a knowing violation places another person in imminent danger of death or serious bodily injury. These serious violations are punishable by fines of up to $250,000 per day and up to 15 years in prison. If the violator is a corporation, the fine may be increased to $1 million per day. Repeat offenses are subject to doubled fines and imprisonment.

**False statements**

The CWA creates a separate class of criminal penalties for parties that file false statements or tamper with monitoring equipment. Violations are punishable by fines of up to $10,000 and jail sentences up to 2 years, with penalties doubled for repeat offenses. The EPA is especially vigorous in prosecuting those who interfere with the flow of information within the NPDES reporting structure. The entire NPDES depends strongly on dischargers obtaining and reporting accurate and complete data. Persons who deliberately withhold or falsify information are a direct threat to the success of such a self-reporting system. Therefore, the EPA is very active in pursuing such cases. The CWA equates withholding of information to falsifying of information.

*It is not advisable at any time to falsify or withhold information from the EPA or state regulators.* The possible criminal penalties resulting from falsifying or withholding information are likely to be much more severe than the civil penalties resulting from honestly reporting the true facts, however unfavorable those facts may be.

## Citizens' Enforcement of the Clean Water Act

### Citizens' suits to enforce the Clean Water Act

Civil suits can be filed in federal district court by citizens' groups as well as the federal or state government. Citizens' suits came into wide use during the 1980s, as environmental and public interest groups learned how to use the *discharge monitoring reports* (DMRs) submitted by NPDES permit holders to determine whether treatment standards were violated. However, several requirements must be met to success-fully prosecute an enforcement action [Stimson et al., 1993]:

1. *Sixty days' notice:*   Before a suit is filed, 60 days' notice must be provided to the alleged violator, to the EPA, and to state authorities about the nature of the threatened suit.

2. *Government priority:*   The federal or state government may decide to proceed with its own enforcement action, and this "diligent pros-ecution" will preclude the citizen from filing suit.

3. *Legal standing:*   The citizen must have legal standing to pursue the action. The CWA defines this as a "person or persons having an interest which is or may be adversely affected" by the violation. The courts have generally interpreted this requirement broadly, such that almost any group of citizens who use a waterway in any man-ner would qualify.

4. *Belief of ongoing violations:*   Since the violator has had 60 days' notice of the proposed suit, the violation may be corrected before the suit can be filed. If this is the case, then the suit cannot be pursued. The citizen may show a "good faith" belief that the violations were ongoing—that they were continuing at the time the suit was filed. However, if the violations are corrected at any time—even after the suit is filed—the suit cannot proceed. Citizen suits cannot be brought for violations which are completely in the past.

If the suit proceeds, and if the federal court decides that the facility was indeed liable for discharge permit violations, the court may fine the violator or issue an injunction to prevent the violation. Fines are paid to the U.S. Treasury.

Usually, these citizen actions end in settlements. The alleged viola-tor pays some fine, but most of the settlement usually goes for pro-grams to benefit the damaged waterway through studies, public education, or cleanup projects [Stimson et al., 1993].

**Citizens' petitions to the EPA**

In addition to citizens' suits, the rules of the NPDES program allow private citizens to petition the EPA or state to rescind general permit coverage for a particular discharger, provided that the citizen is able to show cause why the general permit coverage should be rescinded. The EPA or state would then require an individual permit application from the discharger. (Chapter 5 describes general and individual permit coverage.)

## Compliance with the National Storm Water Program

For the first few months after the October 1, 1992, deadline for storm water discharge permit coverage, the level of compliance among industrial dischargers was very low. The state of California estimated that only about 17 percent of the industries which should have applied for permit coverage actually did so within the first 6 months after permit coverage was required by law. This estimate is based on a comparison of the database of storm water permit applicants with the statewide database of manufacturers available to the state. The nationwide average is probably not any better.

Many of those who have complied with the requirement to submit a *Notice of Intent* (NOI) for general permit coverage may not be complying with other requirements of the National Storm Water Program. Since no other backup information must be submitted to the EPA to show compliance efforts, it is possible that many industrial facilities have submitted an NOI without taking any other real actions toward storm water quality improvement.

Because of the relatively low rate of compliance, EPA and state representatives have continued to attempt to educate regulated industries about the permit program. They generally have not chosen to penalize late applicants, but instead have provided an informal grace period during which industries may submit applications and receive permit coverage without penalty.

Eventually, however, the regulatory agencies will adopt a more aggressive stance. They will undoubtedly impose penalties on dischargers who have ignored permit application requirements. Any dischargers who become aware of the fact that their facility is required to obtain a discharge permit for storm water should contact the EPA or applicable state regulatory authorities and submit a permit application (or NOI for general permit coverage) as soon as possible, without waiting for the regulatory authorities to initiate contact. This type of positive action toward compliance will reduce the possibility that penalties will be imposed, and will lead to a reduction in penalties if they are imposed.

## References

Adams, Thomas L., and Lawrence L. Jensen: "Guidance on Class I Clean Water Act Administrative Penalty Procedures," Environmental Protection Agency (internal memorandum), July 27, 1987.

Jensen, Lawrence L., and Courtney M. Price: "Clean Water Act Civil Penalty Policy," Environmental Protection Agency (internal memorandum), Feb. 11, 1986.

Stimson, James A., Jeffrey J. Kimmel, and Sara Thurin Rollin: *Guide to Environmental Laws from Premanufacture to Disposal,* Bureau of National Affairs, Washington, 1993.

# 3

# Regulated
# Storm Water
# Discharges

This is the third of three chapters providing basic information for all dischargers. This chapter describes what types of storm water discharges must have permits. Chapter 4 provides more details on storm water discharges from industrial areas.

## Regulated Discharges

As noted in Chap. 1, phase I of the National Storm Water Program (NSWP) requires that "storm water discharges from areas of industrial activity" apply for and receive permits from the EPA or authorized states. This requirement applies to well over 100,000 industrial facilities and construction sites in the United States.

Several other types of storm water discharges are also regulated, including large and medium municipal separate storm sewer systems. However, the focus of this book is on industrial discharges, including the construction industry.

The very first step in complying with EPA or state regulations on industrial and construction storm water discharges is to determine whether a particular discharge is regulated. To make this determination, it is important to understand exactly the definitions of such terms as *storm water, discharge, point source, waters of the United States,* and *areas associated with industrial activity.*

## Storm Water

The EPA defines *storm water* as "storm water runoff, snow melt runoff, and surface runoff and drainage" [40 CFR 122.26(b)(13)]. Unless special conditions apply, only these types of discharges are allowed under a storm water discharge permit. Note that the EPA definition includes only discharges which result from precipitation. That is, only water which originates in the form of rainfall, snowfall, or other forms of precipitation can produce storm water discharges.

Water which is carried onto the site in vehicles, is piped or channeled onto the site, or is produced in industrial processes on the site does not fit the definition of storm water. For example, storm water does not include such discharges as water used to flush utility lines, test storage tanks, or any form of process wastewater.

Operators of industrial facilities or construction sites are generally responsible for storm water from upstream adjacent facilities that enters the site or combines with the discharge from a facility submitting a permit application. If such a situation exists, the permit application for the downstream facility needs to address the issue and bring it to the attention of the permitting authority. The permitting authority can then draft appropriate permit conditions to reflect these circumstances. For example, the downstream facility may be required to development management practices or other run-on/runoff controls to segregate or otherwise prevent outside runoff from mixing with on-site storm water discharges. These permit conditions should be acceptable to the owners of the downstream facility, because these conditions will limit the liability for pollutants in such "run-on" storm water.

## Point Source Discharges

The NPDES permit program regulates only point source discharges. The EPA defines a *point source* as "any discernible, confined, and discrete conveyance, including but not limited to any pipe, ditch, channel, tunnel, conduit, well, discrete fissure, container, rolling stock, concentrated animal feeding operation, landfill leachate collection system, vessel or other floating craft from which pollutants are or may be discharged. This term does not include return flows from irrigated agriculture or agricultural storm water runoff" [40 CFR 122.2].

Since only point sources of storm water are regulated, a permit is not generally necessary for *sheet flow,* which is shallow unconcentrated overland flow. However, the definition of point source is written broadly, so as to include most situations which are commonly referred to as sheet flow. According to the EPA definition, the discharge must be considered a point source if there is any *discernible* conveyance. A shallow swale or rill, a depression, or a curb cut could fit such a description. The EPA has indicated that it

> intends to embrace the broadest possible definition of point source consistent with the legislative intent of the CWA and court interpretations to include any identifiable conveyance from which pollutants might enter the waters of the United States. In most court cases interpreting the term "point source," the term has been interpreted broadly. For example, the holding in *Sierra Club v. Abston Construction Co., Inc.*, 620 F. 2d 41 (5th Cir. 1980) indicates that changing the surface of land or establishing grading patterns on land will result in a point source where the runoff from the site is ultimately discharged to waters of the United States. [55 FR 47989 (Nov. 16, 1990)]

A natural channel or rill may form a point source discharge, even if it results only from natural erosion processes and has never been improved in any way at the point of discharge, provided that human activities have increased the amount of impervious cover or have otherwise changed the runoff characteristics of the area drained by the natural channel or rill.

Because of the broad interpretation of *point source* by the EPA and the courts, it is difficult to argue that an industrial area drains entirely by sheet flow, without any discernible conveyances. The EPA recommends that a permit application be submitted along with information on flow conditions, if there is any doubt about whether the flow would be classified as a point source.

It is important to note that a discharge does not occur until the storm water crosses the property boundary of the industrial site or enters waters of the United States (which are defined later in this chapter). Storm water which runs from one part of an industrial site to another part is not a discharge; it is merely an internal transfer of flow, which does not require a permit. Treating an internal flow transfer as a discharge results in unnecessary effort in sampling, permitting, and measuring flows which do not require a permit.

The only types of storm water discharges which are regulated under the National Storm Water Program are discharges into municipal separate storm sewer systems or waters of the United States. Discharges to combined storm sewers (CSSs) are not included, because they are regulated under a separate program. [A *Combined sewer system* (CSS) is a system which carries sanitary sewage under dry-weather conditions, but which is surcharged with runoff under storm conditions. Such systems are present in the older cities of the United States.] The

EPA does not regulate discharges to groundwater[1] (such as from an infiltration basin), although some states do.

If the storm water runoff from an industrial site flows into a retention basin on site with *no possibility* of discharge, then no permit is required. The storm water would then be eliminated by evaporation or infiltration. How large does the retention basin have to be? The answer is not likely to satisfy the engineer or hydrologist. It depends upon the level of risk that the owner of the industrial facility is willing to accept. If the owner is willing to accept the risk of having an unpermitted storm water discharge every 2 years, then the retention basin should be designed with sufficient capacity for the 2-year storm event. The design capacity of the retention basin is left entirely to the discretion of the permittee. However, every time that the capacity of the retention basin is exceeded, resulting in a discharge, the facility is in violation of the Clean Water Act. The penalties described in Chap. 2 may apply. Therefore, it is prudent to provide sufficient capacity in the retention basin for a large storm event.

## Waters of the United States

As noted above, storm water is regulated only if it discharges to a municipal separate storm sewer system or directly to waters of the United States. There are very few terms which have been debated and litigated as much as the term *waters of the United States*. The definition has grown from the original concept of *navigable waters* to a very broad definition which includes most of the bodies of water and wetlands in the country. (Some people claim that the "waters of the United States" are becoming not only "fishable and swimmable" but also "driveable and campable.") The official definition is as follows:

a) All waters which are currently used, were used in the past, or may be susceptible to use in interstate or foreign commerce, including all waters which are subject to the ebb and flow of the tide;

b) All interstate waters, including interstate "wetlands";

c) All other waters such as interstate[2] lakes, rivers, streams (including intermittent streams), mudflats, sandflats, wetlands, sloughs, prairie potholes, wet meadows, playa lakes, or natural ponds the use, degradation, or destruction of which would affect or could affect interstate or foreign commerce including any such waters:

---

[1] Some recent court cases suggest that the EPA may have the right to regulate discharges to groundwater which is hydrologically connected with surface waters.

1) Which are or could be used by interstate or foreign travelers for recreational or other purposes;
2) From which fish or shellfish are or could be taken and sold in interstate or foreign commerce; or
3) Which are used or could be used for industrial purposes by industries in interstate commerce;

d) All impoundments of waters otherwise defined as waters of the United States under this definition;
e) Tributaries of waters identified in paragraphs a) through d) of this definition;
f) The territorial sea; and
g) Wetlands adjacent to waters (other than waters that are themselves wetlands) identified in paragraphs a) through f) of this definition.

Waste treatment systems, including treatment ponds or lagoons designed to meet the requirements of CWA, are not waters of the United States. [40 CFR 122.2]

Note that most wetlands are considered waters of the United States. The definition of *wetlands* is as follows:

"Wetlands" means those areas that are inundated or saturated by surface or groundwater at a frequency and duration sufficient to support, and that under normal conditions do support, a prevalence of vegetation typically adapted for life in saturated soil conditions. Wetlands generally include swamps, marshes, bogs, and similar areas [40 CFR 122.2].

Because of the broad definition of *waters of the United States,* any point source of storm water into a wetlands area, or any of the other bodies of water listed above, is potentially regulated under the NPDES program.

## Permit Requirements for Small Municipalities

Industrial facilities owned or operated by a municipal entity with a total population of less than 100,000 are generally not required to obtain permits to discharge storm water, unless the facility is an airport, powerplant, or uncontrolled sanitary landfill. Construction projects undertaken by small municipalities are also exempt from storm water discharge permit requirements. The broad exemption for small municipalities was granted by Congress in section 1068 of the Intermodal Surface Transportation Efficiency Act, which was passed in December 1991.

The EPA defines a *municipal entity* to include not only incorporated cities but also other entities which provide municipal services, such as counties, sanitary sewer districts, flood control districts, and unincorporated towns and townships. School districts and state agencies are also included. In determining whether a municipal entity has to obtain permit coverage for industrial activities which it owns or operates, the most recent Census will be used as follows:

- *Counties:*  If the county has a population of 100,000 or more, then its construction activities and the industrial operations which it owns or operates must be permitted.

- *Sewage treatment districts:*  Service populations will be used to determine the population of sewage treatment districts which operate publicly owned treatment works (POTWs). Where one sewer district operates a number of plants, the entire service population of the district will be used to determine the applicable population classification of all the treatment works operated by the district. (For example, if a district with a cumulative service population of 150,000 operates two sewage treatment plants, one of which serves 100,000 and the other of which serves 50,000, then both plants will be considered to be a facility that is owned or operated by a municipality with a population of 100,000 or more.)

- *Other special districts:*  Flood control districts and other municipal entities with service populations must obtain permits for industrial or construction operations which they own or operate if their service population is 100,000 or more. School districts must obtain storm water discharge permits if their total resident population (not the number of students) is greater than 100,000.

- *State agencies:*  The state population will be used to determine the population of most state agencies. Under this approach, the EPA would base the population of facilities operated by a state agency on the entire state population rather than the population of the local government entity with land-use authority (e.g., city, town, township, county) in which the facility is physically located. This means that most state-owned facilities and projects would be subject to storm water discharge permit requirements. However, some state agencies with limited service areas (such as a river basin authority) may avoid storm water discharger permit requirements if their total population is less than 100,000.

- *Combined ownership:*  Where an industrial facility is owned or operated by more than one municipality, then the EPA will use the combined populations of the appropriate municipalities in determining population thresholds.

The effect of these rules is to limit the number of municipalities which can escape the storm water discharge permit requirement. However, the exclusion of industrial facilities and construction projects owned by small municipalities effectively removes thousands of storm water discharges from the National Storm Water Program, at least for the time being.

Where a facility is privately owned and operated but has a service contract with a municipality, the facility is not considered to be "municipally operated." For example, a privately owned and operated landfill that receives municipal waste pursuant to a contract with a municipality or some other form of reimbursement from a municipality is not exempt from storm water discharge permit requirements.

## Industries Exempt from Storm Water Discharge Permits

Certain categories of industries are specifically exempt from regulation by storm water discharge permits:

- *Radioactive wastes:*   high-level radioactive wastes regulated under the Atomic Energy Act of 1954.

- *Vessels:*   sewage discharges from vessels [40 CFR 122.2].

- *Oil and gas operations:*   permitted water, gas, or other material injected into wells to aid in the production of oil or gas, so long as ground or surface waters are not degraded [40 CFR 122.3(a)].

- *Agricultural runoff:*   return flows from irrigated agriculture or agricultural storm water runoff [40 CFR 122.2; 40 CFR 122.3(e) and (f)].

- *Non-point-source silvicultural activities:*   No permit is required for discharges from non-point-source silvicultural activities such as tree nurseries, site preparations, restoration and subsequent cultural treatment, thinning, prescribed burning, pest and fire control, tree harvesting operations, surface drainage, or road construction or maintenance from which there is natural runoff [40 CFR 122.3(e)]. At 40 CFR 122.27(b)(1) is defined the term *silvicultural point source* to mean any discrete conveyance related to rock crushing, gravel washing, log sorting, or log storage facilities which are operated in connection with silvicultural activities and from which pollutants are discharged into waters of the United States. Section 122.27(b)(1) also excludes certain sources.

## References

Government Printing Office: *Federal Register,* Office of the Federal Register, National Archives and Records Administration, Washington.
———: *United States Code,* Washington, 1988.
———: *Code of Federal Regulations,* Office of the Federal Register, National Archives and Records Administration, Washington, July 1, 1992.

# 4

# Storm Water Associated with Industrial Activity

This is the first of five chapters which deal with the specific requirements for storm water discharges from *industrial* (nonconstruction) facilities. This chapter describes the types of storm water discharges that must have permits.

Chapter 5 describes the permit application process and the types of applications available. Chapters 6 and 7 describe how to prepare a *storm water pollution prevention plan* (SWPPP) for an industrial facility. Chapter 8 describes the requirements and procedures for storm water sampling.

There is additional information on requirements for specific states in Chap. 14. A copy of the EPA Final General Permit for storm water discharges from areas associated with industrial activity is included in App. A. Appendix C presents an example of an SWPPP for an industrial facility.

## Regulated Discharges

As noted in Chap. 3, only point source discharges of storm water into waters of the United States are regulated by National Pollutant Discharge Elimination System (NPDES) permits. Chapter 3 defined the terms *storm water, discharge, point source,* and *waters of the United States.* A basic understanding of the material presented in Chap. 3 is necessary.

For industrial storm water discharge permits, only storm water discharges *associated with industrial activity* are required to have permits. The EPA definition of this term is quite lengthy and detailed. It includes "the discharge from any conveyance which is used for collecting and conveying storm water and which is directly related to manufacturing, processing, or raw materials storage areas at an industrial plant. The term does not include discharges from facilities or activities excluded from the NPDES program." [40 CFR 122.26(b)(14)]

The EPA definition also provides several examples of industrial activity:

> ...the term includes, but is not limited to, storm water discharges from industrial plant yards; immediate access roads and rail lines used or traveled by carriers of raw materials, manufactured products, waste material, or by-products used or created by the facility; material handling sites; refuse sites; sites used for the application or disposal of process waste waters; sites used for the storage and maintenance of material handling equipment; sites used for residual treatment, storage, or disposal; shipping and receiving areas; manufacturing buildings; storage areas (including tank farms) for raw materials, and intermediate and finished products; and areas where industrial activity has taken place in the past and significant materials remain and are exposed to storm water. [40 CFR 122.26(b)(14)]

The reference to *immediate access roads and rail lines* is limited to those roads which are exclusively or primarily dedicated for use by the industrial facility. The EPA does not intend that these regulations extend to public roads such as county, state, or federal roads and highways. In addition, the materials hauled on these roads must be part of an actual industrial operation, not simply part of a preliminary reconnaissance or sampling program.

The EPA provides examples of material handling activities covered by the storm water regulations: "...material handling activities include the storage, loading and unloading, transportation, or conveyance of any raw material, intermediate product, finished product, by-product or waste product" [40 CFR 122.26(b)(14)].

Pilot plants and research facilities are required to obtain storm water discharge permits, provided that the manufacturing operations of the full-scale facility would require a permit [EPA, 1992].

One important aspect of the EPA definition is the exclusion of storm water discharges from those portions of the industrial facility which are not actively involved in industrial activities: "The term excludes areas located on plant lands separate from the plant's industrial activities, such as office buildings and accompanying parking lots as long as the drainage from the excluded areas is not mixed with storm water drained from the above described areas" [40 CFR 122.26(b)(14)]. In addition, off-site stockpiles of final product from an industrial facility do not require permit coverage, because they are not located at the site of the industrial facility [EPA, 1992].

Areas associated with industrial activity do not include commercial or retail facilities. This is an important distinction; in some cases (such as construction), the EPA has chosen to regulate only those activities which are significant enough to be inherently *industrial* in nature.

There is no exclusion for federal or state-owned facilities. Many military facilities have operations which fit within the categories which must receive permit coverage. Some municipally owned facilities are excluded under the Transportation Act of 1991, as described in Chap. 3.

## Specific Areas Associated with Industrial Activity

The EPA requires storm water discharge permits only for specific types of industrial activities. The activities requiring permits are defined in two ways: by a narrative description or by a *Standard Industrial Classification* (SIC) code. SIC codes are standard numeric codes assigned to each type of industrial process in the United States by the President's Office of Management and Budget [OMB, 1987].

There is an important distinction between these two types of categories: Industrial sites identified by SIC code are required to obtain permit coverage only if the *primary site activity* is within the SIC codes listed. If the listed activity is not the primary site activity, it is considered an *auxiliary activity* which does not require permit coverage. For categories defined by a narrative description, however, a permit is required if *any of the described activity* occurs on site. Therefore, the narrative categories are more inclusive.

There are seven categories of industrial activity defined by narrative description:

1. Subchapter N industries
2. Hazardous waste treatment, storage, or disposal facilities
3. Landfills
4. Power generation facilities
5. Sewage treatment plants
6. Construction activities
7. Water quality violators or significant polluters

These categories are described in detail later in this chapter. Construction activities are also described in Chap. 9.

There are five categories of industrial activity defined by SIC codes:

1. Heavy manufacturing
2. Light manufacturing

3. Mining

4. Recyclers

5. Industrial transportation

These categories are also described in detail later in this chapter.

### Narrative category: Subchapter N industries

Subchapter N of Title 40 of the *Code of Federal Regulation* (CFR) includes all the effluent guidelines and standards for various types of industrial facilities. Subchapter N contains 40 CFR sections 401 through 471. Facilities subject to any of the following types of limitations or guidelines under 40 CFR, subchapter N (except facilities which are exempt under the light-industry exclusion), must obtain NPDES permits to discharge storm water:

- Storm water effluent limitation guidelines
- New source performance standards
- Toxic pollutant effluent standards (water priority pollutants)

According to the EPA, "the industries in these categories have generally been identified by EPA as the most significant dischargers of process wastewaters in the country. As such, these facilities are likely to have storm water discharges associated with industrial activity for which permit applications should be required" [55 FR 47989 (Nov. 16, 1990)].

Because these industries are described as a narrative category, a permit is required if *any* of the described activity occurs on site.

The following sections list the industry groups covered by storm water effluent limitations guidelines, new source performance standards, or toxic pollutant effluent standards. Many of these industry groups overlap. Some also overlap with industry groups required to obtain storm water discharge permits under other provisions of the EPA rules.

**Storm water effluent limitation guidelines.**   The following types of industries are required to obtain NPDES storm water discharge permits because they are covered by storm water effluent limitations or guidelines [EPA, 1992]:

- Cement manufacturing [40 CFR 411]
- Feedlots [40 CFR 412]
- Fertilizer manufacturing [40 CFR 418]
- Petroleum refining [40 CFR 419]

- Phosphate manufacturing [40 CFR 422]
- Steam electric power generation [40 CFR 423]
- Coal mining [40 CFR 434]
- Mineral mining and dressing [40 CFR 436]
- Ore mining and dressing [40 CFR 440]
- Asphalt emulsion [40 CFR 443]

Industries subject to storm water effluent limitations are not eligible for the light-industry exemption from storm water discharge permitting described later in this chapter.

**New source performance standards.**  Most effluent guidelines listed in 40 CFR subchapter N include new source performance standards, and facilities subject to these standards are required to submit a storm water permit application. However, the following types of facilities do *not* have new source performance standards and are therefore *not* required to obtain storm water discharge permits [EPA, 1992]:

- Oil and gas extraction [40 CFR 435]
- Mineral mining and processing [40 CFR 436]
- Gum and wood chemicals manufacturing [40 CFR 454]
- Pesticide chemicals [40 CFR 455]
- Explosives manufacturing [40 CFR 457]
- Photographic processing [40 CFR 459]
- Hospitals [40 CFR 460]

Industries subject to new source performance standards are not eligible for the light-industry exemption from storm water discharge permitting described later in this chapter.

**Toxic pollutant effluent standards.**  This category has been subject to considerable confusion. The EPA originally issued information which indicated that the term *toxic pollutants* refers to the priority pollutants listed in tables II and III of appendix D of 40 CFR part 122 (not 40 CFR part 129). A list of 27 different industries with toxic pollutant effluent standards for at least one subcategory was also published [EPA, 1992].

Later, the EPA revised the definition of *toxic pollutant effluent standards* to include only the standards established pursuant to CWA section 307(a)(2) and codified at 40 CFR part 129. This essentially reverses the earlier definition. Part 129 applies only to manufacturers of six specific pesticide products which are defined as toxic pollutants [EPA, 1993].

Industries subject to toxic pollutant effluent standards may be eligible for the light-industry exemption from storm water discharge permitting described earlier in this chapter, provided that they meet all other qualifications for this exemption.

### Narrative category: Hazardous treatment, storage, or disposal facilities

Hazardous waste treatment, storage, or disposal facilities, including those that are operating under interim status or a permit under subtitle C of the Resource Conservation and Recovery Act (RCRA), must obtain NPDES storm water discharge permits. A facility that stores hazardous waste less than 90 days is not considered to be a treatment, storage, or disposal facility and therefore is not required to submit a storm water discharge permit application [EPA, 1992]. Because these industries are described as a narrative category, a permit is required if *any* of the described activity occurs on site.

Land disposal units and incinerators as well as *boilers and industrial furnaces* (BIFs) that burn hazardous waste may receive a diverse range of industrial wastes. Waste receiving, handling, storage, and processing, in addition to actual waste disposal, can be a significant source of pollutants at waste disposal facilities. The EPA has summarized case studies documenting surface water impacts and groundwater contamination of land disposal units. Evaluation of 163 case studies revealed surface water impacts at 73 facilities. Elevated levels of organic chemicals, including pesticides, and metals have been found in groundwater and/or surface water at many sites [55 FR 47989 (Nov. 16, 1990)].

Incinerators and BIFs burn hazardous materials such as spent solvents, contaminated fuels, and so on. The primary purpose of an incinerator is waste disposal, but the primary purpose of a BIF is to provide heat or steam or to generate electricity for use in manufacturing processes.

Incinerators and BIFs will typically manage the same types of wastes as landfills, and therefore present similar risks with respect to waste transportation, handling, and storage. In addition, a wide range of toxic pollutants potentially present in fuel stocks, material accepted for disposal, air emission particulate, and ash at these facilities have the potential to contaminate storm water runoff.

### Narrative category: Industrial waste landfills

Landfills, land application sites, and open dumps that receive industrial wastes must obtain NPDES storm water discharge permits. *Industrial waste* is waste received from the manufacturing portions of facilities under any of the other industrial categories under this program. It does include construction debris.

The EPA considers the construction of new cells at a landfill to be routine landfill operations that are covered by the landfill's industrial storm water permit. Therefore, no separate construction permit is required to construct the cell, even if the area disturbed by construction of the cell is greater than 5 acres. However, where a new landfill is being constructed and 5 acres or more of land is disturbed, the construction activity should be covered by a construction permit. Some authorized states may address these situations differently [EPA, 1993].

Because these industries are described as a narrative category, a permit is required if *any* of the described activity occurs on site.

Landfills which are capped and closed must be judged on a case-by-case basis. A permit application should be filed for such facilities. The EPA has excluded from coverage under the general permit those storm water discharges from inactive landfills on federal lands where an operator cannot be identified. The EPA is addressing these discharges in conjunction with distinct permitting efforts addressing storm water discharges from inactive mining operations and inactive oil and gas operations on federal lands.

As described in Chap. 3, under section 1068(c) of the Transportation Act of 1991, the EPA shall not require any municipality with a population of less than 100,000 to apply for or obtain a permit for any storm water discharge associated with most industrial activities. However, these municipalities are required to obtain storm water discharge permits for uncontrolled sanitary landfills which they own or operate. Section 1068(d) of the Transportation Act defines *uncontrolled sanitary landfill* to mean a landfill or open dump, whether open or closed, that does not meet the requirements for run-on and runoff controls established pursuant to subtitle D of the Solid Waste Disposal Act (RCRA). Even landfills that are in compliance with subtitle D requirements and that are owned by small municipalities may be required to obtain NPDES permits for storm water discharges if they are significant contributors of pollutants to waters of the United States or if they contribute to a violation of a water quality standard.

The EPA has published criteria for solid waste disposal facilities, including municipal solid waste landfills (MSWLFs), pursuant to subtitle D of the Solid Waste Disposal Act [56 FR 50978 (Oct. 9, 1991)]. Several provisions of these regulations specifically address run-on and runoff from the active portions of regulated units. Owners or operators of all MSWLF units are required to design, construct, and maintain a run-on control system to prevent flow onto the active portion of the MSWLF unit during the peak discharge from a 25-year storm [40 CFR 258.25]. In addition, all MSWLF units are required to design, construct, and maintain a runoff control system from the active portion of the landfill to collect and control at least the water volume resulting from a 24-hour (24-h), 25-year storm.

The EPA rules issued pursuant to subtitle D of the Solid Waste Disposal Act do not require that the collected runoff be sampled or treated. However, the EPA intended that this runoff be subjected to NPDES permit requirements, which may require sampling and/or treatment. Runoff from the active portion of the unit must be handled so that all MSWLF units are operated in compliance with NPDES requirements [40 CFR 258.27(a)]. Any discharges of a nonpoint source of pollution from an MSWLF unit into waters of the United States must also be in conformance with any established water quality management plan developed under the CWA.

Older landfills are of most concern to the EPA because they may have received large volumes of hazardous waste and, in general, their use of design controls was very limited. States have reported to the EPA that of the 1100 municipal solid waste landfills which monitored discharges to surface water, 660 were cited for surface water impacts. The EPA believes that newer and future solid waste landfills may present lower risks because subtitle C regulations keep most hazardous waste out of solid waste landfills. In addition, design controls for solid waste landfills have improved, and are expected to continue to improve with the implementation of subtitle D requirements [56 FR 50981 (Oct. 9, 1991)].

### Narrative category: Steam electric power generation

Steam electric power generating facilities, including coal handling sites, must obtain NPDES storm water discharge permits. This would include single-user facilities, such as a steam electric power generating facility for a university campus. However, steam production for heating and cooling is not covered by permit requirements. Cogeneration facilities are regulated if they are based on use of dual fuels. However, cogeneration facilities based on heat capture only are not regulated.

The EPA originally required storm water discharges from transformer storage sites to receive storm water discharge permits. However, after further investigation, the EPA determined that the Toxic Substances Control Act (TSCA) addresses pollutants associated with transformers that may enter receiving water through storm water discharges. Under TSCA, transformers are required to be stored in a manner that prevents rainwater from reaching the stored PCBs or PCB items [40 CFR 761.65(b)(1)(i)]. Therefore, the EPA does not require storm water discharge permits for transformer storage areas. Storm water discharges from electrical substations are also not regulated [EPA, 1992].

The EPA acknowledges that certain discharges are regulated under the Atomic Energy Act and are therefore exempt from EPA regulation.

However, the EPA may require permits from other storm water discharges from nuclear power facilities.

Coal handling activities at coal-fired steam electric plants can be a significant source of pollutants in storm water discharges. Runoff from coal handling areas can have high levels of total suspended solids, sulfate, iron, aluminum, mercury, copper, arsenic, selenium, and manganese as well as an acidic pH [EPA, 1982]. However, coal piles which are located off site (not at the site of the steam electric power generation) are not required to be permitted, because they are not located on the site of a facility which is engaged in industrial activity [EPA, 1992].

Spills and leaks from fuel handling sites, including loading and unloading areas and storage tanks, at oil-fired steam electric power generating facilities are potential significant sources of pollutants to storm water runoff. Given the large amounts of oil managed at these facilities, many of the pollutant sources associated with oil handling and storage are expected to be similar to those at petroleum refineries [EPA, 1979b].

Because these industries are described as a narrative category, a permit is required if *any* of the described activity occurs on site.

As described in Chap. 3, section 1068(c) of the Transportation Act of 1991 provides that the EPA shall not require any municipality with a population of less than 100,000 to apply for or obtain a permit for most industrial activities. However, power plants owned or operated by such municipalities are still required to obtain permits to discharge storm water.

### Narrative category: Sewage treatment

Sewage treatment plants have been required to obtain NPDES permits to discharge treated sewage effluent since the passage of the Clean Water Act. The Water Quality Act of 1987, however, now requires permit coverage for storm water discharges from such facilities.

Storm water discharge permits must be obtained for treatment works treating domestic sewage or any other sewage sludge or wastewater treatment device or system, used in the storage, treatment, recycling, and reclamation of municipal or domestic sewage, including land dedicated to the disposal of the sewage sludge that is located within the confines of the facility. Off-site pumping stations are not required to obtain storm water discharge permits. Sewage treatment plants typically include sludge composting and storage of chemicals such as ferric chloride, alum, polymers, and chlorine. The plants may experience spills and bubble-overs which contribute to storm water pollution. (See Fig. 4.1.)

Only sewage facilities with a design flow of 1.0 million gallons per day (gal/day) or more, or which are required to have an approved pre-

Figure 4.1  Chemical handling area at sewage treatment plant.

treatment program under 40 CFR part 403, are included. Farmlands, domestic gardens, and lands used for sludge management where sludge is beneficially reused and which are not physically located within the confines of the sewage treatment facility, or areas that are in compliance with section 405 of the Clean Water Act, are not included. (Section 405 of the Clean Water Act regulates the disposal of sewage sludge.) If the facility collects all storm water from the plant site and treats it as part of the normal inflow that is processed through the treatment plant, no storm water discharge permit is required.

As described in Chap. 3, the Transportation Act of 1991 exempted all publicly owned treatment works (POTWs) owned by small municipalities (less than 100,000), regardless of whether they meet the other criteria for regulation described above. However, permit coverage may still be required if the POTW is a significant contributor of pollutants to waters of the United States or if it contributes to a violation of a water quality standard.

Because these industries are described as a narrative category, a permit is required if *any of the described activity* occurs on site.

**Narrative category: Construction activity**

Storm water discharges from construction activities involving at least 5 acres of disturbed land must be covered by an NPDES permit, as discussed in detail in Chap. 9.

**Narrative category: Water quality violators or significant polluters**

The EPA or an authorized state NPDES program administrator may determine that a particular discharge contributes to a violation of a water quality standard or is a significant contributor of pollutants to waters of the United States. This determination, which is made on a case-by-case basis, will result in the requirement that the facility obtain a storm water discharge permit. To make such a determination, the regulatory agency must follow the specific administrative procedures of the Clean Water Act and other applicable regulations. The determination must be based on fact and cannot be arbitrary.

**SIC code category: Heavy manufacturing**

Heavy manufacturing includes several industrial activities and processes which are generally conducted outdoors and exposed to storm water:

- SIC code 24: lumber and wood products (except 2434: wood kitchen cabinets). These facilities are engaged in operating sawmills, planing mills, and other mills engaged in producing lumber and wood basic materials.

- SIC code 26: paper and allied products (except 265: paperboard containers and boxes and 267: converted paper and paperboard products).

- SIC code 28: chemicals and allied products (except 283: drugs and 285: paints, varnishes, lacquers, enamels, etc.).

- SIC code 29: petroleum refining and related activities.

- SIC code 311: leather tanning and finishing. Such processes use chemicals, such as sulfuric acid and sodium dichromate; detergents; and a variety of raw and intermediate materials.

- SIC code 32: stone, clay, glass, and concrete products (except 323: glass products made of purchased glass). These facilities manufacture glass, clay, stone, and concrete products from raw materials in the form of quarried and mined stone, clay, and sand.

- SIC code 33: primary metal industries, including facilities that smelt and refine ferrous and nonferrous metals from ore, pig, or scrap and manufacturing related products.
- SIC code 3441: structural metal fabricating.
- SIC code 373: ship and boat building and repair.

When taken as a group, these industries are expected to have one or many of the following activities or processes occurring on site: storage of raw materials, intermediate products, final products, by-products, waste products, or chemicals outside; smelting; refining; production of significant emissions from stacks or air exhaust systems; loading or unloading of chemical or hazardous substances; use of unhoused manufacturing and heavy industrial equipment; and generation of significant dust or particulates. Accordingly, these are classes of facilities which can be viewed as generating storm water discharges associated with industrial activity requiring a permit.

Because these industrial activities are identified by SIC code, the site is required to obtain permit coverage only if the *primary site activity* is within the SIC codes listed.

**Primary metal industries.**   Primary metal facilities (SIC code 33) are engaged in the manufacturing of ferrous metals and metal products and the primary and secondary smelting and refining of nonferrous metals. In addition, facilities engaged in the molding, casting, or forming of ferrous or nonferrous metals are included in this group.

Due to the nature of processes and activities commonly occurring at these facilities, a number of sources can potentially contribute significant amounts of pollutants to storm water. Sources of pollutants include outdoor storage and material handling activities, particulate and dust generating processes, and slag quench processes. Open-air storage and handling of raw materials, products, and wastes are common practices at many of these facilities. In addition, dust and particulate generating processes, particularly at smelting and refining facilities, are considered potential sources of pollutants in storm water discharges. Many of these types of facilities also use a high volume of water for operations such as spray quenching, heat treating, and die cooling, which when coupled with the old age of many primary metals facilities, can create the potential for nonstorm water to be discharged to the storm water collection systems.

**Ship and boat building and repair.**   A number of industrial activities at shipbuilding and ship repairing facilities can be significant sources of pollutants to storm water discharges, including improper controls on activities such as ship bottom cleaning, bilge water disposal, loading and unloading of fuels, metal fabrication and cleaning operations, and surface preparation and painting [EPA, 1979a, 1991].

### SIC code category: Light manufacturing

Light manufacturing includes a large number of industrial activities and processes which may be conducted indoors so that exposure to storm water is minimal:

- SIC code 20: food and kindred products, including processing foods such as meats, dairy food, fruit, and flour
- SIC code 21: tobacco products, including cigarettes, cigars, chewing tobacco, and related products
- SIC code 22: textile mill products, producing yarn, and so on and/or dye and finishing fabrics
- SIC code 23: apparel and other textile products which produce clothing by cutting and sewing purchased woven or knitted textile products
- SIC code 2434: wood kitchen cabinets
- SIC code 25: furniture and fixtures
- SIC code 265: paperboard containers and boxes
- SIC code 267: converted paper and paperboard products (except containers and boxes)
- SIC code 27: printing and publishing, including bookbinding and plate making
- SIC code 283: drugs (pharmaceuticals)
- SIC code 285: paints, varnishes, lacquers, enamels, and allied products
- SIC code 30: rubber and miscellaneous plastic products
- SIC code 31: leather and leather products (except 311: leather tanning and finishing)
- SIC code 323: glass products made of purchased glass
- SIC code 34: fabricated metal products (except 3441: structural metal fabricating)
- SIC code 35: industrial and commercial machinery and computer equipment
- SIC code 36: electronic and other electric equipment and components

- SIC code 37: transportation equipment (except 373: ship and boat building and repair)

- SIC code 38: instruments and related products, including measuring, analyzing, and controlling instruments; photographic, medical, and optical goods; and watches and clocks

- SIC code 39: miscellaneous manufacturing industries, including jewelry, silverware, plated ware, musical instruments, dolls, toys, games, sporting and athletic goods, pens, pencils, artists' materials, novelties, buttons, notions, brooms, brushes, signs, burial caskets, and hard surface floor coverings

- SIC code 4221: farm products warehousing and storage

- SIC code 4222: refrigerated warehousing and storage

- SIC code 4225: general warehousing and storage

Because these industrial activities are identified by SIC codes, the site is required to obtain permit coverage only if the *primary site activity* is within the SIC codes listed.

Under current EPA regulations, these types of industrial activities can be conducted without obtaining a storm water discharge permit, if no material handling equipment or activities, raw materials, intermediate products, final products, waste materials, by-products, or industrial machinery is exposed to storm water [40 CFR 122.26(b)(14)][1]

When considered as a class, most of the activity at these facilities is undertaken in buildings; emissions from stacks will be minimal or nonexistent; the use of unhoused manufacturing and heavy industrial equipment will be minimal; outside material storage, disposal, or handling generally will not be a part of the manufacturing process; and generating significant dust or particulates would be atypical. As such,

---

[1]After the EPA published the regulations concerning phase I of the National Storm Water Program, the Natural Resources Defense Council (NRDC) filed suit against the EPA on December 10, 1990. The NRDC argued that (1) Congress did not allow an exemption from permit requirements for industries without storm water exposure and (2) these industries should therefore be required to obtain permit coverage in the same manner as the heavy industries discussed above.

The ninth circuit court of appeals remanded this issue to the EPA on June 4, 1992, with instructions that the EPA provide justification for this exemption. The EPA is currently gathering this information. The information will be submitted to the court for final review. Depending upon the final court ruling on this issue, these industries may all be required to obtain storm water discharge permits, regardless of whether materials are exposed to storm water.

The EPA published a notice in the *Federal Register* on December 18, 1992, summarizing the actions of the ninth circuit court of appeals in this case. *The EPA made it clear that until a final ruling is handed down by the court, the existing exemption on light industry remains in effect.*

these industries are more akin or comparable to retail, commercial, or service industries, and storm water discharges from these facilities are not "associated with industrial activity."

The simple fact that a manufacturing building, rail spur, or access road is exposed to storm water does not necessarily constitute exposure of materials. In addition, a covered dumpster does not constitute exposure of materials, provided that the container is completely covered and nothing can drain out of holes in the bottom or can be lost during loading onto a garbage truck. An air vent may constitute exposure of materials if particulate matter has accumulated around the air vent and is subject to wash-off by storm water. Therefore, air vents must be considered on a case-by-case basis.

Some of these types of facilities handle oil drums or other contained materials which are exposed during loading and unloading operations. If there is a reasonable potential for leaks or spills from these containers which could be exposed to storm water, discharges from the exposed area will be subject to storm water permitting requirements [EPA, 1993].

If material handling equipment or activities, raw materials, intermediate products, final products, waste materials, by-products, or industrial machinery is stored outside in a structure with a roof but with no sides, and if wind-blown rain, snow, or runoff comes into contact with the equipment, material, or activities, then discharges from the area will be subject to storm water permitting requirements [EPA, 1993].

Because of the potential savings available by avoiding permit responsibilities for these types of facilities, it is generally worthwhile to make some changes in the facility to eliminate storm water exposure. For example, changing from uncovered to covered dumpsters, eliminating or covering outside material storage areas, and cleaning up exposed waste products or scrap machinery may all be cost-effective and advisable, if these steps eliminate storm water exposure and therefore eliminate storm water discharge permit requirements.

### SIC code category: Mining and oil and gas extraction

According to the EPA, "oil, gas, and mining facilities are among those industrial sites that are likely to discharge storm water runoff that is contaminated by process wastes, toxic pollutants, hazardous substances, or oil and grease. Such contamination can include disturbed soils and process wastes containing heavy metals or suspended or dissolved solids, salts, surfactants, or solvents used or produced in oil and gas operations" [55 FR 47989 (Nov. 16, 1990)]. However, the 1987 Water Quality Act recognized that the storm water in some facilities is "channeled around plants and operations through a series of ditches and other structural devices in order to prevent pollution of the storm water by harmful contaminants." Therefore, there are significant exemptions for facilities which practice good storm water management.

Several categories of active or inactive mining operations and oil and gas exploration, production, processing, or treatment operations, or transmission facilities are required to obtain storm water permit coverage, including the following:

- SIC code 10: metal mining
- SIC code 11: anthracite mining
- SIC code 12: coal mining
- SIC code 13: oil and gas extraction
- SIC code 14: nonmetallic minerals, except fuels

Because these industrial activities are identified by SIC code, the site is required to obtain permit coverage only if the *primary site activity* is within the SIC codes listed.

**Active mining facilities.**    Several major exemptions will allow many mining facilities to operate without permit coverage. Because of these exemptions, only "contaminated" mine discharges are required to be permitted. Any mining area where storm water discharges do not contact any overburden, raw material, intermediate products, finished products, by-products, or waste products is exempt from permit requirements.

Roads for mining operations will not be required to obtain storm water discharge permit coverage unless storm water runoff from such roads mixes with storm water that is contaminated by contact with overburden, raw materials, intermediate products, finished products, by-products, or waste products. When roads are constructed from materials such as overburden or by-products, an application for an NPDES storm water discharge permit is required. [EPA, 1992]

**Mining claims.**    Sites where mining claims are being maintained prior to disturbances associated with the extraction, beneficiation, or processing of mined materials are not included in the permit requirements. Similarly, no discharge permit is required for sites where minimal activities required for the sole purpose of maintaining the mining claim are undertaken.

**Inactive mines.**    Inactive mining areas which have an identifiable owner-operator must be permitted under the same conditions as an active mine, because the EPA believes that some of these mining sites represent a significant source of contaminated storm water runoff. An inactive mining site is one where there has been past extraction, beneficiation, or processing of mining materials, but with no current active mining. However, in such cases the exclusion discussed above for uncontaminated discharges will still apply. The EPA has issued a separate general permit for inactive mining areas on federal lands which have no identifiable owner or operator.

**Reclaimed mines.** Inactive mines which have undergone a complete reclamation do not require storm water discharge permits. These include the following:

- *Reclaimed coal mines:* areas of coal mining operations which no longer meet the definition of a reclamation area under 40 CFR 434.11(1) because the performance bond issued to the facility by the appropriate SMCRA authority has been released.

- *Other reclaimed mines:* areas of noncoal mining operations which have been released from applicable state or federal reclamation requirements after December 17, 1990. The EPA decided to require storm water discharge permits for reclaimed mining areas released prior to this date because "EPA does not have sufficient evidence to suggest that each State's previous reclamation rules and/or Federal requirements, if applicable, were necessarily effective in controlling future storm water contamination [55 FR 47989 (Nov. 16, 1990)].

**Oil and gas extraction.** Most oil and gas operations are exempt from storm water discharge permit requirements. However, if a facility meets one of the following criteria, a discharge permit must be obtained:

- The facility has had a "reportable quantity" discharge in storm water at any time since November 16, 1987, pursuant to 40 CFR 117.21, 40 CFR 302.6, or 40 CFR 110.6.
- The facility contributes to a violation of a water quality standard.

A *reportable quantity* of oil is the amount that violates applicable water quality standards or causes a film or sheen or a discoloration of the water surface or adjoining shorelines or causes a sludge or emulsion to be deposited beneath the surface of the water or upon adjoining shorelines [40 CFR 110.6]. Reportable quantities for other substances are listed in terms of pounds released during any 24-hour period, in 40 CFR 117.3 and 40 CFR 302.4.

Information from sources such as non-point-source assessments developed pursuant to section 319(a) of the CWA indicate that significant water quality impacts can be caused by wet-weather failure of on-site waste disposal systems at oil and gas exploration and production operations (such as storm-induced overflows of reserve pits used to hold spent drilling muds and cuttings).

The American Petroleum Institute (API) estimates that there are about 850,000 active oil and gas wells, 219,000 tank batteries, and 150,000 injection wells in the United States. The API also estimates that *spill prevention control and countermeasure* (SPCC) plans have been developed for about 130,000 of these facilities. Many of these sites include multiple components (e.g., active wells, a tank battery, and injection wells).

Oil and gas facilities that discharge a reportable quantity of oil or a hazardous substance in storm water after October 1, 1992, must submit a Notice of Intent (NOI) to be covered by the EPA general permit within 14 days of their first knowledge of the release, and they must prepare and begin complying with a storm water discharge permit within 60 days.[2]

### SIC code category: Recyclers

Some types of industrial activities which are concerned with the salvage and reclamation of materials are required to obtain storm water discharge permit coverage. These include metal scrap yards, battery reclaimers, salvage yards, and automobile junkyards, including but not limited to those classified as

- SIC code 5015: motor vehicle parts, used
- SIC code 5093: scrap and waste materials, including the following wholesale businesses: automotive wrecking for scrap, bag reclaiming, waste bottles, waste boxes, fur cuttings and scraps, iron and steel scrap, general junk and scrap, metal and waste scrap, nonferrous metals scrap, waste oil, plastics scrap, rags, rubber scrap, scavenging, scrap and waste materials, textile waste, wastepaper (including paper recycling), and wiping rags (including washing and reconditioning)

Figure 4.2 illustrates a typical small automobile parts recycling operation.

---

[2] The procedure for filing a Notice of Intent for general permit coverage is described in Chap. 5, and the requirements for a storm water pollution prevention plan are described in Chaps. 6 and 7.

**Figure 4.2**  Small automotive parts recycling operation.

Only *industrial* recyclers are included in the storm water regulations. *Commercial* recycling operations, such as gas stations or automotive repair shops that collect tires or batteries or municipal waste collection sites that collect bottles, cans, and newspapers, are not regulated.

According to the EPA, automotive fluids and greases from automobile drivelines are a significant potential source of pollutants to storm water discharges from automobile junkyards. Drivelines include the engine, transmission, differential or transaxle, fuel, brake, and coolant (radiator) systems. Automotive fluids and greases from these areas typically include engine oil, fuel, transmission fluid or oil, rear-end oil, suspension joint and bearing greases, antifreeze, brake fluid, power steering fluid, and the oil and grease leaking from and covering various components (e.g., oil and grease on the exterior of an engine). The procedures used for fluids captured during the dismantling process will affect the potential to contribute pollutants to storm water.

Based on an evaluation of the battery reclamation industry, the EPA also identified handling, storage and processing of lead acid batteries, as well as by-product and waste handling at reclamation facilities, as having a significant potential for pollutants in storm water discharges. (See Fig. 4.3.)

Because these industrial activities are identified by SIC code, the site is required to obtain permit coverage only if the *primary site activity* is

**Figure 4.3**   Small battery recycling area.

within the SIC codes listed. If this is an auxiliary activity of the site, permit coverage is not required.

### SIC code category: Industrial transportation

Several types of industrial transportation activities are included in the storm water discharge permit requirements:

- SIC code 40: railroad transportation
- SIC code 41: local and interurban highway passenger transit
- SIC code 42: trucking and warehousing (except 4221: farm products warehousing and storage, 4222: refrigerated warehousing and storage, and 4225: general warehousing and storage)
- SIC code 43: U.S. Postal Service
- SIC code 44: water transportation
- SIC code 45: transportation by air
- SIC code 5171: petroleum bulk stations and terminals

Discharges must be permitted only for facilities which provide vehicle maintenance shops, equipment cleaning operations, or airport deicing operations. Only those portions of the facility that are involved in vehicle maintenance (including vehicle rehabilitation, mechanical repairs, painting, fueling, and lubrication), equipment cleaning operations, or airport deicing operations are covered by the permit requirements. Parking lots used to store vehicles prior to maintenance are considered to be a component of the vehicle maintenance activity and should therefore be covered by a storm water discharge permit.

The presence of a vehicle maintenance or equipment cleaning operation on an industrial site does not trigger a storm water discharge permit requirement, unless industrial transportation (as defined using the SIC codes listed above) is the *primary* industrial activity of the site. (See. Fig. 4.4.)

An off-site vehicle maintenance facility supporting one company would not be required to apply for a storm water discharge permit if that company were not primarily engaged in providing transportation services and therefore would not be classified as SIC code 42. The maintenance facility would be considered an auxiliary operation to the manufacturing facility. The EPA has determined that off-site vehicle maintenance facilities which primarily service trucks used for local transportation of goods or for local services are generally considered supporting establishments which do not assume a transportation SIC code. Such facilities are classified according to the SIC code of the facility they support [EPA, 1993].

**Figure 4.4** Industrial transportation maintenance facility.

If the maintenance facility is located on the same site as the manufacturing operation, it is included in the areas associated with industrial activity and must therefore be covered by a storm water discharge permit [EPA, 1992].

The operation of fire trucks and police cars is classified under public order and safety (SIC code 92). Therefore, the operator of a facility primarily engaged in servicing these vehicles is not required to apply for a storm water discharge permit [EPA, 1992].

Gas stations and commercial automotive repair facilities are not included in the definition of *industrial transportation* because these facilities are commercial or retail in nature.

**Transportation facilities owned by municipal entities.**    As noted in Chap. 3, by section 1068(c) of the Transportation Act of 1991, the EPA shall not require any municipality with a population of less than 100,000 to apply for or obtain a permit for most industrial activities. Therefore, vehicle maintenance facilities and other transportation-related facilities owned and operated by small municipalities may operate without a storm water discharge permit. For this reason, school bus maintenance facilities owned and/or operated by municipal entities (including school boards, school districts, or other municipal entities) are not required to apply for NPDES storm water discharge permits. However, private-contract school bus companies are required to apply [EPA, 1992].

Municipalities are required to obtain storm water discharge permits for airports which they own or operate. Permit coverage may also be required for other industrial transportation facilities if the facility is a significant contributor of pollutants to waters of the United States or if it contributes to a violation of a water quality standard.

**Airport requirements.**    Airports or airline companies must apply for a storm water discharge permit for locations where deicing chemicals are applied. This includes, but is not limited to, runways, taxiways, ramps, and areas used for the deicing of airplanes. The operator of the airport should apply for the storm water discharge permit, while the individual airline companies should be included as coapplicants. The EPA has the discretion to issue individual permits to each discharger or to issue an individual permit to the airport operator and have other dischargers to the same system act as copermittees. Facilities primarily engaged in performing services that incidentally use airplanes (such as crop dusting or aerial photography) are classified according to the service performed [EPA, 1992].

Deicing activities at airports can be a significant source of pollutants to storm water discharges. The amount of deicing fluids used depends on the temperature and the amount and type of precipitation. For example, freezing rain may require more deicing fluids than many snowfalls. Ethylene glycol, urea, and ammonium nitrate are the primary ingredients of other deicing compounds used at airports. These chemicals can have a significant oxygen demand in water. When deicing operations are performed, large volumes of ethylene glycol are sprayed on aircraft and runways. Data from Stapleton International Airport in Denver, Colorado, indicate that storm water discharges contained levels of up to 5050 milligrams per liter (mg/L) ethylene glycol during a monitoring period from December 1986 to January 1987. Deicing fluids have been implicated in several fish kills across the nation.

## References

Environmental Protection Agency: *Development Document for Proposed Effluent Limitations Guidelines and Standards for the Shipbuilding and Repair Point Source Category,* EPA 440/1/-79/076-b, December 1979.

————: *Development Document for Effluent Limitations Guidelines and Standards for Pretreatment Standards for the Petroleum Refineries Point Source Category,* EPA 440/1/-79/014b, 1979b.

————: *Guidance Specifying Management Measures for Sources of Nonpoint Pollution in Coastal Waters,* Office of Water, EPA 840:B-92-002, January 1993.

————: *NPDES Storm Water Program Question and Answer Document,* vol. 1, EPA 833-F-93-002, March 16, 1992.

————: *NPDES Storm Water Program Question and Answer Document,* vol. 2, EPA 833-F-93-002B, July 1993.

Government Printing Office, *Federal Register,* Office of the Federal Register, National Archives and Records Administration, Washington.

————: *Code of Federal Regulations,* Office of the Federal Register, National Archives and Records Administration, Washington, July 1, 1992.

Office of Management and Budget (OMB): *Standard Industrial Classification Manual,* Executive Office of the President, Washington, 1987.

# 5

# Industrial Storm Water Discharge Permit Applications

This is the second of five chapters (Chaps. 4 to 8) which deal with the specific requirements for storm water discharges from industrial (non-construction) facilities. This chapter describes the permit application process and the types of applications available.

## EPA Storm Water Permitting Strategy

In establishing phase I of the National Storm Water Program (NSWP), the EPA set up a "risk-based" permitting strategy which allows for regulation of storm water discharges in at least four tiers [57 FR 11393 (Apr. 2, 1992)]:

- *Tier I: baseline permitting*—permits that establish a minimum set of requirements which must be met by all permittees, regardless of location or type of discharge.

- *Tier II: watershed permitting*—permits that establish a set of more stringent, water-quality-based requirements for targeted permittees discharging into a specific watershed.

- *Tier III: industry-specific permitting*—permits that establish a set of requirements which must be met by permittees within a certain industrial classification, regardless of the location of the discharge.

- *Tier IV: facility-specific permitting*—permits that establish a set of requirements which must be met by a specific permittee for a specific discharge. Some facilities which are not eligible for general permits or group permit applications must submit individual permit applications. EPA or state regulators may require an individual permit application from any regulated discharger.

It is important not to misinterpret the list of tiers as a list of four separate "phases" through which the NSWP will pass. In fact, it is likely that all four tiers of permitting will coexist, each used as appropriate for local circumstances. The EPA is already using three of the four tiers of regulation established according to this strategy. The only tier that is not currently being used by the EPA is watershed permitting. However, some states have established special requirements for particular watersheds, and the EPA also appears to be moving in this direction.

The primary purpose of baseline permitting, through the general permits, is to provide an expedient means of offering permit coverage to most regulated industries. During the 5-year duration of the initial general permits (October 1, 1992, to October 1, 1997), the EPA will gather data and assess the effectiveness of the general permits. As these initial general permits expire, they will likely be replaced by watershed permits, industry permits, facility-specific permits, or revised general permits, as needed.

## Types of NPDES Storm Water Permit Applications

Initially, three types of permit applications were available for complying with the National Pollutant Discharge Elimination System (NPDES) storm water discharge permit requirements:

1. *General permits:* Most authorized states have issued general permits for many types of industrial storm water discharges. For nonauthorized states, the EPA published two general permits on September 9, 1992, one covering construction activities only and one covering all other types of industrial activities. Another separate general permit will be issued later for inactive mining, landfills, and oil and gas operations on federal lands. Coverage under a general permit is usually obtained by filing a Notice of Intent (NOI). Most authorized states have issued NOI forms for general permit coverage. For nonauthorized states, the EPA published an NOI form with the general permits on September 9, 1992. The NOI filing deadline for existing discharges was October 1, 1992, in nonauthorized states. For authorized states, the NOI filing deadlines vary. Facilities which were operating on the NOI filing deadline but which did not submit an NOI or other type of permit application on that date as required should still submit permit applications. The EPA and most states have not chosen

to impose penalties for late filings during the first few months of the program, but they have the authority to do so. In most cases, the chances of being penalized are reduced whenever the applicant contacts the regulatory agency voluntarily, rather than waiting for the regulatory agency to commence enforcement actions.

2. *Group applications:* These applications were received in two parts. Part 1 was due September 30, 1991, and part 2 was due October 1, 1992. There is no such thing as a "group permit." Instead, the group *applications* will result in the issuance of general or individual permits for each discharge. Group applications were not accepted after the deadlines listed above, and new facilities cannot be added to the list of facilities included with each group application.

3. *Individual permit applications,* with a permit application deadline of October 1, 1992. Individual permit applications are still being received for new facilities. Facilities which were operating on October 1, 1992, but which did not submit an individual permit application on that date, as required, may also still submit permit applications.

The EPA and most state regulatory agencies prefer that as many discharges as possible be covered under the general permit, because these agencies do not have the resources to process a large number of individual permit applications. In addition, general permit requirements are likely to be less stringent than individual permit requirements, so there is no incentive for industries to seek individual permit coverage unless they are required to. In fact, most individual permit applicants are likely to receive coverage under the EPA or general permit rather than an individually written permit, simply because the regulatory agencies will have staff available only to write individual permits for facilities which violate water quality standards, have a history of NPDES permit violations, or present special risks of storm water pollution.

Under the EPA general permit for nonauthorized states, certain discharges are not eligible for general permit coverage, and therefore individual permit applications must be filed. The limitations on coverage are applied on a discharge-by-discharge basis, as opposed to a facility-by-facility basis. Limited discharges include the following:

- *Discharges subject to storm water effluent limitation guidelines.* If a facility has multiple storm water discharges, with one or more storm water discharges subject to an effluent limitation guideline and one or more discharges not subject to an effluent limitation guideline, then the discharges that are not subject to an effluent limitation guideline can be covered under the EPA general permit. However, the discharges from the facility that are subject to an effluent limitation guideline may not be covered by the general permit because it does not incorporate the limitations for these discharges.

- *Discharges covered by existing permit.* Discharges which are already covered by an individual NPDES permit are not eligible for general permit coverage. However, facilities with an existing NPDES permit for process wastewaters and/or other non-storm-water discharges are allowed to obtain general permit coverage for their storm water discharges. Only storm water discharges that are authorized by a different NPDES permit cannot be authorized by the general permit. In addition, the discharges covered by the individual permit and the discharges covered by the general permit may be mixed prior to discharge. However, the individual permit should address the monitoring requirements and compliance point for numeric limitations.

- *Discharges mixed with nonstorm water.*  As noted later in this chapter, the EPA general permit allows certain types of nonstorm discharges to be mixed with storm water discharges, without requiring additional permit coverage. The EPA recognizes that discharging some classes of nonstorm water via separate storm sewers or otherwise mixed with storm water discharges is largely unavoidable and/or poses little, if any, environmental risk. However, where a storm water discharge is mixed with *unallowable* types of nonstorm water, the discharger should obtain permit coverage of the non-storm-water portion of the discharge. Some states do not provide coverage for any nonstorm discharges under the general permits for storm water discharges.

- *Discharges excluded by EPA on the basis of water quality concerns and discharges that would adversely affect a listed endangered or threatened species.*   These discharges will be identified on a case-by-case basis.

## State Permitting

As described in Chap. 14, states which administer their own NPDES permitting programs deal with general permits, individual permits, and group permit applications according to the laws and regulations of each state. As noted in Chap. 1, most states have the authority to issue individual and general permits for storm water discharges. Within these states, the general permits for industrial and construction discharges may differ from the EPA general permits. However, there are also many similarities. Some states have chosen to issue general permits for additional industrial categories. In all cases, however, the state permit requirements must meet the minimum standards of the Clean Water Act, as explained in Chap. 1. Generally, this means that state permit requirements are at least as stringent as the EPA permit requirements, although there are exceptions.

## Municipal Notification and Requirements

According to the EPA general permit of September 9, 1992, all industrial facilities which discharge storm water into large or medium municipal separate storm sewer system (MS4) must submit a notification to the operators of the storm sewer system at least 180 days before the first discharge. The municipal notification should include the following information:

- The name of the facility
- The name and phone number of the appropriate contact person associated with the industrial facility
- The location of the discharge
- A description, including SIC code, of the principal products or services provided by the facility
- Any existing NPDES permit number for *any* other discharges of the facility

As described in Chap. 1, a large MS4 is one which serves an urbanized population of at least 250,000. A medium MS4 is one which serves an urbanized population of 100,000 to 250,000. An MS4 includes not only enclosed storm sewer systems but also "roads with drainage systems, municipal streets, catch basins, curbs, gutters, ditches, manmade channels, or storm drains." The system may by operated by an incorporated city, county, special district, or any other public entity created under state law.

During the early portion of the development of regulations to implement the National Storm Water Program, the EPA considered the possibility of regulating industrial storm water discharges by municipal permit requirements only. In other words, industrial facilities discharging into a large or medium municipal storm sewer system would not have been required to obtain EPA or state permits directly. Instead, these dischargers would have been indirectly regulated by the requirements imposed on the municipal separate storm sewer systems receiving discharges from these industrial facilities.

Although the EPA eventually decided to require discharge permits from all industrial dischargers, many industries are still likely to be regulated by municipal operators. Some of the requirements of these municipal operators may exceed the requirements of the facility's NPDES permit for storm water discharges.

The application requirements for large and medium MS4s impose special conditions with respect to certain types of industrial facilities, including

- Landfills
- Hazardous waste treatment, disposal, and recovery facilities
- Facilities subject to SARA Title III, section 313 regulations
- Facilities contributing a substantial pollutant load to the municipal separate storm sewer system

For these types of facilities, the storm water management program developed by the municipal operator must identify priorities and procedures for inspections and for establishing and implementing control measures for these discharges. The municipal operator must also implement a monitoring program for discharges from these facilities. The municipal operator is also required to effectively prohibit non-storm-water discharges.

If an industrial facility discharges into a nonmunicipal storm sewer system (such as a federal government system), then the facility must still obtain an NPDES storm water discharge permit. The industrial facility may also choose to operate as a copermittee with the operator of the nonmunicipal storm sewer system.

### Individual Permit Application

Dischargers not eligible for coverage under the general permits or not participating in group permit applications must apply for coverage under an individual NPDES permit for each discharge. As noted previously, EPA or state regulators may also direct any regulated discharger to submit an individual permit application.

Within nonauthorized states, the requirements for an individual permit application are reflected in EPA Form 1 and Form 2F. There are simplified application requirements for construction activities. For other industrial activities, however, these forms require the development and submittal of relatively detailed site-specific information, including

- A site map showing topography and/or drainage areas and site characteristics
- An estimate of impervious surface areas and total area drained by each outfall
- A narrative description of significant materials and materials management practices
- A certification that outfalls have been tested or evaluated for non-storm-water discharges
- Information on significant leaks and spills of toxic or hazardous pollutants that occurred at the facility in the last 3 years
- Sampling data from one representative storm event

This information is intended to be used to develop the site-specific conditions generally associated with individual permits. The following sections describe each portion of the permit application in greater detail.

### Site maps and site description

The site map, including topography and site drainage, should have arrows indicating the site drainage and entering and leaving points. Existing permit application regulations at 40 CFR 122.21(f)(7) require all permit applicants to submit as part of EPA Form 1 a topographic map extending 1 mile (mi) beyond the property boundaries of the source depicting

- The facility and each intake and discharge structure
- Each hazardous waste treatment, storage, or disposal facility
- Each well where fluids from the facility are injected underground
- Those wells, springs, other surface water bodies, and drinking water wells listed in the map area in public records or otherwise known to the applicant within 0.25 mi of the facility property boundary [47 FR 15304, Apr. 8, 1982]

A narrative description must also be submitted to accompany the drainage map. The narrative will provide a description of on-site features including existing structures (buildings which cover materials and other material covers, dikes, diversion ditches, etc.) and nonstructural controls (employee training, visual inspections, preventive maintenance, and housekeeping measures) that are used to prevent or minimize the potential for release of toxic and hazardous pollutants; a description of significant materials that are currently being treated or in the past have been treated, stored, or disposed outside; and the method of treatment, storage, or disposal used. The narrative will also include a description of activities at materials loading and unloading areas; the location, manner, and frequency with which pesticides, herbicides, soil conditioners, and fertilizers are applied; a description of the soil; and a description of the areas which are predominately responsible for first-flush runoff (defined in Chap. 8).

### Description of significant materials and management practices

The application must include a description of each past or present area used for outdoor storage or disposal of significant materials, including hazardous substances, fertilizers, pesticides, and raw materials used in the production or processing of food. The list must include any chemical the facility is required to report pursuant to section 313 of Title III of SARA. The EPA does not require information on past practices occurring prior to 3 years before the date on which the application is submitted.

### Certification of nonstorm discharges

Permit applicants for storm water discharges associated with industrial activity must also certify that all the outfalls covered in the permit application have been tested or evaluated for non-storm-water discharges which are not covered by an NPDES permit. If this determination can be made by inspection of schematics or piping diagrams, then no testing is required. Chapter 6 provides more details on conducting evaluations for nonstorm discharges.

This requirement is included to assist operators of municipal separate storm sewer systems in meeting their requirement to effectively prohibit non-storm-water discharges to the storm sewer system. The certification requirement would not apply to outfalls where storm water is intentionally mixed with process wastewater streams which are already identified in and covered by a permit.

### Sampling data

The following sampling data must be provided for one representative storm event:

1. Laboratory analysis results for any pollutants limited in an effluent guideline to which the facility is subject
2. Laboratory analysis results for any pollutant listed in an NPDES permit for process wastewater
3. Laboratory analysis results for oil and grease, pH, biochemical oxygen demand (BOD), chemical oxygen demand (COD), total suspended solids (TSS), total phosphorus, nitrate plus nitrite, and total Kjeldahl nitrogen
4. Laboratory analysis results for any pollutant known to be in the discharge
5. Flow measurements or estimates of flow during the storm event
6. Date and duration of storm event

Chapter 8 provides more information on storm water sampling.

### Facilities with existing NPDES permits

If some discharges from the facility are already covered by existing NPDES permits and individual permit coverage is also required for additional storm water discharges, then there are three available strategies for permit issuance:

- *Additional permit:*   The state or the EPA may choose to issue a new permit covering only those storm water discharge points not already covered by the existing NPDES permit for the facility. This would result in two separate permits with different expiration dates.

- *Modified permit:*   The state or the EPA may choose to modify the existing NPDES permit for the facility to include the storm water discharge points not already covered. This would result in a single permit.

- *Transitional permit:*   The state or the EPA may choose to issue a separate permit for the storm water discharges not already covered under the existing NPDES permit. However, it will write the conditions for the new permit to be consistent with the existing NPDES permit for the facility, and it will schedule the expiration date of the new permit to coincide with the expiration date of the existing NPDES permit for the facility. When the permits expire, they will be replaced by a single permit which includes all discharge points.

Discussions with state and EPA regulators in various portions of the country indicate that the third option is the most common.

## Group Applications

As stated earlier, the group application process was made available by the EPA as a temporary option during the initial phase of the National Storm Water Program. Groups of similar industrial facilities were allowed to submit a single application covering all facilities, even though the sites may be in geographically diverse portions of the country. From the EPA's viewpoint, the group application requirements provide information for developing industry-specific general permits. As such, group application requirements correlate with the Tier III permitting activities discussed earlier.

Group applications were submitted in two parts: a part I application which was due September 30, 1991, and a part II application which was due October 1, 1992. The EPA reports that over 1200 part I applications were received, covering more than 60,000 facilities. The part I application presented background information similar to the NOI for general permit coverage.

The part II application, submitted using items 7 through 10 of EPA form 2F, includes quantitative data derived from storm water sampling performed on a small subset of the sites included in the group.

The group application process was designed to culminate in the development of *model permits* which would form the basis for individual permits issued for each group member. The EPA has developed model permits for 32 different industrial sectors:

1. Metal mining (SIC code 10)

2. Coal mining (SIC code 12)

3. Oil and gas extraction (SIC code 13)

4. Mining and quarrying of nonmetallic minerals (SIC code 14)

5. Food and kindred products (SIC code 20) and tobacco products (SIC code 21)

6. Textile mill products (SIC code 22) and apparel and other finished products made from fabrics and similar materials (SIC code 23)

7. Lumber and wood products (SIC code 24)

8. Furniture and fixtures (SIC code 25)

9. Paper and allied products (SIC code 26)

10. Printing, publishing, and allied industries (SIC code 27)

11. Chemicals and allied products (SIC code 28)

12. Petroleum refining and related industries (SIC code 29)

13. Rubber and miscellaneous plastic products (SIC code 30)

14. Leather and leather products (SIC code 31)

15. Stone, clay, glass, and concrete products (SIC code 32)

16. Primary metal industries (SIC code 33)

17. Fabricated metal products, except for machinery and transportation equipment (SIC code 34), and jewelry, silverware, and plated ware (SIC code 29)

18. Industrial and commercial machinery (SIC code 35) except for computer and office equipment (SIC code 357) and transportation equipment (SIC code 37)

19. Electronic equipment, other electrical equipment and components (SIC code 36); computer and office equipment and components (SIC code 357); and measuring, analyzing, and controlling instruments, photographic and optical goods, and watches and clocks (SIC code 38)

20. Shipbuilding and repairing (SIC code 3731) and boat building and repairing (SIC code 3732)

21. Miscellaneous manufacturing industries (SIC code 39, except SIC code 391)

22. Railroad transportation (SIC code 40)

23. Local and suburban transit and interurban highway passenger transportation (SIC code 41), motor freight transportation (SIC code 42), and U.S. Postal Service (SIC code 43)

24. Water transportation (SIC code 44)

25. Transportation by air facilities (SIC code 45)

26. Used motor vehicle parts (SIC code 5015)

27. Scrap and waste materials (SIC code 5093)

28. Petroleum bulk stations and terminals (SIC code 5171)

29. Steam electric power generating facilities

30. Domestic wastewater treatment plants

31. Hazardous waste treatment, storage, and disposal facilities

32. Industrial landfills, land application sites, and open dumps

EPA and state regulators are not required to use the model permits for group members. They have the option of providing general permit coverage for group members. Facilities which have been excluded from a group application, or facilities from a rejected group application, must generally submit an individual permit application.

## General Permit Coverage

As noted in Chap. 1, a series of court rulings have established the authority of the EPA to utilize innovative concepts such as general permits to regulate discharges under the Clean Water Act. The EPA has used general permits as a tool to accommodate the large number of dischargers included in the National Storm Water Program. Most traditional NPDES permits have been individual permits, with requirements specific to the facility named in the permit. In addition, the traditional NPDES permit gives numeric effluent limitations on various pollutants and specifies a minimum discharge sampling interval.

In contrast to the traditional NPDES permit requirements, the EPA general permit for storm water discharges has requirements which are general enough to be applied to a wide range of industrial facilities in many different areas of the United States. The general permit does not require treatment, but instead emphasizes *best management practices,* many of which are nonstructural in nature. The EPA general permit is almost totally devoid of numeric effluent limitations. Finally, the EPA general permit does not require discharge sampling for most types of industrial facilities.

Because of the fundamental differences between the EPA general permit for storm water discharges and previous NPDES permits, some dischargers are confused about exactly how to meet the new permit requirements. The new EPA general permit is so flexible that it is almost like being able to "write your own permit." Some people, even representatives of dischargers, are uncomfortable with having this much flexibility. In the EPA's view, however, this flexibility provides dischargers with the opportunity to develop best management practices which are the most appropriate and effective for each facility.

The EPA issued its *core general permit* for storm water discharges associated with industrial activity on September 9, 1992 (see App. A). This core general permit applies directly to nonauthorized states and serves as the basis for other general permits issued by authorized states. Many authorized states have chosen to tailor the core general permit for various industrial groups.

The EPA core general permit requires the submittal of a Notice of Intent (NOI), which states the permittee's desire to discharge according to the terms and provisions of the general permit. Compliance with the provisions of the general permit involves the preparation and maintenance of a storm water pollution prevention plan (as described in Chaps. 6 and 7). In addition, some types of facilities are required to perform storm water discharge sampling (as described in Chap. 8).

The EPA does not currently assess permit fees for general permit coverage, but several states do. The EPA has worked on a federal permit fee system which would impose fees on permit holders in states without NPDES permit authority. This fee system was developed under the 1990 Budget Reconciliation Act, which required the EPA to develop a system of user fees to pay for services rendered. It is reasonable to expect the EPA to implement a fee system for storm water discharge permit applications.

The existing EPA general permits for industrial and construction activity will expire on October 1, 1997. There is no automatic renewal of general permit coverage. The facility must submit the appropriate NOI or permit application to comply with the program requirements in place at that time.

There is no automatic transfer of general permit coverage to a new facility operator. The new operator must submit a new NOI before assuming operation of the industrial facility.

## EPA general permit NOI requirements

Within nonauthorized states, facilities with industrial activity addressed by the storm water program must submit an NOI at least 2 days prior to the commencement of the industrial activity at the facility. One NOI is generally sufficient for an entire industrial site, including several separate outfalls. However, separate NOIs must be submitted for each separately located industrial facility, even if the facilities are under common ownership. If there are multiple operators at a site, each operator must submit an NOI. The EPA will confirm the receipt of the NOI and will provide the applicant with a permit number and a summary of the guidance on preparing storm water pollution prevention plans [EPA, 1993].

The minimum information on the NOI includes the following:

- *Facility location:* the name, mailing address, and physical location of the facility for which the notice is submitted. If the facility has a street address, this must be provided. Otherwise, the latitude and longitude (or section, township, and range) can be used to identify the site location.

- *Industrial operations:* up to four four-digit Standard Industrial Classification (SIC) codes that best represent the principal products or activities provided by the facility. This information is intended to give the EPA an indication of the nature of the industrial activity at the facility. An alternative indicator of the industrial activity is required for classes of facilities that do not have SIC codes which accurately describe the principal products or services provided (e.g., hazardous waste treatment, storage, or disposal facilities; land disposal facilities that receive or have received any industrial waste; steam electric power generating facilities; or treatment works treating domestic sewage).

- *Operator identification:* the name, address, and telephone number of the operator, along with the ownership status and the status of the operator as a federal, state, local, or private entity.

- *Existing NPDES permits:* the permit number of additional NPDES permits for *any* discharges from the site (including non-storm-water discharges) that are currently authorized by an NPDES permit.

- *Receiving waters or system:* the name of the receiving water(s), which allows the EPA to identify discharges to impaired, sensitive water bodies or high-value water resources that require additional oversight and compliance evaluation. If the discharge is to a large or medium municipal separate storm sewer system, the name of the municipal operator of the storm sewer system must be identified along with the name of the ultimate receiving water(s).

- *Indication of sampling data:* an indication of whether the facility has existing quantitative data describing the concentration of pollutants in storm water discharges. The actual results are not submitted with the NOI; only an indication is needed of whether such results are available.

- *Indication of group participation:* an indication of whether the facility has previously participated in the group application process, which allows the EPA to implement the group application process better and eliminates redundancy or overlap between that process and coverage with general permits.

- *SWPPP certification:* a certification that a storm water pollution prevention plan (SWPPP) has been prepared for the facility. Further details on SWPPPs are presented later in this chapter and in Chaps, 6 and 7.

The person signing the NOI must have a sufficient level of authority and responsibility within the organization to help ensure compliance with the terms and conditions of the permit. For a sole proprietorship, the proprietor must sign the NOI. For a partnership, a general partner must sign.

For a corporation, the person signing the NOI must be a responsible corporate officer, including the president, secretary, treasurer, or vice president of the corporation in charge of a principal business function, or any other person who performs similar policy- or decision-making functions for the corporation.

A corporate plant or facility manager may sign the NOI only under certain conditions. The plant or facility must employ more than 250 persons or have gross annual sales or expenditures exceeding $25 million (in second-quarter 1980 dollars). In addition, the authority to sign documents must have been assigned or delegated to the plant or facility manager in accordance with corporate procedures.

For a municipality, state, federal, or other public agency, the person signing the NOI must be a principal executive officer or ranking elected official. A principal executive officer of a federal agency includes the chief executive officer of the agency or a senior executive officer having responsibility for the overall operations of a principal geographic unit of the agency (e.g., regional administrators of the EPA). Within the military, base commanders represent the appropriate level of authority.

The person signing the NOI is making the following certification:

> I certify under penalty of law that this document and all attachments were prepared under my direction or supervision in accordance with a system

designed to assure that qualified personnel properly gather and evaluate the information submitted. Based on my inquiry of the person or persons who manage the system, or those persons directly responsible for gathering the information, the information submitted is, to the best of my knowledge and belief, true, accurate, and complete. I am aware that there are significant penalties for submitting false information, including the possibility of fine and imprisonment for knowing violations.

### Storm water pollution prevention plan

In nonauthorized states, the EPA general permit requires that a storm water pollution prevention plan (SWPPP) be completed for each existing industrial facility for which an NOI has been submitted. Most authorized states have similar requirements, although some states use different terminology. The SWPPP must be completed and ready to implement at the time the facility begins industrial operations.

Under EPA general permit requirements, the SWPPP is not submitted with the NOI. Instead, the SWPPP is retained on site by the discharger. Federal, state, and local regulatory agencies have the authority to review the SWPPP at any time. If the reviewing agency finds that the SWPPP is not in compliance with general permit requirements, the discharger has 30 days to revise the SWPPP to achieve compliance. Chapters 6 and 7 provide further details on the SWPPP.

### Nonstorm discharges allowed under general permit

The provisions of the EPA general permit prohibit most non-storm-water discharges, except the following:

- Discharges from fire-fighting activities
- Fire hydrant flushing
- Potable water sources, including waterline flushing
- Landscape irrigation drainage
- Lawn watering
- Routine external building wash water (without detergents or other contaminants)
- Pavement wash waters where spills or leaks of toxic or hazardous materials have not occurred (unless all spilled material has been removed) and where detergents are not used
- Air-conditioning condensate (but not including cooling water from cooling towers, heat exchangers, or other sources)
- Springs

- Uncontaminated groundwater

- Foundation or footing drains where flows are not contaminated with process materials such as solvents

To be authorized under the EPA general permit, these sources of non-storm water (except flows from fire-fighting activities) must be identified in the SWPPP prepared for the facility. Where such discharges occur, the plan must also identify and ensure the implementation of appropriate pollution prevention measures for the non-storm-water component(s) of the discharge. Chapter 6 provides further details.

### Special conditions for certain facilities

The EPA general permit provides additional time for complying with the additional requirements for EPCRA section 313 facilities and for facilities with salt piles and coal piles. The portions of the SWPPP addressing these additional requirements must become effective within 3 years of the date of permit coverage. These requirements are described in Chap. 7.

### Notice of Termination

The EPA general permit allows the discharger to submit a Notice of Termination (NOT) form (or photocopy thereof) when the storm water discharges associated with industrial activity from a facility have been eliminated. This assists the EPA in tracking the status of the discharger. The NOT requires the following information:

- *Facility location:* name, mailing address, and location of the facility for which the notification is submitted. Where a street address for the site is not available, the location of the approximate center of the site must be described in terms of the latitude and longitude to the nearest 15 seconds, or the section, township, and range to the nearest quarter.

- *Operator identification:* the name, address, and telephone number of the operator addressed by the Notice of Termination.

- *NPDES permit number:* the NPDES permit number for the storm water discharge associated with industrial activity identified by the NOT.

- *Reason for NOT:* an indication of whether the storm water discharges associated with industrial activity have been eliminated or the operator of the discharges has changed.

- *Certification:* The following certification is required:

I certify under penalty of law that all storm water discharges associated with industrial activity from the identified facility that are authorized by a NPDES general permit have been eliminated or that I am no longer the operator of the facility or construction site. I understand that by submitting this Notice of Termination, I am no longer authorized to discharge storm water associated with industrial activity under this general permit, and that discharging pollutants in storm water associated with industrial activity to waters of the United States is unlawful under the Clean Water Act where the discharge is not authorized by a NPDES permit. I also understand that the submittal of this Notice of Termination does not release an operator from liability for any violations of this permit or the Clean Water Act.

The NOT must be signed in accordance with the signatory requirements of 40 CFR 122.22, which were summarized earlier in this chapter with regard to the NOI form.

## References

Environmental Protection Agency: *NPDES Storm Water Program Question and Answer Document,* vol. 2, EPA 833-F-93-002BRAVO, July 1993.
Government Printing Office: *Federal Register,* Office of the Federal Register, National Archives and Records Administration, Washington.
————: *Code of Federal Regulations,* Office of the Federal Register, National Archives and Records Administration, Washington, July 1, 1992.

Chapter

# 6

# Basic Elements of Industrial Storm Water Pollution Prevention Plans

This is the third of five chapters which deal with the specific requirements for storm water discharges from industrial (nonconstruction) facilities. This chapter describes how to prepare the basic elements of a *storm water pollution prevention plan* (SWPPP) for an industrial facility. Appendix C presents an example of an SWPPP for an industrial facility.

## Requirements for Storm Water Pollution Prevention Plans

The EPA general permit for storm water discharges from industrial activities requires that a storm water pollution prevention plan be completed at the time that the facility operator submits the Notice of Intent (NOI) for general permit coverage. The facility should begin to implement the SWPPP immediately.

A comprehensive SWPPP should have the following basic sections, which are described in this chapter:

- *Pollution prevention team:* This section identifies the specific personnel responsible for developing and implementing the plan, including the specific responsibilities of each individual.

- *Potential pollutant sources:* This part describes and illustrates the existing drainage conditions of the site, presents an inventory of significant materials, and discusses the management practices for these materials. This section also lists any recent spills and leaks, describes the procedures used to evaluate and eliminate nonstorm discharges, and includes any available storm water sampling data for the site. It concludes with a discussion of the risks of storm water pollution at the site.

- *Measures and controls:* This section describes the operations and mechanisms that will be used to eliminate or minimize storm water pollution at the facility. These will include a housekeeping and maintenance plan, spill prevention and response procedures, storm water management controls, inspections and record keeping, employee training, and sediment and erosion controls.

- *Monitoring requirements:* This section describes the required annual site compliance evaluation and certification and any storm water sampling required for the facility.

- *Other regulatory requirements:* This section describes the applicable state and local requirements for the facility and the methods used to ensure compliance with these requirements.

Many storm water pollution prevention plans will also have special sections relating to portions of the site that are regulated by special requirements within the EPA general permit. These special requirements, which are described in Chap. 7, pertain to facilities with salt piles, coal piles, or SARA Title III, section 313 water priority chemicals.

## Philosophy of Storm Water Pollution Prevention Plans

Storm water pollution prevention plans should be dynamic documents which are revised as appropriate to reflect changes in the facility's operations. The EPA general permit requires that the permittee amend the plan whenever there is a change in design, construction, operation, or maintenance which has a significant effect on the potential for the discharge of pollutants to waters of the United States or if the storm water pollution prevention plan proves to be ineffective in eliminating or significantly minimizing pollutants. In addition, permittees are required to inspect their sites and evaluate the accuracy and effectiveness of their plans and modify the plan as necessary.

The use of storm water pollution prevention plans as a means to control pollutants in storm water discharges is a much different approach from the numeric effluent limitations used in traditional National Pollutant Discharge Elimination System (NPDES) permits. It is an example of the flexible and innovative approaches available to the EPA in carrying out the NPDES program. As discussed in Chap. 1, court rulings have established that the EPA has considerable discretionary authority to use pollution prevention requirements when quantitative limitations are unfeasible or unwieldy. The pollution prevention requirements operate as limitations on effluent discharges that reflect the application of best-available technology and best conventional technology, as required by the Clean Water Act.

The EPA believes that the pollution prevention approach is the most environmentally sound and cost-effective way to control the discharge of pollutants in storm water runoff from industrial facilities. This position is supported by the results of a comprehensive technical survey that the EPA completed in 1979. The survey found that there are two classes of management practices used in industry to control the non-routine discharge of pollutants from sources such as storm water runoff, drainage from raw material storage and waste disposal areas, and discharges from places where spills or leaks have occurred. The first class of management practices includes those that are low in cost, are applicable to a broad class of industries and substances, and generally are considered essential to a good pollution control program. Some examples of practices in this class are good housekeeping, employee training, and spill prevention procedures. The second class includes management practices that provide a second line of defense against the release of pollutants. This class addresses containment, mitigation, cleanup, and treatment. The general permit requirements for development and implementation of a storm water pollution prevention plan include both classes of management practices.

## Pollution Prevention Team

As a first step in the process of developing and implementing an SWPPP, permittees must identify a qualified individual or team of individuals to be responsible for developing the plan and assisting the facility or plant manager in its implementation. The team should include the expertise of all relevant departments within the plant to ensure that all aspects of plant operations are considered when the plan is developed. Pollution prevention teams may consist of one individual where appropriate (e.g., in certain small businesses with limited storm water pollution potential).

The pollution prevention team should be specifically identified. It is not sufficient to simply say, "the team shall include representatives of the plant safety office, the operations office, etc." Instead, specific individuals must be identified, if not by name, then at least by position. For example, "the team shall include the director of plant safety, the assistant manager of operations, etc." The team leader must also be identified and must have overall responsibility for preparation and implementation of the SWPPP.

The plan must clearly describe the responsibilities of each team member as they relate to specific components of the plan. In addition to enhancing the quality of communication between team members and other personnel, clear delineation of responsibilities will ensure that every aspect of the plan is addressed by a specified individual or group of individuals.

## Potential Pollutant Sources

Storm water pollution prevention plans must be based on an accurate understanding of the pollution potential of the site. The first part of the plan requires an evaluation of the sources of pollution at a specific industrial site. The permit proposes that the source identification portion of the plan identify all activities and significant materials which may potentially be significant pollutant sources.

The source identification portion of the plan includes the following sections:

1. *Drainage:* a drainage site map with a narrative description
2. *Inventory of exposed materials:* a narrative description of significant materials, materials management practices, pollutant control measures, and storm water treatment
3. *Significant spills and leaks:* a list of significant spills and leaks of toxic or hazardous pollutants that occurred at the facility after the effective date of the permit
4. *Non-storm-water discharges:* a certification that the facility has been tested or evaluated for non-storm-water discharges and that these have been eliminated (except for allowable discharges)
5. *Sampling data:* a summary of existing sampling data describing pollutants in storm water discharges
6. *Risk identification:* an evaluation of activities likely to be significant sources of pollutants to storm water discharges.

Each of these items is discussed in the following sections.

### Drainage

The SWPPP must contain a map of the site that shows the pattern of storm water drainage on the site. The EPA only requires that the portions of the drainage area within the facility's boundaries be identified.

The EPA does not require that the map include site topography, although such information would clearly be pertinent to site drainage. The map should indicate an outline of the portions of the drainage area of each storm water outfall, each existing structural control measure to reduce pollutants in storm water runoff, the location of all surface water bodies (including wetlands), places where significant materials are exposed to rainfall and runoff, and locations of major spills and leaks that occurred in the 3 years prior to the effective date of the permit. Nonstructural features such as grass swales and vegetative buffer strips also should be shown.

The map must show areas where the following activities take place: fueling, vehicle and equipment maintenance and/or cleaning, loading and unloading, material storage (including tanks or other vessels used for liquid or waste storage), material processing, and waste disposal. For areas of the facility that generate storm water discharges with a reasonable potential to contain significant amounts of pollutants, the map must indicate the probable direction of storm water flow and the pollutants likely to be in the discharge. Flows with a significant potential to cause soil erosion must be identified.

### Inventory of exposed materials

Facility operators are required to carefully conduct an inspection of the site and related records to identify significant materials that are or may be exposed to storm water. The inventory must address materials that within 3 years prior to the effective date of the permit have been handled, stored, processed, treated, or disposed of in a manner to allow exposure to storm water. Findings of the inventory must be documented in detail in the pollution prevention plan.

At a minimum, the plan must describe the methods and location of on-site storage or disposal; management practices used to minimize contact of materials with rainfall and runoff; existing structural and nonstructural controls that reduce pollutants in runoff; and any treatment the runoff receives before it is discharged to surface waters or a separate storm sewer system. The description must be updated whenever there is a significant change in the types or amounts of materials, or material management practices, that may affect the exposure of materials to storm water.

The inventory of exposed materials is intended to address materials that potentially may be exposed to precipitation, including chemicals used and by-products formed at the site. Significant materials include, but are not limited to, the following: raw materials; fuels; solvents, detergents, and plastic pellets; finished materials, such as metallic products; raw materials used in food processing or production; hazardous substances designated under section 101(14) of CERCLA; any chemical the facility is required to report pursuant to EPCRA section 313; chemicals or compounds listed in effluent limitations guidelines to which the facility is subject; chemicals or compounds specifically controlled or limited in any other NPDES permit for the facility; fertilizers; pesticides; and waste products, such as ashes, slag, and sludge that have the potential to be released with storm water discharges. [See 40 CFR 122.26(b)(8).]

### Significant spills and leaks

The storm water pollution prevention plan must include a list of any significant spills and leaks of toxic or hazardous pollutants that occurred in the 3 years prior to the effective date of the permit. Significant spills include, but are not limited to, releases of oil or hazardous substances in excess of quantities that are reportable under section 311 of CWA (see 40 CFR 110.10 and 117.21) or section 102 of CERCLA (see 40 CFR 302.4).

Significant spills may also include chronic releases of oil or hazardous substances that are not in excess of reporting requirements. Instances of chronically repeated smaller spills can constitute significant spills if such spills, taken together, add significant amounts of pollutants to storm water discharges.

Significant spills may also include releases of materials that are not classified as oil or a hazardous substance, but that could potentially add significant amounts of pollutants. These discharges can also cause water quality impacts.

The listing should include a description of the causes of each spill or leak, the actions taken to respond to each release, and the actions taken to prevent similar spills or leaks in the future. This effort will aid the facility operator in examining existing spill prevention and response procedures and in developing any additional procedures necessary to comply with the permit.

Some spills, such as those that occur inside buildings which drain to a sanitary sewer, are not potential sources of pollution to storm water discharges and thus do not need to be identified in the SWPPP. However, spills to sumps or secondary containment areas that receive storm water discharges should generally be identified in the SWPPP because such devices can overflow during large or repeated storm events or storm water may be drained and discharged from such devices. It is also important to identify spills that occur on impervious surfaces exposed to precipitation or that otherwise drain to a storm drain even when the spill is cleaned up before any of it enters a storm drain. Listing such events provides an indication of potential pollutant sources that may occur in the future and helps direct priorities for developing and implementing spill response measures.

Storm water pollution prevention plans are to be updated to address significant spills and leaks that occur during the term of the permit.

This information is necessary to ensure that major potential sources of pollution to storm water discharges are identified.

### Non-storm-water discharges

Two types of non-storm-water discharges must be addressed in the SWPPP: allowable non-storm-water discharges and illicit non-storm-water discharges.

**Allowable non-storm-water discharges.**  The provisions of the EPA general permit prohibit most non-storm-water discharges except the following:

- Discharges from fire-fighting activities
- Fire hydrant flushing
- Potable water sources, including waterline flushing
- Landscape irrigation drainage
- Lawn watering
- Routine external building wash water (without detergents or other contaminants)
- Pavement wash waters where spills or leaks of toxic or hazardous materials have not occurred (unless all spilled material has been removed) and where detergents are not used
- Air-conditioning condensate (but not including cooling water from cooling towers, heat exchangers, or other sources)
- Springs
- Uncontaminated groundwater
- Foundation or footing drains where flows are not contaminated with process materials such as solvents

Some state permits prohibit non-storm-water discharges altogether; separate permits are required for all nonstorm discharges. Under the EPA general permit, however, the sources of nonstorm water listed above are allowed, but they must be identified in the SWPPP prepared for the facility. Where such discharges occur, the plan must also identify and ensure the implementation of appropriate pollution prevention measures for the non-storm-water component(s) of the discharge. For example, to reduce pollutants in irrigation drainage, a plan could identify low-maintenance lawn areas that do not require the use of fertilizers or herbicides; for higher-maintenance lawn areas, a plan could identify measures such as limiting fertilizer use based on seasonal and agronomic considerations, decreasing herbicide use with an integrated pest management program, introducing natural vegetation or hardier species, and reducing water use (thereby reducing the volume of irrigation drainage).

Pollution prevention measures are not required to be identified and implemented for non-storm-water flows from fire-fighting activities because these flows will generally be unplanned emergency situations where it is necessary to take immediate action to protect the public.

**Illicit non-storm-water discharges.**   Many facilities have cross-connections between the storm and sanitary sewer systems. In addition, floor drains are commonly connected to the storm sewer system in many industrial plants. These cross-connections and floor drain connections to the storm sewer network are considered to be illicit connections and represent potential non-storm-water discharges. Technically, these connections violate the Clean Water Act unless the facility has already obtained a separate NPDES permit for the connection.

Rinse waters used to clean or cool objects discharge to floor drains that may be connected to separate storm sewers. Large amounts of rinse waters may originate from industries that use regular washdown procedures; e.g., bottling plants use rinse waters for removing waste products, debris, and labels. Rinse waters can be used to cool materials by dipping, washing, or spraying objects with cool water; e.g., rinse water is sometimes sprayed over the final products of a metal plating facility to cool them.

Condensate return lines of heat exchangers often discharge to floor drains. Heat exchangers, particularly those used under stressed conditions such as in the metal finishing and electroplating industry, typically develop pinhole leaks, which may result in contamination of condensate by process wastes.

These and other non-storm-water discharges to a storm sewer may be intentional, based on the belief that the discharge does not contain pollutants, or they may be inadvertent, for the operator may be unaware that a floor drain is connected to the storm sewer. The connection may have been legal at the time of installation. In many cases, operators of industrial facilities may be unaware of illicit discharges or leakage from underground storage tanks or other nonvisible systems.

**Certification of testing for non-storm-water discharges.**   Each pollution prevention plan must include a certification, signed by an authorized individual, that discharges from the site have been tested or evaluated for the presence of non-storm-water discharges. The certification must describe possible significant sources of nonstorm water, the results of any test and/or evaluation conducted to detect such discharges, the test method or evaluation criteria used, the dates on which tests or evaluations were performed, and the on-site drainage points directly observed during the test or evaluation. The certification must be completed within 180 days after submittal of an NOI to be covered by the EPA general permit.

Certification may not be feasible where there is no access to an outfall, manhole, or other point of access to the conduit that ultimately receives the discharge. Where a certification is not feasible, it is not required. However, the source identification section of the SWPPP must indicate why the certification is not feasible and must identify potential significant sources of nonstorm water at the site. The discharger must also notify the EPA that the certification is not feasible.

**Methods of identifying non-storm-water discharges.** A comprehensive evaluation of the storm sewers at a facility may draw on several methods, including the following [EPA, 1990]:

1. *Schematics:* Where they exist, accurate piping schematics can be inspected as a first step in evaluating the integrity of the separate storm sewer system. The use of schematics is limited because schematics usually reflect the design of the piping system and may not reflect the actual configuration constructed. Schematics should be updated or corrected based on additional information found during inspections.

2. *Evaluation of drainage map and inspections:* Drainage maps should identify the key features of the drainage system—each of the inlet and discharge structures, the drainage area of each inlet structure, and units such as storage or disposal units or material loading areas, which may be the source of an illicit discharge or improper dumping. In addition, floor drains and other water disposal inlets that are thought to be connected to the sanitary sewer can be identified. A site inspection can be used to augment and verify map development.

3. *End-of-pipe screening:* Discharge points or other access points such as manhole covers can be inspected for the presence of dry-weather discharges and other signs of non-storm-water discharges. Dry-weather flows can be screened by a variety of methods. Inexpensive on-site tests include measuring pH; observing for oil sheens, scums, and discoloration of pipes and other structures; as well as colormetric detection tests for chlorine, detergents, metals, and other parameters. In some cases, it may be appropriate to collect samples for more expensive analysis in a laboratory for fecal coliform, fecal streptococcus, conventional pollutants, volatile organic carbon, or other appropriate parameters.

4. *Water balance:* Many industrial facilities measure the volume of effluent discharged to the sanitary sewer system and the volume of water supplied to the facility. A significantly higher volume of water supplied to the facility relative to that discharged to the sanitary sewer

and other consumptive uses may be an indication of illicit connections. This method is limited by the accuracy of the flowmeters used.

5. *Dry-weather testing:* Where storm sewers do not discharge during dry-weather conditions, water can be introduced into floor drains, toilets, and other points where non-storm-water discharges are collected. Storm drain outlets are then observed for possible discharges.

6. *Dye testing:* Dry-weather discharges from storm sewers can occur for a number of legitimate reasons including groundwater infiltration or the presence of a continuous discharge subject to an NPDES permit. Where storm sewers do have a discharge during dry-weather conditions, dye testing for illicit connections can be done. Dye testing involves introducing fluorometric or other types of dyes into floor drains, toilets, and other points where non-storm-water discharges are collected. Storm drain outlets are then observed for possible discharges.

7. *Manhole and internal television inspection:* Inspection of manholes and internal inspection of storm sewers either physically or by television are used to identify potential entry points for illicit connections. Dry-weather flows, material deposits, and stains are often indicators of illicit connections. TV inspections are relatively expensive and generally should be used only after a storm sewer has been identified as having illicit connections.

The EPA has specifically not listed smoke tests because of the potential to misapply such tests in evaluating the presence of non-storm-water discharges to storm sewers. Smoke tests (blowing smoke from a downstream point in a pipe up through the pipe) are often ineffective at finding non-storm-water discharges to separate storm sewers, because line traps which are intended to block sewer gas (and will prevent the passage of smoke) are commonly used on non-storm-water drain systems. However, because line traps are less frequently used on storm drains, smoke testing can be useful for detecting cross-connections from storm drains to sanitary sewers. Note that in some industrial facilities which handle explosive vapors, such as refineries, storm drains may have line traps for safety reasons.

### Sampling data

Any existing data on the quality or quantity of storm water discharges from the facility must be described in the SWPPP. These data may be useful for locating areas that have contributed pollutants to storm water. The description should include a discussion of the methods used to collect and analyze the data. Sample collection points should be identified in the plan and shown on the site map.

### Risk identification and summary of potential pollutant sources

The description of potential pollution sources culminates in a narrative discussion of the risk potential that sources of pollution pose to storm water quality. A formal risk assessment is not required, but the discussion should clearly point to activities, materials, and physical features of the facility that have a reasonable potential to contribute significant amounts of pollutants to storm water. Any such activities, materials, or features must be addressed by the measures and controls subsequently described in the plan. Factors to consider in evaluating the reasonable pollution potential of runoff from various portions of an industrial plant include these:

- Loading and unloading of dry bulk materials or liquids

- Outdoor storage of raw materials, intermediate products, by-products, or finished products

- Outdoor manufacturing or processing activities

- Significant dust or particulate generating processes

- Illicit connections or management practices

- On-site waste disposal practices

- The manner and frequency in which pesticides, herbicides, fertilizers, or soil enhancers are applied at the site

Other factors that need to be considered include the toxicity of chemicals; quantity of chemicals used, produced, or discharged; likelihood of these materials coming into contact with storm water and the history of significant leaks or spills of toxic or hazardous pollutants. The assessment must identify the pollutant parameter or parameters (i.e., biochemical oxygen demand, suspended solids, and so on) associated with each source.

Outside drum storage areas, waste dumping sites, and bulk material piles are all obvious sources of potential storm water pollution, but some sources may be less obvious.

Sites previously used for other industrial purposes may have residual matter from former occupants which represent a pollutant source. Facilities located downwind from another industrial facility may contain particulate airborne emissions. A comprehensive soil testing and storm water monitoring program may be required to identify these unexpected pollutant sources.

## Measures and Controls

Following completion of the source identification and assessment phase, the permittee must evaluate, select, and describe the pollution prevention measures, *best management practices* (BMPs), and other controls that will be implemented at the facility. BMPs include processes, procedures, schedules of activities, prohibitions on practices, and other management practices that prevent or reduce the discharge of pollutants in storm water runoff.

The EPA emphasizes the implementation of pollution prevention measures and BMPs that reduce possible pollutant discharges at the source. *Source reduction measures* include, among others, preventive maintenance, chemical substitution, spill prevention, good housekeeping, training, and proper materials management. Where such practices are not appropriate to a particular source or do not effectively reduce pollutant discharges, the EPA supports the use of *source control measures* and BMPs such as material segregation or covering, water diversion, and dust control. Like source reduction measures, source control measures and BMPs are intended to keep pollutants out of storm water. The remaining classes of BMPs, which involve recycling or treatment of storm water, allow the reuse of storm water or attempt to lower pollutant concentrations prior to discharge.

The pollution prevention plan must discuss the reasons why each selected control or practice is appropriate for the facility and how each will address one or more of the potential pollution sources identified in the first part of the plan. The plan must include a schedule specifying the time or times during which each control or practice will be implemented. Not all measures must be implemented immediately; the implementation may be phased over the life of the permit.

In addition, the plan should discuss ways in which the controls and practices relate to one another and, when taken as a whole, produce an integrated and consistent approach for preventing or controlling potential storm water contamination problems.

The EPA recognizes that some facilities will have adequate measures and controls that have been successful in preventing pollutant discharges in storm water. Under the EPA general permit, these facilities are only required to document such practices in a pollution prevention plan and continue them.

### Options for preventing pollutants in storm water

The following five categories describe options for reducing pollutants in storm water discharges from industrial plants:

1. Implement best management practices to prevent pollution.
2. Use traditional storm water management practices.
3. Eliminate pollution sources.
4. Divert storm water discharge to municipal sewage treatment plants.
5. Provide end-of-pipe treatment.

A comprehensive storm water management program for a given plant may include controls from each of these categories. Development of comprehensive control strategies should be based on a consideration of plant characteristics.

**Best management practices.**  The term *best management practices* can describe a wide range of management procedures, schedules of activities, prohibitions on practices, and other management practices to prevent or reduce the pollution of waters of the United States. BMPs also include operating procedures, treatment requirements, and practices to control plant site runoff, drainage from raw-materials storage, spills, or leaks. Many BMPs involve planning, reporting, training, preventive maintenance, and good housekeeping.

Many industrial facilities currently employ BMPs as part of normal plant operation. For example, preventive maintenance and good housekeeping are routinely used in the chemical and related industries to reduce equipment downtime and to promote a safe work environment for employees. Good housekeeping BMPs generally are aimed at preventing spills and similar environmental incidents by stressing the importance of proper management and employee awareness. Experience has shown that many spills of hazardous chemicals can be attributed, in one way or another, to human error. Improper procedures, lack of training, and poor engineering are among the major causes of spills [EPA, 1981]

In preparing an industrial SWPPP, the following categories of BMPs should be considered:

- Good housekeeping
- Preventive maintenance
- Spill prevention and response procedures
- Inspections
- Employee training
- Record-keeping and internal reporting procedures

These BMP categories are described in the following sections.

**Good housekeeping.** Good housekeeping involves using common sense to identify ways to maintain a clean and orderly facility and keep contaminants out of separate storm sewers. It includes establishing protocols to reduce the possibility of mishandling chemicals or equipment and training employees in good housekeeping techniques. These protocols must be described in the plan and communicated to appropriate plant personnel. These measures also ensure that discharges of wash waters to separate storm sewers are avoided.

Where indoor activities are not a potential source of pollutants, good housekeeping measures do not have to be addressed for such areas.

**Preventive maintenance.** Preventive maintenance procedures should be addressed in the plan. Permittees must develop a preventive maintenance program that involves regular inspection and maintenance of storm water management devices and other plant equipment and systems. The program description should identify the devices, equipment, and systems that will be inspected; provide a schedule for inspections and tests; address appropriate adjustment, cleaning, repair, or replacement of devices, equipment, and systems; and maintain complete records on the equipment and systems.

For storm water management devices such as oil-water separators and catch basins, the preventive maintenance program should provide for periodic removal of debris to ensure that the devices are operating efficiently. Maintenance is important because the control measures may be of little or no use if the devices have not been properly maintained.

For other plant equipment and systems, the program should reveal and enable the correction of conditions that could cause breakdowns or failures which could result in the release of pollutants.

**Spill prevention and response procedures.** The SWPPP should reflect requirements for *spill prevention control and countermeasure* (SPCC) plans required under section 311 of the CWA, and may incorporate any part of the SPCC plan into the SWPPP by reference. The SWPPP should also ensure that solid and hazardous waste is managed in accordance with requirements established under the Resource Conservation and Recovery Act (RCRA). Management practices required under RCRA should be expressly incorporated into the SWPPP.

Based on an assessment of possible spill scenarios, the SWPPP must specify appropriate material handling procedures, storage requirements, containment or diversion equipment, and spill cleanup procedures that will minimize the potential for spills and, in the event of a spill, enable proper and timely response. Areas and activities that typically pose a high risk for spills include loading and unloading areas, storage areas, process activities, and waste disposal activities.

Areas where potential spills can occur and their accompanying drainage points should be identified clearly in the SWPPP. Where appropriate, specification of material handling procedures and storage requirements in the plan should be considered. Procedures for cleaning up spills should be identified in the plan and made available to the appropriate personnel. The necessary equipment to implement a cleanup should be available to personnel.

Most facilities already have spill prevention and response plans in place. For storm water pollution prevention, spill response protocols should stress containment and neutralization of the spill, rather than utilization of wash-off procedures. The facility should develop its spill response plan in conjunction with the local fire department to ensure that wash-off procedures will be used only as a last resort in response to a spill incident.

If a release of a hazardous substance or oil occurs above a certain *reportable quantity* (RQ) threshold, the discharger must notify the EPA's National Response Center (NRC) at (800) 424-8802 [or (202) 426-2675 in the Washington, D.C., area] within the first 24 h after the discharger learns of the release [40 CFR parts 110, 117, and 302].

Within 14 days of knowledge of the RQ release, a written description of the release (including the type and estimate of the amount of material released), an account of the circumstances leading to the release, and the date of the release must be incorporated into the SWPPP; and the SWPPP must be reviewed and revised if necessary to identify measures to prevent and respond to such releases. This information also must be submitted to the appropriate EPA regional office within the first 14 days.

If more than one RQ release occurs during a calendar year (or for the first year of the permit, after submittal of an NOI), then each additional release should be reported to the National Response Center. The SWPPP should be revised to include a written description of the dates on which such releases occurred, the type and estimate of the amount of material released, and the circumstances leading to the release. However, these additional releases need not be reported to the EPA regional office.

Any point source discharge of pollutants to waters of the United States without a permit is prohibited under section 301 of the CWA. Therefore, the requirement that a discharge of oil or a hazardous substance be reported only if the amount discharged exceeds the reportable quantity does not imply that the EPA general permit freely allows the discharge of smaller quantities of these substances. The EPA general permit requires dischargers to develop and implement BMPs and pollution prevention measures to reduce and/or control pollutants in the discharge, even in cases where the discharge does not contain hazardous substances or contains hazardous substances at levels significantly lower than reportable quantities.

Facilities subject to SARA Title III section 313 requirements are subject to additional spill prevention requirements, as described in Chap. 7.

**Inspections.** *Inspection* is the process by which you can evaluate if the pollution prevention measures which have already been installed or applied are still effective. In most cases, inspection of pollution prevention measures requires that an inspector look at all the disturbed areas and material storage areas of the site. Typical inspections should include examination of pipes, pumps, tanks, supports, foundations, dikes, and drainage ditches. Material handling areas should be inspected for evidence of, or the potential for, pollutants entering the drainage system.

The EPA general permit refers to two separate classes of inspections: an annual comprehensive site compliance evaluation and more frequent (but less comprehensive) periodic site inspections. The annual comprehensive site compliance evaluation is considered to be a monitoring activity, as described in detail later in this chapter. For the more frequent periodic inspections, qualified facility personnel must be identified to inspect designated equipment and areas of the facility at appropriate intervals specified in the plan. A set of tracking or follow-up procedures must be used to ensure that appropriate actions are taken in response to the inspections.

There are primarily three things an inspector should look for when inspecting a pollution prevention measure:

1. Was the measure installed or performed correctly?
2. Has there been damage to the measure since it was installed or performed?
3. What should be done to correct any problems with the measure?

The inspector should prepare a report documenting the findings of the inspection. The inspector should also request any required maintenance or repair. If the SWPPP should be changed to allow for unexpected conditions, then the inspector should make the changes or notify the appropriate person to make the changes.

There are no formal requirements for inspectors. Any person authorized and considered qualified by the operator may complete inspections and sign the inspection reports. The inspector(s) will generally be key members of the pollution prevention team and will be identified as such in the SWPPP. The EPA recognizes that experience is the best way to develop an understanding for pollution prevention measures. Qualified personnel must have sufficient technical abilities to conduct the inspection or evaluation and should have knowledge of the operations at the facility. The inspector should have detailed knowledge about the site's storm water pollution prevention plan, particularly the following portions:

- The location and type of control measures
- The construction requirements for the control measures
- Maintenance procedures for each of the control measures
- Spill prevention and cleanup measures
- Inspection and maintenance record-keeping requirements

**Employee and contractor training.** The SWPPP must describe a program for informing personnel at all levels of responsibility of the components and goals of the plan. The training program should address topics such as good housekeeping, materials management, and spill response procedures. A schedule for conducting training must be provided in the plan. Where appropriate, contractor personnel also must be trained in relevant aspects of storm water pollution prevention.

**Record-keeping and internal reporting procedures.** The pollution prevention plan must describe procedures for developing and retaining records on the status and effectiveness of plan implementation. A record-keeping system ensures adequate implementation of the SWPPP. The record-keeping requirements begin with the preparation of the SWPPP and NOI (or permit application) and continue through the Notice of Termination (NOT) and afterward. The following records should be maintained on site:

1. *SWPPP:*  The storm water pollution prevention plan should be filed on site for review by regulatory authorities or the public. For convenience, it should be organized into a binder with major sections corresponding to the plan requirements outlined in this chapter.

2. *NOI:*  A copy of the Notice(s) of Intent should be filed with the SWPPP. Copies of any additional NOIs prepared as a result of additional operators becoming involved in the project should also be filed as they are generated.

3. *Inspection reports:*  All inspection reports should be filed with the SWPPP as they are generated. Blank inspection and maintenance forms should be prepared ahead of time. The inspection forms should be specific to the facility. The forms should list each of the measures to be inspected on the site. The form should include blanks for the inspector to fill in: the inspector's name, date of inspection, condition of the measure or area inspected, maintenance

or repair performed, and any changes which should be made to the SWPPP to control or eliminate unforeseen pollution of storm water.

4. *Maintenance reports:*   Reports on regular and special maintenance activities performed on the site, including waste disposal activities.

5. *Industrial activity reports:*   In addition to the inspection and maintenance reports, the operator should keep records of the industrial activity on the site.

6. *Spill reports:*   Records of releases of a hazardous substance in excess of reportable quantities established at 40 CFR 117.3 or 40 CFR 302.4 describing each release that has occurred at any time after the date of 3 years prior to the issuance of this permit, measures taken in response to the release, and measures taken to prevent recurrence must be included in plans.

7. *Other materials:*   Other materials relevant to the permit, including correspondence with regulatory authorities, photographs, and so on.

8. *NOT:*   A copy of the Notice of Termination for the NPDES permit.

The entire file must be kept until at least 1 year after the general permit coverage ends. In addition, all sampling reports must be retained for at least 6 years after the date of sampling or until the termination of permit coverage (whichever is longer).

All SWPPPs required under the permit are considered reports that shall be available to the public under section 308(b) of the CWA. However, if the storm water pollution plan contains trade secrets or other confidential information, the permittee may claim any portion of the plan as confidential in accordance with 40 CFR part 2.

**Traditional storm water management practices.**  "Traditional" storm water management practices are measures which reduce pollutant discharges by reducing the volume of storm water discharges by diverting, infiltrating, reusing, or otherwise managing storm water runoff so as to reduce the discharge of pollutants.

Based on an assessment of the potential of various sources at the plant to contribute pollutants to storm water discharges associated with industrial activity, the SWPPP shall provide that traditional storm water management measures determined to be reasonable and appropriate be implemented and maintained.

Traditional storm water management practices such as grass swales, catch basins, infiltration devices, inlet controls, unlined retention or detention basins, and oil and grit separators can sometimes be applied to an industrial setting. Traditional storm water management practices can include water reuse activities, such as the collection of storm water for later uses such as irrigation or dust control. Appropriate snow removal activities may be considered, such as selecting a site for removed snow and selecting and using deicing chemicals. In addition, other types of controls such as spill prevention measures can be considered to prevent catastrophic events that can lead to surface or groundwater contamination.

The plan must identify practices that are reasonable and appropriate for the facility. The plan should describe the particular pollutant source area or activity to be controlled by each storm water management practice. Reasonable and appropriate practices must be implemented and maintained according to the provisions prescribed in the plan.

In selecting storm water management measures, it is important to consider the potential effects of each method on other water resources, such as groundwater. Although storm water pollution prevention plans primarily focus on storm water management, facilities must also consider potential groundwater pollution problems and take appropriate steps to avoid adversely impacting groundwater quality. For example, if the water table is unusually high in an area, an infiltration pond may contaminate a groundwater source unless special preventive measures are taken. In some cases, it is appropriate to limit traditional storm water management practices to those areas of the drainage system that generate storm water with relatively low levels of pollutants (e.g., many rooftops, parking lots, and so on).

In some instances, facilities may have to develop an elaborate set of structural controls, such as detention and retention ponds to provide treatment to storm water runoff prior to its discharge off site. For most industries, simple modifications to existing facility material handling practices will suffice. Material storage areas can often be enclosed or covered to prevent exposure of the material to storm water runoff. Diversion structures can prevent storm water from entering material storage areas.

The pollution prevention plan must identify areas that, due to topography, activities, soils, cover materials, or other factors, have a high potential for significant soil erosion. The plan must identify measures, such as the placement of vegetation, that will be implemented to limit erosion in these areas and provide filtering of storm water runoff.

**Elimination of pollution sources.**   In some cases, elimination of pollution source may be the most cost-effective way to control pollutants in storm water discharges associated with industrial activity. Options for eliminating pollution sources include reducing on-site air emissions affecting runoff quality, changing chemicals used at the facility, and modifying material management practices such as moving storage areas into buildings.

**Diversion of discharge to sewage treatment plant.** Where storm water discharges contain significant amounts of pollutants that can be removed by a sewage treatment plant, the storm water discharge can be discharged to the sanitary sewage system. Such diversions must be coordinated with the operators of the sewage treatment plant and the collection system to avoid exacerbating problems with *combined sewer overflows* (CSOs), basement flooding, or wet-weather operation of the treatment plant. Where CSO discharges, flooding, or plant operation problems can result, on-site storage followed by a controlled release during dry-weather conditions may be considered.

**End-of-pipe treatment.** At many types of industrial facilities, it may be appropriate to collect and treat the runoff from targeted areas of the facility. This approach was taken with 9 industrial categories with national effluent guideline limitations for storm water discharges. To meet the numeric effluent limitation, most, if not all, facilities must collect and temporarily store on site the runoff from targeted areas of the plant.

The effluent guideline limitations do not apply to discharges whenever a particular rainfall event or a sequence of rainfall events causes an overflow of storage devices designed, constructed, and operated to contain a design storm. The 10-year, 24-h storm or the 25-year, 24-h storm commonly is used as the design storm in the effluent guideline limitations.

Most technology-based treatment standards use relatively simple technologies such as the settling of solids, neutralization, and drum filtration. Potential groundwater impacts should also be considered by operators when storage devices are designed.

## Monitoring Plan

Many facilities are required to perform periodic sampling of their storm water runoff as a condition of the EPA's general permit. Chapter 8 provides details on storm water sampling and monitoring. Sampling data collected during the term of the permits must be summarized in the SWPPP.

Under the EPA general permit, the minimum monitoring requirement for all facilities consists of an annual site compliance evaluation. The SWPPP must describe the scope and content of comprehensive site inspections that qualified personnel will conduct to

1. Confirm the accuracy of the description of potential pollution sources contained in the plan
2. Determine the effectiveness of the plan
3. Assess compliance with the terms and conditions of the permit

The plan must indicate the frequency of such evaluation, which in most cases must be at least once a year. The individual(s) who will conduct the inspections must be identified in the plan and should be members of the pollution prevention team.

Material handling and storage areas and other potential sources of pollution must be visually inspected for evidence of actual or potential pollutant discharges to the drainage system. Inspectors also must observe erosion controls and structural storm water management devices to ensure that each is operating correctly. Equipment needed to implement the pollution prevention plan, such as that used during spill response activities, must be inspected to confirm that it is in proper working order.

The results of each site inspection must be documented in a report signed by an authorized company official. The report must describe the scope of the inspection, the personnel making the inspection, the date(s) of the inspection, and any major observations relating to implementation of the SWPPP.

Based on the results of each inspection, the description of potential pollution sources and measures and controls included in the SWPPP must be revised as appropriate within 2 weeks after each inspection. Changes in the measures and controls must be implemented on the site in a timely manner—and never more than 12 weeks after completion of the inspection.

The pollution prevention plan for the facility must be revised where necessary to address the findings and reflect the recommendations of the inspection. Additionally, an annual certification must be prepared indicating that the SWPPP was evaluated as part of an inspection, that the plan is adequate for control of facility storm water discharges, and that the facility is in compliance with the plan.

Where annual site inspections are shown in the plan to be impracticable for inactive mining sites due to remote location and inaccessibility of the site, comprehensive site compliance evaluations are to be conducted at least once every 3 years. The first site inspection must take place 2 years after the site becomes inactive.

## Other Regulatory Requirements

Many states, cities, and regional water quality agencies have their own requirements for storm water runoff. The pollution prevention plan should be developed with these requirements in mind.

The EPA general permit requires that the SWPPP list all applicable local and state regulatory requirements and summarize the activities undertaken in compliance with these requirements.

Permittees which discharge storm water associated with industrial activity through large or medium municipal separate storm water systems are required to submit a signed copy of their NOI to the operator of the municipal separate storm sewer system.

Facilities covered by these permits must comply with applicable requirements in municipal storm water management programs developed under NPDES permits issued for the discharge of the municipal separate storm sewer system that receives the facility's discharge, provided the discharger has been notified of such conditions. In addition, permittees that discharge storm water associated with industrial activity through a municipal separate storm sewer system serving a population of 100,000 or more must make their pollution prevention plans available to the municipal operator of the system upon request by the municipal operator.

By requiring compliance with local and state regulations, the EPA is effectively putting the full force and authority of the Clean Water Act behind the applicable local and state regulations.

## References

Environmental Protection Agency: *NPDES Best Management Practices Guidance Document,* EPA 600/9-79-045, December 1979.

The Cadmus Group: *Manual of Practice: On-Site Identification of Illicit Connections,* September 1990.

Government Printing Office: *Federal Register,* Office of the Federal Register, National Archives and Records Administration, Washington.

————: *Code of Federal Regulations,* Office of the Federal Register, National Archives and Records Administration, Washington, July 1, 1992.

# 7

# Special Sections of Industrial Storm Water Pollution Prevention Plans

This is the fourth of five chapters which deal with the specific requirements for storm water discharges from industrial (nonconstruction) facilities. This chapter describes how to prepare special sections of a storm water pollution prevention plan (SWPPP) for an industrial facility. Chapter 6 described how to prepare the basic sections of the SWPPP. Appendix C presents an example of an SWPPP for an industrial facility.

## Salt Piles

The EPA general permit contains special requirements for storm water discharges associated with industrial activity from salt storage facilities. Storage piles of salt used for deicing or other commercial or industrial purposes must be enclosed or covered to prevent exposure to precipitation, except for exposure resulting from adding or removing materials from the pile. This requirement applies only to runoff from storage piles discharged to waters of the United States. Facilities that collect all the runoff from their salt piles and reuse it in their processes or discharge it subject to a separate National Pollutant Discharge Elimination System (NPDES) permit do not need to enclose or cover their piles.

Permittees must comply with this requirement as expeditiously as practicable, but no later than September 1995 (3 years after the date that the EPA general permit was issued).

## Coal Piles

The EPA general permit establishes effluent limitations of 50 milligrams per liter (mg/L) total suspended solids and a pH range of 6.0 to 9.0 for coal pile runoff. This effluent limitation is similar to the effluent guideline limitation for coal pile runoff from facilities in the steam electric power generating point source category [see 40 CFR 423.12(b)(9)]. This is the only numeric effluent limitation in the EPA general permit.

The general permit requires that facilities with coal pile runoff comply with the numeric effluent limitations of the permit as expeditiously as possible, but no later than September 1995 (three years from the date of permit issuance). With this exception, however, the deadlines for preparation and compliance of the SWPPP are no different than the deadlines for other types of facilities.

Any untreated overflow from facilities designed, constructed, and operated to treat the volume of coal pile runoff associated with a 10 year, 24 h rainfall event is not subject to the 50 mg/L limitation for total suspended solids. Providing a limit to effluent guidelines for events that exceed a specified storm event provides operators with a basis for installing and operating a treatment system, as the design of the system, particularly the collection devices, will depend on the design storm chosen.

The effluent limitation in the EPA general permit for coal pile runoff is not intended to apply to coal pile runoff from steam electric facilities. Coal pile runoff from steam electric facilities is already subject to an effluent limitation guideline (see 40 CFR 423). The EPA general permit does not provide coverage for storm water discharges that are subject to an effluent limitation guideline.

The pollutants in coal pile runoff can be classified into specific types according to chemical characteristics [EPA, 1982]. The type relates to pH of the coal pile drainage. The pH tends to be of an acidic nature, primarily as a result of the oxidation of iron sulfide in the presence of oxygen and water. The potential influence of pH on the behavior of toxic and heavy metals is of particular concern. Many of the metals are amphoteric with regard to their solubility behavior. The factors affecting acidity, pH, and the subsequent leaching of trace metals are

- Concentration and form of pyritic sulfur in coal
- Size of the coal pile
- Method of coal preparation and clearing prior to storage
- Climatic conditions, including rainfall and temperature
- Concentrations of $CaCO_3$ and other neutralizing substances in the coal

- Concentration and form of trace metals in the coal
- Residence time in the coal pile.

Coal piles can generate runoff with low pH values, with the acid values being quite variable. The suspended-solids levels can be significant, with levels of 2500 mg/L not uncommon. Metals present in the greatest concentrations are copper, iron, aluminum, nickel, and zinc. Others present in trace amounts include chromium, cadmium, mercury, arsenic, selenium, and beryllium.

The effluent limitations for coal pile runoff in the EPA general permit can be achieved by these two primary methods: limiting exposure to coal by use of covers or tarpaulins and collecting and treating the runoff. In some cases, coal pile runoff may be in compliance with the effluent limitations without covering of the pile or collection or treatment of the runoff. In these cases, the operator of the discharge will not have a control cost. The effluent limitations for coal pile runoff in the draft permits can be achieved by limiting exposure of coal to storm water by use of covers or tarpaulins and storm water run-on berms. The use of tarpaulins and berms to prevent exposure is expected to be practical for coal piles smaller than 30,000 cubic meters ($m^3$). The EPA expects that the majority of industrial facilities subject to the requirement will have coal piles smaller than 30,000 $m^3$.

The primary technology options for treating coal pile runoff are (1) equalization, pH adjustment, and settling; and (2) equalization, chemical precipitation treatment, settling, and pH adjustment.

Metals may be removed from wastewater by raising the pH of the wastewater to precipitate them out as hydroxides. Typically, wastewater pH levels of 9 to 12 are required to achieve the desired precipitation levels. Lime is frequently used for pH adjustment. Wastewaters which have a pH greater than 9 after lime addition will require acid addition to reduce the pH before final discharge. Polymer addition may be required to enhance the settling characteristics of the metal hydroxide precipitate. Typical polymer feed concentrations in the wastewater are 1 to 4 parts per million (ppm). The metal hydroxide precipitate is separated from the wastewater in a clarifier or a gravity thickener. Unlike settling ponds, these units continually collect and remove the sludge formed. Filters are typically used for effluent polishing and can reduce suspended-solids levels below 10 mg/L. Sand and coal are the most common filter media. Vacuum filtration is a common technique for dewatering sludge to produce a cake that has good handling properties and minimum volume.

The major equipment requirements for such a system include a lime feed system, mix tank polymer feed system, flocculator-clarifier, deep bed filter, and acid feed system. For wastewaters which have a pH of less than 6, mixers and mixing tanks are made of special materials of construction (stainless steel or lined-carbon steel). For wastewaters with pH levels greater than 6, concrete tanks are typically used. The underflow from the clarifier may require additional treatment with a gravity thickener and a vacuum filter to provide sludge which can be transported economically for landfill disposal.

## SARA Title III, Section 313 (EPCRA) Facilities

The Superfund Amendments and Reauthorization Act (SARA) of 1986 resulted in the enactment of Title III of SARA, the Emergency Planning and Community-Right-to-Know Act. Section 313 of Title III of SARA requires operators of certain facilities that manufacture, import, process, or otherwise use listed toxic chemicals to report annually their releases of those chemicals to any environmental media.

The criteria for facilities that must report under section 313 are given at 40 CFR 372.22. A facility is subject to the annual reporting provisions of section 313 if it meets all three of the following criteria for a calendar year:

- It is included in Standard Industrial Classification (SIC) codes 20 through 39.
- It has 10 or more full-time employees.
- It manufactures (including imports), processes, or otherwise uses a chemical listed in 40 CFR 372.65 in amounts greater than the threshold quantities specified in 40 CFR 372.25. After 1989, the threshold quantity of listed chemicals that the facility must manufacture, import, or process in order to be required to submit a release report is 25,000 pounds per year (lb/yr). The threshold for uses other than manufacturing, importing, or processing of listed toxic chemicals is 10,000 lb/yr.

Of the 329 toxic chemicals listed at 40 CFR 372 which are used to define the scope of SARA Title III, section 313 requirements, approximately 175 chemicals are classified as "section 313 water priority chemicals." These are defined as chemicals or chemical categories which also:

1. Are listed at 40 CFR 372.65 pursuant to SARA Title III, section 313
2. Are present at or above threshold levels at a facility subject to SARA, Title III, section 313 reporting requirements
3. Meet at least one of the following criteria:
    a. Are listed in appendix D of 40 CFR part 122 on table II (organic priority pollutants), table III (certain metals, cyanides, and phe-

nols), or table V (certain toxic pollutants and hazardous substances)

  b.  Are listed as a hazardous substance pursuant to section 311(b)(2)(A) of the CWA at 40 CFR 116.4

  c.  Are pollutants for which the EPA has published an acute or a chronic toxicity criterion

The EPA estimates that 22,000 facilities nationwide will be subject to SARA Title III reporting requirements after 1990. Of these, about 9000 facilities with storm water discharges associated with industrial activity nationwide have section 313 water priority chemicals in threshold amounts.

Applicability to EPCRA section 313 could change in three ways:

1.  The threshold amount of toxic chemicals required to trigger reporting could change.

2.  Requirements could be expanded to facilities other than those classified as SIC 20 to SIC 39.

3.  Specific chemicals or classes of chemicals could be added or deleted from the list of toxic chemicals.

The determination of whether a facility must meet the special requirements for storm water discharges associated with industrial activity from EPCRA section 313 facilities is based on the applicability of EPCRA section 313 on the date of permit issuance. Thus, if the applicability of EPCRA section 313 requirements is expanded to include facilities that use less than current threshold amounts, additional chemicals, or facilities other than those classified as SIC codes 20 through 39, the special requirements in the EPA general permit would not apply to those additional facilities.

If, on the other hand, the applicability of EPCRA section 313 reporting requirements are restricted (e.g., a chemical is deleted from the list of toxic chemicals, the threshold amount of chemicals is raised, or facilities within SIC codes 20 through 39 are exempted), the EPA will not require facilities which are not subject to reporting requirements under the newly restricted requirements under EPCRA section 313 to comply with the special requirements for storm water discharges in the EPA general permits.

Permittees that had to report releases under EPCRA section 313, but during the term of the permit have modified their industrial practices such that they no longer manufacture, process, or otherwise use EPCRA section 313 water priority chemicals on site in amounts that exceed the applicable thresholds under EPCRA section 313, are not subject to the special requirements of the EPA general permit after reductions in use have been made.

Facilities that meet the EPCRA section 313 thresholds for the first time during the term of the permit will be required to comply with the additional requirements in the EPA general permit for EPCRA section 313 facilities 3 years after the date they are first required to report under EPCRA section 313.

### Targeting EPCRA section 313 facilities

The large amounts of toxic chemicals at facilities with section 313 water priority chemicals raise concerns regarding the potential of material handling and storage operations to add pollutants to storm water discharges associated with industrial activity. The material management practices associated with the storage and use of toxic chemicals are a major potential source of pollutants in storm water discharges associated with industrial activity.

The EPA has identified leaks and spills of toxic chemicals associated with material management practices as a major potential source of pollutants in storm water discharges [56 FR 40980 (August 16, 1991)]. Based on a number of studies, the EPA believes that storage systems, truck and rail transfer facilities, and other process areas where significant amounts of toxic chemicals are used and exposed to precipitation may release pollutants if basic accepted engineering practices are not employed. For example, the EPA's *Hazardous Waste Tank Risk Analysis* (EPA, 1986) indicates that the principal causes of reported tank failures are external corrosion, installation problems, structural failure, spills, and overfills due to operator errors, as well as ancillary equipment failure, and that inadequate practices, including those observed at the time of the study, lead to a substantial probability of releases to the environment from such tank failures. The analysis indicated that the major causes of releases from tank systems are usually unrelated to the characteristics of the material stored in the tanks. The analysis also indicated that inadequate management practices allow significant releases to continue undetected until the release becomes obvious. Information from the spill prevention control and countermeasure (SPCC) database and the pollution incident reporting system (PIRS) database indicates that operator error, structural failures, and corrosion were significant causes of releases for aboveground tanks and that failure of ancillary equipment is a significant cause of releases from aboveground systems. These databases indicate that 85 to 90 percent of more than 2000 reported incidents of spills of oil or hazardous substances from ancillary equipment resulted from failures of piping systems (including failures of pumps, flanges, couplings, interconnecting hoses, and valves). Some of the most significant sources of pollutants at these facilities can be attributed to intermittent events, such as significant spills or leaks.

The EPA also believes that the management practices identified in the additional requirements for EPCRA section 313 facilities are typically employed at well-operated facilities that use large amounts of toxic chemicals. Industry practices have been developed in response to concerns about spills and other health and safety issues.

The EPA believes that large spills or releases that are generally associated with releases of a hazardous substance or oil in excess of reportable quantities under 40 CFR part 110, 117, or 302 are only one potential source of pollutants at EPCRA section 313 facilities. Other potential sources of pollutants at these facilities include chronic leaks, smaller spills, management of containers, and storage and/or use of chemicals in solid form. These potential sources can contribute significant amounts of pollutants that are nonetheless below reportable quantities under 40 CFR part 110, 117, or 302.

The special requirements in the EPA general permit for facilities that are subject to EPCRA section 313 reporting requirements apply only to areas of the facilities where EPCRA section 313 chemicals are managed. The other baseline requirements of the EPA general permit apply to other parts of the facility that generate storm water discharges associated with industrial activity.

The special requirements for SWPPPs at facilities that are subject to EPCRA section 313 for section 313 water priority chemicals primarily focus on areas of the facility where equipment used for the management, storage, and processing of section 313 water priority chemicals is exposed to precipitation or can otherwise contribute pollutants to a storm drainage system. The burdens associated with the requirements of the EPA general permit are significantly reduced for facilities that manage (including loading and unloading activities) their toxic chemicals in buildings or under cover such that there is no exposure to precipitation and where the floor drainage in the building is known to be segregated from the storm water collection system.

## Summary of special requirements

The special requirements in the EPA general permit for facilities subject to reporting requirements under EPCRA section 313 for a water priority chemical state that SWPPPs, in addition to the baseline requirements described in Chap. 6 must contain special provisions addressing areas where section 313 water priority chemicals are stored, processed, or otherwise handled. The permit provides that appropriate containment, drainage control, and/or diversionary structures must be provided for such areas. At a minimum, one of the following preventive systems or its equivalent must be used:

- *Drainage controls:*  curbing, culverting, gutters, sewers, or other forms of drainage control to prevent or minimize the potential for storm water run-on to come into contact with significant sources of pollutants
- *Protection measures:*  roofs, covers, or other forms of appropriate protection to prevent storage piles from exposure to storm water and wind

The EPA allows the discharger to choose the preventive system most appropriate for a particular facility. If a leak is discovered which may result in a significant release of a section 313 water priority chemical to waters of the United States, then the EPA general permit requires that permittees either take action to stop the leak or otherwise prevent the significant release of section 313 water priority chemicals to waters of the United States. The temporary use of drip pans, diversions to sumps, or other measures that prevent toxic chemicals from being discharged to waters of the United States until permanent repairs can be made may constitute appropriate action.

The permit also establishes requirements for priority areas of the facility including the following:

1. *Liquid storage areas:*  liquid storage areas where storm water comes into contact with any equipment, tank, container, or other vessel used for section 313 water priority chemicals

2. *Other material storage areas:*  material storage areas for section 313 water priority chemicals other than liquids

3. *Loading and unloading areas:*  truck and railcar loading and unloading areas for liquid section 313 water priority chemicals

4. *Other transfer, process, or handling areas:*  areas where section 313 water priority chemicals are transferred, processed, or otherwise handled

Drainage from these priority areas should be restrained by valves or other positive means to prevent the discharge of a spill or other excessive leakage of section 313 water priority chemicals. Where containment units are employed, such units may be emptied by pumps or ejectors; however, these must be manually activated. Flapper-type drain valves must not be used to drain containment areas, as these will not effectively control spills. Valves used for the drainage of containment areas should, as far as is practical, be of manual, open-and-closed design. If facility drainage does not meet these requirements, the final discharge conveyance of all in-facility storm sewers must be equipped to be equivalent to a diversion system that could, in the event of an uncontrolled spill of section 313 water priority chemicals, return the spilled material or contaminated storm water to the facility. Records must be kept of the frequency and estimated volume (in gallons) of discharges from containment areas.

### Liquid storage areas

Appropriate measures to minimize discharges of section 313 chemicals may include secondary containment provided for at least the entire contents of the largest single tank plus sufficient freeboard to allow for precipitation, a strong spill contingency and integrity testing plan, and/or other equivalent measures.

Where storm water comes into contact with any equipment, tank, container, or other vessel used for section 313 water priority chemicals, the material and construction of tanks or containers used for the storage of a section 313 water priority chemical must be compatible with the material stored and conditions of storage, such as pressure and temperature.

A strong spill contingency plan would typically contain, at a minimum, a description of response plans, personnel needs, and methods of mechanical containment (such as the use of sorbents, booms, and collection devices), steps to be taken for removal of spill chemicals or materials, and procedures to ensure access to and availability of sorbents and other equipment. The testing component of the plan would provide for conducting integrity testing of storage tanks at set intervals, such as once every 5 years, and conducting integrity and leak testing of valves and piping at a minimum frequency, such as once per year. In addition, a strong plan would include a written and actual commitment of work force, equipment, and materials required to comply with the permit and to expeditiously control and remove any quantity of spilled or leaked chemicals that may result in a toxic discharge.

### Dry-material storage areas

Material storage areas for section 313 water priority chemicals other than liquids that are subject to runoff, leaching, or wind must incorporate drainage or other control features to minimize the discharge of section 313 water priority chemicals by reducing storm water contact with these chemicals.

### Truck and railcar loading and unloading areas

Appropriate measures to minimize discharges of section 313 chemicals may include the placement and maintenance of drip pans (including the proper disposal of materials collected in the drip pans) where spillage may occur (such as hose connections, hose reels, and filler nozzles) for use when one is making and breaking hose connections; a strong spill contingency and integrity testing plan; and/or other equivalent measures.

### Other transfer, process, or handling areas

Materials used in piping and equipment must be compatible with the substances handled. Drainage from process and material handling areas must minimize storm water contact with section 313 water priority chemicals. Additional protection such as covers or guards to prevent exposure to wind, spraying, or releases from pressure relief vents to prevent a discharge of section 313 water priority chemicals to the drainage system, and overhangs or door skirts to enclose trailer ends at truck loading and unloading docks must be provided as appropriate. Visual inspections or leak tests must be provided for overhead piping conveying section 313 water priority chemicals without secondary containment.

### Other areas

The EPA general permit provides that site runoff from other industrial areas of the facility that may contain section 313 water priority chemicals or spills of section 313 water priority chemicals must incorporate the necessary drainage or other control features to prevent the discharge of spilled or improperly disposed material and to ensure the mitigation of pollutants in runoff or leachate. The permit also establishes special requirements for preventive maintenance and good housekeeping, facility security, and employee training.

Sampling requirements for storm water discharges from EPCRA section 313 are discussed in Chap. 8. Facilities should review monitoring data and evaluate pollution prevention measures suitable for reducing pollutants in discharges.

### Certification requirements

Storm water pollution prevention plans for facilities subject to these special requirements must be reviewed by a registered professional engineer (PE). The PE must be able to certify that the SWPPP has been prepared in accordance with good engineering practices. The PE must personally examine the facility and be familiar with the requirements of the permit before making a certification.

The permit requires that a PE certification be done every 3 years. Where significant modifications are made to the facility, such as the addition of material handling areas or chemical storage units, permittees are required to obtain an additional PE certification as soon as practicable. The PE certifications do not relieve the discharger of the duty to prepare and implement fully an SWPPP that is in accordance with the permit.

For facilities that do not have an appropriate PE on staff to conduct the certification, employees with appropriate knowledge and experience should assist a PE who is not regularly employed by the facility in making the certification.

## References

Environmental Protection Agency: *Final Development Document for Effluent Limitations Guidelines and Standards and Pretreatment Standards for the Steam Electric Point Source Category,* EPA 440/1-82/-29, November 1982.

Government Printing Office: *Federal Register,* Office of the Federal Register, National Archives and Records Administration, Washington.

———: *Code of Federal Regulations,* Office of the Federal Register, National Archives and Records Administration, Washington, July 1, 1992.

# NPDES Industrial Storm Water Sampling and Monitoring

This is the fifth of five chapters which deal with the specific requirements for storm water discharges from industrial (nonconstruction) facilities. This chapter describes the requirements and procedures for storm water sampling and monitoring.

## Introduction to Storm Water Sampling

Sampling is the process of obtaining small quantities of discharge water and subjecting them to various analytical tests in order to characterize the pollutants within the discharge. National Pollutant Discharge Elimination System (NPDES) permits have traditionally included sampling requirements, so that the effectiveness of pollution control measures can be assessed. However, the EPA does not require sampling for all types of storm water discharges, as described later in this chapter.

Under the Clean Water Act, the EPA is authorized to require dischargers to provide information, monitoring, and record keeping to characterize discharges and to assess permit compliance. Discharge monitoring data can be used to assist in the evaluation of the risk of the discharge by indicating the types and the concentrations of pollutant parameters in the discharge. Monitoring of storm water from an industrial site can assist in evaluating sources of pollutants. Discharge monitoring data can be used in evaluating the potential of the discharge to cause or contribute to water quality impacts and water quality standards violations.

Discharge monitoring data can also be used to evaluate the effectiveness of controls on reducing pollutants in discharges. This monitoring function can be important in evaluating both the effectiveness of source control or pollution prevention measures and the operation of end-of-pipe treatment units.

The EPA has typically required that NPDES permittees [such as publicly owned treatment works (POTWs) and industrial dischargers] submit a *discharge monitoring report* (DMR) at least once per year. However, the amount of storm water sampling required for monitoring of general permit compliance depends upon the type of facility. For all facilities, the EPA requires that dischargers conduct a comprehensive annual site compliance evaluation designed to evaluate the effectiveness of permit implementation and to identify pollutant sources.[1] (See Chap. 6.)

The EPA is authorized under section 308 of the CWA to require particular dischargers to submit sampling monitoring data necessary to carry out the objectives of the CWA. This authority can be used to obtain storm water monitoring data that are not otherwise required under the EPA general permit.

## Types of Storm Water Sampling

As described in Chap. 5, storm water sampling is required for individual discharge permit applications, but no sampling is required for initial coverage under the EPA general permit for storm water discharges associated with industrial activity. Certain states or municipalities may have sampling and/or reporting requirements in addition to those described in this chapter. No sampling is required for discharges not subject to NPDES permit requirements, which are described in Chaps. 3 and 4.

As a part of the application for individual permit coverage, at least one *representative* storm event must be sampled. A representative storm event is defined as having the following characteristics:

- *More than 0.1 inch (in) of total rainfall.* This ensures that a significant volume of runoff will be generated by the storm event. Several

---

[1]The EPA originally proposed that all dischargers perform storm water sampling at least once per year and report the results annually. However, as a result of comments by the federal Office of Management and Budget and others, the EPA eliminated the sampling requirements for certain classes of dischargers and reduced the submittal requirements for others.

EPA studies have established 0.1 in of rainfall as the minimum rainfall depth capable of producing the rainfall and runoff characteristics necessary to generate a sufficient volume of runoff for meaningful sample analysis.

- *More than 72 h since last event of more than 0.1 in of total rainfall.* This time interval allows pollutants to collect on the surface of the drainage area and non-storm-water discharges to build up within the drainage system. Therefore, the pollutants contributed by such sources will be measured.

- *Storm duration and total rainfall volume within 50 percent above or below the average rainfall event for the area of the facility.* This criterion is to be applied wherever feasible. The values in Table 8.1 may be used as estimates of the average rainfall depth and storm duration in each region of the contiguous United States. Figure 8.1 illustrates the boundaries of each region.

In determining whether a particular storm meets these criteria, National Weather Service or other available meteorological data collected as close as possible to the facility may be used. However, it may be advantageous to install a nonrecording rainfall gage at the site, if possible, to directly measure the depth and duration of rainfall and the interval between rainfall events. Later in this chapter, some guidelines are provided for situations in which it is difficult or impossible to find a storm event that meets the criteria listed above.

**TABLE 8.1  Typical Rainfall Depths and Storm Durations**

| Region | Average duration, h | Acceptable range of durations, h | Average rainfall volume, in | Acceptable range of volumes, in |
|---|---|---|---|---|
| Northeast | 11.2 | 5.6–16.8 | 0.50 | 0.25–0.75 |
| Northeast coastal | 11.7 | 5.9–17.5 | 0.66 | 0.33–0.99 |
| Mid-Atlantic | 10.1 | 5.1–15.1 | 0.64 | 0.32–0.96 |
| Central | 9.2 | 4.6–13.8 | 0.62 | 0.31–0.93 |
| North Central | 9.5 | 4.8–14.2 | 0.55 | 0.28–0.83 |
| Southeast | 8.7 | 4.4–13.0 | 0.75 | 0.38–1.13 |
| East Gulf | 6.4 | 3.2–9.6 | 0.80 | 0.40–1.20 |
| East Texas | 8.0 | 4.0–12.0 | 0.76 | 0.38–1.14 |
| West Texas | 7.4 | 3.7–11.1 | 0.57 | 0.29–0.85 |
| Southwest | 7.8 | 3.9–11.7 | 0.37 | 0.19–0.55 |
| West inland | 9.4 | 4.7–14.1 | 0.36 | 0.18–0.54 |
| Pacific South | 11.6 | 5.8–17.4 | 0.54 | 0.27–0.81 |
| Northwest inland | 10.4 | 5.2–15.6 | 0.37 | 0.19–0.55 |
| Pacific Central | 13.7 | 6.9–20.5 | 0.58 | 0.29–0.87 |
| Pacific Northwest | 15.9 | 8.0–23.8 | 0.50 | 0.25–0.75 |

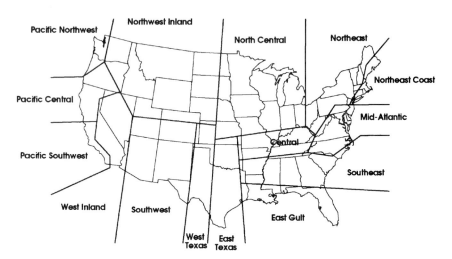

**Figure 8.1** Rainfall zones of the contiguous United States. (*Source: Woodward-Clyde Consultants, 1990.*)

Snow melt is acceptable as a source of runoff for sampling. However, snow melt runoff is typically more contaminated than rainfall runoff.

For individual permit applications, two types of samples must be obtained: a "first-flush" grab sample and a flow-weighted composite sample. For compliance with an existing permit, a first-flush grab sample and a time-weighted composite sample are generally required, although individual permits may have different requirements. Each of these different types of storm water discharge samples is described in the following sections.

**First-flush grab samples**

A *first-flush grab sample* is obtained within the first 30 minutes (min) of discharge. This is generally the most polluted portion of the discharge, because it may contain pollutants that lie on the surface of the drainage area. It may also contain a heavy concentration of non-storm-water discharges, if these are present at the facility. The grab sample should be taken from a well-mixed portion of the flow stream, so that it is representative of the majority of discharge.

The first 30 min of discharge may not coincide with the first 30 min of rainfall. In fact, facilities equipped with detention or retention facilities may experience a considerable delay before the first discharge occurs as a result of a particular rainfall event.

If it is not possible to obtain a grab sample within the first 30 min of discharge, then the grab sample may be obtained within the first 1 h of discharge. However, the monitoring report should note this condition and explain why it was necessary.

Grab samples must be tested in the field for pH and for temperature. Testing for pH provides an indication of the potential availability of metals within the discharge. In some cases it will provide information regarding material management.

Grab samples should be tested in the laboratory for the following "conventional" pollutants:

- *Oil and grease* (mg/L), a common component of storm water discharges which has serious effects on receiving waters. It can indicate materials management, housekeeping, and transportation activities. A value of 30 mg/L is considered to be near the high end of the range of typical values for urban storm water runoff.

- *Total suspended solids (TSS)* (mg/L), a common pollutant which can seriously affect receiving waters. TSS often indicates surface disturbances and material management practices. A value of 400 mg/L is considered to be at the high end of typical values for urban storm water runoff.

- *The 5-day biochemical oxygen demand ($BOD_5$)* (mg/L), the most commonly used indicator of the oxygen depletion potential of the discharge. A value of 50 mg/L is relatively high compared to typical urban storm water runoff.

- *Chemical oxygen demand (COD)* (mg/L), a more inclusive indicator of potential oxygen demand, especially where metals interfere with the $BOD_5$ test. The COD is generally better suited for comparing the oxygen demand of a storm water discharge with that of other discharges.

- *Total Kjeldahl nitrogen (TKN)* (mg/L), a nutrient which can degrade water quality.

- *Nitrate plus nitrite nitrogen* (mg/L), another form of nutrient which can degrade water quality.

- *Total phosphorus* (mg/L), another type of nutrient which can degrade water quality.

In addition to these conventional pollutants, discharges should be analyzed for several other types of pollutants as applicable:

- Pollutants listed in a storm water effluent concentration guideline for the facility. Facilities with storm water effluent guidelines include cement manufacturing [40 CFR 411], feedlots [40 CFR 412], fertilizer manufacturing [40 CFR 418], petroleum refining [40 CFR 419], phosphate manufacturing [40 CFR 422], steam electric power generation [40 CFR 423], coal mining [40 CFR 434], ore mining and dressing [40 CFR 436], and asphalt emulsion [40 CFR 443].

- All components, chemicals, and pollutants limited by any existing NPDES permits for the facility. This may indicate the presence of any cross-contamination of storm water discharges by process water, or the presence of residual contamination which makes its way into the storm water discharge.

- Any other pollutant which may be present as a result of existing or previous operations at the facility. EPA Form 2F prescribes a list of toxic and hazardous substances which must be considered, but other pollutants must also be considered if applicable.

Laboratory testing may be done in-house or by a contract laboratory. Use of an EPA-certified laboratory is not required. However, all tests must be performed using the analytical protocols specified in 40 CFR 136. The analysis of one sample for conventional pollutants will cost about $200. The costs may total more than $1000 for a sample with several other pollutants, although volume discounts are often available.

Individual permit conditions and/or state and municipal requirements may involve additional laboratory tests. Also some states require the use of state-certified laboratories.

Small businesses (with gross total annual sales of less than $100,000 per year for the past 3 years, in second-quarter 1980 dollars) and operators of small coal mines (with a probable annual production of less than 100,000 tons) are exempt from the reporting requirements for organic and toxic pollutants listed in table 2F-3. See the instructions for EPA Form 2F for further details.

### Flow-weighted composite samples

In addition to a grab sample, the second type of sample required for each individual permit application is a *flow-weighted composite sample,* which is a combination of individual "aliquots" (samples) at least 15 min apart, or a minimum of three aliquots per hour for the entire discharge or for the first 3 h of discharge. Ideally, the aliquots are obtained at constant time intervals 20 min apart. The flow rate is measured at the time each aliquot is obtained.

The samples are combined in proportion to the flow rate at the time each sample was obtained. Along with the total volume of discharge, this provides a method of estimating the average pollutant concentration and total pollutant loading in the discharge. After the storm event ends, the maximum flow rate is identified, and the full volume (generally 1000 mL) of the corresponding aliquot is added to the composite sample container. For aliquots obtained at other flow rates, a lesser volume is added to the composite sample container. The volume in each case is determined by the following equation:

$$V = V_{max}(Q/Q_{max})$$

where $V$ = volume of individual aliquot added to composite sample container
$Q$ = flow rate measured at time individual aliquot obtained
$Q_{max}$ = maximum flow rate observed during storm event
$V_{max}$ = volume of aliquot obtained at time of maximum flow rate

Table 8.2 illustrates such a computation for a set of nine aliquots. Note that the peak flow rate is 25 cubic feet per minute ($ft^3$/min), which occurred at the time the third aliquot was obtained. Therefore, the full volume of this aliquot (1000 mL) is added to the composite sample. The volume of each of the other aliquots added to the composite sample is proportional to the flow rate measured at the time each aliquot was obtained. The adjusted-volume column is the volume required to produce a total sample volume of 1000 mL. Figure 8.2 illustrates the relationship between the measured flow rate and computed sample volume for a flow-weighted composite sample.

### Time-weighted composite samples

Although the EPA requires that individual permit applications be accompanied by an analysis of a flow-weighted composite sample, the annual or semiannual monitoring performed as a part of EPA general permit compliance can be based on *time-weighted* composite samples

**TABLE 8.2  Example of Flow-Weighted Composite Sample**

| Sample | Flow rate, $ft^3$/min | Weight | Volume, mL | Adjusted Volume, mL |
|--------|------------------------|--------|------------|----------------------|
| 1 | 10 | 10/25 | 400 | 80 |
| 2 | 20 | 20/25 | 800 | 160 |
| 3 | 25 | 25/25 | 1000 | 200 |
| 4 | 20 | 20/25 | 800 | 160 |
| 5 | 10 | 10/25 | 400 | 80 |
| 6 | 15 | 15/25 | 600 | 120 |
| 7 | 10 | 10/25 | 400 | 80 |
| 8 | 5 | 5/25 | 200 | 40 |
| 9 | 10 | 10/25 | 400 | 80 |
|  |  | Total Volume | 5000 | 1000 |

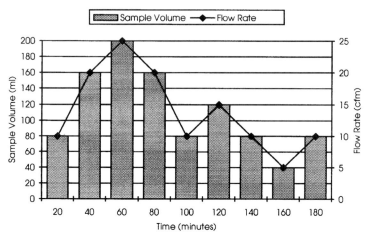

**Figure 8.2** Flow-weighted composite sample.

instead. Although flow-weighted composite samples are more representative of the total pollutant concentrations in the storm water discharge, time-weighted composite samples are easier to prepare, because there is no need to measure the flow rate each time a sample is obtained.

Table 8.3 illustrates the preparation of a time-weighted composite sample, employing the same nine aliquots as used previously. Since the samples are combined without regard to the flow rate which occurred at the time each sample was obtained, an equal volume is added from each of the nine aliquots. Since the desired total volume is 1000 mL, the volume added from each aliquot is simply 1000/9 = 111.11 mL. Figure 8.3 illustrates the relationship between measured flow rate and computed sample volume for a time-weighted composite sample.

**TABLE 8.3   Example of Time-Weighted Composite Sample**

| Sample | Flow rate, $ft^3$/min | Weight | Volume, mL |
|--------|----------------------|--------|------------|
| 1 | 10 | n/a | 111.11 |
| 2 | 20 | n/a | 111.11 |
| 3 | 25 | n/a | 111.11 |
| 4 | 20 | n/a | 111.11 |
| 5 | 10 | n/a | 111.11 |
| 6 | 15 | n/a | 111.11 |
| 7 | 10 | n/a | 111.11 |
| 8 | 5 | n/a | 111.11 |
| 9 | 10 | n/a | 111.11 |
| | | Total:   1000 | |

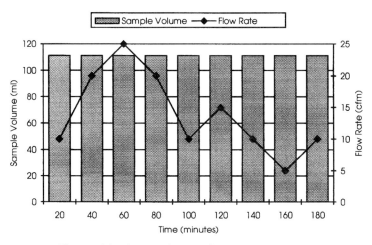

**Figure 8.3**  Time-weighted composite sample.

## Laboratory Analysis of Composite Samples

The analysis requirements for flow-weighted and time-weighted composite samples are almost identical to those requirements for grab samples, except that there is no requirement for field measurement of temperature or pH and there is no requirement for laboratory analysis of oil and grease. Note that the EPA general permit specifies minimum analysis requirements for certain types of facilities, as described later in this chapter. In addition, individual permits will specify the analysis requirements for the facility.

## Reporting Requirements

Discharge monitoring reports and other information may be submitted to the appropriate EPA regional office or state agency, as specified by the permit for the discharge. In addition, copies must be provided to operators of municipal separate storm sewer systems (MS4s) if the facility discharges into a medium or large MS4, as defined in Chap. 1.

EPA Form 2F is used to report the results of storm water sampling in nonauthorized states. For all samples, the following items of information should be reported:

- Outfall locations
- Improvements
- Site drainage map
- Narrative description of pollutant sources

- Non-storm-water discharge certification
- Significant leaks or spills
- Discharge information
- Biological toxicity testing data
- Contract analysis information
- Certification

At each outfall, the following data must be collected:

- Date and duration of storm event
- Time since last measurable event, h
- Flow measurements or estimates
- Total runoff volume for event
- Amount of precipitation, in
- Laboratory test results

### Reducing Sampling Requirements

Because of the expense and time required to obtain and analyze samples and report the results, it is worthwhile to consider measures which may reduce the sampling requirements. Several such measures are available:

1. *Provide annual certification.* In lieu of sampling a particular outfall, the EPA general permit specifies that the discharger may prepare an annual certification, under penalty of law, that material handling equipment or activities, raw materials, intermediate products, final products, waste materials, by-products, industrial machinery or operations, significant materials from past industrial activity, or airport deicing activities are not exposed to storm water within the drainage area of the outfall. This certification should be submitted to the EPA annually and should be included in the SWPPP. (However, the permittee must still comply with other applicable permit requirements which do not address sampling pollutants in discharges.) The EPA intends that this provision act as an incentive for permittees to eliminate exposure of potential pollutant sources to storm water, and will reward facilities that have already done so.

2. *Identify substantially identical outfalls.* The EPA general permit allows sampling requirements to be waived where sampling results are available for another "substantially identical" discharge. In determining whether two are more discharges are substantially identical, the industrial activities, exposed materials, material management

practices, and flow rates must all be substantially identical for each discharge. The EPA sampling guidance document [EPA, 1992] describes an evaluation procedure which should be used to determine if two or more outfalls are substantially identical. This procedure should be used, and this information should be submitted with any discharge monitoring report and included in the SWPPP. (See Chap. 6.)

3. *Sample from a holding pond.* The EPA general permit allows a single grab sample from the holding pond to be substituted for a flow-weighted or time-weighted composite sample, if the runoff from the site passes entirely through a holding pond with a retention time of greater than 24 h (i.e., if the pond volume is greater than the total storm water inflow for the first 24 h of the storm). The grab sample is obtained from the discharge of the holding pond at the end of the runoff event (after essentially all runoff has entered the holding pond). The pond volume averages the pollutant concentrations from all inflows, producing practically the same results as would be obtained by taking a flow-weighted composite sample of the discharge. Note that the holding time is computed for the actual storm event, and not for a particular "design" storm event such as the 2-year, 10-year, or 100-year storm.

4. *Combine outfalls.* It may be possible to construct a temporary or permanent diversion system which diverts flow from one outfall to combine with another. This eliminates an outfall which would otherwise require sampling.

## Sampling Equipment and Laboratories

It is advisable to coordinate the sampling effort in advance with the laboratory which will perform the analyses. The laboratory will generally be able to provide decontaminated sample containers with a shipping container and other necessary supplies. The following equipment is recommended:

- *Weather radio.* The National Weather Service maintains a network of radio stations which provide broadcasts of weather forecasts and warnings. Special weather radio receivers are available at low cost at most consumer electronics stores. These receivers are tuned to the correct frequency to receive the National Weather Service broadcasts.

- *Sample containers.* Plastic sample containers are safer and more convenient, but glass containers may be required for grab samples, because they must be tested for oil and grease. Sample containers should be prelabeled and numbered, so as to avoid any confusion during or after the storm event.

- *Sample scoop.* A wide, flat plastic scoop is used to obtain storm water samples when the depth of flow is not sufficient to fill sample containers directly.

- *Sample logbook with waterproof markers.* This book is used to record sample times, container numbers, and flow rates occurring at each sample time. A survey field book (available at survey supply stores and most engineering reprographics suppliers) serves as a good sample logbook.

- *Ice chest with ice (or refrigerator).* This is used to lower the temperature of samples to about 4°C until they reach the laboratory. All storm water samples must be stabilized so that the chemical composition does not change before the laboratory tests can be performed. Generally, thermal stabilization (refrigeration) is best. However, in some circumstances, when the samples will not reach the testing laboratory within 24 h, chemical stabilization may have to be used. If this may be the case, check with the laboratory for instructions.

- *Thermometer.* It is used to perform field tests on grab samples. These items are readily available from any scientific supply store. A good-quality digital electronic thermometer is recommended.

- *A pH meter.* This is also used for field tests on grab samples and is available from a scientific supply store. A good-quality electronic meter with glass electrodes is required to meet EPA test requirements [40 CFR 136.3] of accuracy to within plus or minus 0.1 pH unit. Pocket-size battery-operated digital pH meters are available for less than $100. For best results, however, a self-calibrating digital pH meter is recommended. These are available for about $500. A pH "strip kit" (pH paper) is not acceptable for pH measurements because of the lack of precision. Other potential problems with pH paper are that it is judged subjectively by comparison to a color chart; is affected by humidity, age, and method of storage; and may be affected by turbidity or suspended solids. In spite of these difficulties, however, the use of a strip kit is recommended as a field check of electronic meter readings. Suppliers of strip kits and pH meters can also supply buffered solutions which may be used to confirm the accuracy of pH meters and test procedures.

- *Container of distilled water.* This is used to clean the pH meter, temperature probe, and sample scoop after each use.

- *Watch or stopwatch.* This is needed to record sample times and/or sample intervals.

- *Rain gear.* This is used to protect employees during field work. Flashlights and other protective equipment may also be necessary.

The chain of custody from the person obtaining the samples to the laboratory should be clearly recorded in writing.

## Manual and Automatic Sampling Methods

An automatic continuous sampler can be used as an alternative to a series of manually collected samples. Manual and automatic sampling methods each have advantages and disadvantages. Manual methods have the advantage of being appropriate for all types of pollutants and requiring minimal equipment. However, manual grab samples are labor-intensive, may involve exposing personnel to hazardous situations, and are subject to human error. Manual flow-weighted composites require that flow measurements be taken during sampling. In addition, it may not be possible to get the sampling personnel and equipment to the outfall location(s) within the required 30 min.

Automatic sampling methods minimize labor requirements, reduce the risk of human error, reduce personnel exposure to hazardous situations, and can be triggered remotely or initiated according to present conditions. The equipment may be battery-operated for remote operation and may include refrigeration systems to stabilize storm water samples.

Automatic sampling methods may eliminate the need for manual compositing of aliquots for flow-weighted composite samples. However, automatic sampling methods may not be representative for oil and grease parameters and cannot be used for volatile organic carbon analysis. The samples may not be appropriate for pH and temperature tests or for other parameters with short holding times (such as fecal streptococcus, fecal coliform, and chlorine). There is also the potential for cross-contamination of the aliquot if the tubing and sample containers are not properly washed. This is especially true for certain pollutants such as pH, temperature, cyanide, total phenols, residual chlorine, oil and grease, fecal coliform, and fecal streptococcus.

Automatic samplers can also be costly ($7000 or more each for battery-powered units). The automated equipment requires installation, maintenance, and operator training, and an accurate flow measurement device must be linked to the automatic sampler.

## Common Problems with Storm Water Sampling

Storm water sampling is considerably more difficult than the sampling of process water discharges, because of the lack of control over sampling times and conditions. Rainfall events do not follow a predetermined schedule. They often occur at night, on weekends and holidays, and with little advance notice.

The EPA general permit has an "adverse climatic conditions" provision allowing a discharger to temporarily waive sampling and submit a description of why samples could not be collected. *Adverse climatic conditions* include insurmountable weather conditions that create dangerous conditions for personnel (such as local flooding, flash floods, high winds, hurricane, tornadoes, and electrical storms) or otherwise make the collection of a sample impracticable (drought, extended frozen conditions, and so on). These events tend to be isolated incidents and should not be used as an excuse for not conducting sampling under more favorable conditions associated with other storm events. This waiver may be used only once during each 2-year period.

The sampling waiver is not intended to apply to difficult logistical conditions, such as remote facilities with few employees or discharge locations which are difficult to access. "Ordinary" difficulties of this sort do not relieve the discharger from the responsibility to collect storm water samples:

- *Lack of rainfall:*  In arid regions or regions experiencing a period of unusually low rainfall, it is advisable to submit whatever samples are available, even if less than nine aliquots have been obtained. Document the conditions under which the available samples have been obtained. In the case of difficult climatic conditions, the EPA will accept sampling data from any storm event of at least 0.1 in total rainfall.

- *Too much rainfall:*  Some regions may experience such frequent rainfall events that there is never a period of 72 h or more between storms. Again, it is advisable to submit the best samples available, even if the 72-h criterion cannot be met. Document the conditions under which the samples were obtained.

- *Short rainfall events:*  If rainfall begins and then ends before at least 3 h of rainfall occurs, then it is advisable to go ahead and perform the laboratory tests on whatever samples were obtained, provided that at least three aliquots are available. Be sure to document the conditions under which the samples were obtained when you submit the test results.

- *Start-and-stop rainfall:*  If rainfall ends before the 3-h duration and then begins again later, it is advisable to continue sampling, provided that no more than a "reasonable" period has passed before the rainfall resumes. What constitutes a reasonable period is left to the judgment of the person obtaining the samples. However, it should not be more than a few hours. As with the other conditions noted above, this condition should be documented when the test results are submitted.

- *Inaccessible outfalls:* Some outfalls are inaccessible, especially during storm events. For example, a storm sewer outfall may be submerged during storm conditions. In such cases, it may be necessary to obtain samples at an upstream location, such as the next manhole or inspection point upstream. (*Note:* Before you begin sampling within manholes, read the safety warnings later in this chapter.) If another manhole or inspection is not available, tap into the pipe or sample at several locations to best represent the total site runoff.

- *Multiple outfalls:* If one person is responsible for sampling at multiple outfall points or multiple sites, it may not be possible to obtain a first-flush grab sample for each outfall for a single storm event. In such cases, it may be necessary to obtain the first-flush sample for different storm events at each outfall or site. For most parameters, automatic samplers may be used to collect samples within the first 30 min, triggered by the amount of rainfall, depth of flow, flow volume, or time.

- *Numerous small point discharges:* If it is not feasible to sample all discharges, impound the discharge channel or combine the discharges by building a weir or digging a ditch to collect discharges at a low point for sampling. This artificial collection point should be lined with plastic to prevent infiltration and/or high levels of sediment.

- *Sampling in manholes:* Sample in manholes only when necessary. Any sampling performed in confined spaces should meet the "SET" test: *s*upported, *e*quipped, and *t*rained. Anyone sampling in a confined space should have a support person monitoring performance and safety. The person doing the sampling should be properly equipped for the task and should be trained in confined-space entry.

- *Run-on from other property:* If possible, estimate the volume of off-site run-on contributions and off-site run-on sources of pollutants to perform a mass-balance calculation. The mass-balance calculation simply provides an estimate of the total volume of run-on times the concentration of various pollutants in the run-on, compared with the total volume and pollutant concentrations of site discharges. Include this information in the permit application. If this estimation is not possible, provide a narrative discussion of the upstream site (e.g., the type of facilities located on the upstream site, the types of pollutants that may be present in discharges, and so on).

- *Commingled discharges:* If process water is known to be mixed with the storm water at a particular outfall, attempt to sample the storm water discharge before it mixes with the non-storm-water discharge. If this is impossible, perform dry-weather sampling of the process water discharge and provide both sets of data to the permitting authority. This will provide an indication of the contribution of pollutants from each source.[2]

### Safety Issues in Storm Water Sampling

By definition, storm water sampling is performed under adverse conditions. These conditions can be merely uncomfortable, or they may be hazardous. Sampling in confined spaces, such as in storm sewer manholes, can be hazardous because of vapors which may collect in such locations. Physical hazards such as lightning and slick surfaces can create significant danger. In addition, there are biological hazards (sometimes known as the "three R's"—roaches, rodents, and reptiles). Finally, sampling personnel may be subjected to crime while outside or in parked vehicles during the 3-h sampling period required for a composite sample. As noted above, the EPA general permit has a temporary sampling waiver for unusually dangerous conditions.

Occupational Safety and Health Administration (OSHA) safety rules should be followed, along with any applicable state and local regulations.

In addition to personal safety and health issues, there are property hazards which must be considered in designing a storm water sampling program. Expensive equipment such as automatic samplers may be subject to theft and vandalism. Appropriate measures should be taken to safeguard such equipment.

### Estimating Flow Rates

It is necessary to be able to estimate the flow rate in order to assemble a flow-weighted composite sample and to fulfill all reporting requirements. The most important thing to understand about flow measurements is that *highly precise primary flow measurement devices such as flumes and weirs are not required by the EPA* (although they are acceptable if used). The EPA has clearly and specifically stated that most dischargers should not have to install expensive flow measurement equipment.

---

[2]Performing meaningful dry-weather sampling can be difficult. One large petrochemical facility had a significant quantity of dry-weather discharge, and the rate of discharge varied considerably, even during a particular 24-h period. Under such conditions, it can be difficult to subtract the contribution of dry-weather flows to total pollutant loading in a system which combines dry-weather flows and storm water runoff.

Acceptable flow rate estimates can generally be prepared by secondary methods using simple principles of hydrology and hydraulics. *Hydrology* is the study of runoff resulting from precipitation. *Hydraulics* is the study of fluid (mainly water) flow.

### Estimating flow rates by hydrologic methods

The most common method for computing the peak rate of runoff from a small drainage area is the *rational method:*

$$Q = CiA$$

where $Q$ = peak flow rate, ft$^3$s—approximate
  $C$ = runoff coefficient of drainage area = fraction of rainfall which appears as runoff at discharge point
  $i$ = average rainfall intensity during time of concentration, in/h
  $A$ = Drainage area, acres

Chapter 10 provides further information on methods of estimating the drainage area and runoff coefficient. The rainfall intensity can be estimated during the actual storm event by reading a rainfall gage periodically.

### Estimating flow rates by hydraulic methods

For all types of conveyances, the flow rate equals the product of the average flow velocity and the cross-sectional area of flow. The cross-sectional area of flow in a channel or culvert may be measured. Then the flow velocity can be measured or computed in one of two ways:

1. *Direct measurement.* One way of measuring flow velocity in a channel or culvert is by the *float method,* in which an object such as an orange is dropped into flowing water. A stopwatch is used to measure the elapsed time required for the orange to move a known distance. Thus the average flow velocity can be easily computed. An orange makes a good "float" for this purpose because it floats very low in the water, so that its velocity represents the flow velocity some distance below the surface, where most of the flow is occurring.

2. *Hydraulic analysis.* The principles of conservation of energy or momentum may be used to relate flow velocity, flow depth, and the characteristics of the conveyance. For open channels, the flow capacity is generally computed by using the *manning equation*

$$Q = \frac{1.486}{n} A \left( \frac{A}{\text{WP}} \right)^{2/3} \sqrt{S}$$

where $Q$ = Flow rate, cubic feet per second (ft$^3$/s)

$n$ = Manning roughness coefficient (depends upon condition of channel)

$A$ = cross-sectional area of flow, square feet (ft$^2$)

WP = wetted perimeter of flow in channel, ft

$S$ = slope of channel, ft/ft

Existing hydraulic structures such as culverts and inlets can also be used to compute flow rates. Charts or equations are generally available for different types of culverts and inlets, relating the depth of flow to the flow rate. Culvert flow is generally analyzed by using charts or equations available from the Federal Highway Administration or various state and local transportation agencies.

Special devices such as flumes and weirs are available to facilitate flow rate measurements. These devices are convenient because they have simple and unique relationships between flow rate and depth of flow. Therefore, it is only necessary to measure the depth of flow, and then the flow rate may be determined from a simple equation or chart.

Even more complex devices are available. Floats may be used to measure the depth of flow. Used in conjunction with a weir or flume, a float makes the use of such a device even more convenient. Ultrasonic transducers are also available to measure the flow depth and velocity.

## Requirements for EPA General Permit Compliance

Under the EPA general permit, sampling is required for some classes of facilities, with requirements similar to those for individual permit applications. At least one representative storm event must be sampled. Two types of samples must be obtained:

- A *first-flush grab sample.*   A single sample obtained within the first 30 min of discharge. Monitoring the first flush is necessary to evaluate the effectiveness of detention and retention devices which may only provide controls for the first portion of the discharge.

- A *time-weighted* or *flow-weighted composite sample.*   Compared with first-flush sampling, composite sampling provides more information for estimating pollutant loads, evaluating certain concentration-based water quality impacts, and generally characterizing storm water discharges. The EPA has authorized either time-weighted or flow-weighted composite samples which may be manually or automatically collected.

## Classifications of industrial facilities

For the purpose of determining storm water monitoring requirements, the EPA has divided industrial facilities into three classifications as follows:

- *Class I (high-risk) facilities:* These include EPCRA section 313 facilities with water priority chemicals, waste disposal sites, land disposal units, incinerators, boiler and industrial furnaces (BIFs), wood preserving facilities, battery reclaimers, coal pile runoff, and primary metal facilities. The EPA has targeted these facilities because they are believed to have a significant potential to contribute toxic pollutants to storm water due to the nature of activities occurring on site and the types of materials handled. Semiannual sampling is required for these facilities, and a discharge monitoring report is submitted annually to the EPA.

- *Class II facilities:* These include larger airports, coal-fired steam electric facilities, animal handling and meat packing, SIC 30 (rubber and miscellaneous plastics products) facilities, SIC 28 (chemicals and allied products) facilities, larger automobile junkyards, lime manufacturing facilities, oil-fired steam electric power generating facilities, cement manufacturing facilities and kilns, ready-mix concrete facilities, and ship building and repairing facilities. Annual storm water sampling is required, but DMRs are retained on site for inspection, rather than submitted to the EPA. The EPA may request the submittal of these DMRs at any time.

- *Class III (low-risk) facilities:* These include all facilities not listed in class I or class II. These facilities do not require sampling—only an annual inspection.

Generally, the industry-specific monitoring requirements are additive and are not intended to be mutually exclusive. Monitoring requirements must be evaluated on an outfall-by-outfall basis. If a particular discharge fits under more than one set of monitoring requirements, the facility must comply with both sets of sampling requirements. This does not mean that dischargers should collect extra samples, but rather that they should analyze samples that are collected for additional parameters. Since the sampling parameters often overlap between the categories, discharges which fit more than one category will often be tested for mostly the same parameters.

For the most part, monitoring requirements are limited to discharges associated with specific industrial activities and do not necessarily apply to all storm water discharges from a site.

### Monitoring requirements for class I facilities

Class I facilities, as noted above, require semiannual monitoring and annual reporting. If the facility discharges into a large or medium municipal separate storm sewer system (MS4), as defined in Chap. 1, copies of the DMRs must be submitted to the MS4. Copies must also be submitted to states that have requested this information. If a class I facility chooses to not monitor a "substantially identical" outfall, the permittee must submit the justification of why an outfall is representative of others with the annual discharge monitoring report.

**Whole effluent toxicity (WET) testing.**    Certain class I facilities require sample testing for acute *whole effluent toxicity* (WET). WET tests involve the exposure of live organisms to undiluted storm water samples. The organisms typically used for these tests are fathead minnows and various species of *Ceriodaphnia* (water fleas), among others. The mortality of the organisms after a certain exposure time determines the acute toxicity of the sample. According to an informal EPA survey of commercial laboratories, 24-h acute toxicity tests conducted on 100 percent effluent cost about $250 per species, or $500 total.

In lieu of WET testing, the discharger may monitor for pollutants identified in tables II and III of App. D of 40 CFR part 122 that the discharger knows or has reason to believe are present at the facility site. The determination of whether a chemical is known or reasonably expected to be present at a facility site will involve the "reasonable best effort" of the permittee to identify that significant quantities of materials or chemicals are present at the facility. The EPA generally believes that only those materials which are present in quantities of 100 kilograms (kg) or 1 barrel (bbl) within the monitoring period are likely to be detectable in storm water discharges, unless there is other evidence to suggest the likelihood of discharge in storm water. This determination can be based on an evaluation of information such as material inventories, industrial activities, raw materials, products, waste materials, and other site-specific considerations. The EPA does not require an exact measurement of whether a chemical is present in amounts that exceed this threshold. For example, where the chemical is a minor constituent of various materials and products used at the facility, where the chemical is present in various products, such as cleaning supplies or other incidental materials not used in an industrial process, or where it is held as a small laboratory stock, there would be no requirement for monitoring.

Therefore, there are two approaches to identify toxic pollution to storm water discharges. The first approach—use of the WET parameter—focuses on the use of a single parameter with the ability to identify the potentially toxic character of mixtures of chemicals in water. This approach might be used at industrial facilities where the storm water may contain a wide range of chemicals, or where the chemicals used at the facility are not well characterized. The WET parameter can be used to provide an initial indication of whether the toxic constituents in a discharge reach toxic levels.

The second approach focuses on analyzing storm water samples for specific chemicals that the discharger knows or has reason to believe are present at the facility site. This approach might be used where the discharger can characterize the chemicals at the facility site. This monitoring approach provides chemical-specific information that may provide a more direct indication than the WET parameter of specific pollutant sources.

When evaluating which of these two monitoring approaches to pursue, permittees should consider the types of chemicals present at the site, the feasibility of collecting sample volumes necessary to conduct WET monitoring, and analytical laboratory costs.

**Toxicity reductions.**  The EPA general permit provides that if acute whole effluent toxicity (statistically significant difference between the 100 percent dilution and control) is detected after October 1, 1995, in storm water discharges required to conduct toxicity testing, the permittee must review the SWPPP and make appropriate modifications to assist in identifying the source(s) of toxicity and to reduce the toxicity of the storm water discharges.

Under section 308 of the CWA, the EPA also has the authority to request a *toxicity identification evaluation* (TIE) or a *toxicity reduction evaluation* (TRE) where toxicity is reported. Similarly, where facilities detect significant levels of other pollutant parameters, the EPA may, where appropriate, request additional information, such as an additional pollutant source evaluation or a pollution prevention evaluation.

**Facilities subject to Title III, section 313 of SARA.**  The EPA believes that facilities that manufacture, import or process, or make other use of large amounts of toxic chemicals can potentially be a significant source of toxic pollutants to storm water. Failures of process, handling, and storage equipment used for EPCRA water priority chemicals associated with operator error, structural failures, and corrosion can result in the release of toxic chemicals.

For section 313 facilities subject to reporting requirements for water priority chemicals, storm water discharges that come into contact with any equipment, tank, container, or other vessel or area used for storage of a section 313 water priority chemical, or storm water discharges from a truck or railcar loading or unloading area where a section 313 water priority chemical is handled, must be tested for the following pollutants:

- Oil and grease, mg/L
- 5-day biochemical oxygen demand, mg/L
- Chemical oxygen demand, mg/L
- Total suspended solids, mg/L
- Total Kjeldahl nitrogen, mg/L
- Total phosphorus, mg/L
- pH
- Acute whole effluent toxicity (see earlier discussion)
- Section 313 water priority chemical for which the facility reports[3]

The sampling periods for section 313 facilities extend from January through June and from July through December. On each January 28, the results from the past two sampling periods (January through December) must be submitted.

**Primary metal industries.** For primary metal industries, all storm water discharges associated with industrial activity must be tested for the following:

- Oil and grease, mg/L
- Chemical oxygen demand, mg/L
- Total suspended solids, mg/L
- pH
- Acute whole effluent toxicity (see discussion earlier in this chapter)
- Total recoverable lead, mg/L
- Total recoverable cadmium, mg/L
- Total recoverable copper, mg/L
- Total recoverable arsenic, mg/L

---

[3] A list of section 313 water priority chemicals is included as an addendum to the EPA final general permit for discharges from areas associated with industrial activity (App. A).

- Total recoverable chromium, mg/L
- Any pollutant limited in an effluent guideline to which the facility is subject

Facilities that manufacture pure silicon and/or semiconductor-grade silicon are not required to monitor for total recoverable cadmium, total recoverable copper, total recoverable arsenic, total recoverable chromium, or whole effluent toxicity.

The sampling period for primary metal facilities extends from March through August and from September through February. On each April 28, the results from the past two sampling periods (March through February) must be submitted.

**Waste disposal facilities.**   Storm water discharges from waste disposal facilities (including land disposal units, incinerators, and boilers and industrial furnaces) must be tested for the following:

- Total recoverable magnesium, mg/L
- Dissolved magnesium, mg/L
- Total Kjeldahl nitrogen, mg/L
- Chemical oxygen demand, mg/L
- Total dissolved solids, mg/L
- Total organic carbon, mg/L
- Oil and grease, mg/L
- pH
- Total recoverable arsenic, mg/L
- Total recoverable barium, mg/L
- Total recoverable cadmium, mg/L
- Total recoverable chromium, mg/L
- Total recoverable cyanide, mg/L
- Total recoverable lead, mg/L
- Total mercury, mg/L
- Total recoverable selenium, mg/L
- Total recoverable silver, mg/L
- Acute whole effluent toxicity (see discussion earlier in this chapter)

These parameters are similar to those addressed by proposed groundwater monitoring requirements for municipal solid waste landfills established under subtitle D of RCRA [53 FR 33372 (Aug. 30, 1988)], except that several parameters have been deleted which are monitored in a groundwater context primarily to detect plume migration and are not necessarily of concern in and of themselves. These parameters include carbonate, calcium, chloride, iron, potassium, sodium, and sulfate.

The sampling periods for waste disposal facilities extend from October through March and from April through September. On each October 28, the results from the past two sampling periods (October through September) must be submitted.

Storm water discharges from active or inactive land disposal units (landfills) without a stabilized cover that have received any waste from industrial facilities other than construction sites must be monitored.

In general, inactive land disposal sites with a final cover that is consistent with specifications for a final cover system for municipal solid waste landfills developed under subtitle D of RCRA will satisfy the requirement of a stabilized final cover for the purposes of monitoring requirements. The subtitle D specifications for a final cover system are provided at 40 CFR 258.60 and include an erosion layer underlaid by an infiltration layer as follows:

1. *Erosion layer:*   a minimum of 6 in of earthen material that is capable of sustaining native plant growth

2. *Infiltration layer:*   a minimum of 18 in of earthen material that has a permeability less than or equal to the permeability of any bottom liner system or natural subsoils present, or a permeability no greater than $1 \times 10^{-5}$ centimeter per second (cm/s), whichever is less

Inactive facilities meeting these requirements will generally not be a significant source of pollutants to storm water discharges and are therefore not required to be monitored.

States may approve alternative final cover designs that include an infiltration layer which achieves an equivalent reduction in infiltration and an erosion layer which provides equivalent protection from wind and water erosion.

**Wood treatment facilities.**   Pollutants in storm water runoff from treated material storage yards at wood preserving facilities were studied by the EPA in 1981 in support of effluent guidelines development and in support of a proposed hazardous waste listing in 1988 [53 FR 53287 (Dec. 30, 1988)]. Several organic pollutants were found at significant concentrations, including pentachlorophenol, fluoranthene, benzo(a)-anthracene, chrysene, phenanthrene, and pyrene.

Wood preserving or wood surface application facilities are divided into several categories according to the type of operations and materials used. For all facilities, storm water discharges from areas that are used for wood treatment, wood surface application, or storage of treated or surface-protected wood must be tested for the following:

- Oil and grease, mg/L
- pH
- Chemical oxygen demand, mg/L
- Total suspended solids,[4] mg/L.

Facilities that use chlorophenolic formulations must also test for pentachlorophenol and acute whole effluent toxicity.

Facilities that use creosote formulations must also test for acute whole effluent toxicity.

Facilities that use chromium-arsenic formulations must also test for total recoverable arsenic (mg/L), total recoverable chromium (mg/L), and total recoverable copper (mg/L).

As a part of RCRA, the EPA has published regulations addressing several wastes from wood preserving facilities, including storage yard drippage [55 FR 50450 (Dec. 6, 1990)]. The RCRA requirements establish a set of controls, including certain management practices, to manage wastes addressed by the rule. The use of these controls does not eliminate or reduce the requirement for storm water discharge monitoring.

The sampling periods for wood treatment facilities extend from January through June and from July through December. On each January 28, the results from the past two sampling periods (January through December) must be submitted.

**Industrial facilities with coal piles.**    Coal pile runoff should be addressed somewhat differently from other runoff because it is subject to a numeric effluent limitation. Coal pile runoff should be monitored before it is commingled with flows from other sources. Thus, coal pile runoff from a primary metal facility, e.g., should be monitored only for the parameters specified for coal pile runoff.

The coal pile runoff limitations correspond to those at 40 CFR part 423. Storm water discharges from coal pile runoff must be tested for the following:

---

[4] The EPA originally proposed that wood treatment facilities monitor phosphorus, nitrate plus nitrite, Kjeldahl nitrogen, and $BOD_5$. However, these requirements were eliminated because nutrients are not expected to be present in significant amounts at wood treatment facilities. In addition, the metals and other toxic materials in samples can limit the accuracy of $BOD_5$ analysis.

- Oil and grease, mg/L
- pH
- Total suspended solids, mg/L
- Total recoverable copper, mg/L
- Total recoverable nickel, mg/L
- Total recoverable zinc, mg/L

The sampling periods for coal pile runoff extend from March through August and from September through February. On each April 28, the results from the past two sampling periods (March through February) must be submitted.

**Battery reclaimers.**  Storm water discharges from areas for storage of lead acid batteries, reclamation products, or waste products and for areas used for lead acid battery reclamation (including material handling activities) must be tested for the following:

- Oil and grease, mg/L
- Chemical oxygen demand, mg/L
- Total suspended solids, mg/L
- pH
- Total recoverable copper, mg/L
- Total recoverable lead, mg/L

Other portions of the facility are not subject to this monitoring requirement.

The sampling periods for battery reclaimer facilities extend from March through August and from September through February. On each April 28, the results from the past two sampling periods (March through February) must be submitted.

### Monitoring requirements for class II facilities

As noted above, class II facilities must monitor discharges annually and retain reports on site for review by the EPA upon request. If the listed activity does not occur at a particular site or if the runoff from that area is treated as a process wastewater, is discharged to a municipal sanitary sewer (with the municipality's permission), or is retained on site, then no sampling is required.

If a class II facility chooses to not monitor a substantially identical outfall, the permittee must develop the justification of why an outfall is representative of others. However, the permittee is not required to submit the justification unless it is requested by the director. These facilities must keep the justification in the SWPPP.

**Large airports.** Airports with over 50,000 flight operations per year must monitor storm water discharges from aircraft or airport deicing areas. A flight operation consists of a single takeoff or landing by an aircraft. These discharges must be tested for the following:

- Oil and grease, mg/L
- 5-day biochemical oxygen demand, mg/L
- Chemical oxygen demand, mg/L
- Total suspended solids, mg/L
- pH
- The primary ingredient used in the deicing materials (e.g., ethylene glycol, propylene glycol, urea)

According to information obtained from the Aircraft Owners and Pilots Association (AOPA) and based on 1990 Federal Aviation Administration data, there are approximately 5078 public-use airports in the United States. Of these, approximately 376 airports (7.4 percent) have 50,000 or more flight operations per year.

**Coal-fired steam electric facilities.** Monitoring parameters will be the same as those required semiannually under the EPA general permit for coal piles, with the same justification of their selection. Because this monitoring requirement does not support a numeric effluent limitation, and because of the more diffuse nature of coal in the coal handling areas, the EPA decided that a monitoring frequency of once per year is adequate.

Storm water discharges from coal handling sites (other than runoff from coal piles which is not eligible for coverage under the general permit) must be tested for the following:

- Oil and grease, mg/L
- pH
- Total suspended solids, mg/L
- Total recoverable copper, mg/L
- Total recoverable nickel, mg/L
- Total recoverable zinc, mg/L

**Animal handling and meat packing facilities.** The nature of potential pollutant sources to runoff from animal handling, manure management areas, and production waste management areas at meat packing plants, poultry packing plants, and facilities that manufacture animal and marine fats with animal waste and/or production wastes is similar to runoff from confined animal feeding operations (feedlots). Animal waste products can be a significant source of pollutants to storm water runoff which can contribute high levels of oxygen-demanding pollutants, nutrients, and fecal bacteria [EPA, 1991, 1974b].

Storm water discharges from animal handling areas, manure management areas, production waste management areas exposed to precipitation at meat packing plants, poultry packing plants, and facilities that manufacture animal and marine fats and oils must test for the following:

- 5-day biochemical oxygen demand, mg/L
- Oil and grease, mg/L
- Chemical oxygen demand, mg/L
- Total suspended solids, mg/L
- Total Kjeldahl nitrogen, mg/L
- Total phosphorus, mg/L
- pH
- Fecal coliform (counts per 100 mL)

**Chemical and allied products and rubber manufacturers.** For chemical and allied products manufacturers and rubber manufacturers (SIC codes 28 and 30), storm water discharges that come into contact with solid chemical storage piles must be tested for the following:

- Oil and grease, mg/L
- Chemical oxygen demand, mg/L
- Total suspended solids, mg/L
- pH
- Any pollutant limited in an effluent guideline to which the facility is subject

**Automobile Junkyards.** Storm water discharges from the following areas must be monitored:

- Areas where over 250 automobile and/or truck bodies with drivelines, 250 drivelines, or any combination thereof (in whole or in parts) is exposed to storm water

- Areas where over 500 automobile and/or truck units (bodies with or without drivelines in whole or in parts) are stored exposed to storm water

- Areas where over 100 units per year are dismantled and drainage or storage of automotive fluids occurs in areas exposed to storm water

These storm water discharges must be tested for the following:

- Oil and grease, mg/L
- Chemical oxygen demand, mg/L
- Total suspended solids, mg/L
- pH
- Any pollutant limited in an effluent guideline to which the facility is subject

**Lime manufacturing facilities.**   Chemical storage piles can have a significant potential for contributing pollutants to storm water discharges. Storm water discharged from areas of exposed lime storage piles at lime manufacturing facilities can have significantly elevated pH levels.

Storm water discharges that have come into contact with lime storage piles must be tested for the following:

- Oil and grease, mg/L
- Chemical oxygen demand, mg/L
- Total suspended solids, mg/L
- pH
- Any pollutant limited in an effluent guideline to which the facility is subject

**Oil-fired steam electric power generating facilities.**   Storm water discharges from oil handling sites must be tested for the following:

- Oil and grease, mg/L
- Chemical oxygen demand, mg/L
- Total suspended solids, mg/L

- pH
- Any pollutant limited in an effluent guideline to which the facility is subject

**Cement manufacturing facilities and cement kilns.**  Loading and unloading activities, raw-material storage, and processing operations at cement manufacturing facilities, cement kilns, and ready-mix concrete facilities can be a significant potential source of pollutants to storm water [EPA, 1974a]. The effluent limitation guidelines for the cement manufacturing category address runoff from the storage of materials used in or derived from the manufacture of cement (see 40 CFR 411.30). Discharges that are covered by the effluent limitation guideline cannot be authorized under the general permit. Individual permit applications must be submitted for such discharges.

Dust generating processes and air deposition of pollutants from smokestacks at cement kilns could also be significant sources of pollutants to storm water. Discharges from cement manufacturing facilities and cement kilns could contain the same constituents limited in the storm water effluent limitation guidelines for cement kilns' material storage piles.

Storm water discharges associated with industrial activity (except those from material storage piles that are not eligible for coverage under the general permit) must be tested for the following:

- Oil and grease, mg/L
- Chemical oxygen demand, mg/L
- Total suspended solids, mg/L
- pH
- Any pollutant limited in an effluent guideline to which the facility is subject

**Ready-mix concrete facilities.**  Discharges from ready-mix concrete facilities could contain the same constituents limited in the storm water effluent limitation guidelines for cement kilns' material storage piles. Storm water discharges associated with industrial activity must be tested for the following:

- Oil and grease, mg/L
- Chemical oxygen demand, mg/L
- Total suspended solids, mg/L

- pH
- Any pollutant limited in an effluent guideline to which the facility is subject

**Ship building and repairing facilities.**   Storm water discharges associated with industrial activity must be tested for the following:

- Oil and grease, mg/L
- Chemical oxygen demand, mg/L
- Total suspended solids, mg/L
- pH
- Any pollutant limited in an effluent guideline to which the facility is subject

### References

Environmental Protection Agency: *Development Document for Effluent Limitation Guidelines and New Source Performance Standards for the Cement Manufacturing Point Source Category,* EPA/440/1-79-005-a, 1974a.

———: *Development Document for Effluent Limitations Guidelines and New Source Performance Standards—Feedlots Point Source Category,* EPA-440/1/74-004-a, 1974b.

———: *Guidance Specifying Management Measures for Sources of Nonpoint Pollution in Coastal Waters,* Office of Water, EPA 840-B-92-002, January 1993.

———: *NPDES Storm Water Sampling Guidance Document,* EPA 833-B-92-001, July 1992.

Woodward-Clyde Consultants, Inc.: *Urban Targeting and BMP Selection: An Information and Guidance Manual for State Nonpoint Source Program Staff Engineers and Managers,* prepared for Region V, Water Division, Watershed Management Unit, Environmental Protection Agency, Chicago, and Office of Water Regulations and Standards, Office of Water Enforcement and Permits, Environmental Protection Agency, Washington. Distributed by The Terrene Institute, Washington, November 1990.

# 9

# Construction
# Storm Water Permitting

This is the first of five chapters which deal with the specific requirements for storm water discharges from construction facilities. This
chapter introduces the requirements for storm water permitting for
such facilities and describes the EPA general permit for storm water
discharges from construction facilities.

Chapter 10 describes how to prepare a storm water pollution prevention plan (SWPPP) for a construction site. Chapter 11 provides
details on stabilization measures (such as vegetation) for erosion and
sediment control and Chap. 12 on structural measures (such as sediment basins) for erosion and sediment control. Chapter 13 describes
other pollution prevention measures for construction sites.

There is additional information on construction permit requirements
for specific states in Chap. 14. A copy of the EPA final NPDES general
permit for storm water discharges from construction sites is included
in App. B. Appendix D presents an example of an SWPPP for a construction site.

## Why EPA Regulates Construction Storm
## Water Discharges

Construction activities produce many different kinds of pollutants
which may cause storm water contamination problems. Grading activities remove grass, rocks, pavement, and other protective ground covers, resulting in the exposure of underlying soil to the elements.
Because the soil surface is unprotected, soil and sand particles are easily picked up by wind and/or washed away by rain or snow melt. This
process is called *erosion*. The water carrying these particles eventually

reaches a stream, river, or lake where the water slows down, allowing the particles to fall onto the bottom of the streambed or lake. This process is called *sedimentation*. Gradually, layers of these clays and silt build up in the streambeds, choking the river and stream channels and covering the areas where fish spawn and plants grow. These particles also cloud waters, causing aquatic respiration problems, and can kill fish and plants growing in the river stream.

Sediment runoff rates from construction sites are typically 10 to 20 times those of agricultural lands, with runoff rates as high as 100 times those of agricultural lands and typically 1000 to 2000 times those of forest lands. Even a small amount of construction may have a significant negative impact on water quality in localized areas. Over a short time, construction sites can contribute more sediment to streams than was deposited previously over several decades.

In addition, the construction of buildings and roads may require the use of toxic or hazardous materials such as petroleum products, pesticides, fertilizers and herbicides, and building materials such as asphalt, sealants, and concrete which may pollute storm water running off the construction site. These materials can be toxic to aquatic organisms and can degrade water for drinking and water-contact recreational purposes.

## Regulated Discharges

As noted in Chap. 1, phase I of the National Storm Water Program requires that "storm water discharges from areas of industrial activity" apply for and receive permits from the EPA or authorized states. Certain types of construction projects are defined as *industrial activity* for the purposes of storm water permitting.

The very first step in complying with EPA or state regulations on construction storm water discharges is to determine whether a particular discharge is regulated. To make this determination, it is important to understand exactly how terms such as *storm water, discharge, point source,* and *waters of the United States* are defined. Chapter 3 provides detailed definitions and a discussion of these terms.

Under the National Storm Water Program, the EPA regulates storm water discharges from construction sites, including clearing, grading, and excavation activities, if the disturbed land area is 5 acres or more.[1]

---

[1] The EPA originally proposed that all construction activities over 1 acre be permitted, but this was changed to 5 acres.

As the EPA published the regulations concerning phase I of the National Storm Water Program, the Natural Resources Defense Council (NRDC) filed suit against the EPA on several issues. One issue raised in the NRDC suit concerned the 5-acre limit on construction sites which must be permitted. The NRDC suit claimed that the EPA had no scientific or technical basis for choosing a 5-acre cutoff for permit requirements.

The Ninth Circuit Court of Appeals in San Francisco ruled on the NRDC case in June

Construction sites with disturbed areas of less than 5 acres may also be regulated, if they are part of a "larger common plan of development or sale." In this way, the EPA prevents projects from being divided into 4.9-acre "projects" merely for the sake of avoiding storm water discharge permit requirements.

The EPA defines "part of a larger common plan of development or sale" as a contiguous area where multiple separate and distinct construction activities may be taking place at different times on different schedules under one plan. Thus, if a distinct construction activity has been identified on site by the time the application would be submitted, that distinct activity should be included as part of the larger plan [EPA, 1992]. For example, if a developer buys a 20-acre lot, builds roads, and installs underground utilities with the intention of constructing homes or other structures sometime in the near future, this is considered a common plan of development or sale. If the land is parceled off or sold, and construction occurs on plots that are *less than* 5 acres by separate, independent builders, then this activity still is subject to storm water permitting requirements if the smaller plots are included on the original site plan [EPA, 1993].

If a construction activity is undertaken at an industrial facility which already holds a permit for industrial storm water discharges, a separate permit must be obtained for the construction activity (assuming that it meets the 5-acre limitation). For construction activities on less than 5 acres, no construction permit is required, but the industrial operator should modify the storm water pollution prevention plan to address all new sources of pollution and runoff from construction activities [EPA, 1993].

The EPA is requiring permits for all storm water discharges from construction activities where the land disturbed meets the requirements established in 40 CFR 122.26(b)(14)(x) and which discharge into waters of the United States. The location of the construction activity and the ultimate land use at the site do not factor into the analysis. The construction activities may include road building; construction of residential houses, office buildings, or industrial buildings; and demolition activity. At a demolition site, disturbed areas might include where building materials, demolition equipment, or

---

1992, instructing the EPA to present further information concerning the 5-acre limit. The EPA is currently gathering this information. The information will be submitted to the court for final review. The court may rule that the existing 5-acre limitation on permit requirements may be modified or eliminated.

The EPA published a notice in the *Federal Register* on December 18, 1992, summarizing the Ninth Circuit Court of Appeals actions in this case. *The EPA made it clear that until a final ruling is handed down by the court, the existing 5-acre limitation remains in effect.*

disturbed soil are situated, which may alter the surface of the land [EPA, 1993].

No permit is required for agricultural or silvicultural activities, including the clearing of land for agricultural purposes, because these are exempt from NPDES permit requirements under 40 CFR 122.4 [EPA, 1992].

Repaving of roads is not regulated under the storm water program unless 5 acres or more of underlying and/or surrounding soil are cleared, graded, or excavated as part of the repaving operation. Maintenance activities for flood control channels or roadside ditches (such as removal of vegetation) must obtain storm water discharge permit coverage if they involve grading, clearing, or excavation activities that disturb 5 acres or more, either individually or as part of a long-term maintenance plan [EPA, 1993].

Off-site borrow pits are not considered part of the on-site construction activity, and their surface area is not considered part of the 5-acre minimum surface area required for construction permitting. If a borrow pit is specifically used for the removal of materials such as sand, gravel, and clay, the pit is considered a mine and is classified under SIC code 14. Such sites are regulated as industrial activities, as explained in Chap. 4. However, if the borrow pit is utilized for the removal of general fill material (such as dirt) and disturbs 5 acres or more of land, the pit is considered a construction activity as defined at 40 CFR 122.26(b)14(x) [EPA, 1993].

As discussed in Chap. 2, the Transportation Act of 1991 exempted all construction projects owned by small municipalities (less than 100,000), in spite of whether the projects meet the other criteria for regulation described above. If the construction activity is owned by a small municipality, it is exempt from permit coverage, even though it may be operated by a private contractor. However, some states may require permit coverage. In addition, permit coverage may still be required if the project is a significant contributor of pollutants to waters of the United States or if it contributes to a violation of a water quality standard.

## Types of Permits for Construction Site Storm Water Discharges

There are two types of NPDES permits available for storm water discharges from construction sites: an individual permit and the general permit. This chapter describes the EPA general permit; App. B gives the text of the permit. Many states have developed their own general permits for construction storm water discharges; review Chap. 14 for further details on state requirements.

Almost all construction activities which require NPDES permit coverage for storm water discharges can be covered under the general permit. Therefore, this book strongly emphasizes the general permit requirements. However, the EPA or state government administering the NPDES permit program has the right to require that a construction project submit an application for an individual permit under certain conditions. These conditions are most likely to be encountered in large, complex, and controversial construction projects, such as new airports, freeways, and other major facilities. These types of facilities often face some opposition from environmental groups, which already use existing permit requirements (such as the requirement for a section 404 wetlands permit) as a means of delaying, altering, or killing the project. The requirement for a permit to discharge storm water provides a new legal means for such groups to oppose such major projects.

## General Permit Coverage

As noted in Chap. 1, a series of court rulings have established the authority of the EPA to utilize innovative concepts such as general permits to regulate discharges under the Clean Water Act. The EPA has used general permits as a tool to accommodate the large number of dischargers included in the National Storm Water Program. Most traditional NPDES permits have been individual permits, with permit requirements which were specific to the facility named in the permit. In addition, the traditional NPDES permit gives numeric effluent limitations on various pollutants and specifies a minimum discharge sampling interval.

The EPA issued its "core" general permit for storm water discharges associated with construction activity on September 9, 1992 (see App. B). This core general permit applies directly to nonauthorized states and also serves as the basis for other general permits issued by authorized states.

The EPA core general permit requires the submittal of a Notice of Intent (NOI), which states the permittee's desire to discharge according to the terms and provisions of the general permit. Compliance with the provisions of the general permit involves the preparation and maintenance of an SWPPP (as described in Chap. 10).

The EPA does not currently assess permit fees for general permit coverage, but several states do. The EPA has worked on a federal permit fee system which would impose fees on permit holders in states without NPDES permit authority. This fee system was developed under the 1990 Budget Reconciliation Act, which required the EPA to develop a system of user fees to pay for "services rendered." It is reasonable to expect the EPA to implement a fee system for storm water discharge permit applications.

The existing EPA general permits for construction activity will expire on October 1, 1997. There is no automatic renewal of general permit coverage. Construction projects which are under way at that time must submit the appropriate NOI or permit application to comply with whatever program requirements are in place at that time.

Complying with EPA regulations involves filing a Notice of Intent with the EPA or the appropriate state agency. The NOI indicates that the operator of the construction site will comply with the terms of the general permit for construction activities.

### EPA definition of *operator*

The NOI is submitted by the operator or operators of the construction site. The EPA defines the term *operator* in two ways:

- *The operator has operational control over site specifications.*  Since the owner of the site generally has the ability to change the construction specifications, this definition tends to include the owner.

- *The operator has day-to-day operational control over the site activities.*  Since the general contractor usually maintains day-to-day control of the site activities. this definition tends to include the general contractor.

Therefore, under EPA definitions, both the owner and the general contractor are responsible for filing an NOI. This can be done in one of three ways:

1. The owner and general contractor can file a joint NOI.

2. The owner and general contractor can file separate NOIs, but these should be filed at the same time (in the same envelope) so as to notify the EPA that they pertain to the same activity.

3. The owner can file an NOI before the general contractor is selected, and then the general contractor can file an amended NOI (to include the contractor's name along with the owner's name) before beginning work on the site.

Several states have different requirements concerning the operator. Some states name the owner as the operator while others name the general contractor; some follow the EPA example and require them to become copermittees.

*The NOI must be filed at least 2 days before construction begins.*[2] If a different owner or operator assumes control of the site, the new owner or operator must file a new NOI at least 2 days before beginning work on the site. The permit coverage of the previous owner or operator does not carry forward to the new owner or operator.

### EPA general permit NOI requirements

The minimum information on the NOI for coverage under the EPA general permit for construction storm water discharges includes the following:

- *Site location:* The name, mailing address, and physical location of the site for which the notice is submitted. If the site has a street address, this must be provided. Otherwise, the latitude and longitude (or section, township, and range) can be used to identify the site location. For linear projects (such as roadways and pipelines), the location of the project given on the NOI should be the midpoint of the project. For projects which span two or more states, the NPDES requirements of both states should be met [EPA, 1993].

- *Owner's address:* The name, address, and telephone number of the project owner.

- *Operator identification:* The name, address, and telephone number of the operator, along with the ownership status and the status of the operator as a federal, state, local, or private entity.

- *Existing NPDES permits:* The permit number of additional NPDES permits for any discharges from the site (including non-storm-water discharges) that are currently authorized by an NPDES permit.

- *Receiving waters or system:* The name of the receiving water(s) allows the EPA to identify discharges to impaired, sensitive water bodies or high-value water resources that require additional oversight and compliance evaluation. If the discharge is to a large or medium municipal separate storm sewer system, the name of the municipal operator of the storm sewer system must be identified along with the name of the ultimate receiving water(s).

---

[2]The EPA had originally proposed that NOIs be filed 90 days before construction begins. This was reduced to 30 days in the draft general permit issued on August 16, 1991, and finally to 2 days in the final general permit of September 9, 1992. Many states require that the NOI be filed more than 2 days before the start of construction.

- *Indication of sampling data:* An indication of whether the facility has existing quantitative data describing the concentration of pollutants in storm water discharges. The actual results are not submitted with the NOI—only an indication of whether such results are available.

- *Project start and completion dates:* The scheduled dates that construction activities requiring permit coverage will begin and end on the site.

- *Disturbed acreage:* The number of acres of soil on the site which will be disturbed by clearing, grading, or excavation during the proposed construction activities.

- *SWPPP certification:* A certification that a storm water pollution prevention plan has been prepared for the facility. Further details on SWPPPs are presented later in this chapter and in Chap. 10.

The person signing the NOI must have a sufficient level of authority and responsibility within the organization to help ensure compliance with the terms and conditions of the permit. For a sole proprietorship, the proprietor must sign the NOI. For a partnership, a general partner must sign.

For a corporation, the person signing the NOI must be a responsible corporate officer, including the president, secretary, treasurer, or vice president of the corporation in charge of a principal business function or any other person who performs similar policy- or decision-making functions for the corporation.

A corporate plant or facility manager may sign the NOI only under certain conditions. The plant or facility must employ more than 250 persons or have gross annual sales or expenditures exceeding $25 million (in second-quarter 1980 dollars). In addition, the authority to sign documents must have been assigned or delegated to the plant or facility manager in accordance with corporate procedures.

For a municipality, state, federal, or other public agency, the person signing the NOI must be a principal executive officer or ranking elected official. A principal executive officer of a federal agency includes the chief executive officer of the agency and a senior executive officer having responsibility for the overall operations of a principal geographic unit of the agency (e.g., regional administrators of the EPA). Within the military, base commanders represent the appropriate level of authority.

The person signing the NOI makes the following certification:

> I certify under penalty of law that this document and all attachments were prepared under my direction or supervision in accordance with a system designed to assure that qualified personnel properly gather and evaluate

the information submitted. Based on my inquiry of the person or persons who manage the system, or those persons directly responsible for gathering the information, the information submitted is, to the best of my knowledge and belief, true, accurate, and complete. I am aware that there are significant penalties for submitting false information, including the possibility of fine and imprisonment for knowing violations.

### Storm water pollution prevention plan

In nonauthorized states, the EPA general permit requires that an SWPPP be completed for each construction project for which an NOI has been submitted. Most authorized states have similar requirements, although some states use different terminology. The SWPPP must be completed and ready to implement at the time the project begins construction.

Under EPA general permit requirements, the SWPPP is not submitted with the NOI. Instead, the SWPPP is retained on site by the discharger. Federal, state, and local regulatory agencies have the authority to review the SWPPP at any time. If the reviewing agency finds that the SWPPP is not in compliance with general permit requirements, the discharger has 30 days to revise the SWPPP to achieve compliance. Chapter 10 provides further details on the SWPPP.

### Notice of termination

The EPA allows the operator(s) to file a Notice of Termination (NOT) with the EPA which certifies that specific activities in the SWPPP have ended and that one of the following conditions is true:

- Final stabilization is complete, and temporary erosion and sediment controls have been removed.

- All discharges from the construction area have been eliminated.

- The operator has changed, and the new operator is responsible for compliance. The new operator is responsible for submitting an NOI if activities continue.

The NOT form requires the following information:

- *Facility location:*   Name, mailing address, and location of the facility for which the notification is submitted. Where a street address for the site is not available, the location of the approximate center of the site must be described in terms of the latitude and longitude to the nearest 15 seconds or the section, township, and range to the nearest quarter.

- *Operator identification:*    The name, address, and telephone number of the operator addressed by the NOT.

- *NPDES permit number:*    The NPDES permit number for the storm water discharge identified by the NOT.

- *Reason for NOT:*    An indication of whether the storm water discharges associated with industrial activity have been eliminated or the operator of the discharges has changed.

- *Certification:*    The following certification:

   I certify under penalty of law that all storm water discharges associated with industrial activity from the identified facility that are authorized by an NPDES general permit have been eliminated or that I am no longer the operator of the facility or construction site. I understand that by submitting this Notice of Termination, I am no longer authorized to discharge storm water associated with industrial activity under this general permit, and that discharging pollutants in storm water associated with industrial activity to waters of the United States is unlawful under the Clean Water Act where the discharge is not authorized by an NPDES permit. I also understand that the submittal of this notice of termination does not release an operator from liability for any violations of this permit or the Clean Water Act.

The NOT must be signed in accordance with the signatory requirements of 40 CFR 122.22, which were summarized earlier in this chapter with regard to the NOI.

### Contractor requirements

The general contractor has several responsibilities with respect to the NPDES permit, including

1. Filing an NOI, as described above.

2. Implementing the storm water management activities and other measures stated in the SWPPP, which must identify the general contractor. (See Chap. 10.)

3. Signing a certification acknowledging the terms and conditions of the permit.

Subcontractors do not need to submit an NOI if the general contractor continues to have day-to-day operational control of the site and has already filed an NOI. However, subcontractors must be identified by name in the SWPPP, must implement the measures stated in the plan, and must sign a certification acknowledging the terms and conditions of the permit.

It is wise to obtain signatures from all subcontractors working on the construction project, even those subcontractors who are not directly involved in clearing, grading, or excavating activities. Other subcontractors, such as paint, electrical, and even drywall contractors, generate construction waste, move vehicles onto and off the site, and perform other actions that affect at least some portions of the SWPPP. The cooperation of these subcontractors is required to fully implement the plan.

### Summary of certification requirements

Compliance with the final general permit for construction activities relies largely on written certifications. Two types of certifications must be made:

- *Certification for true, accurate, and complete information:* The NOI, NOT, SWPPP, and the inspection reports must all include certifications that the information presented is true, accurate, and complete. The EPA has the authority to impose various penalties for making false statements in such certifications.

- *Certification for acknowledging the terms and conditions of the permit:* The general contractor and all subcontractors must certify that they are aware of and will comply with the terms and conditions of the general permit. This certification should be filed with the SWPPP before each contractor begins operations on the site.

### References

Environmental Protection Agency: *NPDES Storm Water Program Question and Answer Document,* vol. 1, EPA Document 833-F-93-002, March 16, 1992.
————: *NPDES Storm Water Program Question and Answer Document,* vol. 2, EPA Document 833-F-93-002B, July 1993.

# 10

# NPDES Construction Permit Storm Water Pollution Prevention Plan

This is the second of five chapters which deal with the specific requirements for storm water discharges from construction facilities. This chapter describes how to prepare a storm water pollution prevention plan (SWPPP) for a construction site. The material in this chapter is derived primarily from information presented in the EPA guidance document for construction best management practices [EPA, 1992]. Appendix D presents an example of an SWPPP for a construction project.

## Concept of the Storm Water Pollution Prevention Plan

Given the nature of construction activities and the resulting pollutants as well as the variable nature of storm events, the EPA determined that the best approach to storm water management for these sites is through the use of SWPPPs *designed by the permittee (the site operators)*. These plans are based on the use of *best management practices* (BMPs). For construction sites, there are three main types of BMP:

1. Those that prevent erosion, including the stabilization practices described in Chap. 11

2. Those that trap pollutants before they can be discharged, including the structural practices described in Chap. 12

3. Those that prevent pollutants from the construction materials from mixing with storm water, including the practices described in Chap. 13

Although these three types of BMP have different functions, the basic principle is the same: These BMPs are designed to prevent, or at least control, the pollution of storm water before it has a chance to affect receiving streams.

## Purpose of the SWPPP

The SWPPP is the focus of the NPDES storm water permit and is the key to controlling pollutants in storm water discharges. Therefore, proper and careful development and implementation of the plan will maximize the potential benefits of pollution prevention and sediment and erosion control measures. The permit consists of specific requirements for the plan, including deadlines and certain storm water control measures. This chapter provides a step-by-step explanation of how to develop and implement an SWPPP which will satisfy the requirements of the EPA general permit for construction activities. Authorized states may have different requirements, and local regulatory authorities may impose additional standards.

## SWPPP Preparation Date

An SWPPP must be prepared before the NOI is submitted, and the operator(s) must begin implementing the plan at the time that the NOI is submitted. The SWPPP is not generally submitted with the NOI; it is filed on site along with contractor and subcontractor certifications and inspection reports (described later in this chapter). Note that some state and local agencies require that the SWPPP be submitted for review and approval.

Each NPDES storm water permit may specify deadlines for plan development and implementation. The sequence described in this chapter assumes that the SWPPP is completed and implemented at the time the project breaks ground and is revised (if necessary) as construction proceeds. The plan should be in place before project initiation because construction operations pose environmental risks as soon as activity begins. The initial rough-grading activities may contribute a significant amount of pollutants to storm water runoff.

The planning for pollution prevention measures should be done while the site construction plan is being developed. The best SWPPPs are developed at the same time as the design of the site plan. However, if the site plan design has been completed before one begins to prepare the SWPPP, much of the information needed for the plan should already be included in the design documents. An SWPPP can be prepared for most construction projects by using information from the existing design and modifying the design to accommodate the controls.

Responsibility for developing an SWPPP typically lies with the operator of the construction project, as defined in Chap. 9.

## Steps in Developing an SWPPP

The process of developing an SWPPP for construction activities has been divided into three steps.

1. *Site evaluation and design development,* including collecting site information, developing the site plan, and preparing the pollution prevention plan site map

2. *Assessment,* including measuring the site area, determining the drainage areas, and calculating the runoff coefficient

3. *Control selection and plan design,* including selecting erosion and sediment controls, selecting other controls, selecting storm water management controls, indicating the location of controls on the site maps, preparing an inspection and maintenance plan, coordinating controls with construction activity, preparing a sequence of major activities, and incorporating state or local requirements

After the SWPPP is developed, three additional steps are needed to implement the plan:

4. *Certification and notification,* including certifying the plan, submitting the Notice of Intent, and determining the plan location and public access

5. *Construction and implementation,* including implementing the controls, inspecting and maintaining the controls, updating and changing the plan, and reporting releases of reportable quantities

6. *Final stabilization and termination,* including final site stabilization and the NOT

The following sections describe the processes involved in each of the steps listed above.

## Step 1: Site Evaluation and Design Development

The first phase in preparing an SWPPP for a construction project is to define the characteristics of the site and of the type of construction which will be done. This phase is broken down into three tasks: collect site information, develop the site plan, and prepare the site map.

### Collect site information

Information must be collected on the site which will be developed. The following items are suggested:

**Existing-conditions site map.** Obtain a map of the existing conditions at the site. The map should be to scale and preferably topographic. The map should indicate the existing land use for the site (i.e., wooded area, open grassed area, pavement, building, etc.) as well as the location of surface waters which are located on or next to the site (including wetlands, streams, rivers, lakes, and ponds).

The best way to obtain a site map is to have the site surveyed by a professional surveyor (either land-based or aerial). If it is not practical to survey the site, then topographic maps may be available from state or local government agencies. A final alternative is to use the U.S. Geological Survey (USGS) topographic maps. USGS maps are least desirable for use as site maps for a pollution prevention plan because they are available only in a very large scale (1:24,000) and the features of an average-size construction site would be very difficult to distinguish.

The scale of the map should be small enough to easily distinguish important features such as drainage swales and control measures.

**Soils information.** Determine the type of soils present on the site. This information should be based on information from a specific site, not regional characteristics. The USDA Soil Conservation Service (SCS) soils map of the area may indicate the type of soil on the site and its potential erodibility.

Even more accurate information may be obtained by performing soil borings at the site; this method is more expensive and is usually only required for some storm water practices such as infiltration. Soil borings may already be required for the design of foundations or other structures.

**Runoff water quality.** Collect any information on the quality of the runoff from the site which may be available. In many cases, there will be little water quality data from runoff collected specifically from a site. However, if a construction site is located on or next to an industrial facility, or if it drains to a municipal separate storm sewer in a city or county with a population greater than 100,000, then water quality data may have been collected which indicate the quality of runoff from the site.

Contact people either at the industrial facility or at the municipal storm sewer authority who will receive the storm water from the proposed construction site and ask if they have performed any analysis on storm water from the site. Runoff water quality information may also be available from the USGS, the USDA Soil Conservation Service, and state or local watershed protection agencies.

**Name of receiving water.**    Identify the name of the body of water(s) which will receive runoff from the construction site. If the receiving water is a tributary, include the name of the ultimate body of water, if possible. Receiving waters could include rivers, lakes, streams, creeks, runs, estuaries, wetlands, bays, and ocean. If the site drains into a *municipal separate storm sewer system* (MS4), identify the system and indicate the receiving water to which the system discharges. This information is usually available from county, state, or USGS maps.

**Rainfall data.**    It is useful to determine the amount of rainfall to anticipate in the design of storm water management measures. These rainfall amounts are often referred to as *design storms*. Design storms are typically described in terms of both the average time that passes before that amount of rain falls again and the duration of the rain (e.g., the 10-year, 24-hour storm). The National Weather Service (NWS) publishes this information [National Weather Service, 1961, 1964, 1977]. Contact state or local storm water program agencies for additional information on the design storm criteria in the project area.

**Develop the site plan**

*Develop a preliminary site plan for the facility which is to be constructed.* The site plan will be developed primarily based upon the goals and objectives of the proposed facility. However, there are several pollution prevention principles which should be considered when the site plan is developed for the project:

- Disturb the smallest vegetated area possible.
- Keep the amount of cut and fill to a minimum.
- Limit impacts within sensitive areas such as steep and/or unstable slopes, surface waters, including wetlands, areas with erodible soils, and existing drainage channels.

In addition to reducing pollution in storm water runoff from the site, incorporating these objectives into the site plan for the project can reduce construction costs for grading and landscaping, reduce the amount of sediment and storm water management controls, and improve the aesthetics of the completed project.

*Once the preliminary design is developed, prepare a narrative description of the nature of the construction activity to include in the SWPPP.* The narrative should provide a brief description of the project including the purpose of the project (the final result), the major soil-disturbing activities that will be necessary to complete the project, and the approximate time it will take to complete the project.

Describe the purpose of construction (goal or project result) as one of the following: residential development, commercial, industrial, institutional, office development, highway projects, roads, streets, or parking lots, recreational areas, or underground utility. The description of the construction activity does not need to address indoor construction activities that have no effect on the quality of storm water.

Describe soil-disturbing activities as one or more of the following: clearing and grubbing, excavation and stockpiling, rough grading, final or finish grading, preparation for seeding or planting, excavation of trenches, and demolition.

### Prepare site map

*When the site plan is complete for the construction project, the information should be transferred to the pollution prevention plan site map.* (*Note:* The construction site plan and the SWPPP site map can be the same.) At this phase in the SWPPP development, three things can be indicated on the site map: the approximate slopes after grading, the drainage pattern, and the areas of disturbance. (Note that surface waters should already be indicated on the map.)

**Approximate slopes after grading.** If possible, indicate the revised grades on the same topographic map as the existing grades. Use two separate symbols for existing contours and proposed contour (i.e., dashed and solid lines). Topographic maps indicating existing and proposed contours for a site make it easy to determine the areas which must be disturbed for regrading.

If a topographic map of the site cannot be prepared, then examine the proposed plan for the site and indicate on the site map the approximate location, direction, and steepness of slopes. The location and direction of the slope may be indicated by arrows (pointing from high to low) and numbers indicating the degree of slope. Slope is usually expressed as a ratio of the length it takes to decrease 1 foot in height; for example, 3:1 indicates that the slope takes 3 feet in length to drop 1 foot in height.

**Areas of soil disturbance.** After the proposed grading is indicated on the site map, indicate the entire area which will be disturbed by the construction activity.

*Draw a limit-of-disturbance line on the site plan.* Draw the limit of disturbance so that any soil-disturbing activity such as clearing, stripping, excavation, backfilling, stockpiling (topsoil or other fill material), and paving will be inside the limit. The limit of disturbance should also include roads for construction vehicles unless those roads are paved (or stabilized) and have measures to reduce tracking of sediments.

When you draw the line, try to leave room for the control structures which may be required (this may be difficult, but the limit of disturbance can be redrawn after the control structures are designed). The limit of disturbance should be a closed boundary line around the entire disturbed area. There can be "islands" of undisturbed area inside the limit of disturbance, e.g., a tree or group of trees which are to be preserved. These islands should be circled with a limit of disturbance.

**Drainage patterns.**    In addition to the slopes anticipated after grading and areas of soil disturbance, *the SWPPP site map should indicate the drainage patterns of the site after the major grading activities.*

If possible, use a topographic map of the site which indicates drainage basin boundaries and drainage channels or pipes. A *drainage basin* is an area of the site in which water, sediments, and dissolved materials drain to a common outlet (such as a swale or storm drain pipe) from the site. There can be one or more drainage basins on a site.

*Drainage boundaries* are closed lines which start and end at the common outlet. Drainage boundaries typically follow the high points on a site including hilltops, ridges, and roads. Drainage areas do not overlap. To determine the drainage basin boundaries, determine where rain falling on each portion flows off the site. Areas that drain to different points are in different drainage areas. Drainage boundaries can be changed by grading and structural controls.

*The site map should indicate the drainage boundaries after the major grading has been done or structural controls have been installed.* It may be necessary to change the drainage boundaries after structural controls are selected.

If a topographic site map cannot be provided, use arrows to indicate the direction in which water will flow. Show the areas where there will be overland flow and the location of swales or channels. If there is a new or proposed underground storm drain system on the site, then this should be indicated on the SWPPP site map as well. The pipe diameter and slope should be included on the site map.

The SWPPP site map is not complete until it includes the locations of the major control structures and the areas where stabilization is expected to occur, as described later in this chapter.

## Step 2: Assessment

After the characteristics of the site and the construction have been defined, the next step in developing an SWPPP is to measure the size of the land disturbance and estimate the impact that the project will have on storm water runoff from the site, from the information developed in step 1. There are three tasks which should be done to assess the project:

1. Measure the site area.

2. Measure the drainage areas.

3. Calculate the runoff coefficient.

### Measure the site area

Typically, NPDES storm water permits may require that the SWPPP include estimates of the total site area and the area which will be disturbed. The area of the site can usually be found on the deed of sale for the property, the record plat, site survey, or site plan. The amount of area to be disturbed is sometimes noted on a site plan or grading plan. If the information is not available from one of these sources, the areas may be measured from the SWPPP site map which clearly shows the site boundary and limits of disturbance.

*The total area of the site should be measured first and should include the area inside the project's property boundaries, easements, and/or rights-of-way.* The total area includes both the disturbed and undisturbed areas.

The area which will be disturbed by the construction project should be measured next. This is the area enclosed by the limit of disturbance drawn on the site map, minus the area of any undisturbed islands within the limit of disturbance. The disturbed area should always be less than or equal to the total site area.

The most accurate method to measure area from the site map employs a planimeter or digitizer. A *planimeter* is a device which can measure the area on a drawing by tracing its outline. Planimeters are available from engineering and surveyor supply stores. A *digitizer* is an electronic device which can be used to trace the outline of a shape on a drawing and transfer the coordinates of the shape to a computer where a program (such as a computer-assisted design program) can compute the enclosed area.

For those who lack access to a planimeter or digitizer, the grid method can be used to estimate the size of an area. The grid method requires only transparent graph or grid paper. Do as follows:

1. *Outline site:*  Place graph or grid paper over the scale drawing, and trace the outline of the entire property.

2. *Determine the grid squares:*  Count the total number of complete squares within the site area, and count every two partial squares along the edges of the site as one square.

3. *Determine the square inches:*  Divide the total number of squares by the number of squares in $1 \text{ in}^2$ of graph or grid paper. This results in an estimate of the number of square inches contained in the outline of the site.

4. *Convert to acres:*  Multiply the result of step 3 by the number of square feet in a 1-in square based on the scale of the drawing. This gives an estimate of the number of square feet on the site. Then divide the number of square feet on the site by $43,560 \text{ ft}^2/\text{acre}$ to find the number of acres. The result is an estimate of the site area in acres.

Repeat this method, using the outline of the disturbed area, to find the estimated acreage of soil-disturbing activities. The area should be expressed to the nearest 0.1 acre, for example, 5.5 acres total site area and 3.5 acres disturbed area.

### Determine the drainage areas

*The size of each drainage basin for each point where concentrated flow will leave the site should also be measured.* Although this information is not required to be included in the pollution prevention plan, it is necessary in order to select and design the sediment control and storm water management measures for the project.

For design of the sediment control measures, the area of the portion of each drainage basin which will be disturbed should also be measured. The disturbed areas of the drainage basins should be measured by the methods suggested above to estimate the area enclosed by the limit of disturbance and/or the drainage boundary (whichever boundary gives the smaller area).

For the design of the storm water management controls and for the calculation of the runoff coefficient, measure the total area of each drainage basin and the areas of each land use which will occur in the basin after the construction is completed. Be sure to include off-site water draining onto the project site when you determine the total size of the drainage basin. See Table 10.1 for a listing of different types of land uses. The area of each land use in the drainage basins should be measured by the methods suggested above to estimate the area

TABLE 10.1   Typical C Values

| Description of area | Runoff coefficients |
|---|---|
| Business: Downtown areas | 0.70–0.95 |
| Business: Neighborhood areas | 0.50–0.70 |
| Residential: Single-family areas | 0.30–0.50 |
| Residential: Multifamily, detached | 0.40–0.60 |
| Residential: Multifamily, attached | 0.60–0.75 |
| Residential (suburban) | 0.25–0.40 |
| Apartment dwelling areas | 0.50–0.70 |
| Industrial: Light areas | 0.50–0.80 |
| Industrial: Heavy areas | 0.60–0.90 |
| Parks, cemeteries | 0.10–0.25 |
| Playgrounds | 0.20–0.35 |
| Railroad yard areas | 0.20–0.40 |
| Unimproved areas | 0.10–0.30 |
| Streets: Asphalt | 0.70–0.95 |
| Streets: Concrete | 0.80–0.95 |
| Streets: Brick | 0.70–0.85 |
| Drives and walks | 0.75–0.85 |
| Roofs | 0.75–0.95 |
| Lawns: Coarse textured soil (> 85% sand) | |
|    Slope: flat (2%) | 0.05–0.10 |
|    Slope: average (2–7%) | 0.10–0.15 |
|    Slope: steep (7%) | 0.15–0.20 |
| Lawns: Fine textured soil (> 40% clay) | |
|    Slope: flat (2%) | 0.13–0.17 |
|    Slope: average (2–7%) | 0.18–0.22 |
|    Slope: steep (7%) | 0.25–0.35 |

SOURCE: American Society of Civil Engineers, 1960.

enclosed by the land-use boundary and/or the drainage boundary (whichever boundary gives the smaller area). Topographic maps are helpful tools to use in determining drainage boundaries.

### Calculate the runoff coefficient

The next step in the assessment phase is to develop an estimate of the development's impact on runoff after construction is completed. This can be done by estimating a runoff coefficient for postconstruction conditions. The *runoff coefficient* or *C value,* is the partial amount of the total rainfall which will become runoff. The runoff coefficient is used in the rational method:

$$Q = CIA$$

where $Q$ = rate of runoff from an area, ft$^3$/s
  $I$ = rainfall intensity, in/h
  $A$ = area of drainage basin, acres

Many methods can be used to estimate the amount of runoff from a site. The EPA does not require the use of the rational method to design storm water conveyances or management measures. State or local design guidelines may describe appropriate methods to use for estimating design flow rates from each development.

The less rainfall that infiltrates into the ground, evaporates, or is otherwise absorbed on site, the higher the $C$ value. For example, the $C$ value of a lawn area is 0.2, which means that only 20 percent of the rainfall landing on that area will run off—the rest will be absorbed or will evaporate. A paved parking area has a $C$ value of 0.9, which means that 90 percent of the rainfall landing on that area will become runoff.

*The C value calculated for the SWPPP is the one that represents the final condition of the site after construction is completed.* A runoff coefficient should be calculated for each drainage basin on the site.

The runoff coefficient or $C$ value for a variety of land uses may be found in Table 10.1. These $C$ values provide an estimate of anticipated runoff for particular land uses.

When a drainage area contains more than one type of surface material with more than one runoff coefficient, a *weighted* $C$ must be calculated. This weighted $C$ will take into account the amount of runoff from all the various parts of the site. This formula is used to determine the weighted $C$:

$$C = \frac{A_1 C_1 + A_2 C_2 + \cdots + A_x C_x}{\sum_{i=1}^{x} A_i}$$

where $A$ = area in acres and $C$ = runoff coefficient.

Therefore, if a drainage area has 15 acres with 5 paved acres ($C$ = 0.9), 5 grassed acres ($C$ = 0.2), and 5 acres in natural vegetation ($C$ = 0.1), a weighted $C$ is calculated as follows:

$$C = \frac{5 \times 0.9 + 5 \times 0.2 + 5 \times 0.1}{5 + 5 + 5} = \frac{4.5 + 1.0 + 0.5}{15} = \frac{6.0}{15} = 0.4$$

## Step 3: Control Selection and Plan Design

After you collect the necessary measurements and other information, the next step is to design a plan to prevent and control pollution of storm water runoff from the construction site. The SWPPP should address the following types of controls:

- Stabilization practices for erosion and sediment control
- Structural measures for erosion and sediment control
- Storm water management controls
- Other pollution prevention measures

### Selection of soil erosion and sediment control practices

Erosion and sediment controls are implemented during the construction period to prevent and/or control the loss of soil from the construction site into the receiving waters. The soil erosion and sediment control portion of the SWPPP should describe temporary or permanent soil erosion and sediment control practices directed toward the following objectives:

- *Stabilize the soil:*  Minimize the amount of disturbed soil, by using stabilization practices such as permanent seeding, sod stabilization, geotextile stabilization, reinforced soil-retaining systems, or gabions. These measures are described in detail in Chap. 11.

- *Dissipate the flow velocity:*  Slow down the runoff flowing across the site, by using measures such as check dams and surface roughening. These measures are described in detail in Chap. 12.

- *Manage storm water:*  Prevent runoff from off-site areas from flowing across disturbed areas, by using measures such as earth dikes, drainage swales, and pipe slope drains. These measures are described in detail in Chap. 12.

- *Capture sediment:*  Remove sediment from on-site runoff before it leaves the site, by using measures such as silt fences, straw bale barriers, sediment traps, storm drain-inlet protection, and brush barriers. These measures are also described in detail in Chap. 12.

How these objectives are met depends primarily on the nature of the construction activity and the characteristics of the site, as determined during the site evaluation and design development and site assessment steps, described earlier in this chapter. *The site operator has substantial control over the control measures selected and implemented at a particular location.*

### Select permanent storm water management controls

The SWPPP should also address storm water management controls. *These are permanent facilities which are constructed to prevent or control pollution of storm water after the construction is completed.* They include the following:

- Storm water detention structures, including wet ponds (see Fig. 10.1)
- Storm water retention structures
- Open vegetated swales
- Natural depressions
- Infiltration measures
- Velocity dissipation measures, such as outlet protection

These may be the same as the structural erosion and sediment control measures. Very little specific guidance is available from the EPA as to what will meet the requirements for storm water management controls. Currently, the interpretation of this requirement is largely left to the facility operator. Chapter 12 provides further information.

As with erosion and sediment controls, the selection of the most appropriate permanent storm water management measures is dependent upon a number of factors, but is most dependent on site conditions. The information collected in the site evaluation, design, and assessment steps is used to select permanent storm water management controls.

**Figure 10.1**  Excavated storm water detention structure.

### Select other controls

In addition to erosion and sediment controls, the pollution prevention plan should address the other potential pollutant sources which may exist on a construction site. They include proper waste disposal, control of off-site vehicle tracking, compliance with applicable state or local waste disposal, sanitary sewer or septic system regulations, and control of allowable non-storm-water discharges. These measures are described in detail in Chap. 13.

The following basic information should be a part of the SWPPP:

- Provide a narrative description of each practice.

- Show the location of each control measure on the site map (if possible).

- Describe the maintenance, inspection, repair, and record-keeping procedures that will ensure that control measures remain effective and in working order during the construction activity.

- Describe the employee training necessary for the operation and maintenance of the practice or control.

### Indicate the location of controls on the site map

*Once the pollution prevention controls have been selected, they should be indicated in the site map.* Provide the location of each measure used for erosion and sediment control, storm water management, and other controls. It may not be feasible to indicate some controls on the site map; e.g., it would be very difficult to indicate appropriate waste control on the site map.

Once the controls have been indicated in the site map, it may be necessary to revise the limit of disturbance and/or the drainage boundaries. The limit of disturbance should be indicated outside any perimeter control, because the construction of most controls does require some soil disturbance. Drainage boundaries are often impacted by diversion structures, which typically divert runoff from one drainage basin to another. The drainage patterns on the site map should reflect the drainage patterns on the site while the controls are in place.

Once the location of the controls is indicated, the site map is ready to be included in the pollution prevention plan. The following items are typically *required* to be indicated on the SWPPP site map:

1. Drainage patterns
2. Approximate slopes after grading

3. Area of soil disturbance

4. Location of major structural and nonstructural controls

5. Areas where stabilization practices are expected to occur

6. Location of surface waters

### Prepare the inspection and maintenance plan

There must be a plan for the inspection and maintenance of vegetation, erosion and sediment control measures, and other protective measures. These controls must be in good operating condition until the area they protect has been completely stabilized or the construction project is completed.

*An inspection and maintenance checklist should be prepared that addresses each of the control measures proposed for the facility.* A blank checklist for the facility should be included in the SWPPP prior to the onset of construction. The inspector should complete a copy of the blank checklist during each inspection. The inspection and maintenance checklist should be prepared based upon the requirements for each individual measure. For example, sediment must be removed from a silt trap when it has been filled to one-third of its depth. Consult state or local manuals for maintenance requirements for control measures.

A good maintenance and inspection plan should include the following:

1. *Areas to be inspected and maintained:*  These should include all the disturbed areas and material storage areas of the site.

2. *Measures to be inspected and maintained:*  These should include all the erosion and sediment controls identified in the SWPPP.

3. *Inspection schedule:*  Provide an inspection schedule for each area and measure, as described in the following section.

4. *Maintenance procedures:*  List the typical maintenance procedures for each measure. Chapters 11 and 12 provide maintenance guidelines for various pollution prevention measures. Maintenance requirements should be considered as measures are selected. Some measures require a good deal more maintenance than others, and this may influence the selection of measures.

5. *Responsible parties:*  Describe the procedure to follow if additional repair is required, e.g., who will be responsible or whom to call.

6. *Inspection and maintenance forms:*  Provide forms and instructions for record-keeping practices.

7. *Personnel:*   List the names of personnel assigned to each task.

8. *Training:*   Indicate what training employees will need to be able to do the job.


**Inspection requirements.**   The EPA general permit requires that inspections of pollution prevention measures be performed at a minimum once every 7 calendar days plus additional inspections within 24 h after any storm event of greater that 0.5 in of rain per 24-h period.

*Inspection* is the process by which you can evaluate whether the pollution prevention measures which have already been installed or applied are still effective. In most cases, inspection of pollution prevention measures requires that an inspector look at all the disturbed areas and sediment controls on the site and make some measurements of sediment accumulation (depending upon the measures.) (See Fig. 10.2.) The inspector should look at each measure to determine if it is still effective. The inspector should consult the description included in the SWPPP and determine if the measures still meet the minimum requirements.

There are primarily three things an inspector should look for when inspecting a pollution prevention measure:

1. Whether the measure was installed or performed correctly

**Figure 10.2**  Illustration of sediment accumulation requiring maintenance.

2. Whether there has been damage to the measure since it was installed or performed

3. What should be done to correct any problems with the measure

**Inspection reports.**  The inspector should prepare an inspection report documenting the findings of the inspection. The inspector should also request any required maintenance or repair. If the SWPPP should be changed to allow for unexpected conditions, then the inspector should make the changes or instruct the appropriate person to make the changes.

**Qualifications of inspectors.**  There are no formal requirements for inspectors. Any person authorized and considered qualified by the operator may complete inspections and sign the inspection reports. The EPA recognizes that experience is the best way to develop an understanding of pollution prevention measures, although formal training in sediment and erosion control can be very helpful.

The inspector should have detailed knowledge about the site's SWPPP, particularly the following portions:

- The location and type of control measures
- The construction requirements for the control measures
- Maintenance procedures for each of the control measures
- Spill prevention and cleanup measures
- Inspection and maintenance record-keeping requirements

**Maintenance.**  Maintenance of pollution prevention measures involves the upkeep and repair of the measures which have been installed to reduce the pollution of storm water. Maintenance is important because the control measures may be of little or no use if they have not been properly maintained. Good maintenance helps to ensure that these measures are in proper working order when they are really needed under storm or spill conditions.

Maintenance should be performed either at an interval specified in the pollution prevention plan or when an inspection finds that maintenance is necessary for the measure to be effective. For example, if an inspector finds that sediment has accumulated in a sediment trap to one-half of its storage depth, she or he should request that the accumulated sediment be removed from the trap. Appropriate maintenance practices for erosion and sediment controls are discussed in Chaps. 11 and 12.

Maintenance activities for erosion and sediment controls are fairly elementary. For example, sedimentation structures require removal (and proper disposal) of accumulated sediments to ensure effective trapping capacity. This technique is also appropriate for temporary sediment traps, sediment basins, and silt fences.

**Record-keeping requirements.** Record keeping is an essential part of compliance with an NPDES storm water discharge permit. The record-keeping requirements begin with the preparation of the SWPPP and NOI (or permit application) and continue through the NOT and afterward. The following records should be maintained on site throughout the effective life of the permit:

1. *SWPPP:* The SWPPP should be filed on site for review by regulatory authorities or the public. For convenience, the SWPPP should be organized in a binder with major sections corresponding to the plan requirements outlined in this chapter.

2. *NOI:* A copy of the Notice(s) of Intent should be filed with the SWPPP. Copies of any additional NOIs prepared as a result of additional operators becoming involved in the project should also be filed as they are generated.

3. *Certifications:* The certifications signed by an authorized representative of the general contractor and subcontractors should be included in, or filed with, the SWPPP. Be sure to obtain certifications from all contractors who should be aware of the terms and requirements of the SWPPP.

4. *Inspection reports:* All inspection reports should be filed with the SWPPP as they are generated. Blank inspection and maintenance forms should be prepared prior to the start of the construction activity. The inspection forms should be specific to the construction project and the SWPPP. The forms should list each of the measures to be inspected on the site. The form should include blanks for the inspector to fill in: his or her name, the date of inspection, the condition of the measure or area inspected, maintenance or repair performed, and any changes which should be made to the SWPPP to control or eliminate unforeseen pollution of storm water.

5. *Maintenance reports:* Reports should be made of regular and special maintenance activities performed on the site, including waste disposal activities.

6. *Construction activity reports:* In addition to the inspection and maintenance reports, the operator should keep records of the construction activity on the site. In particular, the operator should

keep a record of the dates when major grading activities occur in a particular area, when construction activities cease in an area (temporarily or permanently), and when an area is stabilized. These records can be used to make sure that areas where there is no construction activity will be stabilized within the required time frame.

7. *Other materials:*   Other materials relevant to the permit, including spill reports, correspondence with regulatory authorities, and photographs should be kept.

8. *NOT:*   A copy of the Notice of Termination for the NPDES permit should be kept. After the NOT is filed, the formal record-keeping requirements of the permit end. However, the records must be maintained for a minimum of 3 years after the termination of permit coverage.

### Incorporate state or local requirements

Many state and local authorities also have sediment and erosion control or storm water management regulations in place. *The EPA requires that all state and local requirements be met.* The NPDES storm water discharge is not intended to supersede state or local requirements. Instead, the NPDES storm water permit ensures that a minimum level of pollution prevention is required. Where a construction site has taken measures to comply with state and local requirements and with these SWPPP conditions, the applicable measures may be incorporated into the plan.

Consult state or local authorities to determine what requirements, if any, exist for sediment and erosion control on construction projects. Many state and local authorities provide their own design manuals or guidance to assist in preparing a plan which meets their requirements. These state and local requirements should be at least considered in the preparation of the pollution prevention plan. In many cases, the NPDES permit may require that state and local sediment and erosion control or storm water management requirements be incorporated by reference into the plan.

If the state or local authority requires review and approval of the sediment and erosion control plan, then a reviewed and approved copy of that plan should be included in the pollution prevention plan.

Although most of the provisions of the NPDES storm water permits for construction activities are consistent with most state and local requirements, there may be differences in the specific requirements for control measures. *When EPA, state, and local requirements differ, use the most stringent requirement.*

**Prepare a description of controls**

After planning the construction activities and selecting the controls, you should make a list of each type of control planned for the site. Include in this list a description of each control, its purpose, and why it is appropriate in this location. The description should include specific information about the measure such as size, materials, and methods of construction. Read each permit carefully to ensure that the plan includes all the required controls.

**Coordinate controls with construction activity**

Prepare a sequence of major activities that lists all the tasks required for construction of control measures, earth-disturbing construction activities, and maintenance activities for control measures. These should be listed in the order in which they will occur. Specific timing requirements for installation and maintenance of control measures are dependent upon the measures and/or the construction activities. There are, however, several general principles to bear in mind when you develop the sequence of major activities.

- Install downslope and side-slope perimeter controls before the land-disturbing activity occurs.

- Do not disturb an area until it is necessary for construction to proceed.

- Cover or stabilize as soon as possible.

- Time activities to limit the impact from seasonal climate changes or weather events.

- Delay construction of infiltration measures to the end of the construction project when upstream drainage areas have been stabilized.

- Do not remove temporary perimeter controls until all upstream areas have been stabilized.

**Step 4: Certification and Notification**

Once the site description and controls portion of the SWPPP have been prepared, the pollution prevention plan can be certified. The Notice of Intent for coverage under the general permit may be submitted. Chapter 9 provides additional details on the Notice of Intent and certification requirements.

Review the permit carefully to be sure that all required items are included in the SWPPP prior to certifying the plan or submitting a Notice of Intent.

### Regulatory review of SWPPP

Some NPDES storm water permits for construction sites may require that SWPPPs be submitted to the director of the regulatory agency for review. However, the general permit requires only that plans be maintained on site. Permitting authorities may prefer not to require plans to be submitted to reduce the administrative burden of reviewing a large number of pollution prevention plans.

However, when the EPA requests the plan, permittees should submit it in a timely manner. In addition, when requested, permittees should submit their plan to state or local sediment and erosion or storm water management agencies, or to a municipal operator where the site discharges through an NPDES storm water permitted municipal separate storm sewer system. Examine each permit carefully to determine which requirements apply to each facility regarding the submitting of plans.

Regardless of whether the SWPPP should be submitted to the permitting authority or other public agency, *site operators are expected to keep the plan and supporting materials at the site of the construction operations at all times throughout the project.* In maintaining plans on site, keep all records and supporting documents together in an orderly fashion. The EPA general permit requires that all records be maintained for at least 3 years after the project is completed.

### Public access to the SWPPP

*The SWPPP and related documents are considered to be "reports" according to section 308(b) of the Clean Water Act and, therefore, are available to the public.* This is true despite the fact that plans and associated records are not necessarily required to be submitted to the EPA or any other regulatory agency.

Permittees may claim certain portions of their SWPPP as confidential according to the regulations at 40 CFR part 2. Basically, these regulations state that records which contain trade secret information may be claimed as confidential. These confidential portions may be excluded from public access.

## Step 5: Construction and Implementation

The first step in carrying out the SWPPP is to *construct or apply the controls selected for the plan.* The controls should be constructed or applied in accordance with state or local standard specifications. If there are no state or local specifications for control measures, then the controls should be constructed in accordance with good engineering practices. The controls should be constructed and the stabilization measures applied in the order indicated in the sequence of major activities.

To ensure that controls are adequately implemented, it is important that the work crews who install the measures are experienced and/or adequately trained. Improperly installed controls can have little or no effect and may actually increase the pollution of storm water.

It is also important that all other workers on the construction site be made aware of the controls so that they do not inadvertently disturb or remove them.

Inspection and maintenance of the control measures are as important to pollution prevention as proper planning and design. *Inspection should be performed at the frequency specified in the SWPPP and/or the permit.* The inspector should note any damage or deficiencies in the control measures in an inspection report. The operator should correct damage or deficiencies as soon as practicable after the inspection, and any changes that may be required to correct deficiencies in the SWPPP should be made as soon as practicable after the inspection.

In addition to the inspection and maintenance reports, the operator should keep records of the construction activity on the site, to demonstrate compliance with the plan.

### Changing the plan

Storm water pollution prevention plans are developed based on site-specific features and functions. When there are changes in design, construction, operation, or maintenance and those changes will have a significant effect on the potential for discharging pollutants in storm water at a site, the SWPPP should be modified by the permittee to reflect the changes and new conditions. For example, a change in the construction schedule or design specifications should be incorporated in the SWPPP. Also the plan should be modified when it proves ineffective in controlling pollutants. This determination could be based on the results of regular visual inspections.

If, at any time during the effective period of the permit, the permitting authority finds that the plan does not meet one or more of the minimum standards established by the pollution prevention plan requirements, the permitting authority will notify the permittees of required changes necessary to bring the plan up to standard.

## Step 6: Final Stabilization and Termination

The NPDES permit may remain in effect as long as there is a storm water discharge associated with construction activity, as defined in Chap. 9. The need for a permit may end because the storm water discharge is eliminated (e.g., by the construction of a large retention basin), because a new operator has taken over the construction project, or because the construction is finished and final stabilization is completed. Final stabilization requirements may vary from permit to permit. However, typically all temporary measures and controls must be removed, all permanent storm water management measures must be in place and functional, and all areas stabilized by vegetation must exhibit at least a 70 percent viability of the plant cover.

The EPA general permit allows the permit coverage to be terminated by submitting a Notice of Termination. The NOT is typically the final task required to comply with the requirements of an NPDES storm water permit for a construction activity. Chapter 9 provides some additional details on the NOT.

### References

American Society of Civil Engineers: *Design and Construction of Sanitary and Storm Sewers,* Manual of Practice, no. 37, New York, 1967.

Environmental Protection Agency: *Storm Water Management for Construction Activities: Developing Pollution Prevention Plans and Best Management Practices,* EPA Report 832/R-92/005, September 1992.

National Weather Service: *Rainfall Frequency Atlas of the United States,* Technical Paper 40, U.S. Department of Commerce, Washington, 1961.

———: *Two- to Ten-Day Precipitation for Return Periods of 2 to 100 Years in the Contiguous United States,* Technical Paper 49, U.S. Department of Commerce, Washington, 1964.

———: *Five- to 60-Minute Precipitation Frequency for the Eastern and Central United States,* Technical Memorandum NWS HYDRO-35, National Oceanographic and Atmospheric Administration, U.S. Department of Commerce, Silver Spring, Maryland, 1977.

# 11

# Stabilization Practices for Construction Erosion Control

This is the third of five chapters which deal with the specific requirements for storm water discharges from construction facilities. This chapter provides details on stabilization measures (such as vegetation) for erosion control. Most of the information in this chapter is taken directly from the EPA guidance manual on storm water discharge permit compliance [EPA, 1992].

## Erosion and Sediment Controls

Erosion controls, as described in this chapter, provide the first line of defense in preventing off-site sediment movement and are designed to prevent erosion by protecting soils. Sediment controls, as described in Chap. 12, are generally designed to remove sediment from runoff before the runoff is discharged from the site. Soil erosion and sediment control is not a new technology. The USDA Soil Conservation Service and a number of state and local agencies have been developing and promoting the use of erosion and sediment control devices for years. *The EPA general permit requires that stabilization practices be implemented within 14 days after activity in a portion of the site ceases. They are not required if construction resumes within 21 days. State permit requirements may vary.* Stabilization practices include measures to prevent soil loss from disturbed areas, including temporary or permanent seeding, mulching, geotextiles, sodding, vegetative buffer strips, protection of trees, preservation of mature vegetation, and other appropriate measures.

## General Stabilization Guidelines

Several general guidelines pertain to selecting stabilization practices for a construction project:

1. *Minimize the disturbed area.*   Minimizing the amount of disturbed soil on the construction site will decrease the amount of soil which erodes from the site and can decrease the amount of controls required to remove the sediment from the runoff. If possible, clear only those portions of the site necessary for construction. When a smaller area is disturbed for construction, there is less erosion of soil.

2. *Construct the project in stages.*   If the construction project will take place over a widespread area, consider staging or phasing the project so that only a small portion of the site will be disturbed at one time. Phased construction helps to lessen the risk of erosion by minimizing the amount of disturbed soil that is exposed at a given time. There are exceptions to this guideline. For example, if an efficient drainage system for the property is constructed as part of the first phase of construction, then succeeding phases may result in increased sediment downstream because the efficient drainage system will serve to deliver a high proportion of the sediment to the discharge point.

3. *Match existing land contours.*   A construction project site should be selected and laid out so that it fits into existing land contours, whenever possible. When a project significantly changes the grades in an area, there is a corresponding increase in the amount of disturbed soil, which in turn increases the amount of erosion.

4. *Use temporary stabilization.*   If there are disturbed portions of the site that will not be redisturbed for a long period, then these areas should be stabilized with temporary seeding or mulching. This will reduce the amount of erosion from these areas until they are disturbed again.

5. *Use final stabilization.*   By permanently stabilizing the disturbed areas as soon as possible after construction is completed in those areas, the amount of sediment which should be trapped before it leaves the site can be significantly reduced.

6. *In snow-covered areas, wait for snowmelt.*   If snow cover prevents seeding or planting vegetation, then wait until the snow melts before stabilizing the area.

7. *In dry areas, use other methods.*   If there is not enough rainfall on the disturbed area to allow vegetation to grow, then seed and irrigate the disturbed area (if allowed by the permit for the facility) or stabilize the disturbed areas by nonvegetative methods, as described later in this chapter.

The remainder of this chapter describes these common stabilization practices:

- *Vegetative stabilization practices:*  temporary seeding, sod stabilization, permanent seeding and planting, buffer zones, and preservation of natural vegetation

- *Nonvegetative stabilization practices:*  mulching, geotextiles, chemical stabilization, stream bank stabilization, soil-retaining measures, and dust control

## Vegetative Stabilization Practices

*Preserving existing vegetation or revegetating disturbed soil as soon as possible after construction is the most effective way to control erosion* and can provide a sixfold reduction in discharge suspended-sediment levels [Metropolitan Washington Council of Governments, 1990]. Vegetation reduces erosion potential through several different processes:

1. *Rainfall protection:*  shielding the soil surface from the direct erosive impact (kinetic energy) of raindrops.

2. *Flow protection:*  dispersing and decreasing the velocity of surface flow, which reduces erosion and allows sediment to drop out or deposit.

3. *Soil retention:*  physically holding the soil in place with plant roots.

4. *Infiltration:*  improving the soil's water storage porosity and capacity through the incorporation of roots and plant residues, so more water can infiltrate the ground.

5. *Transpiration:*  conducting moisture into plants, where it is eliminated by evaporation. This decreases the soil moisture content and increases the soil's moisture storage capacity.

Vegetative cover can be grass, trees, vines, or shrubs. Grasses are the most common type of cover used for revegetation because they grow quickly, providing erosion protection within days. Other soil stabilization practices such as mulch may be used during nongrowing seasons to prevent erosion. Newly planted shrubs and trees establish root systems more slowly, so keeping existing ones is a more effective practice.

*Vegetative and other site stabilization practices can be either temporary or permanent controls.* Temporary controls provide a cover for exposed or disturbed areas for short periods or until permanent erosion controls are put in place. Permanent vegetative practices are used when activities that disturb the soil are completed or when erosion is occurring on a site that is otherwise stabilized.

### Temporary seeding

*Temporary seeding* means growing a short-term vegetative cover (plants) on disturbed site areas that may be in danger of erosion. Temporary seeding provides for temporary stabilization by establishing vegetation of areas of the site which will be disturbed at some time during the construction operation and where work (other than the initial disturbance) is not conducted until some time later in the project. Soils at these areas may be exposed to precipitation for an extended period, even though work is not occurring on these areas.

For temporary seeding, fast-growing grasses are used whose root systems hold down the soil so that the soil is less apt to be carried off the site by storm water runoff or wind. Temporary seeding also reduces the problems associated with mud and dust from bare soil surfaces during construction. In most climates, temporary seeding is typically appropriate for areas exposed by grading or clearing for more than 7 to 14 days. Temporary seeding practices have been found to be up to 95 percent effective in reducing erosion [USDA Soil Conservation Service, 1985]

Probably the most common type of grass used for temporary seeding is rye grass. (See Fig. 11.1.) Sterile wheat is also used. A new grass which has received favorable reports is vetiver, which is native to India. Sterile varieties of vetiver are available [National Academy Press, 1992].

Temporary seeding should be performed on areas which have been disturbed by construction and which are likely to be redisturbed, but

**Figure 11.1**  Construction site seeded with rye grass.

not for at least 21 days. Typical areas might include denuded areas, soil stockpiles, dikes, dams, sides of sediment basins, and temporary road banks. Temporary seeding should be done as soon as practicable following the last land-disturbing activity in an area.

Temporary seeding may not be an effective practice in arid and semiarid regions where the climate prevents fast plant growth, particularly during the dry seasons. In those areas, mulching or chemical stabilization may be better for the short term, as discussed later in this chapter.

Proper seedbed preparation and the use of high-quality seed are needed to grow plants for effective erosion control. Soil that has been compacted by heavy traffic or machinery may need to be loosened. For successful growth, usually the soil must be tilled before the seed is applied. Placement of topsoil is not necessary for temporary seeding; however, it may improve the chances of establishing temporary vegetation in an area. Seedbed preparation may also require the application of fertilizer and/or lime to the soil to make conditions more suitable for plant growth. Proper fertilizer, seeding mixtures, and seeding rates vary depending on the location of the site, soil types, slopes, and season. Local suppliers, state and local regulatory agencies, and the USDA Soil Conservation Service will supply information on the best seed mixes and soil conditioning methods.

Seeded areas should be covered with mulch to provide protection from the weather. Seeding on slopes of 2:1 or more, in adverse soil conditions, during excessively hot or dry weather, or where heavy rain is expected should be followed by the spreading of mulch. Frequent inspections are needed to check that conditions for growth are good. If the plants do not grow quickly or thickly enough to prevent erosion, the area should be reseeded as soon as possible. Seeded areas should be kept adequately moist. If normal rainfall will not be sufficient, mulching, matting, and controlled watering should be done. If seeded areas are watered, watering rates should be watched so that excessive irrigation (which can cause erosion itself) does not occur.

Temporary-seeding costs average about $1 per square yard, not counting any costs for mulch. This makes it one of the least expensive stabilization measures.

### Sod stabilization

Sod stabilizes an area by immediately covering the surface with vegetation and providing areas where storm water can infiltrate the ground. When installed and maintained properly, sodding can be 99 percent effective in reducing erosion, making it the most effective vegetation practice available [USDA Soil Conservation Service, 1985]. The higher cost of sod stabilization relative to other vegetative controls typically limits its use to exposed soils where a quick vegetative cover is desired and on sites which can be maintained with ground equipment. The average cost of sod is about $4 per square yard. In addition, sod is sensitive to climate and may require intensive watering and fertilizing.

Sodding is appropriate for any graded or cleared area that might erode and where a permanent, long-lived plant cover is needed immediately. Sodding can be used in buffer zones, stream banks, dikes, swales, slopes, outlets, level spreaders, and filter strips. See Fig. 11.2.

Final grading should be complete before the sod is laid down. Topsoil may be needed in areas where the soil textures are inadequate. Lime and fertilizers should be added to the soil to promote good growth conditions. Sodding can be applied in alternating strips or other patterns, or alternate areas can be seeded to reduce expense. Sod should not be planted during very hot or wet weather.

One advantage of sod is that it can withstand some flow soon after installation, especially if it is installed with staggered joints. The sod blocks may also be pegged into the ground to withstand moderate flow velocities.

Sod should not be placed on slopes greater than 3:1 if they are to be mowed. If placed on steep slopes, sod should be laid with staggered joints and/or pegged. In areas such as steep slopes or next to running waterways, chicken wire, jute, or other netting can be placed over the sod for extra protection against lifting. Roll or compact the sod immediately after installation to ensure firm contact with the underlying topsoil.

**Figure 11.2**   Example of sod being placed behind street curb.

Inspect the sod frequently after it is first installed, especially after large storm events, until it is established as permanent cover. Remove and replace dead sod. Watering may be necessary after planting and during periods of intense heat and/or lack of rain (drought).

### Permanent seeding and planting

*Permanent seeding of grass and planting of trees and brush stabilize the soil by holding soil particles in place.* Vegetation reduces sediments and runoff to downstream areas by slowing the velocity of runoff and permitting greater infiltration of the runoff. Vegetation also filters sediments, helps the soil absorb water, improves wildlife habitats, and enhances the aesthetics of a site.

Permanent seeding and planting is appropriate for any graded or cleared area where long-lived plant cover is desired. Some areas where permanent seeding is especially important are filter strips, buffer areas, vegetated swales, steep slopes, and stream banks. This practice is effective in areas where soils are unstable because of their texture, structure, a high water table, high winds, or high slope.

For this practice to work, it is important to select appropriate vegetation, prepare a good seedbed, properly time the planting, and condition the soil. Planting local plants during their regular growing season will increase the chances for success and may lessen the need for watering. Check seeded areas frequently for proper watering and growth conditions.

For seeding in cold climates during fall or winter, cover the area with mulch to provide a protective barrier against cold weather. Seeding should also be mulched if the seeded area has a slope of 4:1 or more, if the soil is sandy or clayey, or if the weather is excessively hot or dry. Plant when conditions are most favorable for growth. When possible, use low-maintenance local plant species.

The average cost of permanent seeding can be estimated at about $1 per square yard, not including mulch costs. However, there is a wide variation according to the desired appearance of the finished project.

*Topsoil should be used on areas where the topsoil has been removed, where the soils are dense or impermeable, or where mulching and fertilizers alone cannot improve the soil quality.* Topsoil placement should be coordinated with the seeding and planting practices and should not be done when the ground is frozen or too wet. Topsoil layers should be at least 2 in deep (or similar to the existing topsoil depth).

To minimize erosion and sedimentation, remove as little existing topsoil as possible. All required structural sediment and erosion control measures should be in place before the topsoil is removed. If topsoil is brought in from another site, its texture must be compatible with the subsoil on site; e.g., sandy topsoil is not compatible with clay subsoil.

Stockpiling of topsoil on site requires good planning so that soils will not obstruct other operations. If soil is to be stockpiled, consider using temporary seeding, mulching, geotextiles, or silt fencing to prevent or control erosion. Inspect the stockpiles frequently for erosion. After topsoil has been spread, inspect it regularly and reseed or replace areas that have eroded.

### Buffer zones

*Buffer zones* are preserved or planted strips of vegetation at the top and bottom of a slope, outlining property boundaries, or adjacent to receiving waters such as streams or wetlands. Buffer zones can slow runoff flows at critical areas, decreasing erosion and allowing sediment deposition. Buffer zones are different from vegetated filter strips (discussed in Chap. 12) because buffer zone effectiveness is not measured by its ability to improve infiltration. The buffer zone can be an area of vegetation that is left undisturbed during construction, or it can be newly planted.

Buffer zones can be used at almost any site that can support vegetation. Buffer zones are particularly effective on floodplains, next to wetlands, along stream banks, and on steep, unstable slopes.

If buffer zones are preserved, existing vegetation, good planning, and site management are needed to protect against disturbances such as grade changes, excavation, damage from equipment, and other activities. Establishing new buffer strips requires the establishment of a good, dense turf, trees, and shrubs.

Careful maintenance is important to ensure healthy vegetation. The need for routine maintenance such as mowing, fertilizing, liming, irrigating, pruning, and weed and pest control will depend on the species of plants and tress involved, soil types, and climatic conditions. Maintaining planted areas may require debris removal and protection against unintended uses or traffic.

Many state and local storm water program or zoning agencies have regulations which define required or allowable buffer zones, especially near sensitive areas such as wetlands. Contact the appropriate state and local agencies for their requirements.

If buffer zones must be established by planting, the costs may be estimated at about $1 per square yard, plus any costs for mulch. If buffer zones consist of existing native vegetation, the costs vary according to the efforts required to preserve and maintain the vegetation.

### Preservation of natural vegetation

The preservation of natural vegetation (existing trees, vines, brushes, and grasses) provides natural buffer zones. Preserving stabilized areas minimizes erosion potential, protects water quality, and provides aesthetic benefits. Preservation of natural vegetation qualifies as a permanent storm water control measure, as described in Chap. 12.

Mature trees have extensive canopy and root systems which help to hold soil in place. Shade trees also keep soil from drying rapidly and becoming susceptible to erosion. Measures taken to protect trees can vary significantly, from simple measures such as installing tree fencing around the drip line and installing tree armoring to more complex measures such as building retaining walls and tree wells.

Areas where preserving vegetation can be particularly beneficial include floodplains, wetlands, stream banks, steep slopes, and other areas where erosion controls would be difficult to establish, install, or maintain.

Preservation of vegetation on a site should be planned before any site disturbance begins. Preservation requires good site management to minimize the impact of construction activities on existing vegetation. Clearly mark the trees to be preserved, and protect them from ground disturbances around the base of the tree.

Proper maintenance is important to ensure healthy vegetation that can control erosion, especially during construction. Different species, soil types, and climatic conditions will require different maintenance activities such as mowing, fertilizing, liming, irrigation, pruning, and weed and pest control.

The EPA originally considered the requirement that 15 percent of the original vegetation be left in place on all sites. However, eventually the EPA rejected this approach because of the need to allow flexibility. However, some state and local regulations require natural vegetation to be preserved in sensitive areas; consult the appropriate state and local agencies for more information on their regulations.

The cost to preserve existing vegetation can vary widely. To protect existing mature trees, costs may be estimated at $30 to $200 per tree, but can be much higher for isolated large trees.

## Nonvegetative Stabilization Practices

Nonvegetative covers such as mulches and stone aggregates protect soils from erosion. Like vegetative covers, these ground covers can shield the soil surface from the impact of failing rain, reduce flow velocity, and disperse flow. Each of these types of cover provides a rough surface that slows the runoff velocity and promotes infiltration and deposition of sediment. The condition as well as the type of ground cover influences the rate and volume of runoff.

Note that although impervious surfaces (such as parking lots) protect the covered area, they prevent infiltration and consequently increase the peak flow rate. This, along with the possible increase in flow velocities due to the hydraulic efficiency of flow over these surfaces, may increase the potential for erosion at the discharge.

### Mulching

*Mulching* is a temporary soil stabilization or erosion control practice in which materials such as grass, hay, wood chips, wood fibers, straw, or gravel are placed on the soil surface. In addition to stabilizing soils, mulching can reduce the speed of storm water runoff over an area. When used together with seeding or planting, mulching can aid in plant growth by holding the seeds, fertilizers, and topsoil in place; by helping to retain moisture; and by insulating against extreme temperatures.

Mulching is often used alone in areas where temporary seeding cannot be used because of the season or climate. Where temporary seeding and permanent seeding are not feasible, exposed soils can be stabilized by applying plant residues or other suitable materials to the soil surface. Although generally not as effective as seeding practices, mulching, by itself, can provide immediate and inexpensive erosion control. On steep slopes and critical areas such as waterways, mulch matting is used with netting or anchoring to hold it in place.

Mulching is also typically used as part of permanent and temporary seeding practices. Mulching in conjunction with seeding practices provides erosion protection prior to the onset of vegetation growth. In addition, mulching protects seeding practices, providing a higher likelihood of success. Seeded and planted areas should be mulched wherever slopes are steeper than 2:1, where runoff is flowing across the area, or when seedlings need protection from bad weather.

Mulch is more effective when it is secured by using a binder or netting or by tacking the mulch to the ground. Mulch binders should be applied according to the manufacturer's recommended rates and methods.

Final grading is not necessary before mulching. Mulched areas should be inspected often to find where mulched material has been loosened or removed. Such areas should be reseeded (if necessary) and the mulch cover replaced immediately.

Mulch costs may be estimated at about $1.25 per square yard.

### Geotextiles

*Geotextiles* are porous fabrics used for erosion control and other construction purposes. Geotextiles are manufactured by weaving or bonding fibers made from synthetic materials such as polypropylene, polyester, polyethylene, nylon, polyvinyl chloride, glass, and various mixtures of these. Geotextiles are typically used as mulch netting, matting, and separators.

Some geotextiles are also biodegradable materials such as mulch matting and netting. Mulch mattings are materials (jute or other wood fibers) that have been formed into sheets of mulch that are more stable than normal mulch. Netting is typically made from jute, other wood fiber, plastic, paper, or cotton and can be used to hold the mulching and matting to the ground. Netting can also be used alone to stabilize soils while the plants are growing. However, netting does not retain moisture or temperature well. Mulch binders (either asphalt or synthetic) are sometimes used instead of netting to hold loose mulches together.

Geotextiles alone can be used as matting. Matting is used to stabilize the flow on channels and swales, and on recently planted slopes to protect seedlings until they become established. Also, matting may be used on tidal or stream banks where moving water is likely to wash out new plantings.

Geotextiles are also used as separators. For example, a geotextile may be placed between riprap and soil to maintain the base of the riprap and prevent the soil from being eroded.

Many types of geotextiles are available for different purposes. State or local requirements, design procedures, and any other applicable requirements should be consulted. In the field, important concerns include regular inspections to determine if cracks, tears, or breaches are present in the fabric, and appropriate repairs should be made.

Effective netting and matting requires firm, continuous contact between the materials and the soil. If there is no contact, the material will not hold the soil and erosion will occur underneath the material.

### Chemical stabilization

*Chemical stabilization* is a temporary erosion control practice in which materials made of vinyl, asphalt, or rubber are sprayed onto the surface of the soil to hold the soil in place and to protect against erosion from storm water runoff and wind. These materials are often referred to as chemical mulch, soil binder, or soil palliative.

Asphalt emulsions, latex emulsions, or resin in water can be sprayed onto mineral soil to serve as soil adhesives. Calcium chloride may be applied by mechanical spreader as loose, dry granules, or flakes.

Chemical stabilization can be used as an alternative in areas where temporary seeding practices cannot be used because of the season or climate. It can provide immediate, effective, and inexpensive erosion control anywhere erosion is occurring on a site.

The application rates and procedures recommended by the manufacturer of a chemical stabilization product should be followed as closely as possible to prevent the products from forming ponds and from creating large areas where moisture cannot get through.

### Stream bank stabilization

Many erosion problems, and a high proportion of sediment volume, result from various types of stream bank erosion and bank failures, rather than erosion from the land surface itself. Stream bank stabilization is used to prevent stream bank erosion from high velocities and quantities of storm water runoff. Typical methods include riprap, gabions, slope paving and bulkheads, log cribbing, grid pavers, and asphalt paving.

*Riprap* is large angular stones placed along the bank line. It protects soil from erosion and is often used on steep slopes built with fill materials that are subject to harsh weather or seepage. Riprap can be used for flow channel liners, inlet and outlet protection at culverts, stream bank protection, and protection of shorelines subject to wave action. It is used where water is turbulent and fast-flowing and where soil may erode under the design flow conditions. Riprap is often placed over a filter blanket (i.e., a gravel layer or filter cloth). Riprap is either a uniform size or graded (different sizes) and usually is applied in an even layer throughout the stream. Figure 11.3 illustrates a typical riprap installation. Riprap costs may be estimated at about $45 per square yard.

*Gabions* are rock-filled wire-mesh cages that are used to create a new stream bank. Gabions should be installed according to the manufacturer's recommendations. Gabions are sometimes placed over a filter blanket, such as a gravel layer or filter cloth. Figure 11.4 illustrates a typical gabion installation.

*Slope paving and bulkheads* replace natural stream banks and create a nonerosive surface. Reinforced-concrete structures may require positive drainage behind the bulkhead or retaining wall to prevent erosion around the structure. Concrete slope paving typically costs about $65 per square yard.

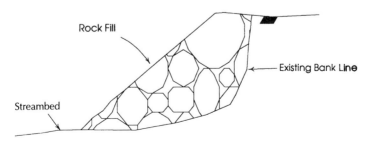

**Figure 11.3** Stream bank stabilization by riprap. (*EPA, 1992.*)

**Figure 11.4**  Stream bank stabilization by gabions.

*Log cribbing* consists of retaining walls built of logs to anchor the soils against erosive forces. These are usually built on the outside of stream bends. Only pressure-treated logs should be used. Figure 11.5 illustrates a typical log cribbing installation.

*Grid pavers* are precast or poured-in-place concrete units that are placed along stream banks to stabilize the stream bank and create open spaces where vegetation can be established. Grid pavers should be

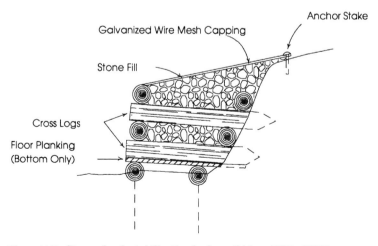

**Figure 11.5**  Stream bank stabilization by log cribbing. (*EPA, 1992.*)

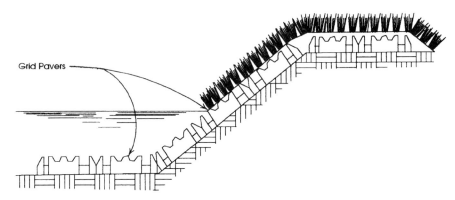

**Figure 11.6**  Stream bank stabilization by grid pavers. (*EPA, 1992.*)

installed according to the manufacturer's recommendations. Figure 11.6 illustrates a typical installation of grid pavers.

*Asphalt paving* is placed along the natural stream bank to create a nonerosive surface. Asphalt paving costs may be estimated at about $35 per square yard.

Stream bank stabilization is used where vegetative stabilization practices are not practical and where the stream banks are subject to heavy erosion from increased flows or disturbance during construction. Stabilization should be achieved prior to any land development in the watershed area. Stabilization can also be retrofitted when erosion of a stream bank occurs, although it is much better to anticipate erosion damage whenever possible.

Stream bank stabilization structures should be planned and designed by a professional engineer licensed in the state where the site is located. Applicable federal, state, and local requirements should be followed. Many types of stream bank stabilization will require permits from the Army Corps of Engineers, under section 404 of the Clean Water Act.

An important design feature of stream bank stabilization methods is the foundation of the structure; the potential for the stream to erode the sides and bottom of the channel should be considered, to ensure that the stabilization measure will be supported properly.

Structures can be designed to protect and improve natural wildlife habitats; e.g., log structures and grid pavers can be designed to keep vegetation. Permanent structures should be designed to handle expected flood conditions.

Stream bank stabilization structures should be inspected regularly and after each large storm event. Structures should be maintained as installed. Structural damage should be repaired as soon as possible to prevent further damage or erosion to the stream bank.

### Soil-retaining measures

*Soil-retaining measures* refer to structures or vegetative stabilization practices used to hold the soil firmly to its original place or to confine as much as possible within the site boundary. There are many different methods for retaining soil; some are used to control erosion while others are used to protect the safety of the workers (i.e., during excavations). Examples of soil-retaining measures include reinforced soil-retaining systems, wind breaks, and stream bank protection by shrubs and reeds.

*Reinforced soil-retaining measures* refer to the use of structural measures to hold in place loose or unstable soil. During excavation, e.g., soil tiebacks and retaining walls are used to prevent cave-ins and accidents. These same methods can be used to retain soils and prevent them from moving. The following types of soil-retaining measures are commonly used:

- *Skeleton sheeting:* Skeleton sheeting, the least expensive soil bracing system, requires cohesive soils, such as clay soils. Construction-grade lumber is used to brace the excavated face of the slope.

- *Continuous sheeting:* Continuous sheeting involves using a material that covers the face of the slope in a continuous manner. Struts and boards are placed along the slope which provide continuous support to the slope face. The material can be steel, concrete, or wood.

- *Permanent retaining walls:* Permanent construction walls may be needed to provide support to the slope well after the construction is completed. In this instance, concrete masonry or wood (railroad tie) retaining walls can be constructed and left in place.

Some sites may have slopes or soils that do not lend themselves to ordinary practices of soil retention, such as vegetation. In these instances, a reinforced soil-retaining measure should be considered.

As emphasized earlier, the use of reinforced soil-retaining practices serves both safety and erosion control purposes. Since safety is the first concern, the design should be performed by qualified and certified engineers. Such design normally requires an understanding of the nature of soil, location of the groundwater table, expected loads, and other important design considerations.

### Dust control

Wind is capable of causing erosion, particularly in dry climates or during the dry season. Wind erosion can occur wherever the surface soil is loose and dry, vegetation is sparse or absent, and the wind is sufficiently strong. Wind erodes soils and transports the sediments off the site, where they may be washed into the receiving water by the next rainstorm. Therefore, various methods of dust control may need to be employed to prevent dust from being carried away from the construction site. There are many ways to accomplish this, and some are described here:

- *Vegetative cover:*   For disturbed areas not subject to traffic, vegetation provides the most practical method of dust control.

- *Mulch:*   When properly applied, mulch offers a fast, effective means of controlling dust.

- *Chemical stabilization:*   Adhesives such as asphalt emulsions, latex emulsions, or resin in water can be sprayed onto mineral soil. Calcium chloride may be applied by mechanical spreader as loose, dry granules or flakes at a rate that keeps the surface moist but not so high as to cause water pollution or plant damage.

- *Water sprinkling:*   The site may be sprinkled until the surface is wet. Sprinkling is especially effective for dust control on haul roads and other traffic routes.

- *Stone:*   Stone is used to stabilize construction roads and can also be effective for dust control.

- *Wind barriers:*   A board fence, wind fence, sediment fence, or similar barrier can control air currents and blowing soil. These fences are normally constructed of wood, and they prevent erosion by obstructing the wind near the ground and preventing the soil from blowing off the site. Barriers can be part of long-term dust control strategy in arid and semiarid areas; however, they are not a substitute for permanent stabilization. A wind barrier generally protects soil downwind for a distance of 10 times the height of the barrier. Perennial grass and stands of existing trees may also serve as wind barriers. Constructed wind barriers typically cost about $2.50 per lineal foot.

Dust control measures should be used when open dry areas of soil are anticipated on the site. Clearing and grading activities create the opportunity for large amounts of dust to be blown; therefore, one or several dust control measures should be considered prior to clearing and grading. Many of the water erosion control measures indirectly prevent wind erosion.

As the distance across bare soil increases, wind erosion becomes more severe. In arid and semiarid regions where rainfall is insufficient to establish vegetative cover, mulching may be used to conserve moisture, prevent surface crusting, reduce runoff and erosion, and help establish vegetation. It is a critical treatment on sites with erosive slopes.

The direction of the prevailing winds and careful planning of clearing activities are important considerations. As a standard practice, any exposed area should be stabilized by using vegetation to prevent both wind and water erosion. If the site is located in an arid or semiarid area, then contact the local USDA Soil Conservation Service representative or the appropriate state or local government agency for additional information.

## References

Environmental Protection Agency: *Storm Water Management for Construction Activities. Developing Pollution Prevention Plans and Best Management Practices,* EPA Report 832/R-92/005, September 1992.

Metropolitan Washington Council of Governments: *Performance of Current Sediment Control Measures at Maryland Construction Sites,* Washington, January 1990.

National Academy Press: *Vetiver: A Thin Green Line Against Erosion,* Washington, 1992.

USDA Soil Conservation Service: *Guides for Erosion and Sediment Control in California,* Davis, CA, 1985.

# 12

# Structural Practices for Construction Sediment Control

This is the fourth of five chapters which deal with the specific requirements for storm water discharges from construction facilities. This chapter provides details on structural measures (such as sediment basins) for erosion and sediment control. The material in this chapter is derived primarily from information presented in the EPA guidance document for construction best management practices [EPA, 1992].

## Erosion and Sediment Controls

Erosion controls, as described in Chap. 11, provide the first line of defense in preventing off-site sediment movement and are designed to prevent erosion by protecting soils. Sediment controls, as described in this chapter, are generally designed to remove sediment before the runoff is discharged from the site. Structural controls are necessary because vegetative controls cannot be employed at areas of the site which are continually disturbed and because a finite time period is required before vegetative practices are fully effective.

Structural practices selected for incorporation into a construction storm water pollution prevention plan (SWPPP) are based on what is attainable at a given site. Structural practices involve the installation of devices to divert flow, store flow, or limit runoff. Options for such controls include straw bale dikes, silt fences, earth dikes, brush barriers, drainage swales, check dams, subsurface drains, pipe slope drains, level spreaders, storm drain inlet protection, outlet protection, sediment traps, and temporary sediment basins.

## Structural Practices

Structural practices generally fall into the following categories:

- *Velocity dissipation:*  Measures which reduce the erosive forces of runoff waters, including outlet protection, check dams, surface roughening, and gradient terraces.

- *Sediment capture:*  Measures which remove sediment runoff before it is carried off site, including silt fences, straw bale dikes, brush barriers, gravel or stone filter berms, storm drain inlet protection, sediment traps, and temporary sediment basins.

- *Temporary storm water management:*  Measures which divert flows away from exposed areas or divert sediment-laden flows into controlled areas, including earth dikes, drainage swales, interceptor dikes and swales, temporary storm drain diversions, pipe slope drains and sub-surface drains.

- *Permanent storm water management:*  Measures which remain in place after the construction has been completed, including on-site infiltration, outfall velocity dissipation devices, storm water retention structures and artificial wetlands, and storm water detention structures. These measures are intended to provide long-term improvements in the quality of runoff from the project site.

## General Permit Requirements

The EPA general permit has several specific requirements for structural erosion and sediment control measures:

1. *Velocity dissipation measures* must be implemented for all construction projects.

2. A *sediment basin* is required if the disturbed area contributing to a common drainage basin is equal to or greater than 10 acres.

3. A *sediment basin and/or sediment traps* must be used as needed if the disturbed area contributing to a common drainage basin is less than 10 acres.

4. *Silt fabric fences* are required for all sideslope and downslope site boundaries. However, if a sediment basin with a volume of 3600 $ft^3$/acre of drainage area is provided, then no other structural practices are required for drainage basins of less than 10 acres.

5. *Permanent storm water management measures* are required for all projects.

The remainder of this chapter describes each of these measures in greater detail.

## Velocity Dissipation Measures

Velocity dissipation measures reduce the erosive forces of runoff waters by decreasing the flow velocity. The quantity and size of the soil particles that are loosened and removed increase with the velocity of the runoff. This is because high runoff velocities reduce infiltration of the soil (and therefore also increase runoff volume) and exert greater forces on the soil particles, causing them to detach. High flow velocities are associated with severe rill and gully erosion. There are several ways in which velocities can be reduced:

1. *Reduce slopes.*   When you prepare the grading plan, try to make grades as gradual as possible without modifying the existing site conditions significantly. Steeper slopes result in faster-moving runoff, which results in greater erosion.

2. *Protect steep slopes.*   Steeply sloped areas can be protected from erosion in a number of ways. Flow can be diverted away from the face of the slope. On the slope itself, gradient terraces should be used to break the slope and slow the speed of the runoff flowing down the hillside. Surface roughening can also be used on sloped areas to slow down overland flow on a steep slope.

3. *Provide vegetative cover.*   In addition to holding soil in place and shielding it from the impact of raindrops, vegetative cover increases the surface roughness, which decreases the flow velocity.

4. *Decrease channel flow velocities.*   Concentrated runoff can be more erosive than overland flow. Runoff concentrated into swales or channels can be slowed by reducing the slope and increasing the width of a channel, or by using check dams. Runoff can also be slowed in channels by establishing a vegetative cover. Sod can provide a quick method of establishing vegetative cover. Geotextiles are often used to hold the channel soil in place while the grass is growing.

The following sections provide additional details on various velocity dissipation measures.

### Velocity dissipation by level spreaders

*Level spreaders* are outlets for dikes and diversions consisting of an excavated depression constructed at zero grade across a slope. Level spreaders convert concentrated runoff to diffuse runoff and release it onto areas stabilized by existing vegetation. Figure 12.1 illustrates a typical level spreader.

### Velocity dissipation by outlet protection

*Outlet protection reduces the speed of concentrated storm water flows,* and therefore it reduces erosion or scouring at the outlet end of culverts

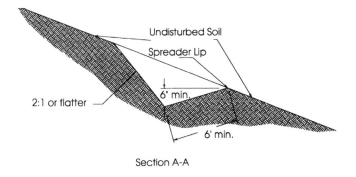

Section A-A

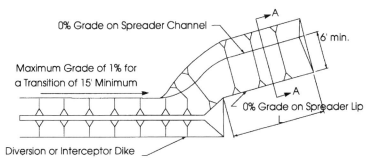

**Figure 12.1** Velocity dissipation by level spreader. (*Harris County, 1992.*)

or paved channel sections. In addition, outlet protection lowers the potential for downstream erosion. This type of protection can be achieved through a variety of techniques, including stone or riprap, concrete aprons, paved sections, and settling basins installed below the storm drain outlet. Figure 12.2 illustrates culvert outlet protection using a riprap apron.

Outlet protection should be installed at all pipe, interceptor dike, swale, or channel section outlets where the velocity of flow may cause erosion at the pipe outlet and in the receiving channel. Outlet protection should also be used at outlets where the velocity of flow at the design capacity may result in plunge pools (small permanent pools formed by erosion). Outlet protection should be installed early during construction activities, but may be added at any time, as necessary.

The exit velocity of the runoff as it leaves the outlet protection structure should be reduced to levels that minimize erosion. Outlet protection should be inspected on a regular schedule to check for erosion and scouring. Repairs should be made promptly.

**Figure 12.2**  Culvert outlet protection.

Outlet velocity protection measures which are properly designed and installed may later be converted to use as a permanent storm water management structure. This may satisfy the requirements of the EPA general permit for permanent storm water control measures, as described later in this chapter.

### Velocity dissipation by check dams

A *check dam* is a small, temporary or permanent dam constructed across a drainage ditch, swale, or channel to lower the speed of concentrated flows. Reduced runoff speed reduces channel erosion and allows sediments to settle out.

A check dam should be installed in steeply sloped swales or in swales where adequate vegetation has not been established. A check dam may be built from logs, stone, covered straw bales, or sandbags filled with pea gravel.

Check dams should be used only in small open channels which will not be overtopped by flow once the dams are constructed. The dams should not be placed in existing natural streams (unless approved by appropriate state authorities). Use the following design guidelines for check dams:

- *Drainage area:*   The drainage area above the check dam should be between 2 and 10 acres.

- *Spacing:*   The dams must be spaced so that the toe of the upstream dam is never any higher than the top of the downstream dam.

- *Height:*   The center of the dam must be 6 to 9 in lower than either edge, and the maximum height of the dam should be 24 in.

- *Width:*   The check dam should be as much as 18 in wider than the banks of the channel, to prevent undercutting as overflow water reenters the channel.

- *Sediment sump:*   Excavating a sediment sump immediately upstream from the check dam improves its effectiveness.

- *Erosion protection:*   Provide outlet stabilization below the lowest check dam where the risk of erosion is greatest.

- *Channel linings:*   Consider the use of channel linings or protection such as plastic sheeting or riprap where there may be significant erosion or prolonged submergence.

For *rock check dams,* use stone 2 to 15 in in diameter. Place the stones on the filter fabric either by hand or by using appropriate machinery; do not simply dump them in place. Extend the stone 18 in beyond the banks, and keep the side slopes 2:1 or flatter. As a suggested option, line the upstream side of the dam with 0.75- to 1.25-in gravel to a depth of 1 ft. Figure 12.3 illustrates a typical rock check dam.

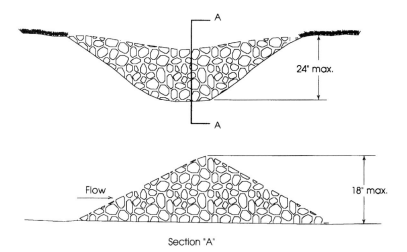

Section "A"

**Figure 12.3**   Rock check dam. (*EPA, 1992.*)

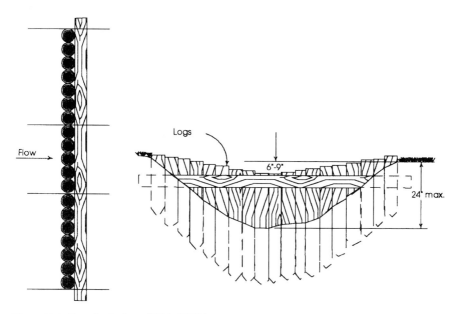

**Figure 12.4**   Log check dam. (*EPA, 1992.*)

For *log check dams,* use logs 6 to 8 in in diameter. Logs must be firmly embedded in the ground; 18 in is the recommended minimum depth. Figure 12.4 illustrates a typical log check dam.

For *sandbag check dams,* use sandbags filled with pea gravel. Be sure that bags are all securely sealed. Place bags by hand or use appropriate machinery.

The cost for the construction of check dams varies with the material used. Rock costs about $100 per dam. Log check dams are usually slightly less expensive than rock check dams. All costs vary depending on the width of channel.

After each significant rainfall, check dams should be inspected for sediment and debris accumulation. Sediment should be removed when it reaches one-half the original dam height. Check for erosion at edges, and repair promptly as required. If sandbags are used, the fabric of the bags should be inspected for signs of deterioration.

Check dams should remain in place and operational until the drainage area and channel are completely stabilized or up to 30 days after the permanent site stabilization is achieved. Restore the channel lining or establish vegetation when each check dam is removed.

It will be important to know the expected erosion rates and runoff flow rate for the swale in which this measure is to be installed. Contact the state or local storm water program agency or a licensed engineer for assistance in designing this measure.

### Velocity dissipation by surface roughening

*Surface roughening* is a temporary erosion control practice. The soil surface is roughened by the creation of horizontal grooves, depressions, or steps that run parallel to the contour of the land. Slopes that are not fine-graded and that are left in a roughened condition can also control erosion. Surface roughening reduces the speed of runoff, increases infiltration, and traps sediment. Surface roughening also helps establish vegetative cover by reducing runoff velocity and giving seed an opportunity to take hold and grow.

To slow erosion, surface roughening should be done as soon as possible after the vegetation has been removed from the slope. Roughening can be used with both seeding and planting and temporary mulching to stabilize an area. For steeper slopes and slopes that will be left roughened for longer periods, a combination of surface roughening and vegetation is appropriate. Surface roughening should be performed immediately after grading activities have ceased in an area, even if grading activities will be resumed later.

Different methods can be used to roughen the soil surface on slopes. They include stair-step grading, grooving with an implement, and tracking (driving a crawler tractor up and down a slope, leaving the cleat imprints parallel to the slope contour). The selection of an appropriate method depends on the grade of the slope, mowing requirements after vegetative cover is established, whether the slope was formed by cutting or filling, and type of equipment available.

**Steep slopes.** Any gradient with a slope greater than 2:1 should be stair-step graded. Each step catches material discarded from above and provides a level site where vegetation can grow. Stairs should be wide enough to work with standard earthmoving equipment.

**Medium slopes.** Cut slopes with a gradient steeper than 3:1 but less than 2:1 should be stair-step graded or groove-cut. Stair-step grading works well with soils containing large amounts of small rock. Grooving can be done by any implement that can be safely operated on the slope, including disks, spring harrows, or teeth on a front-end loader. Grooves should not be less than 3 in deep or more than 15 in apart. Medium slopes should be compacted every 9 in of depth. The face of the slope should consist of loose, uncompacted fill 4 to 6 in deep.

**Mild slopes.** Any cut or filled slope that will be mowed should have a gradient less than 3:1. Such a slope can be roughened with shallow grooves parallel to the slope contour by normal tilling. Grooves should be close together (less than 10 in) and not less than 1 in deep.

It is important to avoid excessive compacting of the soil surface, especially during tracking, because soil compaction inhibits vegetation growth and causes higher runoff speed. Therefore, it is best to limit roughening with tracked machinery to sandy soils that do not compact easily and to avoid tracking on clay soils. Surface-roughened areas should be seeded as quickly as possible. Also regular inspections should be made of all surface-roughened areas, especially after storms. If rills (small watercourses that have steep sides and are usually only a few inches deep) appear, they should be filled, graded again, and reseeded immediately. Proper dust control procedures should be followed during surface roughening.

### Velocity dissipation by gradient terraces

*Gradient terraces* are earth embankments or ridge and channels constructed along the face of a slope at regular intervals. Gradient terraces are constructed at a positive grade. They reduce erosion damage by capturing surface runoff and directing it to a stable outlet at a speed that minimizes erosion. Figure 12.5 illustrates a typical gradient terrace.

Gradient terraces are usually limited to use on long, steep slopes with a water erosion problem, or where it is anticipated that water erosion will be a problem. Gradient terraces should not be constructed on slopes with sandy or rocky soils. They will be effective only where suitable runoff outlets are or will be made available.

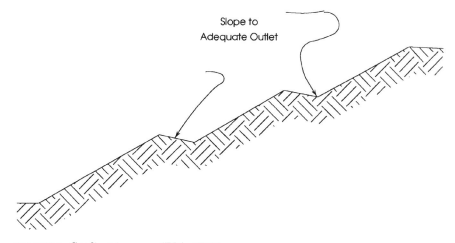

Slope to
Adequate Outlet

**Figure 12.5**   Gradient terraces. (*EPA, 1992.*)

Gradient terraces should be designed and installed according to a plan determined by an engineering survey and layout. It is important that gradient terraces be designed with adequate outlets, such as a grassed waterway, vegetated area, or tile outlet. In all cases, the outlet should direct the runoff from the terrace system to a point where the outflow will not cause erosion or other damage. Vegetative cover should be used in the outlet where possible. The design elevation of the water surface of the terrace should not be lower than the design elevation of the water surface in the outlet at their junction, when both are operating at design flow. Terraces should be inspected regularly, at least once a year and after major storms. Proper stabilization practices should be followed in the construction of these features.

### Sediment Capture Measures

It is necessary to have some disturbed portions of a construction site exposed to possible rainfall, at least briefly. Therefore, it is necessary to install measures which can remove sediment from runoff before it flows off the construction site.

Sediment capture measures prevent sediment from moving off the site by physically interposing a barrier to the movement of the sediment. Such measures include silt fences, straw bale dikes, brush barriers, gravel or stone filter berms, storm drain inlet protection, sediment traps, and temporary sediment basins.

The sediment capture device which is most suitable for large disturbed areas is the *sediment basin*. The EPA general permit for construction storm water discharges requires that a sediment basin be installed at all locations where there is an upstream disturbed area of 10 acres or more, wherever attainable. Authorized states may have different requirements for sediment basins. In addition, many local drainage regulatory agencies and soil conservation districts have regulations affecting construction practices.

*Disturbed areas of less than 10 acres have more variety in the measures which are suitable for sediment capture.* Several types of measures can be used for sediment control, including sediment basins, sediment traps, silt fences, and gravel filter berms. The selection among these measures depends upon a number of situations, including the following:

- *Overland flow:* Runoff which passes over disturbed soil should pass through sediment controls before it can be allowed to flow off the construction site. Therefore, the entire downslope and sideslope borders of the disturbed area should be lined with filtration devices, such as silt fences or gravel filter berms. These methods have limitations regarding the specific conditions in which they are effective. As an alternative, overland flow runoff from a disturbed area can be directed to a sediment trap or a temporary sediment basin by diversion devices such as an earth dike or an interceptor dike and swale.

- *Concentrated flow:*   Sediment should be removed from concentrated runoff by either a sediment trap or a temporary sediment basin, depending on the disturbed area upstream. Filtration measures are generally not effective when used in concentrated flow because flow will overtop the filtering device.

- *Flow into storm drain inlets:*   If there is a yard drain or curb inlet which receives flow from a disturbed area, then a sediment basin, sediment trap, or inlet protection should be constructed to remove the sediment from the runoff before it flows into the inlet.

### Sediment capture by temporary sediment basins

A *temporary sediment basin* is a settling pond with a controlled storm water release structure used to collect and store sediment produced by construction activities. A sediment basin can be constructed by excavation and/or by placing an earthen embankment across a low area or drainage swale. Sediment basins can be designed to maintain a permanent pool or to drain completely dry. The basin detains sediment-laden runoff from larger drainage areas long enough to allow most of the sediment to settle out. Figure 12.6 illustrates a temporary sediment basin.

To meet the requirements of the EPA general permit, the sediment basin must have a volume of at least 3600 ft$^3$/acre of drainage area. This is approximately 1 in of runoff (43,560 ft$^2$/acre÷12 in/ft = 3630 ft$^3$/acre).[1]

---

[1] The EPA indicates that the figure of 3600 ft$^3$/acre was chosen as an approximation for a 2-year storm event. The EPA had originally proposed that sediment basins serving drainage basins of 10 acres or more be large enough to accommodate the runoff from a 25-year storm event. When the draft general permit of August 16, 1991, was released, however, the requirement was reduced to a 10-year storm event. The EPA subsequently received further comments which indicated that some people did not have a good understanding of how to determine the size of the 10-year storm event. Other comments indicated that the 10-year storm event was an unreasonably large requirement for a temporary sediment basin which would be in service for a relatively short time. Therefore, the EPA reduced the final requirement to a 2-year storm event and then simplified the requirements by stating the basin size as a direct function of drainage area, rather than drainage area and local storm intensity.

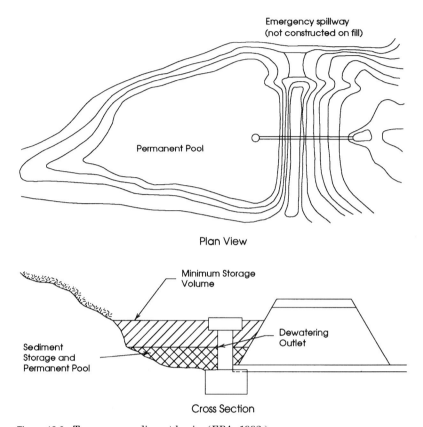

**Figure 12.6** Temporary sediment basin. (*EPA, 1992.*)

A sediment basin may not be attainable at a location under the following conditions:

- *Shallow bedrock* which prevents excavation of a basin.

- *Topographic difficulties* which prohibit the construction of a basin of adequate storage volume.

- *Lack of space* available at the common drainage location to construct a basin, due to the presence of existing structures, pavement, or utilities which cannot be relocated.

- *Lack of property rights* available at the only common drainage location. The only feasible location may be beyond the property line or right-of-way of the construction activity, and a temporary construction easement cannot be obtained.

- *Legal restrictions* as a result of state, local, or other federal regulations that may prohibit a basin or the construction of a basin in the common drainage locations.

If a sediment basin is not economically feasible under the criteria listed above, then sediment traps, silt fences, or other equivalent sediment control measures such as gravel filter berms should be installed instead.

The sediment basin has a riser and pipe outlet with a gravel outlet or spillway to slow the release of runoff and provide some sediment filtration. By removing sediment, the basin helps prevent the clogging of off-site conveyance systems and the sediment loading of receiving waterways. In this way, the basin helps prevent destruction of waterway habitats.

A temporary sediment basin should be installed before clearing and grading are undertaken. It should not be built in an active (existing natural) stream. The creation of a dam in such a site may result in the destruction of aquatic habitats. The risk of flooding damages downstream in case of dam failure should also be considered in the design of the temporary sediment basin.

A temporary sediment basin used in combination with other control measures, such as seeding or mulching, is especially effective for removing sediments. The sediment trapping efficiency is improved by providing the maximum surface area possible. Because finer silts may not settle out completely, additional erosion control measures should be used to minimize the release of fine silt. Runoff should enter the basin as far from the outlet as possible, to provide maximum retention time. To avoid "short-circuit" flows, baffles made of plywood may be installed in the sediment basin to force the flow to follow a longer path from the inlet to the outlet.

The useful life of a temporary sediment basin is dependent upon adequate maintenance. Sediment basins should be readily accessible for maintenance and sediment removal. They should be inspected after each rainfall and cleaned out when about half the volume has been filled with sediment. The sediment basin should remain in operation and be properly maintained until the site area is permanently stabilized by vegetation and/or when permanent structures are in place. The embankment forming the sedimentation pool should be well compacted and stabilized with vegetation. If the pond is located near a residential area, a sign should be posted and the area should be secured by a fence to increase public safety and to reduce the possibility of vandalism.

The cost of sediment basins varies widely according to size and site conditions. Costs typically range from about $5000 to about $50,000 or more.

A well-built temporary sediment basin that is large enough to handle the postconstruction runoff volume may be converted later to use as a permanent storm water management structure. This may satisfy the requirements of the EPA general permit for permanent storm water control measures, as described later in this chapter.

The sediment basin outlet pipe and spillway should be designed by an engineer based upon an analysis of the expected runoff flow rates from the site.

### Sediment capture by sediment traps

A *sediment trap* is formed by excavating a pond or by placing an earthen embankment across a low area or drainage swale. An outlet or spillway is constructed by using large stones or aggregate to slow the release of runoff. The trap retains the runoff long enough to allow most of the silt to settle out. Figure 12.7 illustrates a typical sediment trap.

A temporary sediment trap may be used in conjunction with other temporary measures, such as gravel construction entrances, vehicle wash areas, slope drains, diversion dikes and swales, or diversion channels. Temporary sediment traps are appropriate in the following locations:

- At the outlet of the perimeter controls installed during the first stage of construction

- At the outlet of any structure which concentrates sediment-laden runoff, e.g., at the discharge

- Above a storm water inlet that is in line to receive sediment-laden runoff

Temporary sediment traps may be constructed by excavation alone or by excavation in combination with an embankment. Temporary sediment traps are often used in conjunction with a diversion dike or swale. Sediment traps should not be planned to remain in place longer than about 18 to 24 months.

Sediment traps are suitable for small drainage areas, usually no more than 10 acres total or no more than 5 disturbed acres. The trap should be large enough to allow the sediments to settle and should have a capacity to store the collected sediment until it is removed. The capacity of the sedimentation pool should provide storage volume for at least 3600 ft³/acre of drainage area, and more if conditions require.

The outlet should be designed to provide a 2-ft settling depth and an additional sediment storage area 1.5 ft deep at the bottom of the trap. The embankment height should not exceed 5 ft. The recommended minimum width at the top of the embankment is between 2 and 5 ft. The minimum recommended length of the weir is between 3 and 4 ft, and the maximum length is 12 ft. Table 12.1 illustrates the typical

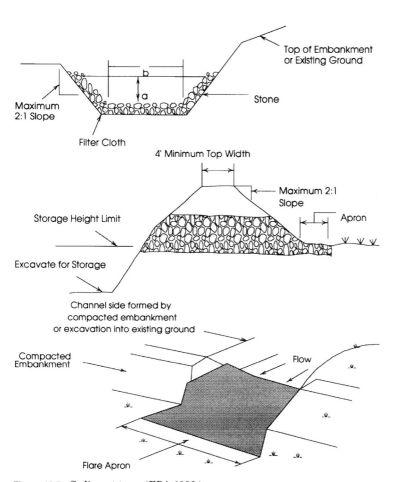

**Figure 12.7** Sediment trap. (*EPA 1992.*)

**TABLE 12.1.  Recommended Dimensions of Sediment Trap**

| Embankment height, ft | Outlet height, ft | Width, ft |
|:---:|:---:|:---:|
| 1.5 | 0.5 | 2.0 |
| 2.0 | 1.0 | 2.0 |
| 2.5 | 1.5 | 2.5 |
| 3.0 | 2.0 | 2.5 |
| 3.5 | 2.5 | 3.0 |
| 4.0 | 3.0 | 3.0 |
| 4.5 | 3.5 | 4.0 |
| 5.0 | 4.0 | 4.5 |

relationship between the embankment height, the height of the outlet, and the width at the top of the embankment.

The following steps are involved in constructing a temporary sediment trap:

1. *Clearing:*  Clear the area of all trees, brush, stumps, or other obstructions.

2. *Embankment:*  Construct the embankment in 8-in lifts, compacting each lift with the appropriate earthmoving equipment. Fill material must be free of woody vegetation, roots, or large stones. Keep cut and fill slopes between 3:1 and 2:1 or flatter.

3. *Filter fabric:*  Line the outlet area with filter fabric prior to placing stone or gravel.

4. *Gravel outlet:*  Construct the gravel outlet, using coarse aggregate between 2 in and 14 in in diameter, and face the upstream side with a 12-in layer of 0.75- to 1.5-in washed gravel on the upstream side.

5. *Stabilization:*  Seed and mulch the embankment as soon as possible to ensure stabilization.

Costs for a sediment trap vary widely based upon the size and the amount of excavation and stone required. It usually can be installed for $500 to $7000.

The effective life of a sediment trap depends upon adequate maintenance. The trap should be readily accessible for periodic maintenance and sediment removal. Traps should be inspected regularly and after each rainfall. Make any repairs necessary to ensure the measure is in good working order. Check the embankment regularly to make sure it is structurally sound. At a minimum, sediment should be removed and the trap restored to its original volume when sediment reaches 50 percent of the original volume. Sediment removed from the trap must be properly disposed of.

The trap should remain in operation and be properly maintained until the site area is permanently stabilized by vegetation and/or when permanent structures are in place.

### Sediment capture by silt fences

A *silt fence,* also called a *filter fence,* is a temporary measure for sedimentation control. The silt fence is used to intercept sediment in diffuse (shallow overland) flow. It usually consists of posts with geotextile fabric (filter cloth) stretched across them and sometimes with a wire support fence. The lower edge of the fence is vertically trenched and covered by backfill. See Fig. 12.8.

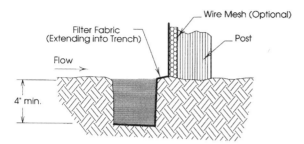

**Figure 12.8**  Silt fence construction detail. (*EPA 1992.*)

A silt fence is used in small drainage areas to detain sediment. These fences are most effective where there is overland flow (runoff that flows over the surface of the ground as a thin, even layer) or in minor swales or drainageways. They prevent sediment from entering receiving waters. Silt fences are also used to catch wind-blown sand and to create an anchor for sand dune creation.

A silt fence is not appropriate for controlling runoff from a large area. For slopes between 50:1 and 5:1, the maximum allowable upstream flow path length to the fence is 100 ft; for slopes of 2:1 and steeper, the maximum is 20 ft. The maximum upslope grade perpendicular to the fence line should not exceed 1:1.

A silt fence should be installed prior to major soil disturbance in the drainage area. The fence should be placed across the bottom of a slope along a contour line (a line of uniform elevation). This will place the fence perpendicular to the direction of flow. It can be used at the outer boundary of the work area. However, the fence does not have to surround the work area completely. In addition, a silt fence is effective where sheet and rill erosion may be a problem. Silt fences should not be constructed in streams or large swales.

Silt fences can be more effective than a straw bale barrier if properly installed and maintained. They may be used in combination with other erosion and sediment practices. Ponding should not be allowed behind silt fences since they will collapse under high pressure; the design should provide sufficient outlets to prevent overtopping.

Aside from the traditional wooden post and filter fabric method, there are several variations of silt fence installation including silt fence fabric which can be purchased with pockets presewn to fit steel fence posts.

The maximum height of the filter fence should range between 18 and 36 in above the ground surface (depending on the amount of upslope ponding expected). The following elements must be considered:

1. *Filter fabric:* Synthetic filter fabric should be a pervious sheet of polypropylene, nylon, polyester, or polyethylene yarn. Synthetic filter fabric should contain ultraviolet ray inhibitors and stabilizers to provide a minimum of 6 months of expected usable construction life at a temperature range of 0 to 120°F. Burlap of 10 oz/yd$^2$ fabric can also be used, but is only acceptable for periods of up to 60 days. The filter fabric should be purchased in a continuous roll to avoid joints. Where joints in the fabric are required, the filter cloth should be spliced together only at a support post, with a minimum 6-in overlap, and securely sealed. See Table 12.2.

2. *Reinforcing wire:* Although it is not required, wire fencing may be used as a backing to reinforce standard-strength filter fabric. The wire fence (14 gage minimum) should be 22 to 48 in wide and should have a maximum mesh spacing of 6 in. If standard-strength filter fabric is to be used, the optional wire mesh support fence may be fastened to the upslope side of the posts by using 1-in heavy-duty wire staples, tie wires, or hog rings. Extend the wire mesh support to the bottom of the trench. The filter fabric should then be stapled or wired to the fence, and 8 to 20 in of fabric should extend into the trench. Extra-strength filter fabric does not require a wire mesh support fence. Staple or wire the filter fabric directly to the posts, and extend 8 to 20 in of fabric into the trench.

3. *Posts:* Posts should be 2 to 4 ft long and should be composed of either 2-in × 2-in or 2-in × 4-in pine (or equivalent) or 1.00 to 1.33 lb/lin ft steel. Steel posts should have projections for fastening wire and fabric to them. Posts should be spaced 8 to 10 ft apart when a wire mesh support fence is used and no more than 6 ft apart when extra-strength filter fabric (without a wire fence) is used. The posts should extend 12 to 30 in into the ground. Trees should not be used as substitutes for posts.

4. *Trench:* A trench should be excavated 4 to 8 in wide and 4 to 12 in deep along the upslope side of the line of posts. Backfill the trench with compacted soil or 0.75-in minimum-diameter gravel placed over the filter fabric.

**TABLE 12.2. Synthetic Filter Fabric Requirements**

| Physical property | Requirements |
|---|---|
| Filtering efficiency | 75–85% (minimum) |
| Tensile strength at 20% (maximum elongation) | Standard strength: 30 lb/lin in (minimum) Extra strength: 50 lb/lin in (minimum) |
| Slurry flow rate | 0.3 gal/(ft$^2 \cdot$ min) (minimum) |

**Figure 12.9** Typical silt fence installation along stream bank.

Silt fence installation costs approximately $6 per linear foot. See Fig. 12.9.

The fence requires frequent inspection and prompt maintenance to maintain its effectiveness. Inspect filter fences daily during periods of prolonged rainfall, immediately after each rainfall event, and weekly during periods of no rainfall. Check for areas where runoff eroded a channel beneath the fence, or where the fence was caused to sag or collapse by runoff flowing over the top. Make any required repairs immediately. Remove and properly dispose of sediment when it is one-third to one-half the height of the fence or after each storm. Take care to avoid damaging the fence during cleanout. See Fig. 12.10.

Filter fences should not be removed until the upslope area has been permanently stabilized. Any sediment deposits remaining in place after the filter fence has been removed should be dressed to conform with the existing grade, prepared, and seeded.

### Sediment capture by straw bale dikes or brush barriers

Straw bales are temporary barriers of straw or similar material used to intercept sediment in runoff from small drainage areas of disturbed soil. When installed and maintained properly, straw bale dikes can remove approximately 67 percent of the sediment in runoff, but this can be achieved only through careful maintenance with special attention to replacing rotted or broken bales.

**Figure 12.10**   Silt fabric fence with sediment accumulated during storm event.

Brush barriers are composed of tree limbs, weeds, vines, root mat, soil, rock, and other cleared materials placed at the toe of a slope.

Many state and local agencies allow straw bales or brush barriers as an alternative to silt fences. However, straw bales and brush barriers are not listed in the EPA general permit because of questions regarding their effectiveness, primarily because of improper installation and inadequate maintenance. Figure 12.11 illustrates a straw bale installation requiring maintenance.

### Sediment capture by gravel or stone filter berms

A *gravel* or *stone filter berm* is a temporary ridge constructed of loose gravel, stone, or crushed rock. It slows and filters flow, diverting it from an exposed traffic area. Diversions constructed of compacted soil may be used where there will be little or no construction traffic within the right-of-way. They are also used for directing runoff from the right-of-way to a stabilized outlet. Figure 12.12 illustrates a typical gravel filter berm.

Gravel or stone filter berms are appropriate where roads and other rights-of-way under construction should accommodate vehicular traffic. Berms are meant for use in areas with gentle slopes. They may also be used at traffic areas within the construction site.

**Figure 12.11**   Straw bales used for curb inlet protection.

Berm material should be well-graded gravel or crushed rock. The spacing of the berms will depend on the steepness of the slope: Berms should be placed closer together as the slope increases.

The diversion should be inspected regularly after each rainfall or if breached by construction or other vehicles. All needed repairs should be performed immediately. Accumulated sediment should be removed and properly disposed of and the filter material replaced, as necessary.

### Sediment capture by storm drain inlet protection

*Storm drain inlet protection* is a filtering measure or excavated impounding area placed around any inlet or drain to trap sediment. This prevents the sediment from entering inlet structures. Additionally, it serves to prevent the silting of inlets, storm drainage systems, or receiving channels.

Storm drain inlet protection is appropriate for small drainage areas where storm drain inlets will be ready for use before final stabilization. Storm drain inlet protection is also used where a permanent storm drain structure is being constructed on the site. Storm drain inlet pro-

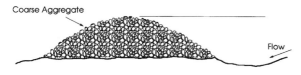

Coarse Aggregate

Flow

**Figure 12.12**   Gravel filter berm. (*EPA, 1992.*)

tection may be constructed of filter fabric, excavated gravel, concrete block and gravel, or other materials. Sod may be used where sediments in the storm water runoff are low. Gravel and mesh filters can be used where flows are higher and subject to disturbance by site traffic. Straw bales are used as storm drain inlet protection in many locations. However, the EPA does not recommend straw bales for this purpose.

The cost of storm drain inlet protection varies depending upon the size and type of inlet to be protected but generally is about $300 per inlet.

Storm drain inlet protection is not meant for use in drainage areas exceeding 1 acre or for large concentrated storm water flows. Installation of this measure should take place before any soil disturbance in the drainage area. The type of material used will depend on the site conditions and the size of the drainage area. Inlet protection should be used in combination with other measures, such as small impoundments or sediment traps, to provide more effective sediment removal.

Inlet protection structures should be inspected regularly, especially after a rainstorm. Repairs and silt removal should be performed as necessary. Storm drain inlet protection structures should be removed only after the disturbed areas are completely stabilized.

**Filter fabric inlet protection.**   Filter fabric is used for inlet protection when storm water flows are relatively small with low velocities. This practice cannot be used where inlets are paved because the filter fabric should be staked. The drainage area should be 1 acre or less, with slopes of 5 percent or less. The area immediately surrounding the inlet should not exceed a slope of 1 percent. Overland flow to the inlet should be no greater than 0.5 ft$^3$/s. Figure 12.13 illustrates a typical filter fabric inlet protection measure.

**Figure 12.13**   Filter fabric storm drain inlet protection.

To avoid failure caused by pressure against the fabric when overtopping occurs, the height of the filter fabric should be limited to 1.5 ft above the crest of the drop inlet. A sediment-trapping sump 1 to 2 ft deep with side slopes of 2:1 is recommended. The following elements must be considered:

1. *Filter fabric:*   This is the same as used for silt fences.

2. *Posts:*   Use wooden posts 2 in × 2 in or 2 in × 4 in with a minimum length of 3 ft. Place a stake at each corner of the inlet and around the edges no more than 3 ft apart. Stakes should be driven into the ground 18 in or at a minimum 8 in.

3. *Framework:*   For stability, a framework of wood strips should be installed around the stakes at the crest of the overflow area 1.5 ft above the crest of the drop inlet. Staple the filter fabric to the wooden stakes with heavy-duty staples at least $\frac{1}{2}$-in long, overlapping the joints to the next stake. Ensure that 12 to 32 in of filter fabric extends at the bottom so it can be formed into the trench.

4. *Trench:*   Excavate a trench of 8 to 12 in deep around the outside perimeter of the stakes. If a sediment-trapping sump is being provided, then the excavation may be as deep as 2 ft. Place the bottom of the fabric in the trench, and backfill the trench all the way around, using washed gravel $\frac{3}{4}$ in in diameter to a minimum depth of 4 in.

Inspect regularly and after every storm. Make sure that the stakes are firmly seated in the ground and that the filter fabric continues to be securely anchored. Make any repairs necessary to ensure the measure is in good working order.

Sediment should be removed and the trap restored to its original dimensions when sediment has accumulated to 50 percent of the design depth of the trap. All removed sediments should be properly disposed of. If the filter fabric becomes clogged, it should be replaced immediately.

Inlet protection should remain in place and operational until the drainage area is completely stabilized or up to 30 days after the permanent site stabilization is achieved.

**Excavated gravel inlet protection.**   Excavated gravel inlet protection may be constructed by excavating around a storm drain inlet located in an unpaved area. The excavation provides storage for sediment. Figure 12.14 illustrates a typical excavated gravel inlet protection measure.

Excavated gravel and mesh inlet protection may be used with most inlets where overflow capability is needed and in areas of heavy flows, 0.5 ft$^3$/s or greater. The drainage area should be fairly flat with slopes of 5 percent or less. The trap should have a sediment-trapping sump of

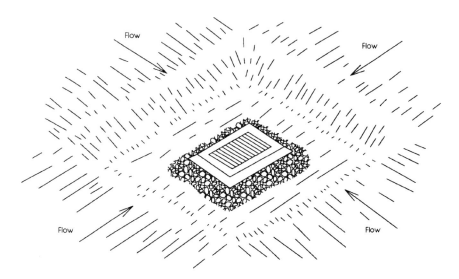

**Figure 12.14**   Excavated gravel inlet protection. (*EPA, 1992.*)

1 to 2 ft measured from the crest of the inlet. Side slopes should be 2:1. The recommended volume of excavation is 35 yd$^3$/acre disturbed. To achieve maximum trapping efficiency, the longest dimension of the basin should be oriented toward the longest inflow area. The following steps are followed in constructing excavated gravel inlet protection:

1. *Excavation:*   Remove any obstructions to excavating and grading. Excavate the sump area, grade the slopes, and properly dispose of the excavated soil.

2. *Inlet grate:*   Secure the inlet grate to prevent seepage of sediment-laden water.

3. *Wire mesh:*   Place hardware cloth or wire mesh with ½-in openings over the drop inlet so that the wire extends a minimum of 1 ft beyond each side of the inlet structure. Overlap the strips of mesh if more than one is necessary.

4. *Filter fabric:*   Place filter fabric (as specified for silt fences) over the mesh, extending it at least 18 in beyond the inlet opening on all sides. Ensure that weep holes in the inlet structure are protected by filter fabric and gravel.

5. *Gravel:*   Place washed gravel ¾ to 4 in in diameter over the fabric and wire mesh to a depth of at least 1 ft.

Inspect regularly and after every storm. Make any repairs necessary to ensure the measure is in good working order. Clean or remove and replace the stone filter or filter fabric if it becomes clogged. Sediment should be removed and the trap restored to its original dimensions when sediment has accumulated to one-half the design depth of the trap.

Inlet protection should remain in place and operational until the drainage area is completely stabilized or up to 30 days after the permanent site stabilization is achieved.

**Block-and-gravel inlet protection.**    Concrete block-and-gravel filters can be used where velocities are higher than those allowed for excavated gravel inlet protection. Figure 12.15 illustrates a typical block-and-gravel inlet protection measure.

Block-and-gravel inlet protection may be used with most types of inlets where overflow capability is needed and in areas of heavy flows of 0.5 ft$^3$/s or greater. The drainage area should not exceed 1 acre. The drainage area should be fairly flat with slopes of 5 percent or less. To achieve maximum trapping efficiency, the longest dimension of the basin should be oriented toward the longest inflow area. Where possible, the trap should have a sediment-trapping sump of 1 to 2 ft deep

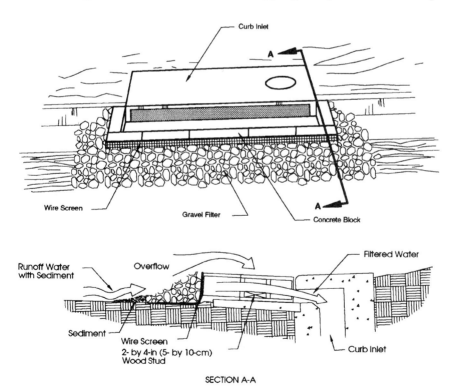

SECTION A-A

**Figure 12.15**   Block and gravel inlet protection. (*Harris County, 1992.*)

with side slopes of 2:1. The following steps are used in constructing this type of inlet protection:

1. *Inlet grate:*   Secure the inlet grate to prevent seepage of sediment-laden water.
2. *Wire mesh:*   Place hardware cloth or wire mesh with $\frac{1}{2}$-in openings over the drop inlet so that the wire extends a minimum of 12 to 18 in beyond each side of the inlet structure. Overlap the strips of mesh if more than one is necessary.
3. *Filter fabric (optional):*   Place filter fabric (as specified for silt fences) over the mesh, and extend it at least 18 in beyond the inlet structure.
4. *Concrete blocks:*   Place concrete blocks (4 to 12 in wide) over the filter fabric in a single row lengthwise on their sides along the sides of the inlet. The foundation should be excavated a minimum of 2 in below the crest of the inlet, and the bottom row of blocks should be against the edge of the structure for lateral support. The open ends of the block should face outward, not upward, and the ends of adjacent blocks should abut. Lay one block on each side of the structure on its side to allow for dewatering of the pool. The block barrier should be at least 12 in high and may be up to a maximum of 24 in high, and it may be from 4 to 12 in deep depending on the size of block used. Prior to backfilling, place wire mesh over the outside vertical end of the blocks so that stone does not wash down the inlet.
5. *Gravel:*   Place washed gravel $\frac{3}{4}$ to 4 in in diameter against the wire mesh to the top of the blocks.

For curb inlets, follow these installation procedures:

1. *Spacer blocks:*   Place two concrete blocks on their sides perpendicular to the curb at either end of the inlet opening.
2. *Front blocks:*   Place concrete blocks on their sides across the front of the opening and abutting the spacer blocks. The openings in the blocks should face outward, not upward.
3. *Retaining stud:*   Cut a $2 \times 4$-in wooden stud the length of the curb inlet plus the width of the spacer blocks. Place the stud through the outer hole of each spacer block to keep the front blocks in place.
4. *Wire mesh:*   Place wire mesh over the outside vertical face (open ends) of the front concrete blocks to prevent stone from being washed through the openings in the blocks. Use chicken wire or hardware cloth with 0.5-in openings.
5. *Gravel:*   Place 2- to 3-in gravel against the wire to the top of the barrier.

Inspect regularly and after every storm. Make any repairs necessary to ensure the measure is in good working order. Sediment should be removed and the trap restored to its original dimensions when sediment has accumulated to one-half the design depth of the trap. All sediments removed should be properly disposed of.

Inlet protection should remain in place and operational until the drainage area is completely stabilized or up to 30 days after the permanent site stabilization is achieved.

## Temporary Storm Water Management Measures

Diverting off-site runoff around a disturbed area reduces the amount of storm water which comes into contact with the exposed soils. If there is less runoff coming in contact with exposed soil, then there will be less erosion of the soil and less storm water which has to be treated to remove sediment. The following conditions may be considered:

- *Off-site flows entering the site:* Overland flow can be diverted around a construction site by installing an earth dike, an interceptor dike and swale, or a drainage swale. The choice of diversion methods depends upon the size of the uphill area and the steepness of the slope that the diversion must go down. Interceptor dikes and swales are effective in diverting overland flows from smaller areas (3 acres or less) down gentle slopes (10 percent or less). A temporary swale is most effective in diverting runoff from concentrated channels, and an earth dike is capable of diverting both sheet and concentrated flows from larger areas down steeper slopes. These devices should be installed from the uphill side of the site down to a point where they can discharge to an undisturbed area on the downhill side of the site.

- *Steep slopes:* Steeply sloped areas are especially susceptible to erosion. If there are steep areas on your site which will be disturbed, then an earth dike or interceptor dike and swale may be used to divert the runoff from the top of the slope to the inlet of a pipe slope drain or to a less steeply sloped area. These measures will minimize the amount of runoff flowing across the face of a slope and will decrease the erosion of that slope.

- *On-site swales or streams:* Swales and streams which run through construction sites must be protected from erosion and sediment because they can be significantly damaged. Streams and other water bodies should be protected by preservation of natural vegetation or buffer zones, as described in Chap. 11. Where possible, these techniques should also be used to protect swales or intermittent streams. Where construction requires that the stream or swale be disturbed, the amount of area and time of disturbance should be kept at a minimum. All stream and channel crossings should be made at right angles to the stream, preferably at the narrowest portion of the channel. Once a stream or swale is disturbed, construction should proceed as quickly as possible in this area. Once completed, the stream banks should be stabilized as described in Chap. 11. Swales and intermittent streams disturbed by construction should be seeded and stabilized with geotextiles as soon as possible.

- *Construction crossings of on-site streams:*  If it is necessary to cross a swale or stream to get to all or parts of your construction site, then before you begin working on the opposite side of the stream, you should construct a temporary stream crossing. Stream crossings can be either permanent or temporary depending upon the need to cross the stream after construction is completed.

The following sections describe storm water management measures for erosion and sediment control.

### Earth dikes

An *earth dike* is a temporary ridge or berm of compacted soil used to protect work areas from upslope runoff or to divert sediment-laden water to appropriate traps or stable outlets. The dike consists of compacted soil and stone, riprap, or vegetation to stabilize the channel. Figure 12.16 illustrates a typical earth dike.

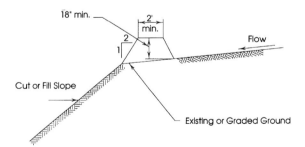

**Figure 12.16**  Earth dike. (*Harris County, 1992.*)

Earth dikes can be used in the following situations:

- Above disturbed existing slopes and above cut or fill slopes to prevent runoff over the slope
- Across unprotected slopes, as slope breaks, to reduce slope length
- Below slopes to divert excess runoff to stabilized outlets
- To divert sediment-laden water to sediment traps
- At or near the perimeter of the construction area to keep sediment from leaving the site
- Above disturbed areas before stabilization to prevent erosion and maintain acceptable working conditions
- To serve as sediment traps when the site has been overexcavated on a flat grade or in conjunction with a sediment fence

Despite an earth dike's simplicity, improper design can limit its effectiveness; therefore, the state or local requirements should be consulted. Some general considerations include proper compaction of the earth dike, appropriate location to divert the intercepted runoff, and properly designed ridge height and thicknesses. Earth dikes should be constructed along a positive grade. There should be no dips or low points in an earth dike where the storm water will collect (other than the discharge point). Also the intercepted runoff from disturbed areas should be diverted to a sediment-trapping device. Runoff from undisturbed areas can be channeled to an existing swale or to a level spreader. Stabilization for the dike and flow channel of the drainage swales should be accomplished as soon as possible. Stabilization materials can include vegetation or stone or riprap.

When the drainage area to the earth dike is greater than 10 acres, the USDA Soil Conservation Service (SCS) standards and specification for diversions should be consulted. Table 12.3 contains suggested dike design criteria.

TABLE 12.3.  Recommended Design Criteria for Earth Dikes

| Drainage area | Under 5 acres | 5 to 10 acres |
|---|---|---|
| Dike height (upstream side) | 18 in | 30 in |
| Dike top width | 24 in | 36 in |
| Dike base width | 6 ft | 8 ft |
| Dike side slopes | 2:1 or less | 2:1 or less |
| Flow width | 4 ft | 6 ft |
| Flow depth | 12 in | 24 in |
| Grade | 0.5–10% | 0.5–10% |

If the dike is constructed from coarse aggregate, the side slopes should be 3:1 or flatter. The channel formed behind the dike should have a positive grade to a stabilized outlet. The channel should be stabilized with vegetative or other stabilization measures. Grades over 10 percent may require an engineering design.

Construct the dike where it will not interfere with major areas of construction traffic so that vehicle damage to the dike will be kept to the minimum. Diversion dikes should be installed prior to the majority of soil-disturbing activity and may be removed when stabilization of the drainage area and outlet is completed.

Clear the area of all trees, brush, stumps, or other obstructions before constructing the dike. Construct the dike to the designed cross section, line, and grade, making sure that there are no irregularities or bank projections to impede the flow. The dike should be compacted by using earthmoving equipment to prevent failure of the dike. The dike must be stabilized as soon as possible after installation.

The cost associated with earth dike construction is roughly $4.50 per linear foot which covers the earthwork involved in preparing the dike. Also added to this cost is approximately $1 per linear foot for stabilization practices. For many construction projects, the cost of earth dike construction is insignificant compared to the overall earthwork project costs.

Inspect the dike, flow channel, and outlet regularly and after every storm, and make any repairs necessary to ensure the measure is in good working order. If material must be added to the dike, be sure it is properly compacted. Reseed or stabilize the dike as needed to maintain its stability regardless of whether there has been a storm event.

### Drainage swales

A *drainage swale* is a channel with a lining of vegetation, riprap, asphalt, concrete, or other material. Drainage swales are installed to convey runoff without causing erosion. They are constructed by excavating a channel and applying the appropriate stabilization.

Drainage swales can be used to convey runoff from the bottom or top of a slope. Temporary drainage swales are appropriate in the following situations:

- To divert upslope flows away from disturbed areas such as cut or fill slopes and to divert runoff to a stabilized outlet
- To reduce the length of the slope that runoff will cross
- At the perimeter of the construction site to prevent sediment-laden runoff from leaving the site
- To direct sediment-laden runoff to a sediment-trapping device.

Since design flows, channel linings, and appropriate outlet devices will need to be considered, consult your state's requirements on such erosion control measures prior to constructing a drainage swale. General considerations include these:

- Divert the intercepted runoff to an appropriate outlet.

- The swale should be lined with geotextiles, grass, sod, riprap, asphalt, or concrete. The selection of the liner is dependent upon the volume and velocity of the anticipated runoff.

- The swale should have a positive grade. There should be no dips or low points in the swale where storm water can collect.

When the drainage area is greater than 10 acres, the USDA Soil Conservation Service standards and specifications for diversions should be consulted.

Swales may have side slopes ranging from 3:1 to 2:1. The minimum channel depth should be between 12 and 18 in. The minimum width at the bottom of the channel should be 24 in, and the bottom should be level. The channel should have a uniform positive grade between 2 and 5 percent, with no sudden decreases where sediments may accumulate and cause overtopping. Grades over 10 percent may require an engineering design. The channel should be stabilized with temporary or permanent stabilization measures. Runoff must discharge to a stabilized outlet.

Construct the swale away from areas of major construction traffic. Clear the area of all trees, brush, stumps, or other obstructions. Construct the swale to the designed cross section, line, and grade, making sure that there are no irregularities or bank projections to impede the flow. The lining should be well compacted by using earthmoving equipment, and stabilization should be initiated as soon as possible. Stabilize lining with grass seed, sod, or riprap. Surplus material should be properly distributed or disposed of so that it does not interfere with the functioning of the swale. Outlet dissipation measures should be used to avoid the risk of erosion.

Inspect the flow channel and outlet for deficiencies or signs of erosion. Inspect regularly and after every storm; make any repairs necessary to ensure the measure is in good working order. If surface of the channel requires material to be added, ensure that it is properly compacted. Reseed or stabilize the channel as needed to prevent erosion during a storm event.

Drainage swales can vary widely depending on the geometry of the swale and the type of lining material: Grass costs $3 per square yard; sod, $4; riprap, $45. No matter which liner type is used, the entire swale must be stabilized (i.e., seeded and mulched at a cost of about $1.25 per square yard).

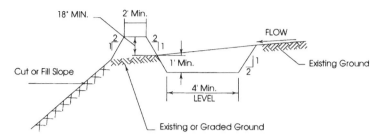

**Figure 12.17**   Interceptor dike and swale. (*Harris County, 1992.*)

## Interceptor dikes and swales

Interceptor dikes (ridges of compacted soil) and swales (excavated depressions) are used to keep upslope runoff from crossing areas where there is a high risk of erosion. The dikes reduce the amount and speed of flow and then guide it to a stabilized outfall (point of discharge) or sediment-trapping area (see sections on sediment traps and sediment basins). Figure 12.17 illustrates a typical interceptor dike and swale.

Interceptor dikes and swales divert runoff by using a combination of earth dike and vegetated swale. Runoff is channeled away from locations where there is a high risk of erosion by placing a diversion dike or swale at the top of a sloping disturbed area. Dikes and swales also collect overland flow, changing it into concentrated flows. Interceptor dikes and swales can be either temporary or permanent storm water control structures.

Interceptor dikes and swales are generally built around the perimeter of a construction site before any major soil-disturbing activity takes place. Temporary dikes or swales may also be used to protect existing buildings, areas such as stockpiles, or other small areas that have not yet been fully stabilized.

When constructed along the upslope perimeter of a disturbed or high-risk area (though not necessarily all the way around it), dikes or swales prevent runoff from uphill areas from crossing the unprotected slope. For short slopes, a dike or swale at the top of the slope reduces the amount of runoff reaching the disturbed area. For longer slopes, several dikes or swales are placed across the slope at intervals. This practice reduces the amount of runoff that accumulates on the face of the slope and carries the runoff safely down the slope. Temporary dikes or swales constructed on the downslope side of the disturbed or high-risk area will prevent runoff that contains sediment from leaving the site before sediment is removed. In all cases, runoff is guided to a sediment-trapping area or a stabilized outfall before release.

Temporary dikes and swales are used in areas of overland flow. If they remain in place longer than 15 days, they should be stabilized. Runoff channeled by a dike or swale should be directed to an adequate sediment-trapping area or stabilized outfall. Care should be taken to provide enough slope for drainage but not so much slope as to cause erosion due to the high runoff flow speed. Temporary interceptor dikes and swales may remain in place as long as 12 to 18 months (with proper stabilization) or may be rebuilt at the end of each day's activities. Dikes or swales should remain in place until the area they were built to protect is permanently stabilized.

Interceptor dikes and swales which are properly designed and installed may later be converted to use as permanent storm water management structures. This may satisfy the requirements of the EPA general permit for permanent storm water control measures, described later in this chapter.

Temporary storm water control measures should be inspected once a week on a regular schedule and after every storm. Repairs necessary to the dike and flow channel should be made promptly.

The cost associated with earth dike construction is roughly $4.50 per linear foot; this covers the earthwork involved in preparing the dike. Drainage swales can vary widely depending on the geometry of the swale and the type of lining material: Grass costs $3 per square yard; sod, $4; riprap, $45. No matter which liner type is used, the entire dike and swale must be stabilized (i.e., seeded and mulched at a cost of about $1.25 per square yard).

### Temporary stream crossings

A *temporary stream crossing* is a bridge or culvert across a stream or watercourse for short-term use by construction vehicles or heavy equipment. Vehicles moving over unprotected stream banks will damage the banks, thereby releasing sediments and degrading the stream banks. A stream crossing provides a means for construction vehicles to cross streams or watercourses without moving sediment to streams, damaging the streambed or channel, or causing flooding.

A temporary stream crossing is used when heavy equipment should be moved from one side of a stream channel to another or when light-duty construction vehicles have to cross the stream channel frequently for a short period of time. Temporary stream crossings should be constructed only when it is necessary to cross a stream and a permanent crossing is not yet constructed.

Where available materials and designs are adequate to bear the expected loadings, *bridges* are preferred as a temporary stream crossing.

*Culverts* are the most common type of stream crossings and are relatively easy to construct. A pipe, which is to carry the flow, is laid into the channel and covered by gravel.

When feasible, always attempt to minimize or eliminate the need to cross streams. Temporary stream crossings are a direct source of pollution; therefore, every effort should be made to use an alternate method (e.g., longer detour), when feasible. When it becomes necessary to cross a stream, a well-planned approach will minimize the damage to the stream bank and will reduce erosion. The design of temporary stream crossings requires knowledge of the design flows and other information; therefore, a professional engineer and specific state and local requirements should be consulted. State and local jurisdictions may require a separate permit for temporary stream crossings; contact them directly to learn about their exact requirements.

The specific loads and the stream conditions will dictate what type of stream crossing to employ. Bridges are the preferred method to cross a stream because they provide the least obstruction to flows and fish migration.

The cost of temporary stream crossings will vary widely according to the size of the stream, the type of equipment using the stream crossing, and other factors. Typically, costs range from $500 to $1500, but they may be much higher.

### Temporary storm drain diversions

A *temporary storm drain* is a pipe which redirects an existing storm drain system or outfall channel to discharge into a sediment trap or basin.

Use storm drain diversions to temporarily divert flow going to a permanent outfall. This diverted flow should be directed to a sediment-trapping device. A temporary storm drain diversion should remain in place as long as the area draining to the storm sewer remains disturbed. Another method is to delay completion of the permanent outfall and instead use temporary diversions to a sediment-trapping device before discharge. Finally, a sediment trap or basin can be constructed below a permanent storm drain outfall. The basin is designed to trap any sediment before final discharge.

Since the existing storm drain systems will be modified, careful consideration should be given to the piping configuration and the resulting impact of installing a temporary storm drain diversion. The temporary diversions will also need to be moved, once the construction has ceased, and it is necessary to restore the original storm drainage systems. Therefore, appropriate restoration measures should be taken such as flushing the storm drain prior to removal of the sediment trap or basin, stabilizing the outfall, and restoration of grade areas. Finally, the state or local requirements should be consulted.

### Slope drains

Slope drains reduce the risk of erosion by discharging runoff to stabilized areas. Made of flexible or rigid pipe or paved chutes, they carry concentrated runoff from the top to the bottom of a slope that has already been damaged by erosion or is at high risk for erosion. Slope drains are also used to drain saturated slopes that have the potential for soil slides. Slope drains can be either temporary or permanent depending on the method of installation and the material used.

Pipe slope drains are appropriate in the following general locations:

- On cut or fill slopes before permanent storm water drainage structures have been installed
- Where earth dikes or other diversion measures have been used to concentrate flows
- On any slope where concentrated runoff crossing the face of the slope may cause gullies, channel erosion, or saturation of slide-prone soils
- As an outlet for a natural drainage way

Temporary pipe slope drains, usually made of flexible tubing or conduit, may be installed prior to the construction of permanent drainage structures. Permanent slope drains may be placed on or beneath the ground surface. Slope drains may be used with other devices, including diversion dikes or swales, sediment traps, and level spreaders (used to spread storm water runoff uniformly over the surface of the ground).

A slope drain constructed on the surface of the slope is called a *paved chute*; it may be covered with a surface of concrete or other impenetrable material. Figure 12.18 illustrates a typical paved chute.

Subsurface slope drains can be constructed of concrete, polyvinyl chloride, clay tile, corrugated metal, or other permanent material. Figure 12.19 illustrates a typical pipe slope drain.

The drainage area for the slope drain may be up to 10 acres; however, in many jurisdictions 5 acres is the recommended maximum. Some guidelines recommend that the slope drain design handle the peak runoff for the 10-year storm. Typical relationships between area and pipe diameter are shown in Table 12.4, although these will vary with local conditions.

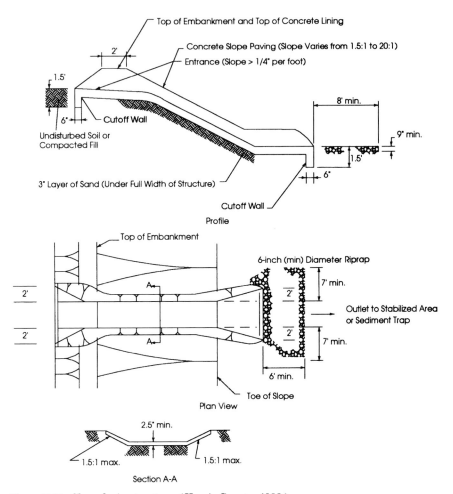

**Figure 12.18**  Slope drain structure. (*Harris County, 1992.*)

The following additional design guidelines may be applied to slope drains:

- *Dike:*  A dike is used to direct water into the pipe inlet and to prevent overtopping the slope. The height at the centerline of the earth dike should range from a minimum of 1.0 ft over the pipe to twice the diameter of the pipe measured from the invert of the pipe. It should also be at least 6 in higher than the adjoining ridge on either side. At no point along the dike will the elevation of the top of the dike be less than 6 in higher than the top of the pipe.

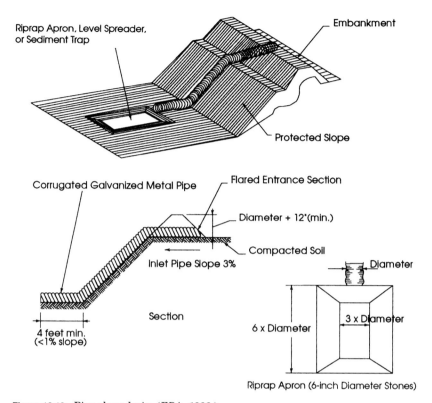

**Figure 12.19**   Pipe slope drain. (*EPA, 1992.*)

**TABLE 12.4.   Recommended Design of Pipe Slope Drains**

| Maximum drainage area, acres | Pipe diameter, in |
|:---:|:---:|
| 0.50 | 12 |
| 0.75 | 15 |
| 1.00 | 18 |

- *Inlet:*   The inlet of a pipe slope drain should be stabilized. A standard flared end section secured with a watertight fitting should be used for the inlet. A standard T-section fitting may also be used. Soil around and under the entrance section must be hand-tamped in 4- to 8-in lifts to the top of the dike to prevent piping failure around the inlet. Place filter cloth under the inlet, extend 5 ft in front of the inlet, and key in 6 in on all sides to prevent erosion. A 6-in metal toe-plate may also be used for this purpose.

- *Base:*   Place the pipe slope drain on undisturbed or well-compacted soil. Ensure firm contact between the pipe and the soil at all points by backfilling around and under the pipe with stable soil material hand compacted in lifts of 4 to 8 in. Securely stake the pipe slope drain to the slope, using grommets provided for this purpose at intervals of 10 ft or less.

- *Pipe material:* Pipe may be heavy-duty flexible tubing designed for this purpose, e.g., nonperforated corrugated plastic pipe, corrugated metal pipe, bituminous fiber pipe, or specially designed flexible tubing. Extension collars should be 12-in-long sections of corrugated pipe. Ensure that all slope drain sections are securely fastened together and have watertight fittings.

- *Discharge:* Extend the pipe beyond the toe of the slope, and discharge at a nonerosive velocity into a stabilized area or to a sedimentation trap or pond. The soil at the discharge end of the pipe should be stabilized with riprap (a combination of large stones, cobbles, and boulders). The riprap should be placed along the bottom of a swale which leads to a sediment-trapping structure or another stabilized area.

The slope drain should have a slope of 3 percent or more. Immediately stabilize all areas disturbed by installation or removal of the slope drain. Do not allow construction traffic to cross the slope drain, and do not place any material on it.

Pipe slope drain costs are generally based upon the pipe type and size (generally, flexible polyvinyl chloride at $5 per linear foot). Also added to this cost are any expenses associated with inlet and outlet structures.

Inspect the slope drain regularly and after every storm. Be sure that the inlet from the pipe is properly installed to prevent bypassing the inlet and undercutting the structure. If necessary, install a headwall, riprap, or sandbags around the inlet. Check the outlet point for erosion, and check the pipe for breaks or clogs. Install outlet protection if needed, and promptly clear breaks and clogs. Make any other necessary repairs. If a sediment trap has been provided, clean it out when the sediment level reaches one-third to one-half the design volume.

The slope drain should remain in place until the slope has been completely stabilized or up to 30 days following permanent slope stabilization.

### Subsurface drains

A *subsurface drain* is a perforated pipe or conduit placed beneath the surface of the ground at a designed depth and grade. It is used to drain an area by lowering the water table. A high water table can saturate soils and prevent the growth of certain types of vegetation. Saturated

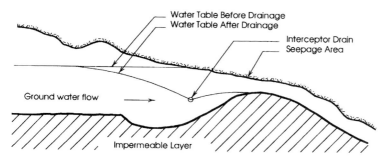

**Figure 12.20**  Effects of subsurface drains on the water table. (*EPA 1992.*)

soils on slopes will sometimes "slip" down the hill. Installing subsurface drains can help prevent these problems. Figure 12.20 illustrates the possible effects of subsurface drains on the water table.

Drains can be made of tile, pipe, or tubing. There are two types of subsurface drains: relief drains and interceptor drains.

*Relief drains* are used to dewater an area where the water table is high. They may be placed in a grid-iron, herringbone, or random pattern. Figure 12.21 illustrates several typical patterns.

*Interceptor drains* are used to remove water where sloping soils are excessively wet or subject to slippage. The drains are usually placed as single pipes instead of in patterns. Generally, subsurface drains are suitable only in areas where the soil is deep enough for proper installation. They are not recommended where they pass under heavy vehicle crossings.

Drains should be placed so that tree roots will not interfere with drainage pipes. The drain design should be adequate to handle the volume of flow. Areas disturbed by the installation of a drain should be stabilized, or else they, too, will be subject to erosion. The soil layer must be deep enough to allow proper installation.

Backfill immediately after the pipe is placed. The material used for backfill should be open granular soil that is highly permeable. The outlet should be stabilized and should direct sediment-laden storm water runoff to a sediment-trapping structure or another stabilized area.

Subsurface drain costs are generally based upon the pipe type and size (generally, drain pipe is about $2.25 per linear foot). Also added to this cost are installation and outlet costs.

Inspect subsurface drains on a regular schedule, and check for evidence of pipe breaks or clogging by sediment, debris, or tree roots. Remove any blockage immediately, replace any broken sections, and restabilize the surface. If the blockage is from tree roots, it may be nec-

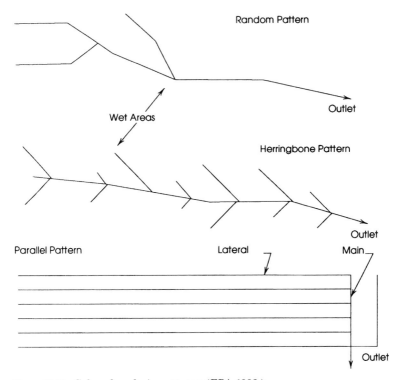

**Figure 12.21**  Subsurface drain patterns. (*EPA 1992.*)

essary to relocate the drain. Check inlets and outlets for sediment or debris. Remove and dispose of these materials properly.

## Permanent Storm Water Management Measures

Permanent storm water management controls are generally those controls which are installed during the construction process, but primarily result in reductions of pollutants in storm water discharged from the site after the construction has been completed.

Construction activities often result in a significant change in land use. These changes in land use typically involve an increase in the overall imperviousness of the site, which can result in dramatic changes in the runoff patterns of a site. As the amount of runoff from a site increases, the amount of pollutants carried by the runoff increases. In addition, activities such as automobile travel on roads can result in higher pollutant concentrations in runoff.

Major classes of storm water management controls include infiltration of runoff on the site; flow attenuation by vegetation or natural depressions; outfall velocity dissipation devices; storm water retention structures and artificial wetlands; and storm water detention structures. For many sites, a combination of these controls may be appropriate.

### Infiltration of runoff on site

A variety of infiltration technologies can be used to reduce the volume and pollutant loadings of storm water discharges from a site, including infiltration trenches and infiltration basins. Infiltration devices tend to mitigate changes to predevelopment hydrologic conditions. Properly designed and installed infiltration devices can reduce peak discharges, provide groundwater recharge, augment low-flow conditions of receiving streams, reduce storm water discharge volumes and pollutant loads, and protect downstream channels from erosion.

Infiltration devices are a feasible option where soils are permeable and the water table and bedrock are well below the surface. Infiltration basins can also be used as sediment basins during construction. Infiltration trenches can be more easily placed into underutilized areas of a development and can be used for small sites and infill developments. However, trenches may require regular maintenance to prevent clogs, particularly where grass inlets or other pollutant-removing inlets are not used. In some situations, such as low-density areas of parking lots, porous pavement can provide for infiltration.

### Flow attenuation by vegetation or natural depressions

Flow attenuation provided by vegetation or natural depressions can provide pollutant removal and infiltration and can lower the erosive potential of flows. Vegetative flow attenuation devices include grass swales and filter strips as well as trees that are either preserved or planted during construction.

Typically, the costs of vegetative controls are small relative to other storm water practices. The use of check dams incorporated into flow paths can provide additional infiltration and flow attenuation. Given the limited capacity to accept large volumes of runoff and the potential erosion problems associated with large concentrated flows, vegetative controls should typically be used in combination with other storm water devices.

Grass swales are typically used in low or medium residential development and highway medians as an alternative to curb and gutter drainage systems.

### Outfall velocity dissipation devices

Outfall velocity dissipation devices include riprap and stone or concrete flow spreaders, described earlier in this chapter. Outfall velocity dissipation devices slow the flow of water discharged from a site to lessen the amount of erosion caused by the discharge.

### Storm water retention structures

Properly designed and maintained storm water retention structures, also referred to as *wet ponds,* can achieve a high removal rate of sediment, biochemical oxygen demand, organic nutrients, and metals. Retention basins are most cost-effective in larger, more intensively developed sites.

### Retention structures and artificial wetlands

Retention structures include ponds and artificial wetlands that are designed to maintain a permanent pool of water. Properly installed and maintained retention structures (also known as wet ponds) and artificial wetlands can achieve a high removal rate of sediment, biochemical oxygen demand, organic nutrients, and metals and are most cost-effective when used to control runoff from larger, intensively developed sites. These devices rely on settling and biological processes to remove pollutants.

### Water quality detention structures

Storm water detention structures include extended detention ponds, which control the rate at which the pond drains after a storm event. Extended detention ponds are usually designed to completely drain in about 24 to 40 h, and they remain dry at other times. They can provide pollutant removal efficiencies that are similar to those of retention ponds. Extended detention systems are typically designed to provide both water quality and water quantity (flood control) benefits. See Fig. 12.22.

**Figure 12.22**    Storm water detention basin.

# References

Environmental Protection Agency: *Storm Water Management for Construction Activities: Developing Pollution Prevention Plans and Best Management Practices,* EPA Report 832/R-92/005, September 1992.

Harris County / Harris County Flood Control District / City of Houston: *Storm Water Management Handbook for Construction Activities,* September 17, 1992.

# 13

# Other Storm Water Pollution Prevention Measures

This is the last of five chapters which deal with the specific requirements for storm water discharges from construction facilities. This chapter describes pollution prevention measures for construction sites other than erosion and sediment control.

## Best Management Practices for Construction Sites

Erosion and sediment are not the only potential sources of pollution from construction activity. Other pollutants, including toxic chemicals, may be present during construction. The controls and practices which limit the discharge of pollutants in storm water are called *best management practices* (BMPs). BMPs are an important part of site-specific controls in a storm water pollution prevention plan (SWPPP). The BMPs in this chapter deal with prevention—limiting contact between storm water and potential pollutants. There are no specific BMPs that are applicable to all construction sites. Only the controls which best address site-specific conditions should be implemented to control or eliminate contamination of storm water.

There are several areas of control (in addition to erosion and sedimentation controls and storm water management) that should be addressed in each SWPPP:

1. *Materials management:* Provide protected storage areas for chemicals, paints, solvents, fertilizers, and other potentially toxic materials.

2. *Waste disposal:*   Provide waste receptacles at convenient locations and provide regular collection of wastes, including building material wastes.

3. *Off-site tracking:*   Minimize off-site tracking of sediments.

4. *Spill prevention and response:*   Make adequate preparations, including training and equipment, to contain spills of oil and hazardous materials.

5. *Sanitation:*   Comply with applicable state or local waste disposal, sanitary sewer, or septic system regulations.

6. *Non-storm-water discharges:*   Use appropriate pollution prevention measures for allowable non-storm-water components of discharge.

Most of these measures involve the day-to-day operations of the construction site. These operations are usually under the control of the general contractor. Therefore, the measures described in this chapter commonly are carried out or directly supervised by the general contractor. However, depending upon the language of the NPDES permit for the construction project, the owner of the project may still be fully responsible for these measures.

Many BMPs could be described as what EPA terms *good housekeeping. Good housekeeping involves keeping a clean, orderly construction site.* One of the first steps toward preventing storm water contamination is to improve housekeeping practices and use common sense. Good housekeeping practices reduce the possibility of accidental spills, improve the response time if there is a spill, and reduce safety hazards as well. Good housekeeping practices are generally inexpensive, relatively easy to implement, and often effective in preventing storm water contamination.

Pollutants that may enter water from construction sites due to poor housekeeping include oils; grease; paints; gasoline; concrete truck wash-down; raw materials used in the manufacture of concrete, including sand, aggregate, and cement; solvents; litter, debris, and sanitary wastes.

## Materials Management

On a construction site, *the material storage area can become a major source of risk* due to possible mishandling of materials or accidental spills. An inventory should be made of the material storage area and of the site. Special care should be taken to identify any materials that have the potential to come in contact with storm water. This will help to raise employee awareness and plan effective controls. See Fig. 13.1.

**Figure 13.1** Construction material (topsoil) stored under highway overpass to reduce storm water contact.

Some of the materials commonly found on a construction site include pesticides, petroleum products, fertilizers and detergents (nutrients), construction chemicals, other pollutants, and hazardous products. (See Fig. 13.2.) The materials inventory list should include these for risk assessment. These questions should be addressed when risks are identified:

- What types of materials are stored on the site?
- How long will the materials be stored before use?
- Are all the materials really needed?
- Can a smaller quantity of each material be stored on the site?
- How are the materials stored and distributed?
- How can potential storm water contact be avoided?

### Storage of pesticides

Pesticides include insecticides, rodenticides, and herbicides which are often used on construction sites. The management practices used to reduce the amounts of pesticides that could contact storm water include the following:

- Handle pesticides as infrequently as possible.
- Leave pesticides in their original shipping containers whenever possible, because those containers often have special handling instructions printed on them.

**Figure 13.2**   Weatherproof material and equipment storage container at construction site.

- Observe all applicable federal, state, and local regulations when using, handling, or disposing of pesticides.
- Store pesticides in a dry, covered area.
- Provide curbs or dikes to contain the pesticide if it should spill.
- Have measures on site to contain and clean up spills of pesticides.
- Strictly follow recommended pesticide application rates and methods.

### Storage of petroleum products

Oil, gasoline, lubricants, and asphaltic substances such as paving materials are petroleum products. These materials should be handled carefully to minimize their exposure to storm water. Petroleum products usually are found in two site areas:

1. Areas where road construction of some type is occurring
2. Vehicle storage areas or areas of on-site fueling or equipment maintenance

These management practices will help reduce the risks of using petroleum products:

- Have equipment to contain and clean up petroleum spills in fuel storage areas or on board maintenance and fueling vehicles.

- Where possible, store petroleum products and fuel vehicles in covered areas, and construct dikes to contain any spills. (See Fig. 13.3.)

- Contain and clean up petroleum spills immediately.

- Perform preventive maintenance for on-site equipment to prevent leakage (e.g., check for and fix gas or oil leaks in construction vehicles on a regular basis).

- Apply asphaltic substances properly, according to the manufacturer's instructions.

### Storage of fertilizers and detergents (nutrients)

Nutrients such as phosphorus and nitrogen are found on construction sites in both fertilizers and detergents. Fertilizers are needed on construction sites to provide the nutrients for plant growth; however, when excess quantities of fertilizers are used or when fertilizers are washed away by storm water runoff, they may be a major source of pollution. An excess of nutrients reaching a body of water can cause an overgrowth of water plants, which then use up the oxygen in the water,

**Figure 13.3** Petroleum storage area without containment dikes or curbs.

creating an unfavorable environment. These steps can be taken to reduce the risks of nutrient pollution:

- Limit the application of fertilizers to the minimum area and the minimum recommended amounts.
- Reduce exposure of nutrients to storm water runoff by working the fertilizer deep into the soil (depth of 4 to 6 in) instead of letting it remain on the surface.
- Apply fertilizer more frequently, but at lower application rates.
- Limit hydroseeding, in which lime and fertilizers are applied to the ground surface in one application.
- Implement good erosion and sediment control to help reduce the amount of fertilizers lost as a result of erosion.
- Limit the use of detergents on the site. Wash water containing detergents should not be discharged in the storm water system. (*Note:* The EPA general permit for storm water discharges from construction sites prohibits the discharge of wash waters containing detergent residues, as discussed later in this chapter.)
- Apply fertilizer and use detergents only in the recommended manner and amounts.

### Storage of hazardous products

Hazardous materials include (but are not limited to) paints, acids for cleaning masonry surfaces, cleaning solvents, chemical additives used for soil stabilization, and concrete curing compounds. Most problem situations involving hazardous materials and other pollutants are the result of carelessness or not using common sense. These practices will help to avoid pollution of storm water by these materials:

- Have equipment to contain and clean up spills of hazardous materials in the areas where these materials are stored or used.
- Contain and clean up spills immediately after they occur.
- Keep materials in a dry, covered area. Store materials in the original manufacturer's containers whenever possible, because special handling instructions are often printed on these containers. (See Fig. 13.4.)

## Waste Disposal

Proper management and disposal of building materials and other construction site wastes is an important part of pollution prevention. The EPA general permit for storm water discharges from construction sites

**Figure 13.4**   Uncovered drum storage area at a construction site.

prohibits the discharge of *floatables* (floating objects) in storm water. (See Fig. 13.5.) Waste materials are generally the largest sources of floatables.

Construction wastes include surplus or refuse building materials as well as hazardous wastes. Possible management practices for these construction wastes include trash disposal, recycling, material handling, and spill prevention and cleanup measures. Controls and practices should also meet other federal, state, and local requirements.

Construction projects tend to generate a great deal of solid waste material which is unique to this activity. Construction wastes may include but are not limited to the following:

- Trees and shrubs removed during clearing and grubbing or other phases of construction

- Packaging materials (including wood, paper, plastic, etc.)

- Scrap or surplus building materials, e.g., scrap metals, rubber, plastic and glass pieces, masonry products, and other solid waste materials

- Paints and paint thinners

- Materials resulting from the demolition of structures (rubble)

The following steps will help ensure proper disposal of construction wastes:

- *Collection area:*   Select a designated waste collection area on the site.

- *Covered containers:*  Provide an adequate number of containers with lids or covers that can be placed over the container prior to rainfall. Whenever possible, locate containers in a covered area. (See Fig. 13.6.)

- *Collection:*  Arrange for waste collection before containers overflow.

- *Spill response:*  If a container spills or overflows, clean up immediately.

- *Adjust collection activity:*  Plan for additional containers and more frequent pickups during the demolition phase of construction.

- *Disposal:*  Ensure that construction waste is collected, removed, and disposed of only at authorized disposal areas.

- *Subcontractor participation:*  Since painting and many other waste-generating construction activities are often performed by subcontractors, make sure that the subcontractors are aware of the requirements of the NPDES permit for the construction project. *All* subcontractors should sign the subcontractor's certification. (See Chap. 9.)

Check with the local solid waste management agency for specific guidance.

**Figure 13.5**  Floatable debris discharged from a construction site.

**Figure 13.6**   Open waste disposal container at a construction site.

### Disposal of hazardous products

Many of the materials found at a construction site may be hazardous to the environment or to personnel. It is always important to *read the labels of the materials or products kept on the site.* At a minimum, consider paints, acids for cleaning masonry surfaces, cleaning solvents, chemical additives used for soil stabilization (e.g., palliative such as calcium chloride), and concrete curing compounds and additives to be hazardous substances.

The following management practices will help avoid problems associated with the disposal of hazardous materials:

- Check with local waste management authorities to determine the requirements for disposing of hazardous materials.

- Use all the product before disposing of the container.

- Do not remove the original product label from the container; it often contains important information.

- Do not mix products unless it is specifically recommended by the manufacturer.

- Follow the manufacturer's recommended method for disposal, which is often found on the label.

### Disposal of contaminated soils

*Contaminated soils* are soils which have been exposed to and still contain hazardous substances. Contaminated soils may be encountered on the site during earthmoving activities or during the cleanup of a spill or leak of a hazardous product. Material storage areas may also have been contaminated by undetected spills. The nature of the contaminants may or may not be known.

State or local solid waste regulatory agencies should be contacted concerning information and procedures necessary to treat or dispose of contaminated soils. Some landfills may accept contaminated soil; however, laboratory tests may be required before a final decision is made. Private firms can also be consulted concerning disposal options.

### Disposal of waste concrete

Most construction projects include some sort of concrete work. Usually, concrete is mixed off site and delivered to the project by mixer truck. The concrete is poured, and there is a residual amount of concrete remaining in the truck. Sometimes, excess concrete is delivered, or the concrete is found to be unacceptable and is rejected by the construction inspector or foreman. The truck must be cleaned and the residual concrete dumped before it "sets up" (hardens) in the truck.

Emptying or washout of excess concrete may be allowed on the site. *Excess concrete and wash water should be disposed of in a manner that prevents contact between these materials and storm water which will be discharged from the site.* For example, dikes could be constructed around the area to contain these materials until they harden, at which time they may be properly disposed of.

If possible, a beneficial use of waste concrete should be found. For example, an area may be set aside where waste concrete can be poured into simple forms to make riprap for channel or outlet protection. Concrete-mixer truck drivers are often under pressure to eliminate waste concrete; providing a beneficial use can reduce or eliminate illicit dumping.

### Disposal of sandblasting grits

Sandblasting is a commonly used technique to remove paint, dirt, etc., from surfaces. Sand is sprayed on the surface to be cleaned. Sandblasting grits consist of both the spent sand and the particles of paint and dirt removed from the surface. *Sandblasting grits are hazardous waste if they were used to clean old structures where lead-, cadmium-, or chrome-based paints were used.*

Sandblasting grits containing hazardous materials should not be washed into the storm or sanitary sewer. A licensed waste management or transport and disposal firm should be contacted to dispose of this type of used grit.

## Off-Site Vehicle Tracking

The EPA general permit for storm water discharges from construction sites states that off-site vehicle tracking of sediments shall be minimized. Stabilized construction entrances and construction access road stabilization can be used to reduce off-site vehicle tracking. In addition to these measures, paved streets adjacent to the site should be swept to remove any excess mud, dirt, or rock tracked from the site. Also deliveries or other traffic may be scheduled at a time when site personnel are available to provide cleanup if necessary.

### Stabilized construction entrance

A *stabilized construction entrance* is a portion of the construction road which is made of filter fabric and large stone. The primary purpose of a stabilized construction entrance is to reduce the amount of soil tracked off the construction site by vehicles leaving the site. The rough surface of the stone will shake and pull the soil off the vehicles' tires as they drive over the entrance. The stone will also reduce erosion and rutting on the portion of the road where it is installed by protecting the soil below.

The filter fabric separates the stone from the soil below, preventing the large stone from being ground into the soil. The fabric also reduces the amount of rutting caused by the vehicle tires by spreading the weight of the vehicles over a larger soil area than just the tire width.

A stabilized construction entrance should be installed (before construction begins on site) *at every point where traffic leaves or enters a disturbed area.* This measure is appropriate in the following locations:

- Wherever vehicles are leaving a construction site and enter onto a public road. If the number of vehicles is less than about 24 per day, then a stabilized construction entrance may not be necessary.

- At any unpaved entrance or exit location where there is risk of transporting mud or sediment onto paved roads.

A stabilized construction entrance should not be installed over an existing pavement (except for a slight overlap). Where the construction will require a permanent access road or driveway, a stabilized construction entrance should be installed before the permanent pavement. See Fig. 13.7.

Figure 13.8 illustrates a typical stabilized construction entrance. Stabilized construction entrances should be wide enough and long enough that the largest construction vehicle will fit in the entrance with room to spare. The width should be at least 10 to 12 ft, or across the entire width of the access. At sites where traffic volume is high, the entrance should be wide enough for two vehicles to pass safely. The length should be 50 to 75 ft. The entrance should be flared where it meets the existing road to provide a turning radius.

If vehicles will be turning onto the paved road or drive from the stabilized construction entrance, an apron should be provided so that vehi-

**Figure 13.7**  Stabilized construction entrance.

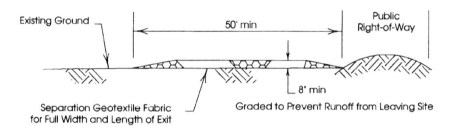

Existing Ground

50' min

Public
Right-of-Way

8' min

Separation Geotextile Fabric
for Full Width and Length of Exit

Graded to Prevent Runoff from Leaving Site

PROFILE VIEW

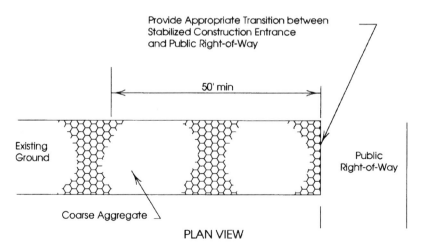

Provide Appropriate Transition between
Stabilized Construction Entrance
and Public Right-of-Way

50' min

Existing
Ground

Public
Right-of-Way

Coarse Aggregate

PLAN VIEW

**Figure 13.8**  Stabilized construction entrance details. (*Harris County, 1992.*)

cles do not go off the stabilized construction entrance before they leave the site.

If the stabilized construction entrance has to cross a swale or stream, then a stream crossing should be provided.

Stabilized construction entrances cost from $1500 to $5000. The following steps are required in the construction of a stabilized construction entrance:

1. *Site preparation:* Clear all vegetation, roots, and other obstructions in preparation for grading. Prior to placing geotextiles, make sure that the entrance is properly graded and compacted.

2. *Geotextile:* To reduce maintenance and loss of aggregate, place geotextiles over the existing ground before placing the stone for the entrance. Table 13.1 lists the required properties of the geotextile.

3. *Stone:* Crushed stone (2 to 4 in in diameter) should be placed to a depth of 6 in or greater for the entire width and length of the entrance. Stone used for the construction entrance should be large enough that it is does not get picked up and tracked off the site by vehicle traffic. Sharp-edged stone should not be used, so as to avoid puncturing tires.

4. *Drainage:* Runoff from a stabilized construction entrance should drain to a sediment trap or sediment basin. If a culvert is placed under the entrance to handle runoff, fill should be placed along the entire length of the culvert to protect it from damage.

5. *Vehicle wash rack:* The construction entrance may be provided with a vehicle wash rack which drains to a temporary sediment trap or other sediment-removing measure. This will allow vehicle tires to be washed prior to leaving the site and will ensure that wash water sediments are removed and can be properly disposed of. Vehicle wash racks, if required, cost about $2000 each.

Stabilized construction entrances should be inspected on a regular basis and after there has been a high volume of traffic or a storm event. Additional stone must be applied periodically and when repair is required. Sediments or any other materials tracked onto the public

**TABLE 13.1.    Geotextile requirements for stabilized construction entrance**

| Physical property | Requirements |
| --- | --- |
| Grab tensile strength | 220 lb (ASTM D1682) |
| Elongation failure | 60% (ASTM D1682) |
| Mullen burst strength | 430 lb (ASTM D3768) |
| Puncture strength | 125 lb (ASTM D751) (modified) |
| Equivalent opening size | 40–80 (U.S. standard sieve) (CW-02215) |

roadway should be removed immediately. Ensure that associated sediment control measures are in good working condition.

### Construction road stabilization

A *stabilized construction road* is a road built to provide a means for construction vehicles to move around the site without causing significant erosion. A stabilized construction road is designed to be well drained so that water does not puddle or flood the road during wet weather. It typically will have a swale along one side or both sides of the road, to collect and carry away runoff. Stabilized construction roads should have a layer of crushed stone or gravel which will cover and protect the soil below from erosion.

A stabilized construction road should be installed in a disturbed area where a high volume of construction traffic is expected. A construction road should be stabilized at the beginning of construction and maintained throughout construction. Construction parking areas should be stabilized as well as the roads. A stabilized construction road should not be located in a cut or fill area until after grading has been performed.

Stabilized construction roads should be built to conform to the site grades; this will require a minimum amount of cut and fill. They should also be designed so that the side slopes and road grades are not excessively steep. Construction roads should not be constructed in areas which are wet or on highly erodible soils.

### Spill Prevention and Response

Spills are a source of storm water contamination, and construction site spills are no exception. Spills can contaminate soil and water, waste materials, and result in potential health risks.

The following measures are appropriate for a spill prevention and response plan:

- *Materials management:* Store and handle materials to prevent spills. Tightly seal containers. Make sure all containers are clearly labeled. Stack containers neatly and securely.

- *Employee training:* Identify personnel responsible for responding to a spill of toxic or hazardous materials. Provide personnel with spill response training. Post the names of spill response personnel. Ensure that cleanup procedures are clearly posted.

- *Spill containment:* Contain any liquid. Stop the source of the spill. Reduce storm water contact if there is a spill.

- *Spill cleanup:*   Cover the spill with absorbent material such as kitty litter or sawdust. Have cleanup materials readily available. Keep the spill area well ventilated. If necessary, use a private firm that specializes in spill cleanup.

- *Disposal:*   Dispose of contaminated materials according to the manufacturer's instructions or state or local requirements.

- *Spill reporting:*   Check the spill reporting requirements listed in the permit. Typically any spill should be reported.

### Sanitary and Septic Disposal

Almost all construction sites have temporary sanitary facilities for on-site personnel. There are three main types:

1. *Portable facilities* that store the sanitary wastes and must be emptied periodically. (See Fig. 13.9.) Domestic waste haulers should be contracted to regularly remove the sanitary and septic wastes and to maintain the facilities in good working order. This will prevent overloading of the system which could allow discharges to storm water

**Figure 13.9**   Portable sanitary facility for construction personnel.

runoff. The state may have a licensing program for waste haulers. If so, only licensed haulers should be used; if not, a reputable hauler should be chosen.

2. *Facilities that employ septic systems* for treatment and disposal of sewage. Wastes should be treated to an appropriate level before discharge. Malfunctioning septic tanks may be a more significant surface runoff pollution problem than a groundwater problem. This is because a malfunctioning septic system is less likely to cause groundwater contamination where a bacterial mat in the soil retards the downward movement of wastewater. Surface malfunctions are caused by clogged or impermeable soils or occur when stopped-up or collapsed pipes force untreated wastewater to the surface. Surface malfunctions can vary in degree from occasional damp patches on the surface to constant pooling or runoff of wastewater. These discharges have high bacteria, nitrate, and nutrient levels and can contain a variety of household chemicals.

3. *Facilities that discharge to a sanitary sewer system.* Facilities should be properly hooked into the sanitary sewer system to prevent illicit discharges.

Untreated, raw sewage or seepage should never be discharged or buried on the site. Sanitary or septic wastes that are generated on the site should be treated or disposed of in accordance with state or local requirements. Many states have regulations concerning *on-site disposal systems* (OSDSs) or discharges to sanitary sewers. Localities often have ordinances which deal with the proper management of sanitary and septic wastes. In addition, if sewage is being discharged to the sanitary sewer, the local *publicly owned treatment works* (POTWs) should be contacted because they may have certain requirements as well.

Contact the proper authorities prior to the development of the SWPPP for the information needed to demonstrate compliance with the appropriate regulations.

## Non-Storm-Water Discharges

NPDES storm water permits for construction activities typically prohibit most non-storm-water discharges. Permits will state that all discharges covered by the permit must be composed entirely of storm water. However, permits may list some non-storm-water discharges that, when combined with storm water discharges, may be authorized by the permit. *These non-storm-water discharges may be allowed,* provided they are addressed in the SWPPP for the site. Common construction activity discharges that fall under the allowable non-storm-water discharges include the following:

- *Fire flows* from fire-fighting activities

- *Fire hydrant and waterline flushing* from the flushing or disinfection of existing or newly installed potable water piping systems

- *Uncontaminated groundwaters* from dewatering of excavated areas

- *Foundation and footing drain discharges* from subsurface drainage systems, where flows are not contaminated with materials such as solvents

- *Natural groundwater discharges,* such as springs, riparian habitats, and wetlands

- *Irrigation tailwater:* Irrigation water discharged during seeding and planting practices

- *Building wash water:* New construction exterior building wash-down discharges, without detergents or other contaminants

- *Pavement wash waters* from dust control and general housekeeping practices, where spills or leaks of toxic or hazardous materials have not occurred and where detergents are not used

- *Air-conditioning condensate* (but not including cooling water from cooling towers, heat exchangers, or other sources)

There are three choices for handling non-storm-water discharges which are not allowed by the NPDES storm water discharge permit:

1. Eliminate the source of the discharge.
2. Apply for a separate NPDES permit for the discharge.
3. Direct the discharge to a sanitary sewer system, after checking with the operator of the sewer system to see whether the material in question can be discharged into the sanitary sewer.

The allowable non-storm-water discharges should be identified in the SWPPP. *For each of the discharges, practices or controls that will be used to prevent pollution from these discharges should be described in detail.* Pollution prevention measures are not required to be identified and implemented for non-storm-water flows from fire-fighting activities, because these flows will generally be unplanned emergency situations where it is necessary to take immediate action to protect the public. The following general practices should be considered to prevent pollution from these discharges:

- All downslope site sedimentation and erosion controls should be in place prior to the discharge.

- Discharges with sediment loads should be discharged so that sediment pollution is minimized. These discharges include dewatering operation discharges and discharges from sediment traps and basins.

- Discharge should be directed only to areas that are stabilized to minimize erosion (e.g., buffer zones, vegetated filter strips, inlet and outlet protection, level spreaders). Do not discharge non-storm-water flows onto disturbed areas.

- Discharges with sediment should be directed to pass through a sediment filtering device. Sediment filtering devices include sediment traps, basins, silt fences, vegetated filter strips, sump pits, and sediment tanks.

At some locations, acid and alkaline solutions from exposed soil or rock units may be a problem. The control of these pollutants involves good site planning and preconstruction geological surveys. Sealing fractures in the bedrock with grout and bentonite will often reduce the amount of acid or alkaline seepage. The remaining runoff may have to be chemically neutralized.

### Dewatering discharges

*Dewatering* is the method used to remove and discharge excess water from a construction site. The most common procedure used is to pump water out of excavated areas, sediment basins, and sediment traps. Dewatering may also include methods used to lower the groundwater table to provide a stabilized area for construction.

Dewatering discharges usually have a very high sediment content; therefore, sediment control should be provided before the discharge enters a receiving water.

Water remaining in excavated areas may be eliminated by dewatering so that construction can proceed on schedule. Sediment traps and basins are often used to remove sediment from dewatering of excavation areas.

Dewatering may be used to remove accumulated water and sediments from sediment traps and basins to ensure their effectiveness throughout the entire project. At the end of the project, dewatering of sediment traps and basins is appropriate prior to removal of the last sediment control measures. Filtering should also be provided when discharge results from dewatering a sediment trap or basin. Methods of filtering the discharge from dewatering a sediment trap or basin include the following:

1. *Sump pit:* This is the preferred method of sediment control for dewatering discharges. The following section provides details.

2. *Floating suction hose:* This is an apparatus which allows clean water at the surface to be pumped out before the hose sinks low enough to pick up sediment-laden water.

3. *Standpipe:* A vertical pipe is attached to the base of the sediment basin riser with slits to control inflow and wrapping of filter fabric to aid in filtering sediments.

**Sump pits**

A *sump pit* is a temporary hole or pit placed so that it can collect water from sediment traps and basins or excavations. In the center of the pit is a slotted or perforated standpipe surrounded by stone. Water that collects in the pit flows through the gravel into the standpipe and is pumped out to a filtering device or, in some cases, directly to a receiving water.

A sump pit may be used to dewater a sediment trap or basin, or it may be used during construction when water collects in an excavation. The number of sump pits and their location will depend on the individual site and any state or local requirements. The standpipe should have holes in it to allow water to flow in and should be extended at least 1 ft over the top of the pit to prevent overflows into the top of the standpipe. If the sump pit is to discharge directly into a receiving water, then the standpipe should be wrapped in filter fabric before the pit is backfilled with stone.

Figure 13.10 illustrates a typical sump pit. The estimated cost of a sump pit ranges from $500 to about $7000, depending upon soil conditions and other factors.

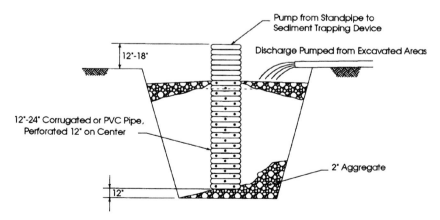

**Figure 13.10** Sump pit for dewatering discharges. (*EPA 1992.*)

## References

Environmental Protection Agency: *Storm Water Management for Construction Activities: Developing Pollution Prevention Plans and Best Management Practices,* EPA Report 832/R-92/005, September 1992.

Harris County / Harris County Flood Control District / City of Houston: *Storm Water Management Handbook for Construction Activities,* September 17, 1992.

# 14

# Storm Water
# Permit Requirements
# for Each State

This chapter provides specific storm water permitting requirements for each state. Rather than describe all the requirements for each state, however, this chapter highlights only those areas in which a particular state's requirements differ from the EPA requirements. Therefore, it is most beneficial to review this chapter after you have already become familiar with the EPA requirements for storm water discharges from industrial facilities (as described in Chaps. 4 through 8) or construction sites (as described in Chaps. 9 through 13).

## Role of the States in NPDES Permitting

The Clean Water Act of 1972 provided for the transfer of some NPDES permitting authority from the federal government to the states. Subsequent amendments to the Clean Water Act (CWA) have allowed and encouraged states to accept greater roles in NPDES permitting. For example, states could not administer the program as it applied to federally owned or operated facilities before 1977, when Congress amended section 313 of the CWA to allow states to have this authority [Jessup, 1990].

The federal Water Quality Act of 1987 also encouraged the transfer of authority to the states, because for the first time Congress authorized the EPA to transfer partial NPDES permitting authority to states. In other words, a state could assume authority for a major category of discharges or a major component of the NPDES program, even though that state was not prepared to fully enforce all other aspects of the NPDES permit program. Congress also allowed for phased program approval over a 5-year period [Jessup, 1990].

As a result of the consistent transfer of NPDES permitting authority from the EPA to the states since 1972, most states are now authorized to manage their own NPDES programs for industrial facilities. However, at the time of this writing, the following states and territories still lack their own NPDES permitting authority: Alaska, Arizona, Florida, Idaho, Louisiana, Maine, New Hampshire, New Mexico, Oklahoma, South Dakota, and Texas; the District of Columbia; the territories of American Samoa, Guam, Northern Mariana Islands, and Puerto Rico. The federal government continues to administer the NPDES permit program on most Native American lands in all states.

## Alabama

Alabama Department of Environmental Management
Water Quality Division
1751 Congressman W.L. Dickinson Drive
Montgomery, AL 36130
John Poole (205) 271-7852

Alabama is an NPDES-delegated state with general permitting authority. The Alabama Department of Environment Management (DEM) has issued 16 general permits for storm water discharges from different types of industries. Two DEM branches are involved in the administration of these permits:

- *DEM industrial branch:* Asphalt/concrete industries; inactive mining sites; lumber and wood products industries; portland cement and portland cement concrete industries; primary metals, metals fabrication, metals finishing industries; transportation terminals and warehousing activities; food and related substances industries; landfills; manufacturing of paint and related products; salvage and recycling activities; plastics and rubber industries; stone, glass, and clay industries; and textile industries.

- *DEM mining and non-point-source section:* Petroleum products and treated groundwater from cleanups involving petroleum products; nonmetallic, non-coal-mining activities; and construction sites and other land-disturbing activities.

To be covered by one of the general permits, a Notice of Intent (NOI), a permit fee, and proof of public notification of the permit application are required.

Within the state of Alabama, the following must obtain storm water discharge permits for their municipal separate storm sewer systems [58 FR 61146 (Nov. 19, 1993)]: Adamsville, Alabaster, Bessemer, Birmingham, Brighton, Brookside, Chickasaw, Creola, Daphne, Fairfield, Fairhope, Fultondale, Gardendale, Graysville, Helena, Homewood, Hoover, Hueytown, Huntsville, Indian Springs, Irondale, Leeds, Lipscomb, Madison, Maytown, Midfield, Mobile, Montgomery, Moody, Mountain Brook, Mulga, Pelham, Pleasant Grove, Prichard, Saraland, Satsuma, Tarrant, Trussville, Vestavia Hills, Baldwin County, Jefferson County (was listed in regulation; however, population dropped below 100,000 in 1990 census), Mobile County (unincorporated areas defined as beginning at the mouth of the South Fork Deer River and extending west to southwest (SW) corner, section 18, township 6 south, range 2 west, then north to northwest (NW) corner, section 6, township 2 south, range 2 west, then east to the Mobile County line, then south along the county line to U.S. Highway 90 bridge), Shelby County (all unincorporated areas of Shelby County within the drainage basin of the Cahaba River upstream of the confluence of Shoal Creek and the Cahaba River), St. Clair County (unincorporated areas of St. Clair County within the drainage basin of the Cahaba River), and the Alabama Highway Department.

## Alaska

Alaska Department of Environmental Conservation (DEC)
3220 Hospital Drive
P.O. Box O
Juneau, AK 99811-1800
(907) 465-2600; (907) 465-2696 (Environmental Quality Division)

Alaska does not have NPDES permitting authority. Therefore, the EPA final general permits are applicable within Alaska. However, the state has certain additional conditions which apply to storm water discharges.

Copies of Notices of Intent, discharge monitoring reports (DMRs), and reportable-quantity (RQ) releases must be sent to the appropriate regional office of the Alaska Department of Environmental Conservation (ADEC) as well as to the EPA region 10 office.

Construction NOIs in Alaska must describe the activities on site, the whole number of acres to be disturbed, the primary pollutants expected to be generated, and the type of treatment to be provided.

Active construction sites must be inspected monthly in arid areas and weekly in other areas, except that all construction sites must be inspected within 24 h of a significant storm event. Sites that have been stabilized must continue to be inspected monthly until a Notice of Termination is submitted for the site.

The Alaska municipality of Anchorage is required to obtain a municipal storm water discharge permit.

## Arizona

Arizona Department of Environmental Quality
Central Palm Plaza Building
2005 North Central Avenue
Phoenix, AZ 85004
(602) 257-2305; (602) 262-8012 (in-state 24-h number)

Arizona does not have NPDES permitting authority. Therefore, the EPA final general permits are applicable within Arizona. However, the state has certain additional conditions which apply to storm water discharges.

Notices of Intent and NOTs must be sent to the Arizona Department of Environmental Quality (DEQ) as well as to the EPA. This requirement applies to industrial as well as construction NOIs and NOTs.

Facilities with section 313 water priority chemicals must use appropriate measures to minimize discharges from liquid storage areas where storm water contacts tanks, containers, vessels, or equipment used to handle such chemicals. Appropriate measures may include secondary containment structures holding at least the volume of the largest single tank plus adequate freeboard to handle a 25-year, 24-h storm event; strong spill contingency and integrity testing plans; and/or equivalent measures.

Within Arizona, Glendale, Mesa, Phoenix, Scottsdale, Tempe, Tucson, Pima County, and the Arizona Department of Transportation must obtain storm water discharge permits for their municipal separate storm sewer systems [58 FR 61146 (Nov. 19, 1993)].

## Arkansas

Arkansas Department of Pollution Control and Ecology (DPCE)
Water Division
8001 National Drive
P.O. Box 8913
Little Rock, AR 72219-8913
Marysia Jastrzebski (501) 562-7444

Arkansas is a delegated NPDES state with general permitting authority. Two general permits are available for storm water discharges: one for construction sites and one for industrial facilities. The requirements of these Arkansas general permits are very similar to those for the baseline EPA general permits, except that the Arkansas industrial permit does not require semiannual sampling for any industrial discharges. Instead, annual sampling is required. However, Arkansas requires that some additional parameters be tested in the discharges of certain types of industries [Thompson Publishing Group, 1994]:

- *Primary metal industries:* 5-day biochemical oxygen demand (BOD).

- *Land disposal units, incinerators, boilers, and industrial furnaces:* Ammonia (as N) and nitrate plus nitrite nitrogen. (These facilities are not required to sample for total Kjeldahl nitrogen.)

- *Wood treatment facilities:*   5-day BOD.

Within Arkansas, the city of Little Rock must obtain storm water discharge permits for its municipal separate storm sewer system [58 FR 61146 (Nov. 19, 1993)].

## California

California Water Resources Control Board
Water Quality Division
P.O. Box 100
901 P Street
Sacramento, CA 95801
Archie Matthews (916) 657-1110; Leo Cosentini (916) 657-1009

California is a delegated NPDES state with general permitting authority. The state has issued two general permits: one for the construction industry and one for all other regulated industries. However, as the program develops, more industry-specific and watershed-specific permits will likely be issued by regional water quality boards. With some exceptions for certain inactive sites and sites which certify that they have no storm water exposure, industrial permittees are required to perform sampling and testing of at least two wet-season (October through April) storm events, in addition to various other monitoring activities. State regulations allow the formation of *group monitoring plans* in which at least 20 percent of a group of facilities is sampled in lieu of sampling the discharges of all facilities. In California, construction storm water discharge permits are issued to the owner of the construction site [Thompson Publishing Group, 1994].

Within California, the following must obtain storm water discharge permits for their municipal separate storm sewer systems [58 FR 61146 (Nov. 19, 1993)]: Agoura Hills, Alameda, Albany, Alhambra, Anaheim, Arcadia, Artesia, Atherton, Azusa, Bakersfield, Baldwin Park, Bell, Bellflower, Bell Gardens, Belmont, Berkeley, Beverly Hills, Big Bear Lake, Bradbury, Brentwood, Brisbane, Burbank, Burlingame,

Camarillo, Campbell, Carlsbad, Carson, Cerritos, Chula Vista, Claremont, Clayton, Colma, Commerce, Compton, Concord, Contra Costa County (15 cities), Coronado, Covina, Cudahy, Culver City, Cupertino, Daly City, Del Mar, Diamond Bar, Downey, Duarte, Dublin, East Palo Alto, El Cajon, El Monte, El Segundo, Emeryville, Encinitas, Escondido, Fairfield, Fillmore, Folsom, Foster City, Fremont, Fresno, Fullerton, Galt, Gardena, Garden Grove, Gilroy, Glendale, Glendora, Half Moon Bay, Hawaiian Gardens, Hawthorne, Hayward, Hermosa Beach, Hidden Hills, Hillsborough, Huntington Beach, Huntington Park, Imperial Beach, Industry, Inglewood, Irvine, Irwindale, La Canada Flintridge, Laguna Beach, Lake Tahoe Basin, Lakewood, La Mesa, La Mirada, La Palma, La Puente, La Verne, Lawndale, Lemon Grove, Livermore, Lomita, Long Beach, Los Alamitos, Los Altos, Los Altos Hills, Los Angeles, Los Gatos, Lynwood, Manhattan Beach, Maywood, Menlo Park, Millbrae, Milpitas, Modesto, Monrovia, Montebello, Monterey Park, Monte Sereno, Moorpark, Moreno Valley, Mountain View, National City, Newark, Norwalk, Oakland, Oceanside, Ojai, Ontario, Orange, Orange County (17 cities), Oxnard, Pacifica, Palo Alto, Palos Verdes Estates, Paramount, Pasadena, Pico Rivera, Piedmont, Pleasanton, Pomona, Port Hueneme, Poway, Rancho Cucamonga, Rancho Palos Verdes, Redondo Beach, Redwood City, Riverside, Riverside County (10 cities), Rolling Hills, Rolling Hills Estates, Rosemead, Sacramento, Salinas, San Bernardino, San Bernardino County (13 cities), San Bruno, San Carlos, San Diego, San Dimas, San Fernando, San Gabriel, San Jose, San Leandro, San Marcos, San Marino, San Mateo, Santa Ana, Santa Clara, Santa Clarita, Santa Fe Springs, Santa Monica, Santa Paula, Santa Rosa, Santee, Saratoga, Seal Beach, Sierra Madre, Signal Hill, Simi Valley, Solana Beach, South El Monte, South Gate, South Pasadena, South San Francisco, Stockton, Suisun City, Sunnyvale, Temple City, Thousand Oaks, Torrance, Union City, Vallejo, Vernon, Vista, Walnut, West Covina, West Hollywood, Westlake Village, Whittier, Woodside; Alameda, Contra Costa County, Kern County, Lake Tahoe Basin (two counties), Los Angeles County, Orange County, Riverside County, Sacramento County, San Bernardino County, San Diego County, San Mateo County, Santa Clara County, Ventura County; the Alameda County Flood Control District, zone 7 of the Alameda County Flood Control District, the California Department of Transportation, the Coachella Valley area, the Contra Costa County Flood Control District, the Orange County Flood Control District, the Riverside Flood Control District, the San Bernardino Flood Control District, the San Diego Unified Port District, and the Santa Clara Valley Water District.

## Colorado

Colorado Department of Health
Water Quality Control Division
4210 East 11th Avenue
Denver, CO 80220
Sara Plocher (303) 692-3609

Colorado is a delegated NPDES state with general permitting authority. Four or five general permits are available for storm water discharges from various categories of industry: heavy industry (those with
numeric effluent limitations), light industry, construction activity,
metal mining, nonmetallic mining, and surface coal mining. Permit
requirements are similar to those for the EPA baseline general permits
[Thompson Publishing Group, 1994].

Within Colorado, Aurora, Colorado Springs, Denver, Englewood,
Lakewood, Pueblo, Arapahoe County, the Colorado Department of
Transportation, and the Colorado Highway Department must obtain
storm water discharge permits for their municipal separate storm
sewer systems [58 FR 61146 (Nov. 19, 1993)].

## Connecticut

Connecticut Department of Environmental Protection (DEP)
Water Management Bureau
Water Discharge Management
165 Capitol Avenue
Hartford, CT 06106
Richard Mason (203) 566-7167

Connecticut is a delegated NPDES state with general permitting
authority. The state has issued two general permits for storm water
discharges: one for construction sites and the other for industrial activities. Any industrial site discharging within 100 ft of a nonfreshwater
tidal wetland must discharge through a system designed to store the
storm water runoff volume generated by 1 in of rainfall on the site.
General permit applications must be certified by an independent professional engineer registered to practice in the state [Thompson
Publishing Group, 1994].

At least 15 days' notice is required before construction can begin
under the general permit for construction activities. The construction
permit authorizes the discharges of construction site storm water
runoff and excavation dewatering discharges only. The construction
general permit requires the installation of a sediment basin for all dis-

turbed areas of 5 acres or more draining to a common discharge point. The basin must have a volume of 134 yd$^3$/acre of drainage area. This is approximately the same as the EPA baseline general permit requirement of 3600 ft$^3$/acre. The Connecticut construction permit requires that permanent storm water control measures be installed which will remove 80 percent of the total suspended solids from the storm water discharge after construction ends. Permanent velocity dissipation devices are also required [Thompson Publishing Group, 1994].

Industrial dischargers must perform semiannual sampling for the following constituents:

- Total oil and grease
- pH
- Chemical oxygen demand
- Total suspended solids
- Total phosphorus
- Total Kjeldahl nitrogen
- Nitrate as nitrogen
- Fecal coliform
- Total copper
- Total zinc
- Total lead
- Other pollutants listed in existing NPDES permits or effluent limitation guidelines for the facility

Additional requirements for acute toxicity testing apply under certain conditions [Thompson Publishing Group, 1994].

Within Connecticut, the city of Stamford must obtain a storm water discharge permit for its municipal separate storm sewer system [58 FR 61146 (Nov. 19, 1993)].

## Delaware

Delaware Department of Natural Resources and Environmental Control
Division of Water Resources
Water Pollution Control Branch
NPDES Storm Water Program
P.O. Box 1401
89 Kings Highway
Dover, DE 19903
Chuck Schadel (302) 739-5731

Delaware is a delegated NPDES state with general permitting authority. The state has issued a general permit for storm water discharges with two parts: part 1 for industrial activities and part 2 for construction activities. The state is developing industry-specific permit provisions for the following industries:

- Temporary asphalt and/or concrete batch plants at construction sites
- Extractive activities such as mining
- Wood products facilities
- Chemicals and related products
- Hazardous waste handling activities
- Recycling centers
- Transportation maintenance
- Food and related products
- Metal fabrication and manufacturing
- Textiles, printing, publishing, and warehousing and storage

At least 180 days' advance notice is required before permit coverage can be obtained for an industrial facility. Sampling is required only for facilities handling SARA Title III, section 313 water priority chemicals [Thompson Publishing Group, 1994].

For construction activities, the NOI must be submitted through an approved agency such as a state agency, conservation district, or municipality. This agency will review and approve the NOI and the related *sediment and storm water management plan* (SSMP). The state requires approved sediment control plans for all construction activities disturbing at least 5000 ft$^2$. Permanent storm water management measures are required to remove at least 80 percent of the total suspended solids from postconstruction discharges and must be designed for the 2-year, 10-year, and 100-year storm events. One employee from each construction site must attend a 3.5-h training course [Thompson Publishing Group, 1994].

Within Delaware, Arden, Ardencroft, Ardentown, Bellefonte, Delaware City, Elsmere, Middletown, Newark, New Castle, Newport, Odessa, Townsend, Wilmington, New Castle County, and the Delaware Department of Transportation must obtain storm water discharge permits for their municipal separate storm sewer systems [58 FR 61146 (Nov. 19, 1993)].

## District of Columbia

District of Columbia Environmental Control Division
Housing and Environmental Regulation Administration
Department of Consumer and Regulatory Affairs
2100 Martin Luther King Boulevard, SE
Washington, DC 20020
Program manager (202) 727-7395

The District of Columbia does not have NPDES permitting authority. Storm water permitting is performed through the EPA region 3 office in Philadelphia. The provisions of the EPA baseline general permits apply, except that dischargers may have to comply with additional requirements for nutrient removal and coal pile runoff.

In the District of Columbia, the city of Washington must obtain storm water discharge permits for its municipal separate storm sewer system.

## Florida

Florida Department of Environmental Regulation (DER)
Storm Water/Nonpoint Source Management Section
Twin Towers Office Building
2600 Blair Stone Road
Tallahassee, FL 32399-2400
Eric H. Livingston (904) 488-4805

Florida does not have NPDES permitting authority. Storm water permitting is performed through the EPA region 4 office in Atlanta. The provisions of the EPA baseline general permits apply, except that construction site operators must submit copies of the construction SWPPP to the appropriate state agency for approval. Permanent storm water management controls are required to achieve 80 to 95 percent removal of total suspended solids from postconstruction discharges, when the discharge enters certain designated streams. Construction site inspections are required as described in the EPA baseline general permit, except that the minimum depth of rainfall required for an additional inspection is 0.25 in rather than the EPA-specified 0.5 in. [Thompson Publishing Group, 1994].

Within Florida the following must obtain storm water discharge permits for their municipal separate storm sewer systems [58 FR 61146 (Nov. 19, 1993)]: Apopka, Atlantic Beach, Atlantis, Auburndale, Bal Harbour, Bartow, Bay Harbor Islands, Bay Lake, Belleair, Belleair Beach, Belleair Bluffs, Belle Glade, Belle Isle, Boca Raton, Boynton Beach, Briny Breezes, Century, Clearwater, Cloud Lake, Coconut Creek, Cooper City, Coral Gables, Coral Springs, Dania, Davenport, Davie,

Deerfield Beach, Delray Beach, Dundee, Dunedin, Eagle Lake, Eatonville, Edgewood, Fort Lauderdale, Fort Meade, Frostproof, Glen Ridge, Golden Beach, Golf, Golfview, Greenacres City, Gulfport, Gulf Stream, Haines City, Hallandale, Haverhill, Hialeah, Hialeah Gardens, Highland Beach, Highland Park, Hillcrest Heights, Hollywood, Homestead, Hypoluxo, Indian Creek, Indian Rocks Beach, Jacksonville Beach, Jacksonville, Juno Beach, Jupiter, Jupiter Inlet Colony, Key Biscayne, Kenneth City, Lake Alfred, Lake Buena Vista, Lake Clarke Shores, Lake Hamilton, Lakeland, Lake Park, Lake Wales, Lake Worth, Lantana, Largo, Lauderdale-by-the-Sea, Lauderdale Lakes, Lauderhill, Lighthouse Point, Longboat Key, Madeira Beach, Maitland, Manalapan, Mangonia Park, Margate, Medley, Miami, Miami Beach, Miami Shores, Miami Springs, Miramar, Mulberry, Neptune Beach, North Bay Village, North Lauderdale, North Miami, North Miami Beach, North Palm Beach, North Port, North Redington Beach, Oakland Park, Ocean Ridge, Ocoee, Oldsmar, Opa-locka, Orlando, Pahokee, Palm Beach, Palm Beach Gardens, Palm Beach Shores, Palm Springs, Parkland, Pembroke Park, Pembroke Pines, Pennsuco, Pensacola, Pinellas Park, Plantation, Plant City, Polk City, Pompano Beach, Redington Beach, Redington Shores, Riviera Beach, Royal Palm Beach, Safety Harbor, St. Petersburg Beach, St. Petersburg, Sarasota, Sea Ranch Lakes, Seminole, South Bay, South Miami, South Palm Beach, South Pasadena, Sunrise, Surfside, Sweetwater, Tallahassee, Tamarac, Tampa, Tarpon Springs, Temple Terrace, Tequesta, Treasure Island, Venice, West Miami, West Palm Beach, Wilton Manors, Winter Garden, Winter Haven, Winter Park; Broward County, Dade County, Escambia County, Hillsborough County, Lee County, Manatee County, Orange County, Palm Beach County, Pasco County, Pinellas County, Polk County, Sarasota County, Seminole County; the Florida Department of Transportation; and the urban water control districts.

## Georgia

Georgia Department of Natural Resources (DNR)
Environmental Protection Division (EPD)
Industrial Wastewater Program
Floyd Towers, East
205 Butler Street, SE
Atlanta, GA 30334
Will Salter (404) 656-4887

Georgia is a delegated NPDES state with general permitting authority. The state has issued separate general permits for storm discharges from construction sites and from industrial facilities. The construction

permit resulted in litigation because it failed to include effluent turbidity limitations as required under state law. Permit requirements
are similar to those for the EPA baseline general permits, except that
no industries are required to perform semiannual storm water sampling. There are also differences in the sampling parameters for certain
industries [Thompson Publishing Group, 1994].

Georgia state law requires permits for all activities disturbing land
areas of more than 1.1 acres, with certain exceptions. Specific requirements apply to the control of sediment from such activities [Thompson
Publishing Group, 1994].

Within Georgia, the following must obtain storm water discharge
permits for their municipal separate storm sewer systems [58 FR
61146 (Nov. 19, 1993)]: Acworth, Alpharetta, Atlanta, Austell,
Bloomingdale, Buford, Chamblee, Clarkston, College Park, Columbus,
Decatur, Doraville, Duluth, East Point, Fairburn, Forest Park, Garden
City, Hapeville, Jonesboro, Kennesaw, Lawrenceville, Lilburn,
Lithonia, Macon, Marietta, Morrow, Norcross, Palmetto, Payne,
Pooler, Powder Springs, Riverdale, Roswell, Savannah, Smyrna,
Snellville, Stone Mountain, Sugar Hill, Suwanee, Thunderbolt, Union
City; Bibb County, Chatham County, Clayton County, Cobb County,
DeKalb County, Fulton County, Gwinnett County, Muscogee County,
and Richmond County.

## Hawaii

Hawaii State Department of Health (DOH)
Clean Water Branch
P.O. Box 3378
1250 Punchbowl Street
Honolulu, HI 96801
Edward Chen (808) 586-4309

Hawaii is a delegated NPDES state with general permitting authority.
The state has issued separate general permits for storm water discharges from construction sites and from industrial facilities. The NOI
for general permit coverage must be submitted at least 90 days before
industrial or construction activities may begin. The construction NOI
is quite comprehensive, containing most of the elements normally
required for a storm water pollution prevention plan. The construction
general permit does not authorize any non-storm-water discharges;
separate permit coverage is required for excavation dewatering discharges and other non-storm-water discharges. All industrial dischargers must perform annual sampling and submit the discharge
monitoring reports for review.

Within Hawaii, Honolulu County and the Hawaii Department of Transportation must obtain storm water discharge permits for their municipal separate storm sewer systems [58 FR 61146 (Nov. 19, 1993)].

## Idaho

Idaho Department of Health and Welfare
Division of Environment
5150 Kendall Street
Boise, ID 83720
(208) 334-5840; Water Quality Bureau (208) 334-3860

Idaho does not have NPDES permitting authority. Therefore, the EPA final general permits are applicable within Idaho. In contrast to most other non-NPDES states, however, Idaho has not added conditions to the EPA general permits. Therefore, the EPA general permits represent the complete requirements within Idaho, except that storm water discharges must meet the state's water quality standards for groundwater.

Within Idaho, Boise City, Garden City, and the Idaho Department of Transportation must obtain storm water discharge permits for their municipal separate storm water sewer systems [58 FR 61146 (Nov. 19, 1993)].

## Illinois

Illinois Environmental Protection Agency (IEPA)
Water Pollution Control Division
2200 Churchill Road
P.O. Box 19276
Springfield, IL 62794-9276
Sue Epperson, Tim Kluge, or Rick Pinneo (217) 782-0610

Illinois is a delegated NPDES state with general permitting authority. The state has issued separate general permits for storm water discharges from construction sites and from industrial facilities. The requirements of these permits are very similar to those for the EPA general baseline permits. However, the Illinois permit for industrial discharges requires sampling as a part of the application process for certain industries. The Illinois permit does not require any storm water sampling after permit coverage is obtained. The NOI for industrial permit coverage must be submitted at least 180 days before the industrial operation begins. Annual inspection reports must be submitted to the state. The NOI for construction permit coverage must be submitted at least 48 h prior to the commencement of construction [Thompson Publishing Group, 1994].

Within Illinois, Rockford, Springfield, and the Illinois Department of Transportation must obtain storm water discharge permits for their municipal separate storm sewer systems [58 FR 61146 (Nov. 19, 1993)].

## Indiana

Indiana Department of Environmental Management (DEM)
Water Management Office
NPDES Permits Group
100 North Senate Avenue
P.O. Box 6015
Indianapolis, IN 46206
Laura Bieberich (317) 233-6725

Indiana is a delegated NPDES state with general permitting authority. The state has issued separate general permits for storm water discharges from construction sites and from industrial facilities. Permit requirements are similar to those for the EPA baseline general permits, except that all industrial facilities must sample one storm event before implementing the SWPPP and two additional storm events after implementation of the SWPPP. Thereafter, only semiannual visual inspections are required, unless the state determines that further sampling is needed. Industrial dischargers must submit annual reports [Thompson Publishing Group, 1994].

Within Indiana, Fort Wayne, Indianapolis, and the Indiana Department of Transportation must obtain storm water discharge permits for their municipal separate storm sewer systems [58 FR 61146 (Nov. 19, 1993)].

## Iowa

Iowa Department of Natural Resources (DNR)
Surface and Groundwater Protection Bureau
Wallace State Office Building
900 East Grand Avenue
Des Moines, IA 50319-0034
Monica Wnuk (515) 281-7017

Iowa is a delegated NPDES state with general permitting authority. The state has issued separate general permits for storm water discharges from construction sites and from industrial facilities. Permit requirements are similar to those for the EPA baseline general permits. However, the requirements for the NOI differ somewhat. For example, the applicant must submit proof that a public notice of the application has been published in at least two newspapers. In addition, the advance-notice requirement for industrial dischargers is 24 h. There are also differences in the sampling requirements and parameters for various industrial discharges [Thompson Publishing Group, 1994].

Within Iowa, Cedar Rapids, Davenport, and Des Moines must obtain storm water discharge permits for their municipal separate storm sewer systems [58 FR 61146 (Nov. 19, 1993)].

## Kansas

Kansas Department of Health and Environment
Water Bureau
Forbes Field, Building 740
Topeka, KS 66620
Don Carlson (913) 296-5547

Kansas is a delegated NPDES state with general permitting authority. The state has issued separate general permits for storm water discharges from construction sites and from industrial facilities. Permit requirements are similar to those for the EPA baseline general permits [Thompson Publishing Group, 1994].

Within Kansas, Kansas City, Overland Park, Topeka, Wichita, the Fairfax Drainage District, and the Kaw Valley Drainage District must obtain storm water discharge permits for their municipal separate storm sewer systems [58 FR 61146 (Nov. 19, 1993)].

## Kentucky

Kentucky Department of Environmental Protection
Water Division
KPDES Branch
18 Reilly Road
Frankfort, KY 40601
Douglas Allgeier (502) 564-3410

Kentucky is a delegated NPDES state with general permitting authority. The state has issued eight separate general permits for storm water discharges from construction sites and from seven different classes of industrial facilities. Permit requirements are similar to those for the EPA baseline general permits, except that no special containment controls are required for SARA Title III, section 313 water priority chemicals. In addition, there are differences in the sampling requirements and parameters for certain industries [Thompson Publishing Group, 1994].

Within Kentucky, Lexington-Fayette, Louisville, and Jefferson County must obtain storm water discharge permits for their municipal separate storm sewer systems [58 FR 61146 (Nov. 19, 1993)].

## Louisiana

Louisiana Department of Environmental Quality (DEQ)
Office of Water Resources
Water Pollution Control Division
Natural Resources Building
625 N. Fourth Street
P.O. Box 82215
Baton Rouge, LA 70884-2215
Darlene Bernard (504) 765-0525

Louisiana does not have NPDES permitting authority. Therefore, the EPA final general permits are applicable in Louisiana. However, the state has certain additional conditions which apply to storm water dischargers.

The state requires that industrial dischargers meet additional numeric limitations on certain storm water contaminants. All industrial dischargers must meet these limits on total organic carbon and oil and grease by October 1995. Oil and gas facilities also must have complied with numeric limits for chemical oxygen demand and chlorides by October 1, 1992.

Louisiana requires that some tests be performed for more pollutants than the EPA general permit. These include total organic carbon and 5-day BOD for certain industrial categories.

Whole effluent toxicity (WET) testing is required for certain industrial dischargers. WET tests must compare grab samples of undiluted storm water discharges with control samples composed of synthetic dilution water.

Within Louisiana, Baton Rouge, New Orleans, Shreveport, East Baton Rouge Parish, Jefferson Parish, and the Louisiana Department of Transportation must obtain storm water discharge permits for their municipal separate storm sewer systems [58 FR 61146 (Nov. 19, 1993)].

## Maine

Maine Department of Environmental Protection (DEP)
Water Bureau
State House, Station 17
Augusta, ME 04333
Norm Marcotte (207) 289-7693

Maine does not have NPDES permitting authority. Therefore, the EPA final general permits are applicable in Maine. However, the state has certain additional conditions which apply to storm water dischargers.

Maine requires that Whole Effluent Toxicity (WET) tests be performed using *Ceriodaphnia dubia* and brook trout, rather than fathead minnows, as required in the EPA general permit.

None of the municipalities in Maine are required to obtain municipal storm water discharge permits.

## Maryland

Maryland Department of the Environment (MDOE)
Water Management Administration
Wastewater Discharge Permit Program
2500 Broening Highway
Baltimore, MD 21224
Ed Gertler (410) 631-3652

Maryland is a delegated NPDES state with general permitting authority. The state has issued separate general permits for storm water discharges from construction sites and from industrial facilities. The state has had controls on sediment discharges for several years, and the construction general permit incorporates these controls. An erosion and sediment control plan must be submitted for approval before construction permit coverage is obtained. Sediment controls are required for all projects disturbing 5000 ft$^2$ or at least 100 yd$^3$ of earth. Industrial permit requirements are similar to those for the EPA baseline general permit, except that fewer additional requirements are imposed on SARA Title III, section 313 facilities. In addition, no sampling is required for industrial dischargers [Thompson Publishing Group, 1994].

Within Maryland, Baltimore, Anne Arundel County, Baltimore County, Carroll County, Charles County, Frederick County, Harford County, Howard County, Montgomery County, Prince George's County, Washington County, and the Maryland State Highway Administration must obtain storm water discharge permits for their municipal separate storm sewer systems [58 FR 61146 (Nov. 19, 1993)].

## Massachusetts

Massachusetts MEPA Unit
Executive Office of Environmental Affairs (EOEA)
Leverett Saltonstall Building 20th floor
100 Cambridge Street
Boston, MA 02202
(617) 727-5830; water pollution control (617) 292-5673

Massachusetts does not have NPDES permitting authority. Therefore, the EPA baseline general permits for industrial and construction storm water discharges are available through the EPA region 1 office in Boston.

Within Massachusetts, Boston and Worcester must obtain storm water discharge permits for their municipal separate storm sewer systems [58 FR 61146 (Nov. 19, 1993)].

## Michigan

Michigan Department of Natural Resources
Surface Water Division
P.O. Box 30038
Lansing, MI 48909
Dave Drullinger or Gary Borsen (517) 373-8088

Michigan is a delegated NPDES state, but the state's general permitting authority was suspended by the EPA in late 1993. The state has proposed separate general permits for storm water discharges from construction sites and from industrial facilities. Permit requirements are similar to those for the EPA baseline general permits, except that each discharger must have its storm water treatment and control measures under the direct supervision of a certified storm water operator. In addition, no sampling is required for industrial discharges. However, until the current issues related to EPA general permitting authority are resolved, dischargers in Michigan must seek individual permit coverage [Thompson Publishing Group, 1994].

Within Michigan, Ann Arbor, Flint, Grand Rapids, Sterling Heights, Warren, the University of Michigan, and the Michigan Department of Transportation must obtain storm water discharge permits for their municipal separate storm sewer systems [58 FR 61146 (Nov. 19, 1993)].

## Minnesota

Minnesota Pollution Control Agency (MPCA)
Water Quality Division
520 Lafayette Road
St. Paul, MN 55155
Scott Thompson (612) 296-7203

Minnesota is a delegated NPDES state with general permitting authority. The state has issued separate general permits for storm water discharges from construction sites and from industrial facilities. Permit requirements are similar to those for the EPA baseline general permits, except that no industries are required to perform storm water sampling. However, semiannual inspection reports must be submitted. There are certain differences in the construction general permit, including the requirement that sediment basins be designed for 1800 ft$^3$/acre of drainage area [Thompson Publishing Group, 1994].

Within Minnesota, Minneapolis, St. Louis, St. Paul, and the Minnesota Department of Transportation must obtain storm water discharge permits for their municipal separate storm sewer systems [58 FR 61146 (Nov. 19, 1993)].

## Mississippi

Mississippi Department of Environmental Quality
Bureau of Pollution Control
Industrial Wastewater Branch
P.O. Box 10385
2380 Highway 80 West
Jackson, MS 39289-0385
Louis LaVallee (601) 961-5074

Mississippi is a delegated NPDES state with general permitting authority. The state has issued separate general permits for storm water discharges from construction sites and from eight other classes of industrial facilities. Permit requirements are similar to those for the EPA baseline general permits, except that certain special provisions are included for each separate class of industry [Thompson Publishing Group, 1994].

Within Mississippi, no municipalities must obtain storm water discharge permits for their municipal separate storm sewer systems [58 FR 61146 (Nov. 19, 1993)].

## Missouri

Missouri Department of Natural Resources (DNR)
Water Pollution Control Program
Jefferson State Office Building
P.O. Box 176
Jefferson City, MO 65102
Karl Fett (314) 526-2928; (800) 334-6946 (toll free in Missouri)

Missouri is a delegated NPDES state with general permitting authority. The state has issued separate general permits for storm water discharges from construction sites and from 11 different classes of industrial facilities. Permit requirements are similar to those for the EPA baseline general permits, except that there are specific requirements for certain industries [Thompson Publishing Group, 1994].

Within Missouri, Independence, Kansas City, and Springfield must obtain storm water discharge permits for their municipal separate storm sewer systems [58 FR 61146 (Nov. 19, 1993)].

## Montana

Montana Department of Health and Environmental Sciences (DHES)
Water Quality Bureau
Cogswell Building, Room A206
Helena, MT 59620
Roxann Lincoln (406) 444-2406

Montana is a delegated NPDES state with general permitting authority. The state has issued separate general permits for storm water discharges from construction sites, from general industrial facilities, and from oil and gas and mining activities. Permit requirements are similar to those for the EPA baseline general permits, except that more information is required on the NOI form for industrial discharges, including information on BMPs and a certification of testing for non-storm-water discharges. In addition, the NOI must be submitted at least 30 days before the discharge begins, and the discharger must receive approval before beginning to discharge. Similarly, construction dischargers must submit a *storm water erosion control plan* (SECP) at least 30 days before construction begins and must receive approval before commencing construction. The industrial permit also imposes additional sampling requirements, including the requirement for acute Whole Effluent Toxicity (WET) testing for all SARA Title III, section 313 facilities (not just water priority chemicals). In addition, industrial dischargers must submit a certificate of compliance each year [Thompson Publishing Group, 1994].

None of the municipalities in Montana are required to obtain municipal storm water discharge permits.

## Nebraska

Nebraska Department of Environmental Control
Water Quality Division
P.O. Box 98922
Lincoln, NE 68509-8922
David Ihrie (402) 471-4239

Nebraska is a delegated NPDES state with general permitting authority. The state has issued separate general permits for storm water discharges from construction sites and from industrial facilities. Permit requirements are similar to those for the EPA baseline general permits, except that annual submittal of monitoring reports is required. Some other miscellaneous differences also exist [Thompson Publishing Group, 1994].

Within Nebraska, Lincoln and Omaha must obtain storm water discharge permits for their municipal separate storm sewer systems [58 FR 61146 (Nov. 19, 1993)].

## Nevada

Nevada Department of Conservation and Natural Resources
Environmental Protection Division
123 West Nye Lane
Carson City, NV 89710
John Nelson (702) 687-4670

Nevada is a delegated NPDES state with general permitting authority. The state has issued separate general permits for storm water discharges from construction sites and from two classes of industrial facilities: metal mining and other industries. Permit requirements are similar to those for the EPA baseline general permits. However, no storm water sampling is required for any facilities except subchapter N mining facilities. Special requirements apply within the Lake Tahoe drainage basin, and state water quality standards vary widely throughout the state [Thompson Publishing Group, 1994].

Within Nevada, Las Vegas, North Las Vegas, Reno, Sparks, Clark County, Washoe County, the Clark County Flood Control District, and the Nevada Department of Transportation must obtain storm water discharge permits for their municipal separate storm sewer systems [58 FR 61146 (Nov. 19, 1993)].

## New Hampshire

New Hampshire Department of Environmental Services
Hazen Drive
Concord, NH 03301
(603) 271-3503

New Hampshire does not have NPDES permitting authority. Therefore, the EPA final general permits are applicable in New Hampshire. In contrast to most other non-NPDES states, however, the state has not added conditions to the EPA general permits. The EPA general permits represent the complete requirements in New Hampshire.

None of the municipalities in New Hampshire are required to obtain municipal storm water discharge permits.

## New Jersey

New Jersey Department of Environmental Protection and Energy
401 East State Street
Trenton, NJ 08625-0029
(609) 633-7026

New Jersey is a delegated NPDES state with general permitting authority. The state has issued separate general permits for storm water discharges from large construction sites and from industrial facilities. Permit requirements differ from those for the EPA baseline general permits in several areas:

- Public notice is required of a Request for Authorization (RFA) to discharge. This is similar to the EPA Notice of Intent.

- Coverage under the New Jersey industrial general permit is limited to storm water which has no contact with significant materials.

- New Jersey does not regulate rooftop drainage, unless an industrial activity is conducted on the rooftop.

- Construction requirements are based upon state requirements already in place prior to the EPA storm water discharge regulations. These requirements include sedimentation and soil erosion controls for most construction disturbing more than 5000 ft$^2$.

Some other miscellaneous differences also exist [Thompson Publishing Group, 1994].

Within New Jersey, no municipalities are required to obtain storm water discharge permits for their municipal separate storm sewer systems [58 FR 61146 (Nov. 19, 1993)].

## New Mexico

New Mexico Water Quality Control Commission
1190 St. Francis Road
Harold Runnels Building
P.O. Box 26110
Santa Fe, NM 87502
Glenn Saums (505) 827-2795

New Mexico does not have NPDES permitting authority. Therefore, the EPA final general permits are applicable in New Mexico. However, the state has certain additional conditions which apply to storm water discharges.

New Mexico requires that certain notifications be sent to the New Mexico Environmental Department as well as to the EPA. The state also requires Whole Effluent Toxicity (WET) tests to be performed within 180 days of the issuance of the general permit. The WET testing must include a comparison of undiluted grab samples of storm water discharges with control samples of synthetic dilution water.

Certain waters are designated as *domestic water supplies* by the state. Discharges to these waters must be tested for two radium isotopes; total mercury; and dissolved arsenic, barium, cadmium, chromium, cyanide, lead, nitrate, selenium, silver, and uranium. The state must be notified if any of these pollutants are present above specified levels.

Within New Mexico, the Albuquerque Metropolitan Flood Control Authority and the New Mexico Department of Transportation must obtain storm water discharge permits for their municipal separate storm sewer systems [58 FR 61146 (Nov. 19, 1993)].

### New York

New York Department of Environmental Conservation
50 Wolf Road
Albany, NY 12233-3500
Ken Stevens (518) 457-1157

New York is a delegated NPDES state with general permitting authority. The state has issued separate general permits for storm water discharges from construction sites and from industrial facilities. Industrial permit requirements are similar to those for the EPA baseline general permit. However, the construction general permit is somewhat more stringent. For example, the construction general permit requires submittal of the SWPPP to applicable local regulatory agencies and requires that streams not be substantially degraded as a result of construction storm water discharges [Thompson Publishing Group, 1994].

Within New York, New York City, the Bronx, Brooklyn, Manhattan, Queens, and Staten Island must obtain storm water discharge permits for their municipal separate storm sewer systems [58 FR 61146 (Nov. 19, 1993)].

### North Carolina

North Carolina Department of Environment, Health, and Natural Resources
Department of Environmental Management
Water Quality Planning
512 North Salisbury Street
P.O. Box 29535
Raleigh, NC 27626-0535
Bill Mills or Steve Ulmer (919) 733-5083

North Carolina is a delegated NPDES state with general permitting authority. The state has issued 13 separate general permits for storm water discharges from various categories of industrial facilities, including construction activities. Most permit requirements are similar to those for the EPA baseline general permits, except for some specific monitoring requirements and other miscellaneous differences [Thompson Publishing Group, 1994].

Within North Carolina, Charlotte, Durham, Fayetteville, Greensboro, Raleigh, Winston-Salem, Cumberland County, and the North Carolina Department of Transportation must obtain storm water discharge permits for their municipal separate storm sewer systems [58 FR 61146 (Nov. 19, 1993)].

## North Dakota

North Dakota State Department of Health and Consolidated Laboratories
Water Quality Division
1200 Missouri Avenue
P.O. Box 5520
Bismarck, ND 58502-5520
Jim Collins (701) 221-5242

North Dakota is a delegated NPDES state with general permitting authority. The state has issued separate general permits for storm water discharges from construction sites, from industrial facilities, and from mining activities. Permit requirements are similar to those for the EPA baseline general permits [Thompson Publishing Group, 1994].

None of the municipalities in North Dakota are required to obtain municipal storm water discharge permits.

## Ohio

Ohio Environmental Protection Agency (EPA)
Water Pollution Control Division
P.O. Box 1049
1800 WaterMark Drive
Columbus, OH 43266-0149
Bob Phelps (614) 644-2001

Ohio is a delegated NPDES state with general permitting authority. The state has issued separate general permits for storm water discharges from construction sites and from industrial facilities. Industrial permit requirements are similar to those for the EPA baseline general permits. However, construction permit requirements differ significantly, because the Ohio permit requirements are based on previous state standards and regulations for sediment and erosion control. Major differences include timing requirements as to when stabilization must take place, specific requirements to protect state waters, and requirements for sediment basins for large projects [Thompson Publishing Group, 1994].

Within Ohio, Akron, Cincinnati, Cleveland, Columbus, Dayton, Toledo, and the Ohio Department of Transportation must obtain storm water discharge permits for their municipal separate storm sewer systems [58 FR 61146 (Nov. 19, 1993)].

## Oklahoma

Oklahoma State Department of Health
P.O. Box 53551
1000 Northeast Tenth Street
Oklahoma City, OK 73152
(405) 271-8056

Oklahoma does not have NPDES permitting authority. Therefore, the EPA final general permits are applicable in Oklahoma. However, the state has certain additional conditions which apply to storm water discharges.

The state prohibits new point source discharges of storm water to waters designated by the state as *outstanding resource waters* and *scenic rivers* as well as certain other designations.

Oklahoma requires Whole Effluent Toxicity (WET) testing by certain industrial dischargers. WET testing must include a comparison of grab samples of storm water discharges with a control sample of synthetic dilution water.

Within Oklahoma, the Oklahoma Department of Transportation must obtain a storm water discharge permit for its municipal separate storm sewer system [58 FR 61146 (Nov. 19, 1993)].

## Oregon

Oregon Department of Environmental Quality (DEQ)
Water Quality Division
811 Southwest Sixth Avenue
Portland, OR 97204
Ranei Namura (503) 229-5256

Oregon is a delegated NPDES state with general permitting authority. The state has issued 13 separate general permits for storm water discharges from various classes of industrial facilities, including construction. Permit requirements are similar to those for the EPA baseline general permits, except that the construction general permit requires the submittal of an *erosion control plan* (ECP) to the state at least 30 days before construction may begin. Other portions of the application must be submitted at least 90 days before construction may begin. All industrial permits require semiannual monitoring, and these vary somewhat from the EPA baseline permit requirements [Thompson Publishing Group, 1994].

Within Oregon the following must obtain storm water discharge permits for municipal separate storm sewer systems [58 FR 61146 (Nov. 13, 1993)]: Banks, Barlow, Beaverton, Canby, Cornelius, Durham, Estacada, Eugene, Fairview, Forest Grove, Gaston, Gladstone, Gresham, Happy Valley, Hillsboro, Johnson, King City, Lake Oswego, Milwaukie, Molalla, North Plains, Oregon City, Portland, Rivergrove, Salem, Sandy, Sherwood, Tigard, Tualatin, West Linn, Wilsonville; Clackamas County, Multnomah County, Washington County; the Oregon Department of Transportation; and the Port of Portland.

## Pennsylvania

Pennsylvania Department of Environmental Resources (DER)
Water Quality Management Bureau
Division of Permits and Compliance
MSSPB, 10th floor
200 North 3rd Street
P.O. Box 8465
Harrisburg, PA 17105-8465
Cuong Vu (717) 787-8184

Pennsylvania is a delegated NPDES state with general permitting authority. The state has issued separate general permits for storm water discharges from construction sites and from industrial facilities. Permit requirements differ from those for the EPA baseline permit requirements in several respects. Industrial dischargers must submit a Notice of Intent at least 180 days before beginning to discharge. In addition, the Pennsylvania permit sets a limit of 7 mg/L for dissolved iron and a pH limit of 6.0 to 9.0. Sampling requirements differ from the EPA baseline permit requirements in certain circumstances. The state requires a *preparedness, prevention, and contingency (PPC) plan* for most dischargers. For construction dischargers, the PPC plan is required only when there is a potential for accidental pollution of the environment or public endangerment through the release of pollutants. However, erosion and sediment control plans are required for all construction permittees. Individual storm water discharge permits are required for projects disturbing 25 acres or more [Thompson Publishing Group, 1994].

Within Pennsylvania, Philadelphia and the Pennsylvania Department of Transportation must obtain storm water discharge permits for their municipal separate storm sewer systems [58 FR 61146 (Nov. 19, 1993)].

## Rhode Island

Rhode Island Department of Environmental Management (DEM)
Division of Water Resources
291 Promenade Street
Providence, RI 02908
Angelo Liberti (401) 277-6519

Rhode Island is a delegated NPDES state with general permitting authority. The state has issued separate general permits for storm water discharges from construction sites and from industrial facilities. Permit requirements are similar to those for the EPA baseline general permits, except for some differences in sampling requirements and other miscellaneous variations [Thompson Publishing Group, 1994].

## South Carolina

South Carolina Department of Health and Environmental Control
Bureau of Water Pollution Control
2600 Bull Street
P.O. Box 11628
Columbia, SC 29201
Arturo Ovalles or Harvey Daniels (803) 734-5300

South Carolina is a delegated NPDES state with general permitting authority. The state has issued separate general permits for storm water discharges from construction sites and from industrial facilities. Permit requirements are similar to those for the EPA baseline general permits [Thompson Publishing Group, 1994].

Within South Carolina, Greenville County, Richland County, and the Harbor of Charleston must obtain storm water discharge permits for their municipal separate storm sewer systems [58 FR 61146 (Nov. 19, 1993)].

## South Dakota

South Dakota Department of Environment and Natural Resources
Division of Environmental Regulation
Joe Foss Building
523 East Capitol
Pierre, SD 57501-3181
Norma Job (605) 773-3546

South Dakota does not have NPDES permitting authority. Therefore, the EPA final general permits are applicable in South Dakota. In contrast to most other non-NPDES states, however, the state has not added conditions to the EPA general permits.

EPA region 8, which has jurisdiction over South Dakota, has additional requirements for Whole Effluent Toxicity (WET) testing. These requirements include a 48-h replacement test using a *Ceriodaphnia* species and an acute 96-h static replacement test using fathead minnows.

Within South Dakota, Sioux Falls must obtain storm water discharge permits for its municipal separate storm sewer systems [58 FR 61146 (Nov. 19, 1993)].

## Tennessee

Tennessee Department of Health and Conservation
Division of Water Pollution Control
L&C Annex, 6th floor
401 Church Street
Nashville, TN 37243-1534
Michael Uss or Robert Haley (615) 532-0625

Tennessee is a delegated NPDES state with general permitting authority. The state has issued separate general permits for storm water discharges from construction sites and from industrial facilities. Permit requirements are similar to those for the EPA baseline general permits [Thompson Publishing Group, 1994].

Within Tennessee, Bartlett, Belle Meade, Berry Hill, Chattanooga, Collierville, East Ridge, Forest Hills, Germantown, Goodlettsville, Knoxville, Lakewood, Memphis, Nashville-Davidson, Oak Hill, Red Bank, Ridgetop, and the Tennessee Department of Transportation must obtain storm water discharge permits for their municipal separate storm sewer systems [58 FR 61146 (Nov. 19, 1993)].

## Texas

Texas Natural Resource Conservation Commission (TNRCC)
P.O. Box 13087, Capitol Station
Austin, TX 78711
(512) 463-7898; Water Quality Division (512) 463-8412

Texas does not have NPDES permitting authority. Therefore, the EPA final general permits are applicable in Texas. However, the state has certain additional conditions which apply to storm water discharges.

Texas has placed numeric effluent limitations on arsenic, barium, cadmium, chromium, copper, lead, manganese, mercury, nickel, selenium, silver, and zinc, for both inland and tidal waters.

Whole Effluent Toxicity (WET) testing is required for all wood treatment facilities in Texas. The WET testing must be performed using freshwater test organisms. The WET testing must indicate a survival rate of greater than 50 percent over 24 h in undiluted grab samples of storm water effluent. Additional WET tests must be conducted to cover a range of five different dilution levels. The WET test must be repeated at least four times with at least five *Daphnia pulex* organisms included in each test and at least four additional times with at least 10 fathead minnow organisms in each test.

Within Texas, Abilene, Amarillo, Arlington, Austin, Beaumont, Corpus Christi, Dallas, El Paso, Fort Worth, Garland, Houston, Irving, Laredo, Lubbock, Mesquite, Pasadena, Plano, San Antonio, Waco, Harris County, the Harris County Flood Control District, and the Texas Department of Transportation must obtain storm water discharge permits for their municipal separate storm sewer systems [58 FR 61146 (Nov. 19, 1993)].

## Utah

Utah Division of Environmental Quality
Division of Water Quality
103 South Main Street
Salt Lake City, UT 84114-4870
Harry Campbell (801) 538-6146

Utah is a delegated NPDES state with general permitting authority. The state has issued separate general permits for storm water discharges from construction sites and from industrial facilities. Permit requirements are similar to those for the EPA baseline general permits, except that the state regulates discharges to groundwater [Thompson Publishing Group, 1994].

Within Utah, Salt Lake County and the Utah Department of Transportation must obtain storm water discharge permits for their municipal separate storm sewer systems [58 FR 61146 (Nov. 19, 1993)].

## Vermont

Vermont Department of Environmental Conservation
Permits, Compliance, and Protection Division
103 South Main Street
Waterbury, VT 05676
Brian Kooiker or Randy Bean (802) 241-3822

Vermont is a delegated NPDES state with general permitting authority. The state has issued separate general permits for storm water discharges from construction sites and from industrial facilities. Permit requirements are similar to those for the EPA baseline general permits, except that no monitoring is likely to be required for low-risk industrial facilities [Thompson Publishing Group, 1994].

None of the municipalities in Vermont must obtain storm water discharge permits for their municipal separate storm sewer systems.

## Virginia

Virginia Department of Environmental Quality
Water Division
9th Street Office Building
P.O. Box 11143
Richmond, VA 23230-1143
Michelle Hooper, Burton Tuxford, or Cathy Boatright (804) 527-5083

Virginia is a delegated NPDES state with general permitting authority. The state has issued four separate general permits for storm water discharges from construction sites and from some classes of industrial facilities. General permits for other classes of industrial facilities are being developed. Permit requirements are similar to those for the EPA baseline general permits. However, 14 days' advance notice is required before discharges are permitted under the construction general permit. The monitoring requirements of the current Virginia industrial permits also vary somewhat from those of the EPA baseline general permit [Thompson Publishing Group, 1994].

Within Virginia, Chesapeake, Hampton, Newport News, Norfolk, Portsmouth, Richmond, Roanoke, Virginia Beach, Chesterfield County, Fairfax County, Henrico County, and Prince William County must obtain storm water discharge permits for their municipal separate storm sewer systems [58 FR 61146 (Nov. 19, 1993)].

## Washington

Washington Department of Ecology (DOE)
Office of Water Programs
Mail Stop PV-11
St. Martin's College Campus—Lacey
Olympia, WA 98504-8711
Linda Matlock or Kathy Flynn (206) 438-7614

Washington is a delegated NPDES state with general permitting authority. The state has issued a single general permit for storm water discharges both from construction sites and from industrial facilities. Other industry-specific permits may become available. Permit requirements are similar to those for the EPA baseline general permits, except for several miscellaneous details. The general permit requires dischargers to implement all BMPs that do not require capital investment by November 18, 1994. BMPs that require capital investment must be implemented by November 18, 1995. No storm water sampling is required, but industrial dischargers must conduct semiannual inspections. Sampling requirements may be added after November 18, 1995 [Thompson Publishing Group, 1994].

Within Washington, Seattle, Tacoma, Clark County, King County, Pierce County, Snohomish County, and Spokane County must obtain storm water discharge permits for their municipal separate storm sewer systems [58 FR 61146 (Nov. 19, 1993)].

## West Virginia

West Virginia Department of Commerce, Labor, and Natural Resources
Office of Water Resources
Industrial Branch
1201 Greenbrier Street
Charleston, WV 25311
Art Vickers (304) 558-8855

West Virginia is a delegated NPDES state with general permitting authority. The state has issued a single general permit for storm water discharges from both construction sites and industrial facilities. Permit coverage is required for construction activities that disturb at least 3 acres. Industrial permit requirements are similar to those for the EPA baseline general permits, except for variations in the sampling requirements. Construction dischargers must apply for permit coverage at least 30 days before construction begins. The state also maintains a voluntary permit program for construction sites disturbing at least 1 acre but less than 3 acres [Thompson Publishing Group, 1994].

None of the municipalities in West Virginia are required to obtain municipal storm water discharge permits.

## Wisconsin

Wisconsin Department of Natural Resources (DNR)
Bureau of Wastewater Management
101 South Webster Street
P.O. Box 7921
Madison, WI 53707
Jim Helm or Kim Knudsen (608) 264-6262

Wisconsin is a delegated NPDES state with general permitting authority. The state has issued separate general permits for storm water discharges from construction sites and from industrial facilities. Permit requirements are similar to those for the EPA baseline general permits, except that the state regulates discharges of storm water into groundwater [Thompson Publishing Group, 1994].

Within Wisconsin, the Wisconsin Department of Transportation and the University of Wisconsin must obtain storm water discharge permits for their municipal separate storm sewer systems [58 FR 61146 (Nov. 19, 1993)].

## Wyoming

Wyoming Department of Environmental Quality (DEQ)
122 West 25th Street
Herschler Building, 4th floor
Cheyenne, WY 82002
John Wagner (307) 777-7082

Wyoming has issued two general permits: one for industrial discharges and one for construction activities. The coverage and requirements of the industrial storm water discharge permit are similar to those for the EPA baseline general permit for discharges from industrial activities. According to the DEQ, the purpose of the industrial general permit is to prevent or minimize pollution to state waters. Therefore, only minimal runoff controls may be required in desert areas, but extensive controls may be required for discharges on steep terrain or near sensitive waters. Best management practices or other controls must be designed so that discharges meet state water quality standards. Most dischargers are not required to perform storm water sampling, only on-site inspections [Thompson Publishing Group, 1994].

Construction sites with runoff that affects bodies of water which are perennially wet must not increase turbidity by more than 10 to 15 turbidity units above background levels. Other dischargers are not subject to the turbidity limitation, but are prohibited from discharging sediments that degrade the aesthetics or habitat characteristics of the water body. Storm water management controls must be designed to remove 80 percent of the total suspended solids from all flows exceeding predevelopment levels. If this goal is not attainable, the permittee must supply justification of why particular management measures are not implemented. Other requirements are similar to those for the EPA baseline general permit, except that the frequency of inspection may be reduced to once per quarter during seasonal shutdowns and after the completion of construction but before the site has returned to "approximate preconstruction conditions" [Thompson Publishing Group, 1994].

None of the municipalities in Wyoming are required to obtain municipal storm water discharge permits.

## References

Jessup, Deborah Hitchcock: *Guide to State Environmental Programs,* 2d ed., Bureau of National Affairs, Rockville, MD, 1990.
Thompson Publishing Group: *Stormwater Permit Manual,* Washington, 1994.

# NPDES General Permits for Storm Water Discharges Associated with Industrial Activity

This appendix presents the text of the EPA's final NPDES general permits for storm water discharges associated with industrial activity. This text was originally published in the *Federal Register* [57 FR 41235 (Sept. 9, 1992)]. This appendix should be a useful reference for Chaps. 4 through 8 of this book, which describe the storm water discharge permit requirements for areas associated with industrial activity.

This general permit is directly applicable only in nondelegated states (states in which the EPA regional offices write NPDES storm water discharge permits). Delegated states write their own NPDES storm water discharge permits, and the general permit conditions in these states may differ from those of the EPA's baseline general permit.

## PREFACE

The CWA provides that storm water discharges associated with industrial activity from a point source (including discharges through a municipal separate storm sewer system) to waters of the United States are unlawful, unless authorized by a National Pollutant Discharge Elimination System (NPDES) permit. The terms "storm water discharge associated with industrial activity", "point source" and "waters of the United States" are critical to determining whether a facility is subject to this requirement. Complete definitions of these terms are found in the definition section (Part X) of this permit. In order to determine the applicability of the requirement to a particular facility, the facility operator must examine its activities in relationship to the eleven categories of industrial facilities described in the definition of "storm water discharge associated with industrial activity".

Category (xi) of the definition, which address facilities with activities classified under Standard Industrial Classifications (SIC) codes 20, 21, 22, 23, 2434, 25, 265, 267, 27, 283, 31 (except 311), 34 (except 3441), 35, 36, 37 (except 373), 38, 39, 4221-25, (and which are not otherwise included within categories (i)-(x)), differs from other categories listed in that it only addresses storm water discharges where material handling equipment or activities, raw materials, intermediate products, final products, waste materials, by-products, or industrial machinery are exposed to storm water.[1]

## Part I. COVERAGE UNDER THIS PERMIT

### A. Permit Area

The permit covers all areas of:

Region I-for the States of Maine and New Hampshire; for Indian lands located in Massachusetts, New Hampshire, and Maine.

Region IV-for the State of Florida; and for Indian lands located in Florida, Mississippi, and North Carolina. Region VI-for the States of Louisiana, New Mexico, Oklahoma, and Texas; and for Indian lands located in Louisiana, New Mexico (except Navajo lands and Ute Mountain Reservation lands), Oklahoma, and Texas.

Region VIII-for the State of South Dakota; for Indian lands located in Colorado, Montana, North Dakota, South Dakota, Utah (except Goshute Reservation and Navajo Reservation lands), and Wyoming; for Federal facilities in Colorado; and for the Ute Mountain Reservation in Colorado, and New Mexico.

Region IX-for the State of Arizona; for the Territories of Johnston Atoll, and Midway and Wake Island; and for Indian lands located in California, and Nevada; and for the Goshute Reservation in Utah and Nevada, the Navajo Reservation in Utah, New Mexico, and Arizona, the Duck Valley Reservation in Nevada and Idaho.

---

[1] On June 4, 1992, the United States Court of Appeals for the Ninth Circuit remanded the exclusion for manufacturing facilities in category (xi) which do not have materials or activities exposed to storm water to the EPA for further rulemaking. (Natural Resources Defense Council v. EPA,Nos. 90-70671 and 91-70200).

Region X-for the State of Alaska, and Idaho; for Indian lands located in Alaska, Idaho (except Duck Valley Reservation lands), and Washington; and for Federal facilities in Washington.

## B. Eligibility

1. This permit may cover all new and existing point source discharges of storm water associated with industrial activity to waters of the United States, except for storm water discharges identified under paragraph I.B.3.
2. This permit may authorize storm water discharges associated with industrial activity that are mixed with storm water discharges associated with industrial activity from construction activities provided that the storm water discharge from the construction activity is in compliance with the terms, including applicable notice of intent (NOI) or application requirements, of a different NPDES general permit or individual permit authorizing such discharges.
3. Limitations on Coverage. The following storm water discharges associated with industrial activity are not authorized by this permit:
   a. storm water discharges associated with industrial activity that are mixed with sources of non-storm water other than non-storm water discharges that are:
      (i) in compliance with a different NPDES permit; or
      (ii) identified by and in compliance with Part III.A.2 (authorized non-storm water discharges) of this permit.
   b. storm water discharges associated with industrial activity which are subject to an existing effluent limitation guideline addressing storm water (or a combination of storm water and process water)[2]
   c. storm water discharges associated with industrial activity that are subject to an existing NPDES individual or general permit; are located at a facility that where an NPDES permit has been terminated or denied; or which are issued in a permit in accordance with paragraph VII.M (requirements for individual or

---

[2]For the purpose of this permit, the following effluent limitation guidelines address storm water (or a combination of storm water and process water): cement manufacturing (40 CFR 411); feedlots (40 CFR 412); fertilizer manufacturing (40 CFR 418); petroleum refining (40 CFR 419); phosphate manufacturing (40 CFR 422); steam electric (40 CFR 423); coal mining (40 CFR 434); mineral mining and processing (40 CFR 436); ore mining and dressing (40 CFR 440); and asphalt emulsion (40 CFR 443 Subpart A). This permit may authorize storm water discharges associated with industrial activity which are not subject to an effluent limitation guideline even where a different storm water discharge at the facility is subject to an effluent limitation guideline.

alternative general permits) of this permit. Such discharges may be authorized under this permit after an existing permit expires provided the existing permit did not establish numeric limitations for such discharges;

d. storm water discharges associated with industrial activity from construction sites, except storm water discharges from portions of a construction site that can be classified as an industrial activity under 40 CFR 122.26(b)(14) (i) through (ix) or (xi) (including storm water discharges from mobile asphalt plant, and mobile concrete plants);

e. storm water discharges associated with industrial activity that the Director (EPA) has determined to be or may reasonably be expected to be contributing to a violation of a water quality standard;

f. storm water discharges associated with industrial activity that may adversely affect a listed or proposed to be listed endangered or threatened species or its critical habitat; and

g. storm water discharges associated with industrial activity from inactive mining, inactive landfills, or inactive oil and gas operations occurring on Federal lands where an operator cannot be identified.

4. Storm water discharges associated with industrial activity which are authorized by this permit may be combined with other sources of storm water which are not classified as associated with industrial activity pursuant to 40 CFR 122.26(b)(14), so long as the discharger is in compliance with this permit.

## C. Authorization

1. Dischargers of storm water associated with industrial activity must submit a Notice of Intent (NOI) in accordance with the requirements of Part II of this permit, using a NOI form provided by the Director (or photocopy thereof), to be authorized to discharge under this general permit.

2. Unless notified by the Director to the contrary, owners or operators who submit such notification are authorized to discharge storm water associated with industrial activity under the terms and conditions of this permit 2 days after the date that the NOI is postmarked.

3. The Director may deny coverage under this permit and require submittal of an application for an individual NPDES permit based on a review of the NOI or other information.

## Part II. NOTICE OF INTENT REQUIREMENTS

### A. Deadlines for Notification

1. Except as provided in paragraphs II.A.4 (rejected or denied municipal group applicants), II.A.5 (new operator) and II.A.6 (late NOIs), individuals who intend to obtain coverage for an existing storm water discharge associated with industrial activity under this general permit shall submit a Notice of Intent (NOI) in accordance with the requirements of this part on or before October 1, 1992;

2. Except as provided in paragraphs II.A.3 (oil and gas operations), II.A.4 (rejected or denied municipal group applicants), II.A.5 (new operator), and II.A.6 (late NOI) operators of facilities which begin industrial activity after October 1, 1992 shall submit a NOI in accordance with the requirements of this part at least 2 days prior to the commencement of the industrial activity at the facility;

3. Operators of oil and gas exploration, production, processing, or treatment operations or transmission facilities, that are not required to submit a permit application as of October 1, 1992 in accordance with 40 CFR 122.26(c)(1)(iii), but that after October 1, 1992 have a discharge of a reportable quantity of oil or a hazardous substance for which notification is required pursuant to either 40 CFR 110.6, 40 CFR 117.21 or 40 CFR 302.6, must submit a NOI in accordance with the requirements of Part II.C of this permit within 14 calendar days of the first knowledge of such release.

4. Storm water discharges associated with industrial activity from a facility that is owned or operated by a municipality that has participated in a timely Part 1 group application and where either the group application is rejected or the facility is denied participation in the group application by EPA, and that are seeking coverage under this general permit shall submit a NOI in accordance with the requirements of this part on or before the 180th day following the date on which the group is rejected or the denial is made, or October 1, 1992, whichever is later.

5. Where the operator of a facility with a storm water discharge associated with industrial activity which is covered by this permit changes, the new operator of the facility must submit an NOI in accordance with the requirements of this part at least 2 days prior to the change.

6. An operator of a storm water discharge associated with industrial activity is not precluded from submitting an NOI in accordance with the requirements of this part after the dates provided in Parts II.A.1, 2, 3, or 4 (above) of this permit. In such instances, EPA may bring appropriate enforcement actions.

## B. Contents of Notice of Intent

The Notice of Intent shall be signed in accordance with Part VII.G (signatory requirements) of this permit and shall include the following information:

1. The street address of the facility for which the notification is submitted. Where a street address for the site is not available, the location of the approximate center of the facility must be described in terms of the latitude and longitude to the nearest 15 seconds, or the section, township and range to the nearest quarter section;

2. Up to four 4-digit Standard Industrial Classification (SIC) codes that best represent the principal products or for hazardous waste treatment, storage or disposal facilities, land disposal facilities that receive or have received any industrial waste, steam electric power generating facilities, or treatment works treating domestic sewage, a narrative identification of those activities;

3. The operator's name, address, telephone number, and status as Federal, State, private, public or other entity;

4. The permit number(s) of additional NPDES permit(s) for any discharge(s) (including non-storm water discharges) from the site that are currently authorized by an NPDES permit;

5. The name of the receiving water(s), or if the discharge is through a municipal separate storm sewer, the name of the municipal operator of the storm sewer and the ultimate receiving water(s) for the discharge through the municipal separate storm sewer;

6. An indication of whether the owner or operator has existing quantitative data describing the concentration of pollutants in storm water discharges (existing data should not be included as part of the NOI);

7. Where a facility has participated in Part 1 of an approved storm water group application, the number EPA assigned to the group application shall be supplied; and

8. For any facility that begins to discharge storm water associated with industrial activity after October 1, 1992, a certification that a storm water pollution prevention plan has been prepared for the facility in accordance with Part IV of this permit. (A copy of the plan should not be included with the NOI submission).

## C. Where to Submit

Facilities which discharge storm water associated with industrial activity must use a NOI form provided by the Director (or photocopy thereof). The form in the Federal Register notice in which this permit was published may be photocopied and used. Forms are also available by calling (703) 821-4823. NOIs must be signed in accordance with Part

VII.G (signatory requirements) of this permit. NOIs are to be submitted to the Director of the NPDES program in care of the following address: Storm Water Notice of Intent, P.O. Box 1215, Newington, VA 22122.

## D. Additional Notification

Facilities which discharge storm water associated with industrial activity through large or medium municipal separate storm sewer systems (systems located in an incorporated city with a population of 100,000 or more, or in a county identified as having a large or medium system (see definition in Part X of this permit and Appendix E of this notice)) shall, in addition to filing copies of the Notice of Intent in accordance with paragraph II.D, also submit signed copies of the Notice of Intent to the operator of the municipal separate storm sewer through which they discharge in accordance with the deadlines in Part II.A (deadlines for notification) of this permit.

## E. Renotification

Upon issuance of a new general permit, the permittee is required to notify the Director of their intent to be covered by the new general permit.

## Part III. SPECIAL CONDITIONS

### A. Prohibition on Non-Storm Water Discharges

1. Except as provided in paragraph III.A.2 (below), all discharges covered by this permit shall be composed entirely of storm water.
2. a. Except as provided in paragraph III.A.2.b (below), discharges of material other than storm water must be in compliance with a NPDES permit (other than this permit) issued for the discharge.
   b. The following non-storm water discharges may be authorized by this permit provided the non-storm water component of the discharge is in compliance with paragraph IV.D.3.g.(2) (measures and controls for non-storm water discharges): discharges from fire fighting activities; fire hydrant flushings; potable water sources including waterline flushings; irrigation drainage; lawn watering; routine external building washdown which does not use detergents or other compounds; pavement washwaters where spills or leaks of toxic or hazardous materials have not occurred (unless all spilled material has been removed) and where detergents are not used; air conditioning condensate; springs; uncontaminated ground water; and foundation or footing drains where flows are not contaminated with process materials such as solvents.

## B. Releases in Excess of Reportable Quantities

1. The discharge of hazardous substances or oil in the storm water discharge(s) from a facility shall be prevented or minimized in accordance with the applicable storm water pollution prevention plan for the facility. This permit does not relieve the permittee of the reporting requirements of 40 CFR part 117 and 40 CFR part 302. Except as provided in paragraph III.B.2 (multiple anticipated discharges) of this permit, where a release containing a hazardous substance in an amount equal to or in excess of a reporting quantity established under either 40 CFR 117 or 40 CFR 302, occurs during a 24 hour period.
   a. The discharger is required to notify the National Response Center (NRC) (800-424-8802; in the Washington, DC metropolitan area 202-426-2675) in accordance with the requirements of 40 CFR 117 and 40 CFR 302 as soon as he or she has knowledge of the discharge;
   b. The storm water pollution prevention plan required under Part IV (storm water pollution prevention plans) of this permit must be modified within 14 calendar days of knowledge of the release to: provide a description of the release, the circumstances leading to the release, and the date of the release. In addition, the plan must be reviewed by the permittee to identify measures to prevent the reoccurrence of such releases and to respond to such releases, and the plan must be modified where appropriate; and
   c. The permittee shall submit within 14 calendar days of knowledge of the release a written description of: the release (including the type and estimate of the amount of material released), the date that such release occurred, the circumstances leading to the release, and steps to be taken in accordance with paragraph III.B.1.b (above) of this permit to the appropriate EPA Regional Office at the address provided in Part VI.D.1.d (reporting: where to submit) of this permit.
2. Multiple Anticipated Discharges
   Facilities which have more than one anticipated discharge per year containing the same hazardous substance in an amount equal to or in excess of a reportable quantity established under either 40 CFR 117 or 40 CFR 302, which occurs during a 24 hour period, where the discharge is caused by events occurring within the scope of the relevant operating system shall:
   a. submit notifications in accordance with Part III.B.1.b (above) of this permit for the first such release that occurs during a calendar year (or for the first year of this permit, after submittal of an NOI); and

b. shall provide in the storm water pollution prevention plan required under Part IV (storm water pollution prevention plan) a written description of the dates on which all such releases occurred, the type and estimate of the amount of material released, and the circumstances leading to the release. In addition, the plan must be reviewed to identify measures to prevent or minimize such releases and the plan must be modified where appropriate.
3. Spills
This permit does not authorize the discharge of hazardous substances or oil resulting from an on-site spill.

## Part IV. STORM WATER POLLUTION PREVENTION PLANS

A storm water pollution prevention plan shall be developed for each facility covered by this permit. Storm water pollution prevention plans shall be prepared in accordance with good engineering practices and in accordance with the factors outlined in 40 CFR 125.3(d) (2) or (3) as appropriate. The plan shall identify potential sources of pollution which may reasonably be expected to affect the quality of storm water discharges associated with industrial activity from the facility. In addition, the plan shall describe and ensure the implementation of practices which are to be used to reduce the pollutants in storm water discharges associated with industrial activity at the facility and to assure compliance with the terms and conditions of this permit. Facilities must implement the provisions of the storm water pollution prevention plan required under this part as a condition of this permit.

### A. Deadlines for Plan Preparation and Compliance

1. Except as provided in paragraphs IV.A.3 (oil and gas operations) 4 (facilities denied or rejected from participation in a group application) 5 (special requirements) and 6 (later dates) the plan for a storm water discharge associated with industrial activity that is existing on or before October 1, 1992:
   a. shall be prepared on or before April 1, 1993 (and updated as appropriate);
   b. shall provide for implementation and compliance with the terms of the plan on or before October 1, 1993;
2. a. The plan for any facility where industrial activity commences after October 1, 1992, but on or before December 31, 1992 shall be prepared, and except as provided elsewhere in this permit, shall provide for compliance with the terms of the plan and this

permit on or before the date 60 calendar days after the commencement of industrial activity (and updated as appropriate);

b. The plan for any facility where industrial activity commences on or after January 1, 1993 shall be prepared, and except as provided elsewhere in this permit, shall provide for compliance with the terms of the plan and this permit, on or before the date of submission of a NOI to be covered under this permit (and updated as appropriate);

3. The plan for storm water discharges associated with industrial activity from an oil and gas exploration, production, processing, or treatment operation or transmission facility that is not required to submit a permit application on or before October 1, 1992 in accordance with 40 CFR 122.26(c)(1)(iii), but after October 1, 1992 has a discharge of a reportable quantity of oil or a hazardous substance for which notification is required pursuant to either 40 CFR 110.6, 40 CFR 117.21 or 40 CFR 302.6, shall be prepared and except as provided elsewhere in this permit, shall provide for compliance with the terms of the plan and this permit on or before the date 60 calendar days after the first knowledge of such release (and updated as appropriate);

4. The plan for storm water discharges associated with industrial activity from a facility that is owned or operated by a municipality that has participated in a timely group application where either the group application is rejected or the facility is denied participation in the group application by EPA,

a. shall be prepared on or before the 365th day following the date on which the group is rejected or the denial is made, (and updated as appropriate);

b. except as provided elsewhere in this permit, shall provide for compliance with the terms of the plan and this permit on or before the 545th day following the date on which the group is rejected or the denial is made; and

5. Portions of the plan addressing additional requirements for storm water discharges from facilities subject to Parts IV.D.7 (EPCRA Section 313 and IV.D.8 (salt storage) shall provide for compliance with the terms of the requirements identified in Parts IV.D.7 and IV.D.8 as expeditiously as practicable, but except as provided below, not later than either October 1, 1995. Facilities which are not required to report under EPCRA Section 313 prior to July 1, 1992, shall provide for compliance with the terms of the requirements identified in Parts IV.D.7 and IV.D.8 as expeditiously as practicable, but not later than three years after the date on which the facility is first required to report under EPCRA Section 313. However, plans for facilities subject to the additional requirements of Part

IV.D.7 and IV.D.8 shall provide for compliance with the other terms and conditions of this permit in accordance with the appropriate dates provided in Part IV.1, 2, 3, or 5 of this permit.

6. Upon a showing of good cause, the Director may establish a later date in writing for preparing and compliance with a plan for a storm water discharge associated with industrial activity that submits a NOI in accordance with Part II.A.2 (deadlines for notification-new dischargers) of this permit (and updated as appropriate).

### B. Signature and Plan Review

1. The plan shall be signed in accordance with Part VII.G (signatory requirements), and be retained on-site at the facility which generates the storm water discharge in accordance with Part VI.E (retention of records) of this permit.

2. The permittee shall make plans available upon request to the Director, or authorized representative, or in the case of a storm water discharge associated with industrial activity which discharges through a municipal separate storm sewer system, to the operator of the municipal system.

3. The Director, or authorized representative, may notify the permittee at any time that the plan does not meet one or more of the minimum requirements of this Part. Such notification shall identify those provisions of the permit which are not being met by the plan, and identify which provisions of the plan requires modifications in order to meet the minimum requirements of this Part. Within 30 days of such notification from the Director, (or as otherwise provided by the Director), or authorized representative, the permittee shall make the required changes to the plan and shall submit to the Director a written certification that the requested changes have been made.

### C. Keeping Plans Current

The permittee shall amend the plan whenever there is a change in design, construction, operation, or maintenance, which has a significant effect on the potential for the discharge of pollutants to the waters of the United States or if the storm water pollution prevention plan proves to be ineffective in eliminating or significantly minimizing pollutants from sources identified under Part IV.D.2 (description of potential pollutant sources) of this permit, or in otherwise achieving the general objectives of controlling pollutants in storm water discharges associated with industrial activity. Amendments to the plan may be reviewed by EPA in the same manner as Part IV.B (above).

## D. Contents of Plan

The plan shall include, at a minimum, the following items:

### 1. Pollution Prevention Team

Each plan shall identify a specific individual or individuals within the facility organization as members of a storm water Pollution Prevention Team that are responsible for developing the storm water pollution prevention plan and assisting the facility or plant manager in its implementation, maintenance, and revision. The plan shall clearly identify the responsibilities of each team member. The activities and responsibilities of the team shall address all aspects of the facility's storm water pollution prevention plan.

### 2. Description of Potential Pollutant Sources

Each plan shall provide a description of potential sources which may reasonably be expected to add significant amounts of pollutants to storm water discharges or which may result in the discharge of pollutants during any dry weather from separate storm sewers draining the facility. Each plan shall identify all activities and significant materials which may potentially be significant pollutant sources. Each plan shall include, at a minimum:

#### a. Drainage

1. A site map indicating an outline of the portions of the drainage area of each storm water outfall that are within the facility boundaries, each existing structural control measure to reduce pollutants in storm water runoff, surface water bodies, locations where significant materials are exposed to precipitation, locations where major spills or leaks identified under Part IV.D.2.c (spills and leaks) of this permit have occurred, and the locations of the following activities where such activities are exposed to precipitation: fueling stations, vehicle and equipment maintenance and/or cleaning areas, loading/unloading areas, locations used for the treatment, storage or disposal of wastes, liquid storage tanks, processing areas and storage areas.

2. For each area of the facility that generates storm water discharges associated with industrial activity with a reasonable potential for containing significant amounts of pollutants, a prediction of the direction of flow, and an identification of the types of pollutants which are likely to be present in storm water discharges associated with industrial activity. Factors to consider include the toxicity of chemical; quantity of chemicals used, produced or discharged; the likelihood of contact with storm water; and history of significant leaks or spills of toxic or hazardous pollutants. Flows with a significant potential for causing erosion shall be identified.

### b. Inventory of Exposed Materials

An inventory of the types of materials handled at the site that potentially may be exposed to precipitation. Such inventory shall include a narrative description of significant materials that have been handled, treated, stored or disposed in a manner to allow exposure to storm water between the time of three years prior to the date of the issuance of this permit and the present; method and location of on-site storage or disposal; materials management practices employed to minimize contact of materials with storm water runoff between the time of three years prior to the date of the issuance of this permit and the present; the location and a description of existing structural and non-structural control measures to reduce pollutants in storm water runoff; and a description of any treatment the storm water receives.

### c. Spills and Leaks

A list of significant spills and significant leaks of toxic or hazardous pollutants that occurred at areas that are exposed to precipitation or that otherwise drain to a storm water conveyance at the facility after the date of three years prior to the effective date of this permit. Such list shall be updated as appropriate during the term of the permit.

### d. Sampling Data

A summary of existing discharge sampling data describing pollutants in storm water discharges from the facility, including a summary of sampling data collected during the term of this permit.

### e. Risk Identification and Summary of Potential Pollutant Sources

A narrative description of the potential pollutant sources from the following activities: loading and unloading operations; outdoor storage activities; outdoor manufacturing or processing activities; significant dust or particulate generating processes; and on-site waste disposal practices. The description shall specifically list any significant potential source of pollutants at the site and for each potential source, any pollutant or pollutant parameter (e.g. biochemical oxygen demand, etc.) of concern shall be identified.

### 3. Measures and Controls

Each facility covered by this permit shall develop a description of storm water management controls appropriate for the facility, and implement such controls. The appropriateness and priorities of controls in a plan shall reflect identified potential sources of pollutants at the facility. The description of storm water management controls shall address the following minimum components, including a schedule for implementing such controls:

### a. Good Housekeeping

Good housekeeping requires the maintenance of areas which may contribute pollutants to storm waters discharges in a clean, orderly manner.

### b. Preventive Maintenance

A preventive maintenance program shall involve timely inspection and maintenance of storm water management devices (e.g. cleaning oil/water separators, catch basins) as well as inspecting and testing facility equipment and systems to uncover conditions that could cause breakdowns or failures resulting in discharges of pollutants to surface waters, and ensuring appropriate maintenance of such equipment and systems.

### c. Spill Prevention and Response Procedures

Areas where potential spills which can contribute pollutants to storm water discharges can occur, and their accompanying drainage points shall be identified clearly in the storm water pollution prevention plan. Where appropriate, specifying material handling procedures, storage requirements, and use of equipment such as diversion valves in the plan should be considered. Procedures for cleaning up spills shall be identified in the plan and made available to the appropriate personnel. The necessary equipment to implement a clean up should be available to personnel.

### d. Inspections

In addition to or as part of the comprehensive site evaluation required under Part IV.4 of this permit, qualified facility personnel shall be identified to inspect designated equipment and areas of the facility at appropriate intervals specified in the plan. A set of tracking or follow-up procedures shall be used to ensure that appropriate actions are taken in response to the inspections. Records of inspection shall be maintained.

### e. Employee Training

Employee training programs shall inform personnel responsible for implementing activities identified in the storm water pollution prevention plan or otherwise responsible for storm water management at all levels of responsibility of the components and goals of the storm water pollution prevention plan. Training should address topics such as spill response, good housekeeping and material management practices. A pollution prevention plan shall identify periodic dates for such training.

### f. Recordkeeping and Internal Reporting Procedures

A description of incidents (such as spills, or other discharges), along with other information describing the quality and quantity of storm water discharges shall be included in the plan required under this part. Inspections and maintenance activities shall be documented and records of such activities shall be incorporated into the plan.

### g. Non-Storm Water Discharges.

1. The plan shall include a certification that the discharge has been tested or evaluated for the presence of non-storm water discharges. The certification shall include the identification of potential significant sources of non-storm water at the site, a description of the results of any test and/or evaluation for the presence of non-storm water discharges, the evaluation criteria or testing method used, the date of any testing and/or evaluation, and the on-site drainage points that were directly observed during the test. Certifications shall be signed in accordance with Part VII.G of this permit. Such certification may not be feasible if the facility operating the storm water discharge associated with industrial activity does not have access to an outfall, manhole, or other point of access to the ultimate conduit which receives the discharge. In such cases, the source identification section of the storm water pollution plan shall indicate why the certification required by this part was not feasible, along with the identification of potential significant source of non-storm water at the site. A discharger that is unable to provide the certification required by this paragraph must notify the Director in accordance with Part VI.A (failure to certify) of this permit.

2. Except for flows from fire fighting activities, sources of non-storm water listed in Part III.A.2 (authorized non-storm water discharges) of this permit that are combined with storm water discharges associated with industrial activity must be identified in the plan. The plan shall identify and ensure the implementation of appropriate pollution prevention measures for the non-storm water component(s) of the discharge.

### h. Sediment and Erosion Control

The plan shall identify areas which, due to topography, activities, or other factors, have a high potential for significant soil erosion, and identify structural, vegetative, and/or stabilization measures to be used to limit erosion.

### i. Management of Runoff

The plan shall contain a narrative consideration of the appropriateness of traditional storm water management practices (practices other than those which control the generation or source(s) of pollutants) used to divert, infiltrate, reuse, or otherwise manage storm water runoff in a manner that reduces pollutants in storm water discharges from the site. The plan shall provide that measures that the permittee determines to be reasonable and appropriate shall be implemented and maintained. The potential of various sources at the facility to contribute pollutants to storm water discharges, associated with industrial activity (see Parts IV.D.2. (description of potential pollutant sources) of this permit) shall be considered when determining reasonable and appropriate measures. Appropriate measures may include: vegetative swales and practices, reuse of collected storm water (such as for a process or as an irrigation source), inlet controls (such as oil/water separators), snow management activities, infiltration devices, and wet detention/retention devices.

### 4. Comprehensive Site Compliance Evaluation

Qualified personnel shall conduct site compliance evaluations at appropriate intervals specified in the plan, but, except as provided in paragraph IV.D.4.d (below), in no case less than once a year. Such evaluations shall provide:

a. Areas contributing to a storm water discharge associated with industrial activity shall be visually inspected for evidence of, or the potential for, pollutants entering the drainage system. Measures to reduce pollutant loadings shall be evaluated to determine whether they are adequate and properly implemented in accordance with the terms of the permit or whether additional control measures are needed. Structural storm water management measures, sediment and erosion control measures, and other structural pollution prevention measures identified in the plan shall be observed to ensure that they are operating correctly. A visual inspection of equipment needed to implement the plan, such as spill response equipment, shall be made.

b. Based on the results of the inspection, the description of potential pollutant sources identified in the plan in accordance with Part IV.D.2 (description of potential pollutant sources) of this permit and pollution prevention measures and controls identified in the plan in accordance with paragraph IV.D.3 (measures and controls) of this permit shall be revised as appropriate within two weeks of such inspection and shall provide for implementation of any changes to the plan in a timely manner, but in no case more than twelve weeks after the inspection.

c. A report summarizing the scope of the inspection, personnel making the inspection, the date(s) of the inspection, major observations relating to the implementation of the storm water pollution prevention plan, and actions taken in accordance with paragraph IV.D.4.b (above) of the permit shall be made and retained as part of the storm water pollution prevention plan for at least one year after coverage under this permit terminates. The report shall identify any incidents of non-compliance. Where a report does not identify any incidents of non-compliance, the report shall contain a certification that the facility is in compliance with the storm water pollution prevention plan and this permit. The report shall be signed in accordance with Part VII.G (signatory requirements) of this permit.

d. Where annual site inspections are shown in the plan to be impractical for inactive mining sites due to the remote location and inaccessibility of the site, site inspections required under this part shall be conducted at appropriate intervals specified in the plan, but, in no case less than once in three years.

### 5. Additional requirements for storm water discharges associated with industrial activity through municipal separate storm sewer systems serving a population of 100,000 or more.

a. In addition to the applicable requirements of this permit, facilities covered by this permit must comply with applicable requirements in municipal storm water management programs developed under NPDES permits issued for the discharge of the municipal separate storm sewer system that receives the facility's discharge, provided the discharger has been notified of such conditions.

b. Permittees which discharge storm water associated with industrial activity through a municipal separate storm sewer system serving a population of 100,000 or more shall make plans available to the municipal operator of the system upon request.

### 6. Consistency with Other Plans

Storm water pollution prevention plans may reflect requirements for Spill Prevention Control and Countermeasure (SPCC) plans developed for the facility under section 311 of the CWA or Best Management Practices (BMP) Programs otherwise required by an NPDES permit for the facility as long as such requirement is incorporated into the storm water pollution prevention plan.

### 7. Additional requirements for storm water discharges associated with industrial activity from facilities subject to EPCRA Section 313 requirements

In addition to the requirements of Parts IV.D.1 through 4 of this permit and other applicable conditions of this permit, storm water pollution prevention plans for facilities subject to reporting requirements under EPCRA Section 313 for chemicals which are classified as 'Section 313 water priority chemicals' in accordance with the definition in Part X of this permit, shall describe and ensure the implementation of practices which are necessary to provide for conformance with the following guidelines:

a. In areas where Section 313 water priority chemicals are stored, processed or otherwise handled, appropriate containment, drainage control and/or diversionary structures shall be provided. At a minimum, one of the following preventive systems or its equivalent shall be used:

(1) Curbing, culverting, gutters, sewers or other forms of drainage control to prevent or minimize the potential for storm water run-on to come into contact with significant sources of pollutants; or

(2) Roofs, covers or other forms of appropriate protection to prevent storage piles from exposure to storm water, and wind.

b. In addition to the minimum standards listed under Part IV.D.7.a (above) of this permit, the storm water pollution prevention plan shall include a complete discussion of measures taken to conform with the following applicable guidelines, other effective storm water pollution prevention procedures, and applicable State rules, regulations and guidelines:

(1) Liquid storage areas where storm water comes into contact with any equipment, tank, container, or other vessel used for Section 313 water priority chemicals.

(a) No tank or container shall be used for the storage of a Section 313 water priority chemical unless its material and construction are compatible with the material stored and conditions of storage such as pressure and temperature, etc.

(b) Liquid storage areas for Section 313 water priority chemicals shall be operated to minimize discharges of Section 313 chemicals. Appropriate measures to minimize discharges of Section 313 chemicals may include secondary containment provided for at least the entire contents of the largest single tank plus sufficient freeboard to allow for precipitation, a strong spill contingency and integrity testing plan, and/or other equivalent measures.

(2) Material storage areas for Section 313 water priority chemicals other than liquids

Material storage areas for Section 313 water priority chemicals other than liquids which are subject to runoff, leaching, or wind shall incorporate drainage or other control features which will minimize the discharge of Section 313 water priority chemicals by reducing storm water contact with Section 313 water priority chemicals.

(3) Truck and rail car loading and unloading areas for liquid Section 313 water priority chemicals

Truck and rail car loading and unloading areas for liquid Section 313 water priority chemicals shall be operated to minimize discharges of Section 313 water priority chemicals. Protection such as overhangs or door skirts to enclose trailer ends at truck loading/unloading docks shall be provided as appropriate. Appropriate measures to minimize discharges of Section 313 chemicals may include: the placement and maintenance of drip pans (including the proper disposal of materials collected in the drip pans) where spillage may occur (such as hose connections, hose reels and filler nozzles) for use when making and breaking hose connections; a strong spill contingency and integrity testing plan; and/or other equivalent measures.

(4) Areas where Section 313 water priority chemicals are transferred, processed or otherwise handled

Processing equipment and materials handling equipment shall be operated so as to minimize discharges of Section 313 water priority chemicals. Materials used in piping and equipment shall be compatible with the substances handled. Drainage from process and materials handling areas shall minimize storm water contact with Section 313 water priority chemicals. Additional protection such as covers or guards to prevent exposure to wind, spraying or releases from pressure relief vents from causing a discharge of Section 313 water priority chemicals to the drainage system shall be provided as appropriate. Visual inspections or leak tests shall be provided for overhead piping conveying Section 313 water priority chemicals without secondary containment.

(5) Discharges from areas covered by paragraphs (1), (2), (3) or (4).

(a) Drainage from areas covered by paragraphs (1), (2), (3) or (4) of this part should be restrained by valves or other positive means to prevent the discharge of a spill or other excessive leakage of Section 313 water priority chemicals. Where containment units are employed, such units may be emptied by pumps or ejectors; however, these shall be manually activated.

(b) Flapper-type drain valves shall not be used to drain containment areas. Valves used for the drainage of containment areas should, as far as is practical, be of manual, open-and-closed design.

(c) If facility drainage is not engineered as above, the final discharge of all in-facility storm sewers shall be equipped to be equivalent with a diversion system that could, in the event of an uncontrolled spill of Section 313 water priority chemicals, return the spilled material to the facility.

(d) Records shall be kept of the frequency and estimated volume (in gallons) of discharges from containment areas.

(6) Facility site runoff other than from areas covered by (1), (2), (3) or (4)

Other areas of the facility (those not addressed in paragraphs (1), (2), (3) or (4)), from which runoff which may contain Section 313 water priority chemicals or spills of Section 313 water priority chemicals could cause a discharge shall incorporate the necessary drainage or other control features to prevent discharge of spilled or improperly disposed material and ensure the mitigation of pollutants in runoff or leachate.

(7) Preventive maintenance and housekeeping

All areas of the facility shall be inspected at specific intervals identified in the plan for leaks or conditions that could lead to discharges of Section 313 water priority chemicals or direct contact of storm water with raw materials, intermediate materials, waste materials or products. In particular, facility piping, pumps, storage tanks and bins, pressure vessels, process and material handling equipment, and material bulk storage areas shall be examined for any conditions or failures which could cause a discharge. Inspection shall include examination for leaks, wind blowing, corrosion, support or foundation failure, or other forms of deterioration or noncontainment. Inspection intervals shall be specified in the plan and shall be based on design and operational experience. Different areas may require different inspection intervals. Where a leak or other condition is discovered which may result in significant releases of Section 313 water priority chemicals to waters of the United States, action to stop the leak or otherwise prevent the significant release of section 313 water priority chemicals to waters of the United States shall be immediately taken or the unit or process shut down until such action can be taken. When a leak or noncontainment of a Section 313 water priority chemical has occurred, contaminated soil, debris, or other material must be promptly removed and disposed in accordance with Federal, State, and local requirements and as described in the plan.

(8) Facility security

Facilities shall have the necessary security systems to prevent accidental or intentional entry which could cause a discharge. Security systems described in the plan shall address fencing, lighting, vehicular traffic control, and securing of equipment and buildings.

(9) Training

Facility employees and contractor personnel that work in areas where Section 313 water priority chemicals are used or stored shall be trained in and informed of preventive measures at the facility. Employee training shall be conducted at intervals specified in the plan, but not less than once per year, in matters of pollution control laws and regulations, and in the storm water pollution prevention plan and the particular features of the facility and its operation which are designed to minimize discharges of Section 313 water priority chemicals. The plan shall designate a person who is accountable for spill prevention at the facility and who will set up the necessary spill emergency procedures and reporting requirements so that spills and emergency releases of Section 313 water priority chemicals can be isolated and contained before a discharge of a Section 313 water priority chemical can occur. Contractor or temporary personnel shall be informed of facility operation and design features in order to prevent discharges or spills from occurring.

(10) Engineering certification

The storm water pollution prevention plan for a facility subject to EPRCA Section 313 requirements for chemicals which are classified as 'section 313 water priority chemicals' shall be reviewed by a Registered Professional Engineer and certified to by such Professional Engineer. A Registered Professional Engineer shall recertify the plan every three years thereafter or as soon as practicable after significant modification are made to the facility. By means of these certifications the engineer, having examined the facility and being familiar with the provisions of this part, shall attest that the storm water pollution prevention plan has been prepared in accordance with good engineering practices. Such certifications shall in no way relieve the owner or operator of a facility covered by the plan of their duty to prepare and fully implement such plan.

### 8. Additional Requirements for Salt Storage

Storage piles of salt used for deicing or other commercial or industrial purposes and which generate a storm water discharge associated with industrial activity which is discharged to a waters of the United States shall be enclosed or covered to prevent exposure to precipitation, except for exposure resulting from adding or removing materials from the pile. Dischargers shall demonstrate compliance with this provision as expeditiously as practicable, but in no event later than October 1, 1995. Piles do not need to be enclosed or covered where storm water from the pile is not discharged to waters of the United States.

## Part V. NUMERIC EFFLUENT LIMITATIONS

### A. Coal Pile Runoff

Any discharge composed of coal pile runoff shall not exceed a maximum concentration for any time of 50 mg/L total suspended solids. Coal pile runoff shall not be diluted with storm water or other flows in order to meet this limitation. The pH of such discharges shall be within the range of 6.0-9.0. Any untreated overflow from facilities designed, constructed and operated to treat the volume of coal pile runoff which is associated with a 10 year, 24 hour rainfall event shall not be subject to the 50 mg/L limitation for total suspended solids. Failure to demonstrate compliance with these limitations as expeditiously as practicable, but in no case later than October 1, 1995, will constitute a violation of this permit.

## Part VI. MONITORING AND REPORTING REQUIREMENTS

### A. Failure to Certify

Any facility that is unable to provide the certification required under paragraph IV.D.3.g.(1) (testing for non-storm water discharges), must notify the Director by October 1, 1993 or, for facilities which begin to discharge storm water associated with industrial activity after October 1, 1992, 180 days after submitting a NOI to be covered by this permit. If the failure to certify is caused by the inability to perform adequate tests or evaluations, such notification shall describe: the procedure of any test conducted for the presence of non-storm water discharges; the results of such test or other relevant observations; potential sources of non-storm water discharges to the storm sewer; and why adequate tests for such storm sewers were not feasible. Non-storm water discharges to waters of the United States which are not authorized by an NPDES permit are unlawful, and must be terminated or dischargers must submit appropriate NPDES permit application forms.

### B. Monitoring Requirements

#### 1. Limitations on Monitoring Requirements

a. Except as required by paragraph b., only those facilities with activities specifically identified in Parts VI.B.2 (semi-annual monitoring requirements) and VI.B.3 (annual monitoring requirements) of this permit are required to conduct sampling of their storm water discharges associated with industrial activity.

   b. The Director can provide written notice to any facility otherwise exempt from the sampling requirements of Parts VI.B.2 (semi-annual monitoring requirements) or VI.B.3 (annual monitoring requirements), that it shall conduct the annual discharge sampling required by Part VI.B.3.d (additional facilities), or specify an alternative monitoring frequency or specify additional parameters to be analyzed.

### 2. Semi-Annual Monitoring Requirements

During the period beginning on the effective date and lasting through the expiration date of this permit, permittees with facilities identified in Parts VI.B.2.a through f must monitor those storm water discharges identified below at least semi-annually (2 times per year) except as provided in VI.B.5 (sampling waiver), VI.B.6 (representative discharge), and VI.C.1 (toxicity testing). Permittees with facilities identified in Parts VI.B.2.a through f (below) must report in accordance with Part VI.D (reporting: where to submit). In addition to the parameters listed below, the permittee shall provide the date and duration (in hours) of the storm event(s) sampled; rainfall measurements or estimates (in inches) of the storm event which generated the sampled runoff; the duration between the storm event sampled and the end of the previous measurable (greater than 0.1 inch rainfall) storm event; and an estimate of the total volume (in gallons) of the discharge sampled;

#### a. Section 313 of EPCRA Facilities

In addition to any monitoring required by Parts VI.B.2.b through f. or Parts VI.B.3.a through d, facilities with storm water discharges associated with industrial activity that are subject to Section 313 of EPCRA for chemicals which are classified as 'Section 313 water priority chemicals' are required to monitor storm water that is discharged from the facility that comes into contact with any equipment, tank, container or other vessel or area used for storage of a Section 313 water priority chemical, or located at a truck or rail car loading or unloading area where a Section 313 water priority chemical is handled for: Oil and Grease (mg/L); Five Day Biochemical Oxygen Demand (BOD5) (mg/L); Chemical Oxygen Demand (COD) (mg/L); Total Suspended Solids (mg/L); Total Kjeldahl Nitrogen (TKN) (mg/L); Total Phosphorus (mg/L): pH; acute whole effluent toxicity; and any Section 313 water priority chemical for which the facility is subject to reporting requirements under section 313 of the Emergency Planning and Community Right to Know Act of 1986.

### b. Primary Metal Industries

Facilities with storm water discharges associated with industrial activity classified as Standard Industrial Classification (SIC) 33 (Primary Metal Industry) are required to monitor such storm water that is discharged from the facility for: oil and grease (mg/L); Chemical Oxygen Demand (COD) (mg/L); total suspended solids (mg/L); pH; acute whole effluent toxicity; total recoverable lead (mg/L); total recoverable cadmium (mg/L); total recoverable copper (mg/L); total recoverable arsenic (mg/L); total recoverable chromium (mg/L); and any pollutant limited in an effluent guideline to which the facility is subject. Facilities that are classified as SIC 33 only because they manufacture pure silicon and/or semiconductor grade silicon are not required to monitor for total recoverable cadmium, total recoverable copper, total recoverable arsenic, total recoverable chromium or acute whole effluent toxicity, but must monitor for other parameters listed above.

### c. Land Disposal Units/Incinerators/BIFs

Facilities with storm water discharges associated with industrial activity from any active or inactive landfill, land application sites or open dump without a stabilized final cover that has received any industrial wastes (other than wastes from a construction site); and incinerators (including Boilers and Industrial Furnaces (BIFs)) that burn hazardous waste and operate under interim status or a permit under Subtitle C of RCRA, are required to monitor such storm water that is discharged from the facility for: Magnesium (total recoverable) (mg/L), Magnesium (dissolved) (mg/L), Total Kjeldahl Nitrogen (TKN) (mg/L), Chemical Oxygen Demand (COD) (mg/L), Total Dissolved Solids (TDS) (mg/L), Total Organic Carbon (TOC) (mg/L), oil and grease (mg/L), pH, Total recoverable arsenic (mg/L), Total recoverable Barium (mg/L), Total recoverable Cadmium (mg/L), Total Chromium (mg/L), Total recoverable Cyanide (mg/L), Total recoverable Lead (mg/L), Total Mercury (mg/L), Total recoverable Selenium (mg/L), Total recoverable Silver (mg/L), and acute whole effluent toxicity.

### d. Wood Treatment

Facilities with storm water discharges associated with industrial activity from areas that are used for wood treatment, wood surface application or storage of treated or surface protected wood at any wood preserving or wood surface facilities are required to monitor such storm water that is discharged from the facility for: oil and grease (mg/L), pH, COD (mg/L), and TSS (mg/L). In addition, facilities that use chlorophenolic formulations shall measure pentachlorophenol (mg/L) and acute whole effluent toxicity; facilities which use creosote formulations shall measure acute whole effluent toxicity; and facilities that use chromium-arsenic formulations shall measure total recoverable arsenic (mg/L), total recoverable chromium (mg/L), and total recoverable copper (mg/L).

### e. Coal Pile Runoff

Facilities with storm water discharges associated with industrial activity from coal pile runoff are required to monitor such storm water that is discharged from the facility for: oil and grease (mg/L), pH, TSS (mg/L), total recoverable copper (mg/L), total recoverable nickel (mg/L) and total recoverable zinc (mg/L).

### f. Battery Reclaimers

Facilities with storm water discharges associated with industrial activity from areas used for storage of lead acid batteries, reclamation products, or waste products, and areas used for lead acid battery reclamation (including material handling activities) at facilities that reclaim lead acid batteries are required to monitor such storm water that is discharged from the facility for: Oil and Grease (mg/L); Chemical Oxygen Demand (COD) (mg/L); Total Suspended Solids (TSS) (mg/L); pH; total recoverable copper (mg/L); and total recoverable lead (mg/L).

### 3. Annual Monitoring Requirements

During the period beginning on the effective date and lasting through the expiration date of this permit, permittees with facilities identified in Parts VI.B.3.a through d. (below) must monitor those storm water discharges identified below at least annually (1 time per year) except as provided in VI.B.5 (sampling waiver), and VI.B.6 (representative discharge). Permittees with facilities identified in parts VI.B.3.a through d. (below) are not required to submit monitoring results, unless required in writing by the Director. However, such permittees must retain monitoring results in accordance with Part VI.E (retention of records). In addition to the parameters listed below, the permittee shall provide the date and duration (in hours) of the storm event(s) sampled; rainfall measurements or estimates (in inches) of the storm event which generated the sampled runoff; the duration between the storm event sampled and the end of the previous measurable (greater than 0.1 inch rainfall) storm event; and an estimate of the total volume (in gallons) of the discharge sampled;

### a. Airports

At airports with over 50,000 flight operations per year, facilities with storm water discharges associated with industrial activity from areas where aircraft or airport deicing operations occur (including runways, taxiways, ramps, and dedicated aircraft deicing stations) are required to monitor such storm water that is discharged from the facility when deicing activities are occurring for: Oil and Grease (mg/L); Five Day Biochemical Oxygen Demand (BOD5) (mg/L); Chemical Oxygen Demand (COD) (mg/L); Total Suspended Solids (TSS) (mg/L); pH; and the primary ingredient used in the deicing materials used at the site (e.g. ethylene glycol, urea, etc.).

### b. Coal-fired Steam Electric Facilities

Facilities with storm water discharges associated with industrial activity from coal handling sites at coal fired steam electric power generating facilities (other than discharges in whole or in part from coal piles subject to storm water effluent guidelines at 40 CFR 423-which are not eligible for coverage under this permit) are required to monitor such storm water that is discharged from the facility for: Oil and grease (mg/L), pH, TSS (mg/L), total recoverable copper (mg/L), total recoverable nickel (mg/L) and total recoverable zinc (mg/L).

### c. Animal Handling / Meat Packing

Facilities with storm water discharges associated with industrial activity from animal handling areas, manure management (or storage) areas, and production waste management (or storage) areas that are exposed to precipitation at meat packing plants, poultry packing plants, and facilities that manufacture animal and marine fats and oils, are required to monitor such storm water that is discharged from the facility for: Five Day Biochemical Oxygen Demand (BOD5) (mg/L); oil and grease (mg/L); Total Suspended Solids (TSS) (mg/L); Total Kjeldahl Nitrogen (TKN) (mg/L); Total Phosphorus (mg/L); pH; and fecal coliform (counts per 100 mL).

### d. Additional Facilities

Facilities with storm water discharges associated with industrial activity that:

(i)   come in contact with storage piles for solid chemicals used as raw materials that are exposed to precipitation at facilities classified as SIC 30 (Rubber and Miscellaneous Plastics Products) or SIC 28 (Chemicals and Allied Products);

(ii)  are from those areas at automobile junkyards with any of the following: (A) over 250 auto/truck bodies with drivelines (engine, transmission, axles, and wheels), 250 drivelines, or any combination thereof (in whole or in parts) are exposed to storm water; (B) over 500 auto/truck units (bodies with or without drivelines in whole or in parts) are stored exposed to storm water; or (C) over 100 units per year are dismantled and drainage or storage of automotive fluids occurs in areas exposed to storm water;

(iii)   come into contact with lime storage piles that are exposed to storm water at lime manufacturing facilities;

(iv)   are from oil handling sites at oil fired steam electric power generating facilities;

(v)    are from cement manufacturing facilities and cement kilns (other than discharges in whole or in part from material storage piles subject to storm water effluent guidelines at 40 CFR 411-which are not eligible for coverage under this permit);

(vi)   are from ready-mixed concrete facilities; or

(vii)  are from ship building and repairing facilities;
        are required to monitor such storm water discharged from the facility for: Oil and Grease (mg/L); Chemical Oxygen Demand (COD) (mg/L); Total Suspended Solids (TSS) (mg/L); pH; and any pollutant limited in an effluent guideline to which the facility is subject.

### 4. Sample Type

For discharges from holding ponds or other impoundments with a retention period greater than 24 hours, (estimated by dividing the volume of the detention pond by the estimated volume of water discharged during the 24 hours previous to the time that the sample is collected) a minimum of one grab sample may be taken. For all other discharges, data shall be reported for both a grab sample and a composite sample. All such samples shall be collected from the discharge resulting from a storm event that is greater than 0.1 inches in magnitude and that occurs at least 72 hours from the previously measurable (greater than 0.1 inch rainfall) storm event. The grab sample shall be taken during the first thirty minutes of the discharge. If the collection of a grab sample during the first thirty minutes is impracticable, a grab sample can be taken during the first hours of the discharge, and the discharger shall submit with the monitoring report a description of why a grab sample during the first thirty minutes was impracticable. The composite sample shall either be flow-weighted or time-weighted. Composite samples may be taken with a continuous sampler or as a combination of a minimum of three sample aliquots taken in each hour of discharge for the entire discharge or for the first three hours of the discharge, with each aliquot being separated by a minimum period of fifteen minutes. Grab samples only must be collected and analyzed for the determination of pH, cyanide, whole effluent toxicity, fecal coliform, and oil and grease.

### 5. Sampling Waiver

When a discharger is unable to collect samples due to adverse climatic conditions, the discharger must submit in lieu of sampling data a description of why samples could not be collected, including available documentation of the event. Adverse weather conditions which may prohibit the collection of samples includes weather conditions that create dangerous conditions for personnel (such as local flooding, high winds, hurricane, tornadoes, electrical storms, etc.) or otherwise make the collection of a sample impracticable (drought, extended frozen conditions, etc.). Dischargers are precluded from exercising this waiver more than once during a two year period.

### 6. Representative Discharge

When a facility has two or more outfalls that, based on a consideration of industrial activity, significant materials, and management practices and activities within the area drained by the outfall, the permittee reasonably believes discharge substantially identical effluents, the permittee may test the effluent of one of such outfalls and report that the quantitative data also applies to the substantially identical outfalls provided that the permittee includes in the storm water pollution prevention plan a description of the location of the outfalls and explaining in detail why the outfalls are expected to discharge substantially identical effluents. In addition, for each outfall that the permittee believes is representative, an estimate of the size of the drainage area (in square feet) and an estimate of the runoff coefficient of the drainage area (e.g. low (under 40 percent), medium (40 to 65 percent) or high (above 65 percent)) shall be provided in the plan. Permittees required to submit monitoring information under Parts VI.D.1.a, b or c of this permit shall include the description of the location of the outfalls, explanation of why outfalls are expected to discharge substantially identical effluents, and estimate of the size of the drainage area and runoff coefficient with the Discharge Monitoring Report.

### 7. Alternative Certification

A discharger is not subject to the monitoring requirements of Parts VI.B.2 or 3 of this permit provided the discharger makes a certification for a given outfall, on an annual basis, under penalty of law, signed in accordance with Part VII.G (signatory requirements), that material handling equipment or activities, raw materials, intermediate products, final products, waste materials, by-products, industrial machinery or operations, significant materials from past industrial activity, or, in the case of airports, deicing activities, that are located in areas of the facility that are within the drainage area of the outfall are not presently exposed to storm water and will not be exposed to storm water for the certification period. Such certification must be retained in the storm water pollution prevention plan, and submitted to EPA in accordance with Part VI.D of this permit.

### 8. Alternative to WET Parameter

A discharger that is subject to the monitoring requirements of Parts VI.B.2.a through d may, in lieu of monitoring for acute whole effluent toxicity, monitor for pollutants identified in Tables II and III of Appendix D of 40 CFR 122 (see Addendum A of this permit) that the discharger knows or has reason to believe are present at the facility site. Such determinations are to be based on reasonable best efforts to identify significant quantities of materials or chemicals present at the facility. Dischargers must also monitor for any additional parameter identified in Parts VI.B.2.a through d.

### C. Toxicity Testing

Permittees that are required to monitor for acute whole effluent toxicity shall initiate the series of tests described below within 180 days after the issuance of this permit or within 90 days after the commencement of a new discharge.

1. Test Procedures.
    a. The permittee shall conduct acute 24 hour static toxicity tests on both an appropriate invertebrate and an appropriate fish (vertebrate) test species (EPA/600/4-90-027 Rev. 9/91, Section 6.1). Freshwater species must be used for discharges to freshwater water bodies. Due to the non-saline nature of rainwater, freshwater test species should also be used for discharges to estuarine, marine or other naturally saline waterbodies.
    b. All test organisms, procedures and quality assurance criteria used shall be in accordance with Methods for Measuring the Acute Toxicity of Effluents and Receiving Waters to Freshwater and Marine Organisms, EPA/600/4-90-027 (Rev. September 1991). EPA has proposed to establish regulations regarding these test methods (December 4, 1989, 53 FR 50216).
    c. Tests shall be conducted semiannually (twice per year) on a grab sample of the discharge. Tests shall be conducted using 100 effluent (no dilution) and a control consisting of synthetic dilution water. Results of all tests conducted with any species shall be reported according to EPA/600/4-90-027 (Rev. September 1991), Section 12, Report Preparation, and the report submitted to EPA with the Discharge Monitoring Reports (DMR's). On the DMR, the permittee shall report "0" if there is no statistical difference between the control mortality and the effluent mortality for each dilution. If there is statistical difference (exhibits toxicity), the permittee shall report "1" on the DMR.
2. If acute whole effluent toxicity (statistically significant difference between the 100% dilution and the control) is detected on or after

October 1, 1995, in storm water discharges, the permittee shall review the storm water pollution prevention plan and make appropriate modifications to assist in identifying the source(s) of toxicity and to reduce the toxicity of their storm water discharges. A summary of the review and the resulting modifications shall be provided in the plan.

### D. Reporting: Where to Submit.

1. a. Permittees which are required to conduct sampling pursuant to Parts VI.B.2.(a) (EPCRA Section 313), and (d) (Wood Treatment facilities), shall monitor samples collected during the sampling periods running from January to June and during the sampling period from July to December. Such permittees shall submit monitoring results obtained during the reporting period running from January to December on Discharge Monitoring Report Form(s) postmarked no later than the 28th day of the following January. A separate Discharge Monitoring Report Form is required for each sampling period. The first report may include less than twelve months of information.

   b. Permittees which are required to conduct sampling pursuant to Parts VI.B.2.(b) (Primary Metal facilities), (e) (Coal Pile Runoff), and (f) (Battery Reclaimers) shall monitor samples collected during the sampling period running from March to August and during the sampling period running from September to February. Such permittees shall submit monitoring results obtained during the reporting period running from April to March on Discharge Monitoring Report Form(s) postmarked no later than the 28th day of the following April. A separate Discharge Monitoring Report Form is required for each event sampling period. The first report may include less than twelve months of information.

   c. Permittees which are required to conduct sampling pursuant to Parts VI.B.2.(c) (Land disposal facilities), shall monitor samples collected during the sampling period running from October to March and during the sampling period running from April to September. Such permittees shall submit monitoring results obtained during the reporting period running from October to September on Discharge Monitoring Report Form(s) postmarked no later than the 28th day of October. A separate Discharge Monitoring Report Form is required for each sampling period. The first report may include less than twelve months of information.

   d. Signed copies of discharge monitoring reports required under Parts VI.D.1.a, VI.D.1.b, and VI.D.1.c, individual permit applications and all other reports required herein, shall be submitted to the Director of the NPDES program at the address of the appropriate Regional Office:

1. CT, MA, ME, NH, RI, VT United States EPA, Region I, Water Management Division, (WCP-2109), Storm Water Staff, John F. Kennedy Federal Building, Room 2209, Boston, MA 02203.

2. NJ, NY, PR, VI United States EPA, Region II, Water Management Division, (2WM-WPC), Storm Water Staff, 26 Federal Plaza, New York, NY 10278.

3. DE, DC, MD, PA, VA, WV United States EPA, Region III, Water Management Division, (3WM55), Storm Water Staff, 841 Chestnut Building, Philadelphia, PA 19107.

4. AL, FL, GA, KY, MS, NC, SC, TN United States EPA, Region IV, Water Management Division, (FPB-3), Storm Water Staff, 345 Courtland Street, NE, Atlanta, GA 30365.

5. IL, IN, MI, MN, OH, WI United States EPA, Region V, Water Quality Branch, (5WQP), Storm Water Staff, 77 West Jackson Boulevard, Chicago, IL 60604.

6. AR, LA, NM (except see Region IX for Navajo lands, and see Region VIII for Ute Mountain Reservation lands), OK, TX United States EPA, Region VI, Water Management Division, (6W-EA), Storm Water Staff, First Interstate Bank Tower at Fountain Place, 1445 Ross Avenue, 12th Floor, Suite 1200, Dallas, TX 75202.

7. IA, KS, MO, NE United States EPA, Region VII, Water Management Division, Compliance Branch, Storm Water Staff, 726 Minnesota Avenue, Kansas City, KS 66101.

8. CO, MT, ND, SD, WY, UT (except see Region IX for Goshute Reservation and Navajo Reservation lands) United States EPA, Region VIII, Water Management Division, NPDES Branch (8WM-C), Storm Water Staff, 999 18th Street, Denver, CO 80202-2466.

   Note.-For Montana Indian Lands, please use the following address:

   United States EPA, Region VIII, Montana Operations Office, Federal Office Building, Drawer 10096, 301 South Park, Helena, MT 59620-0026.

9. AZ, CA, HI, NV, Guam, American Samoa, the Goshute Reservation in UT and NV, the Navajo Reservation in UT, NM, and AZ, the Duck Valley Reservation in NV and ID United States EPA, Region IX, Water Management Division, ( -5-1), Storm Water Staff, 75 Hawthorne Street, San Francisco, CA 94105.

10. AK, ID (except see Region IX for Duck Valley Reservation lands), OR, WA United States EPA, Region X, Water Management Division, (WD-134), Storm Water Staff, 1200 Sixth Street, Seattle, WA 98101(i). e. Permittees with facilities identified in Parts VI.B.3 (annual monitoring) are not required to submit monitoring results, unless required in writing by the Director.

2. Additional Notification.

In addition to filing copies of discharge monitoring reports in accordance with Part VI.D.1 (reporting: where to submit), facilities with at least one storm water discharge associated with industrial activity through a large or medium municipal separate storm sewer system (systems serving a population of 100,000 or more) must submit signed copies of discharge monitoring reports to the operator of the municipal separate storm sewer system in accordance with the dates provided in paragraph VI.D.1 (reporting: where to submit). Facilities not required to report monitoring data under Part VI.B.3 (annual monitoring requirements), and facilities that are not otherwise required to monitor their discharges, need not comply with this provision.

## E. Retention of Records.

1. The permittee shall retain the pollution prevention plan developed in accordance with Part IV (storm water pollution prevention plans) of this permit until at least one year after coverage under this permit terminates. The permittee shall retain all records of all monitoring information, copies of all reports required by this permit, and records of all data used to complete the Notice of Intent to be covered by this permit, until at least one year after coverage under this permit terminates. This period may be explicitly modified by alternative provisions of this permit (see paragraph VI.E.2 (below) of this permit) or extended by request of the Director at any time.

2. For discharges subject to sampling requirements pursuant to Part VI.B (monitoring requirements), in addition to the requirements of paragraph VI.E.1 (above), permittees are required to retain for a six year period from the data of sample collection or for the term of this permit, which ever is greater, records of all monitoring information collected during the term of this permit. Permittees must submit such monitoring results to the Director upon the requests of the Director, and submit a summary of such result as part of renotification requirements in accordance with Part II.F (renotification).

## Part VII. STANDARD PERMIT CONDITIONS

### A. Duty to Comply.

1. The permittee must comply with all conditions of this permit. Any permit noncompliance constitutes a violation of CWA and is grounds for enforcement action; for permit termination, revocation and reissuance, or modification; or for denial of a permit renewal application.
2. Penalties for Violations of Permit Conditions.
   a. Criminal.
      1. Negligent violations.-The CWA provides that any person who negligently violates permit conditions implementing Sections 301, 302, 306, 307, 308, 318, or 405 of the Act is subject to a fine of not less than $2,500 nor more than $25,000 per day of violation, or by imprisonment for not more than 1 year, or both.
      2. Knowing violations.-The CWA provides that any person who knowingly violates permit conditions implementing Sections 301, 302, 306, 307, 308, 318, or 405 of the Act is subject to a fine of not less than $5,000 nor more than $50,000 per day of violation, or by imprisonment for not more than 3 years, or both.
      3. Knowing endangerment.-The CWA provides that any person who knowingly violates permit conditions implementing Sections 301, 302, 306, 307, 308, 318, or 405 of the Act and who knows at that time that he is placing another person in imminent danger of death or serious bodily injury is subject to a fine of not more than $250,000, or by imprisonment for not more than 15 years, or both.
      4. False statement.-The CWA provides that any person who knowingly makes any false material statement, representation, or certification in any application, record, report, plan, or other document filed or required to be maintained under the Act or who knowingly falsifies, tampers with, or renders inaccurate, any monitoring device or method required to be maintained under the Act, shall upon conviction, be punished by a fine of not more than $10,000 or by imprisonment for not more than 2 years, or by both. If a conviction is for a violation committed after a first conviction of such person under this paragraph, punishment shall be by a fine of not more than $20,000 per day of violation, or by imprisonment of not more than 4 years, or by both. (See section 309(c)(4) of the Clean Water Act).

   b. Civil penalties.-The CWA provides that any person who violates a permit condition implementing Sections 301, 302, 306, 307, 308, 318, or 405 of the Act is subject to a civil penalty not to exceed $25,000 per day for each violation.

   c. Administrative penalties.-The CWA provides that any person who violates a permit condition implementing Sections 301, 302, 306, 307, 308, 318, or 405 of the Act is subject to an administrative penalty, as follows:

      1. Class I penalty.-Not to exceed $10,000 per violation nor shall the maximum amount exceed $25,000.

      2. Class II penalty.-Not to exceed $10,000 per day for each day during which the violation continues nor shall the maximum amount exceed $125,000.

### B. Continuation of the Expired General Permit

This permit expires on October 1, 1997. However, an expired general permit continues in force and effect until a new general permit is issued. Permittees must submit a new NOI in accordance with the requirements of Part II of this permit, using a NOI form provided by the Director (or photocopy thereof) between August 1, 1997 and September 29, 1997 to remain covered under the continued permit after October 1, 1997. Facilities that had not obtained coverage under the permit by October 1, 1997 cannot become authorized to discharge under the continued permit.

### C. Need to Halt or Reduce Activity Not a Defense

It shall not be a defense for a permittee in an enforcement action that it would have been necessary to halt or reduce the permitted activity in order to maintain compliance with the conditions of this permit.

### D. Duty to Mitigate

The permittee shall take all reasonable steps to minimize or prevent any discharge in violation of this permit which has a reasonable likelihood of adversely affecting human health or the environment.

### E. Duty to Provide Information

The permittee shall furnish to the Director, within a time specified by the Director, any information which the Director may request to determine compliance with this permit. The permittee shall also furnish to the Director upon request copies of records required to be kept by this permit.

## F. Other Information

When the permittee becomes aware that he or she failed to submit any relevant facts or submitted incorrect information in the Notice of Intent or in any other report to the Director, he or she shall promptly submit such facts or information.

## G. Signatory Requirements

All Notices of Intent, Notices of Termination, storm water pollution prevention plans, reports, certifications or information either submitted to the Director (and/or the operator of a large or medium municipal separate storm sewer system), or that this permit requires be maintained by the permittee, shall be signed.

1. All Notices of Intent shall be signed as follows:
   a. For a corporation: by a responsible corporate officer. For the purpose of this section, a responsible corporate officer means: (1) A president, secretary, treasurer, or vice-president of the corporation in charge of a principal business function, or any other person who performs similar policy or decision-making functions for the corporation; or (2) the manager of one or more manufacturing, production or operating facilities employing more than 250 persons or having gross annual sales or expenditures exceeding $25,000,000 (in second-quarter 1980 dollars) if authority to sign documents has been assigned or delegated to the manager in accordance with corporate procedures;
   b. For a partnership or sole proprietorship: by a general partner or the proprietor, respectively; or
   c. For a municipality: State, Federal, or other public agency: by either a principal executive officer or ranking elected official. For purposes of this section, a principal executive officer of a Federal agency includes (1) the chief executive officer of the agency, or (2) a senior executive officer having responsibility for the overall operations of a principal geographic unit of the agency (e.g. Regional Administrators of EPA).
2. All reports required by the permit and other information requested by the Director shall be signed by a person described above or by a duly authorized representative of that person. A person is a duly authorized representative only if:

   a. The authorization is made in writing by a person described above and submitted to the Director.
   b. The authorization specifies either an individual or a position having responsibility for the overall operation of the regulated facility or activity, such as the position of manager, operator,

superintendent, or position of equivalent responsibility or an individual or position having overall responsibility for environmental matters for the company. (A duly authorized representative may thus be either a named individual or any individual occupying a named position).

c. Changes to authorization. If an authorization under paragraph VII.G.2. is no longer accurate because a different individual or position has responsibility for the overall operation of the facility, a new notice of intent satisfying the requirements of paragraph II.C must be submitted to the Director prior to or together with any reports, information, or applications to be signed by an authorized representative.

d. Certification. Any person signing documents under this section shall make the following certification:

"I certify under penalty of law that this document and all attachments were prepared under my direction or supervision in accordance with a system designed to assure that qualified personnel properly gathered and evaluated the information submitted. Based on my inquiry of the person or persons who manage the system, or those persons directly responsible for gathering the information, the information submitted is, to the best of my knowledge and belief, true, accurate, and complete. I am aware that there are significant penalties for submitting false information, including the possibility of fine and imprisonment for knowing violations."

### H. Penalties for Falsification of Reports

Section 309(c)(4) of the Clean Water Act provides that any person who knowingly makes any false material statement, representation, or certification in any record or other document submitted or required to be maintained under this permit, including reports of compliance or noncompliance shall, upon conviction, be punished by a fine of not more than $10,000, or by imprisonment for not more than 2 years, or by both.

### I. Penalties for Falsification of Monitoring Systems

The CWA provides that any person who falsifies, tampers with, or knowingly renders inaccurate any monitoring device or method required to be maintained under this permit shall, upon conviction, be punished by fines and imprisonment described in section 309 of the CWA.

### J. Oil and Hazardous Substances Liability

Nothing in this permit shall be construed to preclude the institution of any legal action or relieve the permittee from any responsibilities, liabilities, or penalties to which the permittee is or may be subject under section 311 of the CWA or section 106 of the Comprehensive Environmental Response, Compensation and Liability Act of 1980 (CERCLA).

### K. Property Rights

The issuance of this permit does not convey any property rights of any sort, nor any exclusive privileges, nor does it authorize any injury to private property nor any invasion of personal rights, nor any infringement of Federal, State or local laws or regulations.

### L. Severability

The provisions of this permit are severable, and if any provision of this permit, or the application of any provision of this permit to any circumstance, is held invalid, the application of such provision to other circumstances, and the remainder of this permit shall not be affected thereby.

### M. Requiring an Individual Permit or an Alternative General Permit

1. The Director may require any person authorized by this permit to apply for and/or obtain either an individual NPDES permit or an alternative NPDES general permit. Any interested person may petition the Director to take action under this paragraph. The Director may require any owner or operator authorized to discharge under this permit to apply for an individual NPDES permit only if the owner or operator has been notified in writing that a permit application is required. This notice shall include a brief statement of the reasons for this decision, an application form, a statement setting a deadline for the owner or operator to file the application, and a statement that on the effective date of issuance or denial of the individual NPDES permit or the alternative general permit as it applies to the individual permittee, coverage under this general permit shall automatically terminate. Individual permit applications shall be submitted to the address of the appropriate Regional Office shown in Part VI.D.1.d (reporting: where to submit) of this permit. The Director may grant additional time to submit the application upon request of the applicant. If an owner or operator fails to submit in a timely manner an individual NPDES permit application as required by the Director, then the applicability of this permit to the individual NPDES permittee is automatically terminated at the end of the day specified for application submittal.

2. Any owner or operator authorized by this permit may request to be excluded from the coverage of this permit by applying for an indi-

vidual permit. The owner or operator shall submit an individual application (Form 1 and Form 2F) with reasons supporting the request to the Director. Individual permit applications shall be submitted to the address of the appropriate Regional Office shown in Part VI.D.1.c. of this permit. The request may be granted by the issuance of any individual permit or an alternative general permit if the reasons cited by the owner or operator are adequate to support the request.

3. When an individual NPDES permit is issued to an owner or operator otherwise subject to this permit, or the owner or operator is authorized for coverage under an alternative NPDES general permit, the applicability of this permit to the individual NPDES permittee is automatically terminated on the effective date of the individual permit or the date of authorization of coverage under the alternative general permit, whichever the case may be. When an individual NPDES permit is denied to an owner or operator otherwise subject to this permit, or the owner or operator is denied for coverage under an alternative NPDES general permit, the applicability of this permit to the individual NPDES permittee is automatically terminated on the date of such denial, unless otherwise specified by the Director.

### N. State/Environmental Laws

1. Nothing in this permit shall be construed to preclude the institution of any legal action or relieve the permittee from any responsibilities, liabilities, or penalties established pursuant to any applicable State law or regulation under authority preserved by section 510 of the Act.

2. No condition of this permit shall release the permittee from any responsibility or requirements under other environmental statutes or regulations.

### O. Proper Operation and Maintenance

The permittee shall at all times properly operate and maintain all facilities and systems of treatment and control (and related appurtenances) which are installed or used by the permittee to achieve compliance with the conditions of this permit and with the requirements of storm water pollution prevention plans. Proper operation and maintenance also includes adequate laboratory controls and appropriate quality assurance procedures. Proper operation and maintenance requires the operation of backup or auxiliary facilities or similar systems, installed by a permittee only when necessary to achieve compliance with the conditions of the permit.

## P. Monitoring and Records

1. Samples and measurements taken for the purpose of monitoring shall be representative of the monitored activity.
2. The permittee shall retain records of all monitoring information including all calibration and maintenance records and all original strip chart recordings for continuous monitoring instrumentation, copies of the reports required by this permit, and records of all data used to complete the application for this permit, for a period of at least 6 years from the date of the sample, measurement, report or application. This period may be extended by request of the Director at any time.
3. Records contents.-Records of monitoring information shall include:
   a. The date, exact place, and time of sampling or measurements;
   b. The initials or name(s) of the individual(s) who performed the sampling or measurements;
   c. The date(s) analyses were performed;
   d. The time(s) analyses were initiated;
   e. The initials or name(s) of the individual(s) who performed the analyses;
   f. References and written procedures, when available, for the analytical techniques or methods used; and
   g. The results of such analyses, including the bench sheets, instrument readouts, computer disks or tapes, etc., used to determine these results.
4. Monitoring must be conducted according to test procedures approved under 40 CFR Part 136, unless other test procedures have been specified in this permit.

## Q. Inspection and Entry

The permittee shall allow the Director or an authorized representative of EPA, the State, or, in the case of a facility which discharges through a municipal separate storm sewer, an authorized representative of the municipal operator or the separate storm sewer receiving the discharge, upon the presentation of credentials and other documents as may be required by law, to:

1. Enter upon the permittee's premises where a regulated facility or activity is located or conducted or where records must be kept under the conditions of this permit;
2. Have access to and copy at reasonable times, any records that must be kept under the conditions of this permit; and
3. Inspect at reasonable times any facilities or equipment (including monitoring and control equipment).

## R. Permit Actions

This permit may be modified, revoked and reissued, or terminated for cause. The filing of a request by the permittee for a permit modification, revocation and reissuance, or termination, or a notification of planned changes or anticipated noncompliance does not stay any permit condition.

## S. Bypass of Treatment Facility

### 1. Notice:

#### a. Anticipated bypass

If a permittee subject to the numeric effluent limitation of Part V.A of this permit knows in advance of the need for a bypass, he or she shall submit prior notice, if possible, at least ten days before the date of the bypass; including an evaluation of the anticipated quality and effect of the pass.

#### b. Unanticipated bypass

The permittee subject to the numeric effluent limitation of Part V.A of this permit shall submit notice of an unanticipated bypass. Any information regarding the unanticipated bypass shall be provided orally within 24 hours from the time the permittee became aware of the circumstances. A written submission shall also be provided within 5 days of the time the permittee became aware of the circumstances. The written submission shall contain a description of the bypass and its cause; the period of the bypass; including exact dates and times, and if the bypass has not been corrected, the anticipated time it is expected to continue; and steps taken or planned to reduce, eliminate, and prevent reoccurrence of the bypass.

### 2. Prohibition of bypass:

  a. Bypass is prohibited and the Director may take enforcement action against a permittee for a bypass. Unless:

    1. The bypass was unavoidable to prevent loss of life, personal injury, or severe property damage;

    2. There were no feasible alternatives to the bypass, such as the use of auxiliary facilities, retention of untreated wastes, or maintenance during normal periods of equipment downtime. This condition is not satisfied if the permittee should, in the exercise of reasonable engineering judgment, have installed adequate backup equipment to prevent a bypass which occurred during normal periods of equipment downtime or preventive maintenance; and

3.  The permittee submitted notices of the bypass.
b.  The Director may approve an anticipated bypass after consider-
ing its adverse effects, if the Director determines that it will meet
the three conditions listed in Part VII.S.2.a.

### T. Upset Conditions

1.  An upset constitutes an affirmative defense to an action brought for
noncompliance with technology-based numeric effluent limitations
in Part V.A of this permit if the requirements of paragraph 2 below
are met. No determination made during administrative review of
claims that noncompliance was caused by upset, and before an
action for noncompliance, if final administrative action subject to
judicial review.
2.  A permittee who wishes to establish the affirmative defense of an
upset shall demonstrate, through properly signed, contemporane-
ous operating logs, or other relevant evidence, that:
    a.  An upset occurred and that the permittee can identify the spe-
cific cause(s) of the upset:
    b.  The permitted facility was at the time being properly operated;
and
    c.  The permittee provided oral notice of the upset to EPA within 24
hours from the time the permittee became aware of the circumstances. A written submission shall also be provided within 5
days of the time the permittee became aware of the circumstances. The written submission shall contain a description of
the upset and its cause; the period of the upset; including exact
dates and times, and if the upset has not been corrected, the
anticipated time it is expected to continue; and steps taken or
planned to reduce, eliminate, and prevent reoccurrence of the
upset.
3.  In any enforcement proceeding the permittee seeking to establish
the occurrence of an upset has the burden of proof.

## Part VIII. REOPENER CLAUSE

A.  If there is evidence indicating potential or realized impacts on water
quality due to any storm water discharge associated with industrial activity covered by this permit, the owner or operator of such discharge may be required to obtain individual permit or an
alternative general permit in accordance with Part VII.M (requiring
an individual permit or alternative general permit) of this permit or
the permit may be modified to include different limitations and/or
requirements.

B. Permit modification or revocation will be conducted according to 40 CFR 122.62, 122.63, 122.64 and 124.5.

## Part IX. TERMINATION OF COVERAGE

### A. Notice of Termination

Where all storm water discharges associated with industrial activity that are authorized by this permit are eliminated, or where the operator of storm water discharges associated with industrial activity at a facility changes, the operator of the facility may submit a Notice of Termination that is signed in accordance with Part VII.G (signatory requirements) of this permit. The Notice of Termination shall include the following information:

1. Name, mailing address, and location of the facility for which the notification is submitted. Where a street address for the site is not available, the location of the approximate center of the site must be described in terms of the latitude and longitude to the nearest 15 seconds, or the section, township and range to the nearest quarter section;

2. The name, address and telephone number of the operator addressed by the Notice of Termination;

3. The NPDES permit number for the storm water discharge associated with industrial activity identified by the Notice of Termination;

4. An indication of whether the storm water discharges associated with industrial activity have been eliminated or the operator of the discharges has changed; and

5. The following certification signed in accordance with Part VII.G (signatory requirements) of this permit:

> "I certify under penalty of law that all storm water discharges associated with industrial activity from the identified facility that are authorized by a NPDES general permit have been eliminated or that I am no longer the operator of the industrial activity. I understand that by submitting this notice of termination, that I am no longer authorized to discharge storm water associated with industrial activity under this general permit, and that discharging pollutants in storm water associated with industrial activity to waters of the United States is unlawful under the Clean Water Act where the discharge is not authorized by a NPDES permit. I also understand that the submittal of this notice of termination does not release an operator from liability for any violations of this permit or the Clean Water Act."

## B. Addresses

All Notices of Termination are to be sent, using the form provided by the Director (or a photocopy thereof), to the Director of the NPDES program in care of the following address: Storm Water Notice of Termination, PO Box 1185, Newington, VA 22122.

## Part X. DEFINITIONS

**Best Management Practices ("BMPs")** means schedules of activities, prohibitions of practices, maintenance procedures, and other management practices to prevent or reduce the pollution of waters of the United States. BMPs also include treatment requirements, operating procedures, and practices to control facility site runoff, spillage or leaks, sludge or waste disposal, or drainage from raw material storage.

**Bypass** means the intentional diversion of waste streams from any portion of a treatment facility.

**Coal pile runoff** means the rainfall runoff from or through any coal storage pile.

**CWA** means Clean Water Act (formerly referred to as the Federal Water Pollution Control Act or Federal Water Pollution Control Act Amendments of 1972).

**Director** means the Regional Administrator or an authorized representative.

**Flow-weighted composite sample** means a composite sample consisting of a mixture of aliquots collected at a constant time interval, where the volume of each aliquot is proportional to the flow rate of the discharge.

**Landfill** means an area of land or an excavation in which wastes are placed for permanent disposal, and which is not a land application unit, surface impoundment, injection well, or waste pile.

**Land application unit** means an area where wastes are applied onto or incorporated into the soil surface (excluding manure spreading operations) for treatment or disposal.

**Large and medium municipal separate storm sewer system** means all municipal separate storm sewers that are either: (i) located in an incorporated place (city) with a population of 100,000 or more as determined by the latest Decennial Census by the Bureau of Census (these cities are listed in Appendices F and G of 40 CFR Part 122); or (ii) located in the counties with unincorporated urbanized populations of 100,000 or more, except municipal separate storm sewers that are located in the incorporated places, townships or towns within such counties (these counties are listed in Appendices H and I of 40 CFR Part 122); or (iii) owned or operated by a municipality other than those described in paragraph (i) or (ii) and that are designated by the Director as part of the large or medium municipal separate storm sewer system.

**NOI** means notice of intent to be covered by this permit (see Part II of this permit.)

**NOT** means notice of termination (see Part II of this permit.)

**Point source** means any discernible, confined, and discrete conveyance, including but not limited to, any pipe, ditch, channel, tunnel, conduit, well, discrete fissure, container, rolling stock, concentrated animal feeding operation, landfill leachate collection system, vessel or other floating craft from which pollutants are or may be discharges. This term does not include return flows from irrigated agriculture or agricultural storm water runoff.

**Section 313 water priority chemical** means a chemical or chemical categories which: 1) Are listed at 40 CFR 372.65 pursuant to Section 313 of the Emergency Planning and Community Right-to-Know Act (EPCRA) (also known as Title III of the Superfund Amendments and Reauthorization Act (SARA) of 1986); 2) are present at or above threshold levels at a facility subject to EPCRA Section 313 reporting requirements; and 3) that meet at least one of the following criteria: (i) Are listed in Appendix D of 40 CFR 122 on either Table II (organic priority pollutants), Table III (certain metals, cyanides, and phenols) or Table V (certain toxic pollutants and hazardous substances); (ii) are listed as a hazardous substance pursuant to section 311(b)(2)(A) of the CWA at 40 CFR 116.4; or (iii) are pollutants for which EPA has published acute or chronic water quality criteria. See Addendum B of this permit.

**Significant materials** includes, but is not limited to: raw materials; fuels; materials such as solvents, detergents, and plastic pellets; finished materials such as metallic products; raw materials used in food processing or production; hazardous substances designated under section 101(14) of CERCLA; any chemical the facility is required to report pursuant to EPCRA Section 313; fertilizers; pesticides; and waste products such as ashes, slag and sludge that have the potential to be released with storm water discharges. Significant spills includes, but is not limited to: releases of oil or hazardous substances in excess of reportable quantities under section 311 of the Clean Water Act (see 40 CFR 110.10 and CFR 117.21) or section 102 of CERCLA (see 40 CFR 302.4).

**Storm water** means storm water runoff, snow melt runoff, and surface runoff and drainage.

**Storm water associated with industrial activity** means the discharge from any conveyance which is used for collecting and conveying storm water and which is directly related to manufacturing, processing or raw materials storage areas at an industrial plant. The term does not include discharges from facilities or activities excluded from the NPDES program. For the categories of industries identified in paragraphs (i) through (x) of this definition, the term includes, but is not limited to, storm water discharges from industrial plant yards; immediate access roads and rail lines used or traveled by carriers of raw materials, manufactured products, waste material, or by-products used or created by the facility; material handling sites; refuse sites; sites used for the application or disposal of process waste waters (as defined at 40 CFR 401); sites used for the storage and maintenance of material handling equipment; sites used for residual treatment, storage, or disposal; shipping and receiving areas; manufacturing buildings; storage areas (including tank farms) for raw materials, and intermediate and finished products; and areas where industrial activity has taken place in the past and significant materials remain and are exposed to storm water. For the categories of industries identified in paragraph (xi) of this definition, the term includes only storm water discharges from all areas (except access roads and rail lines) listed in the previous sentence where material handling equipment or activities, raw materials, intermediate products, final products, waste materials, by-products, or industrial machinery are exposed to storm water. For the purposes of this paragraph, material handling activities include the: storage, loading and unloading, transportation, or conveyance of any raw material, intermediate product, finished product, by-product or waste product. The term excludes areas located on plant lands separate from the plant's industrial activities, such as office buildings and accompanying parking lots as long as the drainage from the excluded areas is not mixed with storm water drained from the above described areas. Industrial facilities (including industrial facilities that are Federally, State or municipally owned or operated that meet the description of the facilities listed in this paragraph (i)-(xi) of this definition) include those facilities designated under 122.26(a)(1)(v). The following categories of facilities are considered to be engaging in "industrial activity" for purposes of this subsection:

(i)    Facilities subject to storm water effluent limitations guidelines, new source performance standards, or toxic pollutant effluent standards under 40 CFR subchapter N (except facilities with toxic pollutant effluent standards which are exempted under category (xi) of this definition);

(ii)    Facilities classified as Standard Industrial Classifications 24 (except 2434), 26 (except 265 and 267), 28 (except 283), 29, 311, 32 (except 323), 33, 3441, 373;

(iii)   Facilities classified as Standard Industrial Classifications 10 through 14 (mineral industry) including active or inactive mining operations (except for areas of coal mining operations no longer meeting the definition of a reclamation area under 40 CFR 434.11(1) because the performance bond issued to the facility by the appropriate SMCRA authority has been released, or except for areas of non-coal mining operations which have been released from applicable State or Federal reclamation requirements after December 17, 1990) and oil and gas exploration, production, processing, or treatment operations, or transmission facilities that discharge storm water contaminated by contact with or that has come into contact with, any overburden, raw material, intermediate products, finished products, byproducts or waste products located on the site of such operations; inactive mining operations are mining sites that are not being actively mined, but which have an identifiable owner/operator;

(iv)    Hazardous waste treatment, storage, or disposal facilities, including those that are operating under interim status or a permit under Subtitle C of RCRA;

(v)     Landfills, land application sites, and open dumps that have received any industrial wastes (waste that is received from any of the facilities described under this subsection) including those that are subject to regulation under Subtitle D of RCRA;

(vi)    Facilities involved in the recycling of materials, including metal scrapyards, battery reclaimers, salvage yards, and automobile junkyards, including but limited to those classified as Standard Industrial Classification 5015 and 5093;

(vii)   Steam electric power generating facilities, including coal handling sites;

(viii)  Transportation facilities classified as Standard Industrial Classifications 40, 41, 42 (except 4221-25), 43, 44, 45 and 5171 which have vehicle maintenance shops, equipment cleaning operations, or airport deicing operations. Only those portions of the facility that are either involved in vehicle maintenance (including vehicle rehabilitation, mechanical repairs, painting, fueling, and lubrication), equipment cleaning operations, airport deicing operations, or which are otherwise identified under paragraphs (i)-(vii) or (ix)-(xi) of this subsection are associated with industrial activity;

(ix)   Treatment works treating domestic sewage or any other sewage sludge or wastewater treatment device or system, used in the storage treatment, recycling, and reclamation of municipal or domestic sewage, including land dedicated to the disposal of sewage sludge that are located within the confines of the facility, with a design flow of 1.0 mgd or more, or required to have an approved pretreatment program under 40 CFR 403. Not included are farm lands, domestic gardens or lands used for sludge management where sludge is beneficially reused and which are not physically located in the confines of the facility, or areas that are in compliance with 40 CFR 503;

(x)    Construction activity including clearing, grading and excavation activities except: operations that result in the disturbance of less than five acres of total land area which are not part of a larger common plan of development or sale;

(xi)   Facilities under Standard Industrial Classifications 20, 21, 22, 23, 2434, 25, 265, 267, 27, 283, 285, 30, 31 (except 311), 323, 34 (except 3441), 35, 36, 37 (except 373), 38, 39, 4221-25, (and which are not otherwise included within categories (i)-(x)).*

**Time-weighted composite** means a composite sample consisting of a mixture of equal volume aliquots collected at a constant time interval.

**Upset** means an exceptional incident in which there is unintentional and temporary noncompliance with the numeric effluent limitations of part V of this permit because of factors beyond the reasonable control of the permittee. An upset does not include noncompliance to the extent caused by operational error, improperly designed treatment facilities, inadequate treatment facilities, lack of preventive maintenance, or careless or improper operation.

**Waste pile** means any noncontainerized accumulation of solid, non-flowing waste that is used for treatment or storage.

**Waters of the United States** means:

(a)   All waters which are currently used, were used in the past, or may be susceptible to use in interstate or foreign commerce, including all waters which are subject to the ebb and flow of the tide;

(b)   All interstate waters, including interstate "wetlands";

---

*On June 4, 1992, the United States Court of Appeals for the Ninth Circuit remanded the exclusion for manufacturing facilities in category (xi) which do not have materials or activities exposed to storm water to the EPA for further rulemaking. (Nos. 90-70671 and 91-70200).

(c) All other waters such as interstate lakes, rivers, streams (including intermittent streams), mudflats, sandflats, wetlands, sloughs, prairie potholes, wet meadows, playa lakes, or natural ponds the use, degradation, or destruction of which would affect or could affect interstate or foreign commerce including any such waters:

1.  Which are or could be used by interstate or foreign travelers for recreational or other purposes;
2.  From which fish or shellfish are or could be taken and sold in interstate or foreign commerce; or
3.  Which are used or could be used for industrial purposes by industries in interstate commerce;

(d) All impoundments of waters otherwise defined as waters of the United States under this definition;
(e) Tributaries of waters identified in paragraphs (a) through (d) of this definition;
(f) The territorial sea; and
(g) Wetlands adjacent to waters (other than waters that are themselves wetlands) identified in paragraphs (a) through (f) of this definition.

Waste treatment systems, including treatment ponds or lagoons designed to meet the requirements of CWA are not waters of the United States.

## Part XI. STATE SPECIFIC CONDITIONS

(See original Federal Register notice for this section.)

## Addendum A: Pollutants identified in Tables II and III of Appendix D of 40 CFR 122.

*Table II   Organic Toxic Pollutants in Each of Four Fractions in Analysis by Gas Chromatography/Mass Spectroscopy (GS/MS)*

### Volatiles

| | |
|---|---|
| acrolein | 1,2-dichloropropane |
| acrylonitrile | 1,3-dichloropropylene |
| benzene | ethylbenzene |
| bromoform | methyl bromide |
| carbon tetrachloride | methyl chloride |
| chlorobenzene | methylene chloride |
| chlorodibromomethane | 1,1,2,2-tetrachloroethane |
| chloroethane | tetrachloroethylene |
| 2-chloroethylvinyl ether | toluene |
| chloroform | 1,2-trans-dichloroethylene |
| dichlorobromomethane | 1,1,1-trichloroethane |
| 1,1-dichloroethane | 1,1,2-trichloroethane |
| 1,2-dichloroethane | vinyl chloride |
| 1,1-dichloroethylene | |

### Pesticides

| | |
|---|---|
| aldrin | endrin |
| alpha-BHC | endrin aldehyde |
| beta-BHC | heptachlor |
| gamma-BHC | heptachlor epoxide |
| delta-BHC | PCB-1242 |
| chlordane | PCB-1254 |
| 4,4'-DDT | PCB-1221 |
| 4,4'-DDE | PCB-1232 |
| 4,4'-DDD | PCB-1248 |
| dieldrin | PCB-1260 |
| alpha-endosulfan | PCB-1016 |
| beta-endosulfan | toxaphene |
| endosulfan sulfate | |

### Acid Compounds

| | |
|---|---|
| 2-chlorophenol | 4-nitrophenol |
| 2,4-dichlorophenol | p-chloro-m-cresol |
| 2,4-dimethylphenol | pentachlorophenol |
| 4,6-dinitro-o-cresol | phenol |
| 2,4-dinitrophenol | 2,4,6-trichlorophenol |
| 2-nitrophenol | |

*Table II   Organic Toxic Pollutants in Each of Four Fractions in Analysis by Gas Chromatography/Mass Spectroscopy (GS/MS) (Continued)*

### Base/Neutral

| | |
|---|---|
| acenaphthene | anthracene |
| acenaphthylene | benzidine |
| benzo(a)anthracene | 1,2-dichlorobenzene |
| benzo(a)pyrene | 1,3-dichlorobenzene |
| 3,4-benzofluoranthene | 1,4-dichlorobenzene |
| benzo(ghi)perylene | 3,3'-dichlorobenzidine |
| benzo(k)fluoranthene | diethyl phthalate |
| bis(2-chloroethoxy)methane | dimethyl phthalate |
| bis(2-chloroethyl)ether | di-n-butyl phthalate |
| bis(2-chloroisopropyl)ether | 2,4-dinitrotoluene |
| bis(2-ethylhexyl)phthalate | 2,6-dinitrotoluene |
| 4-bromophenyl phenyl ether | di-n-octyl phthalate |
| butylbenzyl phthalate | 1,2-diphenylhydrazine (as azobenzene) |
| 2-chloronaphthalene | fluroranthene |
| 4-chlorophenyl phenyl ether | fluorene |
| chrysene | hexachlorobenzene |
| dibenzo(a,h)anthracene | hexachlorobutadiene |
| indeno(1,2,3-cd)pyrene | hexachlorocyclopentadiene |
| isophorone | hexachloroethane |
| napthalene | N-nitrosodi-n-propylamine |
| nitrobenzene | N-nitrosodiphenylamine |
| N-nitrosodimethylamine | phenanthrene |
| 1, 2, 4-trichlorobenzene | pyrene |

*Table III   Other Toxic Pollutants (Metals and Cyanide) and Total Phenols*

| | |
|---|---|
| Antimony, Total | Nickel, Total |
| Arsenic, Total | Selenium, Total |
| Beryllium, Total | Silver, Total |
| Cadmium, Total | Thallium, Total |
| Chromium, Total | Zinc, Total |
| Copper, Total | Cyanide, Total |
| Lead, Total | Phenols, Total |
| Mercury, Total | |

## Addendum B: Section 313 Water Priority Chemicals.

| CAS Number | Common Name |
|---|---|
| 75-07-0 | Acetaldehyde |
| 75865 | Acetane cynohydrin |
| 107-02-8 | Acrolein |
| 107-13-1 | Acrylonitrile |
| 309-00-2 | Aldrin 1,4:5,8-dimethanonaphthalene, 1,2,3,4,10, 10-hexachloro-1,4,4a,5,8,8a-hexahydro-(1.alpha., 4.alpha., 4a.beta., 5.alpha., 8.alpha., 8a.beta.)- |
| 107-05-1 | Allyl Chloride |
| 7429-90-5 | Aluminum (fume or dust) |
| 7664-41-7 | Ammonia |
| 62-53-3 | Aniline |
| 120-12-7 | Anthracene |
| 7440-36-0 | Antimony |
| 7647189 | Antimony pentachloride |
| 28300745 | Antimony potassium tartrate |
| 7789619 | Antimony tribromide |
| 10025919 | Antimony trichloride |
| 7783564 | Antimony trifluoride |
| 1309644 | Antimony trioxide |
| 7440-38-2 | Arsenic |
| 1303328 | Arsenic disulfide |
| 1303282 | Arsenic pentoxide |
| 7784341 | Arsenic trichloride |
| 1327533 | Arsenic trioxide |
| 1303339 | Arsenic trisulfide |
| 1332-21-4 | Asbestos (friable) |
| 542621 | Barium cyanide |
| 71-43-2 | Benzene |
| 92-87-5 | Benzidine |
| 100470 | Benzonitrile |
| 98-88-4 | Benzoyl chloride |
| 100-44-7 | Benzyl chloride |
| 7440-41-7 | Beryllium |
| 7787475 | Beryllium chloride |

| CAS Number | Common Name |
|---|---|
| 7787497 | Beryllium fluoride |
| 7787555 | Beryllium nitrate |
| 111-44-4 | Bis(2-chloroethyl) ether |
| 75-25-2 | Bromoform |
| 74-83-9 | Bromomethane (Methyl bromide) |
| 85-68-7 | Butyl benzyl phthalate |
| 7440-43-9 | Cadmium |
| 543908 | Cadmium acetate |
| 7789426 | Cadmium bromide |
| 10108642 | Cadmium chloride |
| 7778441 | Calcium arsenate |
| 52740166 | Calcium arsenite |
| 13765190 | Calcium chromate |
| 592018 | Calcium cyanide |
| 133-06-2 | Captan 1H-Isoindole-1,3(2H)-dione,3a,4,7,7a-tetrahydro-2-(trichloromethyl)thio- |
| 63-25-2 | Carbaryl 1-Naphthalenol, methylcarbamate |
| 75-15-0 | Carbon disulfide |
| 56-23-5 | Carbon tetrachloride |
| 57-74-9 | Chlordane 4,7-Methanoindan,1,2,4,5,6,7,8,8-octachloro-2,3,3a,4,7,7a-hexahydro- |
| 7782-50-5 | Chlorine |
| 59-50-7 | Chloro-4-methyl-3-phenol p-Chloro-m-cresol |
| 108-90-7 | Chlorobenzene |
| 75-00-3 | Chloroethane (Ethyl chloride) |
| 67-66-3 | Chloroform |
| 74-87-3 | Chloromethane (Methyl chloride) |
| 95-57-8 | 2-Chlorophenol |
| 106-48-9 | 4-Chlorophenol |
| 1066304 | Chromic acetate |
| 11115745 | Chromic acid |
| 10101538 | Chromic sulfate |
| 7440-47-3 | Chromium |
| 1308-14-1 | Chromium (Tri) |
| 10049055 | Chromous chloride |
| 7789437 | Cobaltous bromide |
| 544183 | Cobaltous formate |

| CAS Number | Common Name |
|---|---|
| 14017415 | Cobaltous sulfamate |
| 7440-50-8 | Copper |
| 108-39-4 | m-Cresol |
| 9548-7 | o-Cresol |
| 106-44-5 | p-Cresol |
| 1319-77-3 | Cresol (mixed isomers) |
| 142712 | Cupric acetate |
| 12002038 | Cupric acetoarsenite |
| 7447394 | Cupric chloride |
| 3251238 | Cupric nitrate |
| 5893663 | Cupric oxalate |
| 7758987 | Cupric sulfate |
| 10380297 | Cupric sulfate, ammoniated |
| 815827 | Cupric tartrate |
| 57-12-5 | Cyanide |
| 506774 | Cyanogen chloride |
| 110-82-7 | Cyclohexane |
| 94-75-7 | 2,4-D Acetic acid, (2,4-dichlorophenoxy)- |
| 106-93-4 | 1,2-Dibromoethane (Ethylene dibromide) |
| 84-74-2 | Dibutyl phthalate |
| 25321-22-6 | Dichlorobenzene (mixed isomers) |
| 95-50-1 | 1,2-Dichlorobenzene |
| 541-73-1 | 1,3-Dichlorobenzene |
| 106-46-7 | 1,4-Dichlorobenzene |
| 91-94-1 | 3,3 minutes-Dichlorobenzidine |
| 75-27-4 | Dichlorobromomethane |
| 107-06-2 | 1,2-Dichloroethane (Ethylene dichloride) |
| 540-59-0 | 1,2-Dichloroethylene |
| 120-83-2 | 2,4-Dichlorophenol |
| 78-87-5 | 1,2-Dichloropropane |
| 542-75-6 | 1,3-Dichloropropylene |
| 62-73-7 | Dichlorvos Phosphoric acid, 2,2-dichloroethenyl dimethyl ester |
| 115-32-2 | Dicofol Benzenemethanol, 4-chloro-.alpha.-(4-chlorophenyl)-.alpha.-(trichloromethyl)- |
| 177-81-7 | Di-(2-ethylhexyl phthalate (DEHP) |
| 84-66-2 | Diethyl phthalate |

| CAS Number | Common Name |
|---|---|
| 105-67-9 | 2,4-Dimethylphenol |
| 131-11-3 | Dimethyl phthalate |
| 534-52-1 | 4,6-Dinitro-o-cresol |
| 51-28-5 | 2,4-Dinitrophenol |
| 121-14-2 | 2,4-Dinitrotoluene |
| 606-20-2 | 2,6-Dinitrotoluene |
| 117-84-0 | n-Dioctyl phthalate |
| 122-66-7 | 1,2-Diphenylhydrazine (Hydrazobenzene) |
| 106-89-8 | Epichlorohydrin |
| 100-41-4 | Ethylbenzene |
| 106934 | Ethylene dibromide |
| 50-00-0 | Formaldehyde |
| 76-44-8 | Heptachlor 1,4,5,6,7,8,8-Heptachloro-3a,4,7,7a-tetrahydro-4,7-methano-1H-indene |
| 118-74-1 | Hexachlorobenzene |
| 87-68-3 | Hexachloro-1,3-butadiene |
| 77-47-4 | Hexachlorocyclopentadiene |
| 67-72-1 | Hexachloroethane |
| 7647-01-0 | Hydrochloric acid |
| 74-90-8 | Hydrogen cyanide |
| 7664-39-3 | Hydrogen fluoride |
| 7439-92-1 | Lead |
| 301042 | Lead acetate |
| 7784409 | Lead arsenate |
| 7645252 | Lead arsenate |
| 10102484 | Lead arsenate |
| 7758954 | Lead chloride |
| 13814965 | Lead fluoborate |
| 7783462 | Lead fluoride |
| 10101630 | Lead iodide |
| 10099748 | Lead nitrate |
| 7428480 | Lead stearate |
| 1072351 | Lead stearate |
| 52652592 | Lead stearate |
| 7446142 | Lead sulfate |
| 1314870 | Lead sulfide |
| 592870 | Lead thiocyanate |

| CAS Number | Common Name |
|---|---|
| 58-89-9 | Lindane Cyclohexane, 1,2,3,4,5,6-hexachloro-(1.alpha.,3.beta.,4.alpha.,5.alpha.,6.beta.)- |
| 14307358 | Lithium chromate |
| 108-31-6 | Maleic anhydride |
| 592041 | Mercuric cyanide |
| 10045940 | Mercuric nitrate |
| 7783359 | Mercuric sulfate |
| 592858 | Mercuric thiocyanate |
| 7782867 | Mercurous nitrate |
| 7439-97-6 | Mercury |
| 72-43-5 | Methoxychlor Benzene, 1,1 minutes-(2,2,2-trichloroethylidene)bis 4-methoxy- |
| 80-62-6 | Methyl methacrylate |
| 91-20-3 | Naphthalene |
| 7440-02-0 | Nickel |
| 15699180 | Nickel ammonium sulfate |
| 37211055 | Nickel chloride |
| 7718549 | Nickel chloride |
| 12054487 | Nickel hydroxide |
| 14216752 | Nickel nitrate |
| 7786814 | Nickel sulfate |
| 7697-37-2 | Nitric acid |
| 98-95-3 | Nitrobenzene |
| 88-75-5 | 2-Nitrophenol |
| 100-02-7 | 4-Nitrophenol |
| 62-75-9 | N-Nitrosodimethylamine |
| 86-30-6 | N-Nitrosodiphenylamine |
| 621-64-7 | N-Nitrosodi-n-propylamine |
| 56-38-2 | Parathion Phosphorothioic acid, O,O-diethyl-O-(4-nitrophenyl) ester |
| 87-86-5 | Pentachlorophenol (PCP) |
| 108-95-2 | Phenol |
| 75-44-5 | Phosgene |
| 7664-38-2 | Phosphoric acid |
| 7723-14-0 | Phosphorus (yellow or white) |
| 1336-36-3 | Polychlorinated biphenyls (PCBs) |
| 7784410 | Potassium arsenate |

| CAS Number | Common Name |
|---|---|
| 10124502 | Potassium arsenite |
| 7778509 | Potassium bichromate |
| 7789006 | Potassium chromate |
| 151508 | Potassium cyanide |
| 75-56-9 | Propylene oxide |
| 91-22-5 | Quinoline |
| 7782-49-2 | Selenium |
| 7446084 | Selenium oxide |
| 7440-22-4 | Silver |
| 7761888 | Silver nitrate |
| 7631892 | Sodium arsenate |
| 7784465 | Sodium arsenite |
| 10588019 | Sodium bichromate |
| 7775113 | Sodium chromate |
| 143339 | Sodium cyanide |
| 10102188 | Sodium selenite |
| 7782823 | Sodium selenite |
| 7789062 | Strontium chromate |
| 100-42-5 | Styrene |
| 7664-93-9 | Sulfuric acid |
| 79-34-5 | 1,1,2,2-Tetrachloroethane |
| 127-18-4 | Tetrachloroethylene (Perchloroethylene) |
| 935-95-5 | 2,3,5,6-Tetrachlorophenol |
| 78002 | Tetraethyl lead |
| 7440-28-0 | Thallium |
| 10031591 | Thallium sulfate |
| 108-88-3 | Toluene |
| 8001-35-2 | Toxaphene |
| 52-68-6 | Trichlorfon Phosphonic acid, (2,2,2-trichloro-1-hydroxyethyl)-dimethylester |
| 120-28-1 | 1,2,4-Trichlorobenzene |
| 71-55-6 | 1,1,1-Trichloroethane (Methyl chloroform) |
| 79-00-5 | 1,1,2-Trichloroethane |
| 79-01-6 | Trichloroethylene |
| 95-95-4 | 2,4,5-Trichlorophenol |
| 88-06-2 | 2,4,6-Trichlorophenol |
| 7440-62-2 | Vanadium (fume or dust) |

| CAS Number | Common Name |
|---|---|
| 108-05-4 | Vinyl acetate |
| 75-01-4 | Vinyl chloride |
| 75-35-4 | Vinylidene chloride |
| 108-38-3 | m-Xylene |
| 95-47-6 | o-Xylene |
| 106-42-3 | p-Xylene |
| 1330-20-7 | Xylene (mixed isomers) |
| 7440-66-6 | Zinc (fume or dust) |
| 557346 | Zinc acetate |
| 14639975 | Zinc ammonium chloride |
| 14639986 | Zinc ammonium chloride |
| 52628258 | Zinc ammonium chloride |
| 1332076 | Zinc borate |
| 7699458 | Zinc bromide |
| 3486359 | Zinc carbonate |
| 7646857 | Zinc chloride |
| 557211 | Zinc cyanide |
| 7783495 | Zinc fluoride |
| 557415 | Zinc formate |
| 7779864 | Zinc hydrosulfite |
| 7779886 | Zinc nitrate |
| 127822 | Zinc phenolsulfonate |
| 1314847 | Zinc phosphide |
| 16871719 | Zinc silicofluoride |
| 7733020 | Zinc sulfate |

# Final NPDES General Permits for Storm Water Discharges from Construction Sites

This appendix presents the text of the EPA final NPDES general permits for storm water discharges from construction activities. This text was originally published in the *Federal Register* [57 FR 41175 (Sept. 9, 1992)]. This appendix should be a useful reference for Chaps. 9 through 13 of this book, which describe the storm water discharge permit requirements for construction sites.

This general permit is directly applicable only in nondelegated states (states in which the EPA regional offices write NPDES storm water discharge permits). Delegated states write their own NPDES storm water discharge permits, and the general permit conditions in these states may differ from those of the EPA baseline general permit.

## PREFACE

The Clean Water Act (CWA) provides that storm water discharges associated with industrial activity from a point source (including discharges through a municipal separate storm sewer system) to waters of the United States are unlawful, unless authorized by a National Pollutant Discharge Elimination System (NPDES) permit. The terms "storm water discharge associated with industrial activity", "point source" and "waters of the United States" are critical to determining whether a facility is subject to this requirement. Complete definitions of these terms are found in the definition section (Part IX) of this permit.

## Part I. COVERAGE UNDER THIS PERMIT

### A. Permit Area

The permit covers all areas of:

Region I-for the States of Maine and New Hampshire; for Indian lands located in Massachusetts, New Hampshire, and Maine.

Region II-for the Commonwealth of Puerto Rico.

Region IV-for Indian lands located in Florida (two tribes), Mississippi, and North Carolina.

Region VI-for the States of Louisiana, New Mexico, Oklahoma, and Texas; and for Indian lands located in Louisiana, New Mexico (except Navajo lands and Ute Mountain Reservation lands), Oklahoma, and Texas.

Region VIII-for the State of South Dakota; for Indian lands located in Colorado (including the Ute Mountain Reservation in Colorado), Montana, North Dakota, Utah (except Goshute Reservation and Navajo Reservation lands), and Wyoming; for Federal facilities in Colorado; and for the Ute Mountain Reservation New Mexico.

Region IX-for the State of Arizona; for the Territories of Johnston Atoll, and Midway and Wake Island; and for Indian lands located in California, and Nevada; and for the Goshute Reservation in Utah and Nevada, the Navajo Reservation in Utah, New Mexico, and Arizona, the Duck Valley Reservation in Nevada and Idaho.

Region X-for the State of Alaska, and Idaho; for Indian lands located in Alaska, Idaho (except Duck Valley Reservation lands), and Washington; and for Federal facilities in Washington.

### B. Eligibility

1. This permit may authorize all discharges of storm water associated with industrial activity from construction sites, (those sites or common plans of development or sale that will result in the disturbance of five or more acres total land area[1]), (henceforth referred to as storm water discharges from construction activities) occurring after the effective date of this permit (including discharges occurring

---

[1] On June 4, 1992, the United States Court of Appeals for the Ninth Circuit remanded the exemption for construction sites of less than five acres to the EPA for further rulemaking. (Nos. 90-70671 and 91-70200).

after the effective date of this permit where the construction activity was initiated before the effective date of this permit), except for discharges identified under paragraph I.B.3.

2. This permit may only authorize a storm water discharge associated with industrial activity from a construction site that is mixed with a storm water discharge from an industrial source other than construction, where:

   a. the industrial source other than construction is located on the same site as the construction activity;

   b. storm water discharges associated with industrial activity from the areas of the site where construction activities are occurring are in compliance with the terms of this permit; and

   c. storm water discharges associated with industrial activity from the areas of the site where industrial activity other than construction are occurring (including storm water discharges from dedicated asphalt plants and dedicated concrete plants) are covered by a different NPDES general permit or individual permit authorizing such discharges.

3. Limitations on Coverage
   The following storm water discharges from construction sites are not authorized by this permit:

   a. storm water discharges associated with industrial activity that originate from the site after construction activities have been completed and the site has undergone final stabilization.

   b. discharges that are mixed with sources of non-storm water other than discharges which are identified in Part III.A of this permit and which are in compliance with Part IV.D.5 (non-storm water discharges) of this permit.

   c. storm water discharges associated with industrial activity that are subject to an existing NPDES individual or general permit or which are issued a permit in accordance with paragraph VI.L (requiring an individual permit or an alternative general permit) of this permit. Such discharges may be authorized under this permit after an existing permit expires provided the existing permit did not establish numeric limitations for such discharges;

   d. storm water discharges from construction sites that the Director (EPA) has determined to be or may reasonably be expected to be contributing to a violation of a water quality standard; and

   e. storm water discharges from construction sites if the discharges may adversely affect a listed or proposed to be listed endangered or threatened species or its critical habitat.

## C. Authorization

1. A discharger must submit a Notice of Intent (NOI) in accordance with the requirements of Part II of this permit, using a NOI form provided by the Director (or a photocopy thereof), in order for storm water discharges from construction sites to be authorized to discharge under this general permit.

2. Where a new operator is selected after the submittal of an NOI under Part II, a new Notice of Intent (NOI) must be submitted by the operator in accordance with Part II, using a NOI form provided by the Director (or a photocopy thereof).

3. Unless notified by the Director to the contrary, dischargers who submit an NOI in accordance with the requirements of this permit are authorized to discharge storm water from construction sites under the terms and conditions of this permit 2 days after the date that the NOI is postmarked. The Director may deny coverage under this permit and require submittal of an application for an individual NPDES permit based on a review of the NOI or other information (see Part VI.L of this permit).

## Part II. NOTICE OF INTENT REQUIREMENTS

### A. Deadlines for Notification

1. Except as provided in paragraphs II.A.2, II.A.3, and II.A.5, individuals who intend to obtain coverage for storm water discharges from a construction site (where disturbances associated with the construction project commence before October 1, 1992), under this general permit shall submit a Notice of Intent (NOI) in accordance with the requirements of this Part on or before October 1, 1992.

2. Individuals who intend to obtain coverage under this general permit for storm water discharges from a construction site where disturbances associated with the construction project commence after October 1, 1992, shall submit a Notice of Intent (NOI) in accordance with the requirements of Part at least 2 days prior to the commencement of construction activities (e.g. the initial disturbance of soils associated with clearing, grading, excavation activities, or other construction activities);

3. For storm water discharges from construction sites where the operator changes, (including projects where an operator is selected after a NOI has been submitted under Parts II.A.1 or II.A.2) a NOI in

accordance with the requirements of this Part shall be submitted at least 2 days prior to when the operator commences work at the site; and

4. EPA will accept an NOI in accordance with the requirements of this part after the dates provided in Parts II.A.1, 2 or 3 of this permit. In such instances, EPA may bring appropriate enforcement actions.

### B. Contents of Notice of Intent

The Notice(s) of Intent shall be signed in accordance with Part VI.G of this permit by all of the entities identified in Part II.B.2 and shall include the following information:

1. The mailing address of the construction site for which the notification is submitted. Where a mailing address for the site is not available, the location of the approximate center of the site must be described in terms of the latitude and longitude to the nearest 15 seconds, or the section, township and range to the nearest quarter section;

2. The name, address and telephone number of the operator(s) with day to day operational control that have been identified at the time of the NOI submittal, and operator status as a Federal, State, private, public or other entity. Where multiple operators have been selected at the time of the initial NOI submittal, NOIs must be attached and submitted in the same envelope. When an additional operator submits an NOI for a site with a preexisting NPDES permit, the NOI for the additional operator must indicate the number for the preexisting NPDES permit;

3. The name of the receiving water(s), or if the discharge is through a municipal separate storm sewer, the name of the municipal operator of the storm sewer and the ultimate receiving water(s);

4. The permit number of any NPDES permit(s) for any discharge(s) (including any storm water discharges or any non-storm water discharges) from the site;

5. An indication of whether the operator has existing quantitative data which describes the concentration of pollutants in storm water discharges (existing data should not be included as part of the NOI); and

6. An estimate of project start date and completion dates, estimates of the number of acres of the site on which soil will be disturbed, and a certification that a storm water pollution prevention plan has been prepared for the site in accordance with Part IV of this permit, and such plan provides compliance with approved State and/or local sediment and erosion plans or permits and/or storm water management plans or permits in accordance with Part IV.D.2.d of this permit. (A copy of the plans or permits should not be included with the NOI submission).

## C. Where to Submit

1. Facilities which discharge storm water associated with industrial activity must use a NOI form provided by the Director (or photocopy thereof). The form in the Federal Register notice in which this permit was published may be photocopied and used. Forms are also available by calling (703) 821-4823. NOIs must be signed in accordance with Part VI.G of this permit. NOIs are to be submitted to the Director of the NPDES program in care of the following address: Storm Water Notice of Intent, PO Box 1215, Newington, VA 22122.

2. A copy of the NOI or other indication that storm water discharges from the site are covered under an NPDES permit, and a brief description of the project shall be posted at the construction site in a prominent place for public viewing (such as alongside a building permit).

## D. Additional Notification

Facilities which are operating under approved State or local sediment and erosion plans, grading plans, or storm water management plans shall submit signed copies of the Notice of Intent to the State or local agency approving such plans in accordance with the deadlines in Part II.A of this permit (or sooner where required by State or local rules), in addition to submitting the Notice of Intent to EPA in accordance with paragraph II.C.

## E. Renotification

Upon issuance of a new general permit, the permittee is required to notify the Director of his intent to be covered by the new general permit.

## Part III. SPECIAL CONDITIONS, MANAGEMENT PRACTICES, AND OTHER NON-NUMERIC LIMITATIONS

### A. Prohibition on Non-Storm Water Discharges

1. Except as provided in paragraph I.B.2 and III.A.2, all discharges covered by this permit shall be composed entirely of storm water.

2. a. Except as provided in paragraph III.A.2.(b), discharges of material other than storm water must be in compliance with a NPDES permit (other than this permit) issued for the discharge.

   b. The following non-storm water discharges may be authorized by this permit provided the non-storm water component of the discharge is in compliance with paragraph IV.D.5: discharges from fire fighting activities; fire hydrant flushings; waters used to wash vehicles or control dust in accordance with Part IV.D.2.c.(2); potable water sources including waterline flushings; irrigation drainage; routine external building washdown which does not use detergents; pavement washwaters where spills or leaks of toxic or hazardous materials have not occurred (unless all spilled material has been removed) and where detergents are not used; air conditioning condensate; springs; uncontaminated ground water; and foundation or footing drains where flows are not contaminated with process materials such as solvents.

### B. Releases in Excess of Reportable Quantities

1. The discharge of hazardous substances or oil in the storm water discharge(s) from a facility shall be prevented or minimized in accordance with the applicable storm water pollution prevention plan for the facility. This permit does not relieve the permittee of the reporting requirements of 40 CFR part 117 and 40 CFR part 302. Where a release containing a hazardous substance in an amount equal to or in excess of a reporting quantity established under either 40 CFR 117 or 40 CFR 302, occurs during a 24-hour period:
   a. The permittee is required to notify the National Response Center (NRC) (800-424-8802; in the Washington, DC metropolitan area 202-426-2675) in accordance with the requirements of 40 CFR 117 and 40 CFR 302 as soon as he or she has knowledge of the discharge;
   b. The permittee shall submit within 14 calendar days of knowledge of the release a written description of: the release (including the type and estimate of the amount of material released), the date that such release occurred, the circumstances leading to the release, and steps to be taken in accordance with Part III.B.3 of this permit to the appropriate EPA Regional office at the address provided in Part V.C (addresses) of this permit; and
   c. The storm water pollution prevention plan required under Part IV of this permit must be modified within 14 calendar days of knowledge of the release to: Provide a description of the release, the circumstances leading to the release, and the date of the release. In addition, the plan must be reviewed to identify measures to prevent the reoccurrence of such releases and to respond to such releases, and the plan must be modified where appropriate.
2. Spills. This permit does not authorize the discharge of hazardous substances or oil resulting from an on-site spill.

## Part IV. STORM WATER POLLUTION PREVENTION PLANS

A storm water pollution prevention plan shall be developed for each construction site covered by this permit. Storm water pollution prevention plans shall be prepared in accordance with good engineering practices. The plan shall identify potential sources of pollution which may reasonably be expected to affect the quality of storm water discharges from the construction site. In addition, the plan shall describe and ensure the implementation of practices which will be used to reduce the pollutants in storm water discharges associated with industrial activity at the construction site and to assure compliance with the terms and conditions of this permit. Facilities must implement the provisions of the storm water pollution prevention plan required under this part as a condition of this permit.

### A. Deadlines for Plan Preparation and Compliance

The plan shall:

1. Be completed (including certifications required under Part IV.E) prior to the submittal of an NOI to be covered under this permit and updated as appropriate;

2. For construction activities that have begun on or before October 1, 1992, except for sediment basins required under Part IV.D.2.a(2) (structural practices) of this permit, the plan shall provide for compliance with the terms and schedule of the plan beginning on October 1, 1992. The plan shall provide for compliance with sediment basins required under Part IV.D.2.a.(a) of this permit by no later than December 1, 1992;

3. For construction activities that have begun after October 1, 1992, the plan shall provide for compliance with the terms and schedule of the plan beginning with the initiation of construction activities.

### B. Signature and Plan Review

1. The plan shall be signed in accordance with Part VI.G, and be retained on-site at the facility which generates the storm water discharge in accordance with Part V (retention of records) of this permit.

2. The permittee shall make plans available upon request to the Director; a State or local agency approving sediment and erosion plans, grading plans, or storm water management plans; or in the case of a storm water discharge associated with industrial activity which discharges through a municipal separate storm sewer system with an NPDES permit, to the municipal operator of the system.

3. The Director, or authorized representative, may notify the permittee at any time that the plan does not meet one or more of the minimum requirements of this part. Such notification shall identify those provisions of the permit which are not being met by the plan, and identify which provisions of the plan requires modifications in order to meet the minimum requirements of this part. Within 7 days of such notification from the Director, (or as otherwise provided by the Director), or authorized representative, the permittee shall make the required changes to the plan and shall submit to the Director a written certification that the requested changes have been made.

## C. Keeping Plans Current

The permittee shall amend the plan whenever there is a change in design, construction, operation, or maintenance, which has a significant effect on the potential for the discharge of pollutants to the waters of the United States and which has not otherwise been addressed in the plan or if the storm water pollution prevention plan proves to be ineffective in eliminating or significantly minimizing pollutants from sources identified under Part IV.D.2 of this permit, or in otherwise achieving the general objectives of controlling pollutants in storm water discharges associated with industrial activity. In addition, the plan shall be amended to identify any new contractor and/or subcontractor that will implement a measure of the storm water pollution prevention plan (see Part IV.E). Amendments to the plan may be reviewed by EPA in the same manner as Part IV.B above.

## D. Contents of Plan

The storm water pollution prevention plan shall include the following items:

### 1. Site description.

Each plan shall, provide a description of pollutant sources and other information as indicated:
   a. A description of the nature of the construction activity;
   b. A description of the intended sequence of major activities which disturb soils for major portions of the site (e.g. grubbing, excavation, grading);
   c. Estimates of the total area of the site and the total area of the site that is expected to be disturbed by excavation, grading, or other activities;
   d. An estimate of the runoff coefficient of the site after construction

activities are completed and existing data describing the soil or the quality of any discharge from the site;

e. A site map indicating drainage patterns and approximate slopes anticipated after major grading activities, areas of soil disturbance, an outline of areas which not be disturbed, the location of major structural and nonstructural controls identified in the plan, the location of areas where stabilization practices are expected to occur, surface waters (including wetlands), and locations where storm water is discharged to a surface water; and

f. The name of the receiving water(s), and areal extent of wetland acreage at the site.

## 2. Controls.

Each plan shall include a description of appropriate controls and measures that will be implemented at the construction site. The plan will clearly describe for each major activity identified in Part IV.D.1.b appropriate control measures and the timing during the construction process that the measures will be implemented. (For example, perimeter controls for one portion of the site will be installed after the clearing and grubbing necessary for installation of the measure, but before the clearing and grubbing for the remaining portions of the site. Perimeter controls will be actively maintained until final stabilization of those portions of the site upward of the perimeter control. Temporary perimeter controls will be removed after final stabilization). The description and implementation of controls shall address the following minimum components:

### a. Erosion and sediment controls

(1) stabilization practices.

A description of interim and permanent stabilization practices, including site-specific scheduling of the implementation of the practices. Site plans should ensure that existing vegetation is preserved where attainable and that disturbed portions of the site are stabilized. Stabilization practices may include: temporary seeding, permanent seeding, mulching, geotextiles, sod stabilization, vegetative buffer strips, protection of trees, preservation of mature vegetation, and other appropriate measures. A record of the dates when major grading activities occur, when construction activities temporarily or permanently cease on a portion of the site, and when stabilization measures are initiated shall be included in the plan. Except as provided in paragraphs IV.D.2.(a).(1).(a), (b), and (c) below, stabilization measures shall be initiated as soon as practicable in portions of the site where construction activities have temporarily or permanently ceased, but in no case more than 14 days after the construction activity in that portion of the site has temporarily or permanently ceased.

(a). Where the initiation of stabilization measures by the 14th day after construction activity temporary or permanently cease is precluded by snow cover, stabilization measures shall be initiated as soon as practicable.

(b). Where construction activity will resume on a portion of the site within 21 days from when activities ceased, (e.g. the total time period that construction activity is temporarily ceased is less than 21 days) then stabilization measures do not have to be initiated on that portion of site by the 14th day after construction activity temporarily ceased.

(c). In arid areas (areas with an average annual rainfall of 0 to 10 inches) and semi-arid areas (areas with an average annual rainfall of 10 to 20 inches), where the initiation of stabilization measures by the 14th day after construction activity has temporarily or permanently ceased is precluded by seasonal arid conditions, stabilization measures shall be initiated as soon as practicable.

(2) Structural practices.

A description of structural practices to divert flows from exposed soils, store flows or otherwise limit runoff and the discharge of pollutants from exposed areas of the site to the degree attainable. Such practices may include silt fences, earth dikes, drainage swales, sediment traps, check dams, subsurface drains, pipe slope drains, level spreaders, storm drain inlet protection, rock outlet protection, reinforced soil retaining systems, gabions, and temporary or permanent sediment basins. Structural practices should be placed on upland soils to the degree attainable. The installation of these devices may be subject to Section 404 of the CWA.

(a) For common drainage locations that serve an area with 10 or more disturbed acres at one time, a temporary (or permanent) sediment basin providing 3,600 cubic feet of storage per acre drained, or equivalent control measures, shall be provided where attainable until final stabilization of the site. The 3,600 cubic feet of storage area per acre drained does not apply to flows from offsite areas and flows from onsite areas that are either undisturbed or have undergone final stabilization where such flows are diverted around both the disturbed area and the sediment basin. For drainage locations which serve 10 or more disturbed acres at one time and where a temporary sediment basin providing

3,600 cubic feet of storage per acre drained, or equivalent controls is not attainable, smaller sediment basins and/or sediment traps should be used. At a minimum, silt fences, or equivalent sediment controls are required for all sideslope and downslope boundaries of the construction area.

(b) For drainage locations serving less than 10 acres, sediment basins and/or sediment traps should be used. At a minimum, silt fences or equivalent sediment controls are required for all sideslope and downslope boundaries of the construction area unless a sediment basin providing storage for 3,600 cubic feet of storage per acre drained is provided.

**b. Storm water management.**

A description of measures that will be installed during the construction process to control pollutants in storm water discharges that will occur after construction operations have been completed. Structural measures should be placed on upland soils to the degree attainable. The installation of these devices may be subject to Section 404 of the CWA. This permit only addresses the installation of storm water management measures, and not the ultimate operation and maintenance of such structures after the construction activities have been completed and the site has undergone final stabilization. Permittees are only responsible for the installation and maintenance of storm water management measures prior to final stabilization of the site, and are not responsible for maintenance after storm water discharges associated with industrial activity have been eliminated from the site.

(1). Such practices may include: storm water detention structures (including wet ponds); storm water retention structures; flow attenuation by use of open vegetated swales and natural depressions; infiltration of runoff onsite; and sequential systems (which combine several practices). The pollution prevention plan shall include an explanation of the technical basis used to select the practices to control pollution where flows exceed predevelopment levels.

(2). Velocity dissipation devices shall be placed at discharge locations and along the length of any outfall channel for the purpose of providing a non-erosive velocity flow from the structure to a water course so that the natural physical and biological characteristics and functions are maintained and protected (e.g., no significant changes in the hydrological regime of the receiving water).

**c. Other controls**

(1) Waste disposal. No solid materials, including building materials, shall be discharged to waters of the United States, except as authorized by a Section 404 permit.

(2) Off-site vehicle tracking of sediments and the generation of dust shall be minimized.

(3) The plan shall ensure and demonstrate compliance with applicable State and/or local waste disposal, sanitary sewer or septic system regulations.

#### d. Approved State or local plans.

(1) Permittees which discharge storm water associated with industrial activity from construction activities must include in their storm water pollution prevention plan procedures and requirements specified in applicable sediment and erosion site plans or site permits, or storm water management site plans or site permits approved by State or local officials. Permittees shall provide a certification in their storm water pollution prevention plan that their storm water pollution prevention plan reflects requirements applicable to protecting surface water resources in sediment and erosion site plans or site permits, or storm water management site plans or site permits approved by State or local officials. Permittees shall comply with any such requirements during the term of the permit. This provision does not apply to provisions of master plans, comprehensive plans, non-enforceable guidelines or technical guidance documents that are not identified in a specific plan or permit that is issued for the construction site.

(2) Storm water pollution prevention plans must be amended to reflect any change applicable to protecting surface water resources in sediment and erosion site plans or site permits, or storm water management site plans or site permits approved by State or local officials for which the permittee receives written notice. Where the permittee receives such written notice of a change, the permittee shall provide a recertification in the storm water pollution plan that the storm water pollution prevention plan has been modified to address such changes.

(3) Dischargers seeking alternative permit requirements shall submit an individual permit application in accordance with Part VI.L of the permit at the address indicated in Part V.C of this permit for the appropriate Regional Office, along with a description of why requirements in approved State or local plans or permits, or changes to such plans or permits, should not be applicable as a condition of an NPDES permit.

#### 3. Maintenance.

A description of procedures to ensure the timely maintenance of vegetation, erosion and sediment control measures and other protective measures identified in the site plan in good and effective operating condition.

## 4. Inspections.

Qualified personnel (provided by the discharger) shall inspect disturbed areas of the construction site that have not been finally stabilized, areas used for storage of materials that are exposed to precipitation, structural control measures, and locations where vehicles enter or exit the site at least once every seven calendar days and within 24 hours of the end of a storm that is 0.5 inches or greater. Where sites have been finally stabilized, or during seasonal arid periods in arid areas (areas with an average annual rainfall of 0 to 10 inches) and semi-arid areas (areas with an average annual rainfall of 10 to 20 inches) such inspection shall be conducted at least once every month.

a. Disturbed areas and areas used for storage of materials that are exposed to precipitation shall be inspected for evidence of, or the potential for, pollutants entering the drainage system. Erosion and sediment control measures identified in the plan shall be observed to ensure that they are operating correctly. Where discharge locations or points are accessible, they shall be inspected to ascertain whether erosion control measures are effective in preventing significant impacts to receiving waters. Locations where vehicles enter or exit the site shall be inspected for evidence of offsite sediment tracking.

b. Based on the results of the inspection, the site description identified in the plan in accordance with paragraph IV.D.1 of this permit and pollution prevention measures identified in the plan in accordance with paragraph IV.D.2 of this permit shall be revised as appropriate, but in no case later than 7 calendar days following the inspection. Such modifications shall provide for timely implementation of any changes to the plan within 7 calendar days following the inspection.

c. A report summarizing the scope of the inspection, name(s) and qualifications of personnel making the inspection, the date(s) of the inspection, major observations relating to the implementation of the storm water pollution prevention plan, and actions taken in accordance with paragraph IV.D.4.b of the permit shall be made and retained as part of the storm water pollution prevention plan for at least three years from the date that the site is finally stabilized. Such reports shall identify any incidents of non-compliance. Where a report does not identify any incidents of non-compliance, the report shall contain a certification that the facility is in compliance with the storm water pollution prevention plan and this permit. The report shall be signed in accordance with Part VI.G of this permit.

## 5. Non-Storm Water Discharges.

Except for flows from fire fighting activities, sources of non-storm water listed in Part III.A.2 of this permit that are combined with storm water discharges associated with industrial activity must be identified in the plan. The plan shall identify and ensure the implementation of appropriate pollution prevention measures for the non-storm water component(s) of the discharge.

### E. Contractors

1. The storm water pollution prevention plan must clearly identify for each measure identified in the plan, the contractor(s) and/or subcontractor(s) that will implement the measure. All contractors and subcontractors identified in the plan must sign a copy of the certification statement in Part IV.E.2 of this permit in accordance with Part VI.G of this permit. All certifications must be included in the storm water pollution prevention plan.

2. Certification Statement. All contractors and subcontractors identified in a storm water pollution prevention plan in accordance with Part IV.E.1 of this permit shall sign a copy of the following certification statement before conducting any professional service identified in the storm water pollution prevention plan:

> I certify under penalty of law that I understand the terms and conditions of the general National Pollutant Discharge Elimination System (NPDES) permit that authorizes the storm water discharges associated with industrial activity from the construction site identified as part of this certification.

The certification must include the name and title of the person providing the signature in accordance with Part VI.G of this permit; the name, address and telephone number of the contracting firm; the address (or other identifying description) of the site; and the date the certification is made.

### Part V. RETENTION OF RECORDS

A. The permittee shall retain copies of storm water pollution prevention plans and all reports required by this permit, and records of all data used to complete the Notice of Intent to be covered by this permit, for a period of at least three years from the date that the site is finally stabilized. This period may be extended by request of the Director at any time.

B. The permittee shall retain a copy of the storm water pollution prevention required by this permit at the construction site from the date of project initiation to the date of final stabilization.

C. Addresses. Except for the submittal of NOIs (see Part II.C of this permit), all written correspondence concerning discharges in any State, Indian land or from any Federal Facility covered under this permit and directed to the U.S. Environmental Protection Agency, including the submittal of individual permit applications, shall be sent to the address of the appropriate Regional Office listed below:

1.  CT, MA, ME, NH, RI, VT United States EPA, Region I, Water Management Division (WCP- 2109), Storm Water Staff, John F. Kennedy Federal Building, Room 2209, Boston, MA 02203.

2.  NJ, NY, PR, VI United States EPA, Region II, Water Management Division (2WM-WPC), Storm Water Staff, 26 Federal Plaza, New York, NY 10278.

3.  DE, DC, MD, PA, VA, WV United States EPA, Region III, Water Management Division (3WM55), Storm Water Staff, 841 Chestnut Building, Philadelphia, PA 19107.

4.  AL, FL, GA, KY, MS, NC, SC, TN United States EPA, Region IV, Water Management Division (FPB-3), Storm Water Staff, 345 Courtland Street, NE., Atlanta, GA 30365.

5.  IL, IN, MI, MN, OH, WI United States EPA, Region V; Water Quality Branch (5WQP), Storm Water Staff, 77 West Jackson Boulevard, Chicago, IL 60604.

6.  AR, LA, NM (Except See Region IX for Navajo Lands, and See Region VIII for Ute Mountain Reservation Lands), OK, TX United States EPA, Region VI, Water Management Division (6W-EA), Storm Water Staff, First Interstate Bank Tower at Fountain Place, 1445 Ross Avenue, 12th Floor, Suite 1200, Dallas, TX 75202.

7.  IA, KS, MO, NE United States EPA, Region VII, Water Management Division, Compliance Branch, Storm Water Staff, 726 Minnesota Avenue, Kansas City, KS 66101.

8.  CO, MT, ND, SD, WY, UT (Except See Region IX for Goshute Reservation and Navajo Reservation Lands) United States EPA, Region VIII, Water Management Division, NPDES Branch (8WM-C), Storm Water Staff, 999 18th Street, Denver, CO 80202-2466. Note-For Montana Indian Lands, please use the following address: United States EPA, Region VIII, Montana Operations Office, Federal Office Building, Drawer 10096, 301 South Park, Helena, MT 59620-0026.

9.  AZ, CA, HI, NV, Guam, American Samoa, the Goshute Reservation in UT and NV, the Navajo Reservation in UT, NM, and AZ, the Duck Valley Reservation in NV and ID United States EPA, Region IX, Water Management Division (W-5-1), Storm Water Staff, 75 Hawthorne Street, San Francisco, CA 94105.

10. AK, ID (Except See Region IX for Duck Valley Reservation Lands), OR, WA United States EPA, Region X, Water

Management Division (WD-134), Storm Water Staff, 1200 Sixth Street, Seattle WA 98101.

## Part VI. STANDARD PERMIT CONDITIONS

### A. Duty to Comply

1. The permittee must comply with all conditions of this permit. Any permit noncompliance constitutes a violation of CWA and is grounds for enforcement action; for permit termination, revocation and reissuance, or modification; or for denial of a permit renewal application.
2. Penalties for Violations of Permit Conditions
   a. Criminal
      (1) Negligent Violations

      The CWA provides that any person who negligently violates permit conditions implementing Sections 301, 302, 306, 307, 308, 318, or 405 of the Act is subject to a fine of not less than $2,500 nor more than $25,000 per day of violation, or by imprisonment for not more than 1 year, or both.

      (2) Knowing Violations

      The CWA provides that any person who knowingly violates permit conditions implementing Sections 301, 302, 306, 307, 308, 318, or 405 of the Act is subject to a fine of not less than $5,000 nor more than $50,000 per day of violation, or by imprisonment for not more than 3 years, or both.

      (3) Knowing Endangerment

      The CWA provides that any person who knowingly violates permit conditions implementing Sections 301, 302, 306, 307, 308, 318, or 405 of the Act and who knows at that time that he is placing another person in imminent danger of death or serious bodily injury is subject to a fine of not more than $250,000, or by imprisonment for not more than 15 years, or both.

      (4) False Statement

      The CWA provides that any person who knowingly makes any false material statement, representation, or certification in any application, record, report, plan, or other document filed or required to be maintained under the Act or who knowingly falsifies, tampers with, or renders inaccurate, any monitoring device or method required to be maintained under the Act, shall upon conviction, be punished by a fine of not more than $10,000 or by imprisonment for not more than 2 years, or by both. If a conviction is for a violation committed after a first conviction of such person under this paragraph, punishment shall be by a fine of not more than $20,000 per day of violation, or by imprisonment of not more than 4 years, or by both. (See Section 309.c.4 of the Clean Water Act).

b. Civil Penalties

The CWA provides that any person who violates a permit condition implementing Sections 301, 302, 306, 307, 308, 318, or 405 of the Act is subject to a civil penalty not to exceed $25,000 per day for each violation.

c. Administrative Penalties

The CWA provides that any person who violates a permit condition implementing Sections 301, 302, 306, 307, 308, 318, or 405 of the Act is subject to an administrative penalty, as follows:

(1) Class I penalty Not to exceed $10,000 per violation nor shall the maximum amount exceed $25,000.

(2) Class II penalty Not to exceed $10,000 per day for each day during which the violation continues nor shall the maximum amount exceed $125,000.

## B. Continuation of the Expired General Permit

This permit expires on October 1, 1997. However, an expired general permit continues in force and effect until a new general permit is issued. Permittees must submit a new NOI in accordance with the requirements of Part II of this permit, using a NOI form provided by the Director (or photocopy thereof) between August 1, 1997 and September 29, 1997 to remain covered under the continued permit after October 1, 1997. Facilities that had not obtained coverage under the permit by October 1, 1997 cannot become authorized to discharge under the continued permit.

## C. Need to Halt or Reduce Activity Not a Defense

It shall not be a defense for a permittee in an enforcement action that it would have been necessary to halt or reduce the permitted activity in order to maintain compliance with the conditions of this permit.

## D. Duty to Mitigate

The permittee shall take all reasonable steps to minimize or prevent any discharge in violation of this permit which has a reasonable likelihood of adversely affecting human health or the environment.

## E. Duty to Provide Information

The permittee shall furnish to the Director; an authorized representative of the Director; a State or local agency approving sediment and erosion plans, grading plans, or storm water management plans; or in the case of a storm water discharge associated with industrial activity which discharges through a municipal separate storm sewer system with an NPDES permit, to the municipal operator of the system, any information which is requested to determine compliance with this permit or other information.

## F. Other Information

When the permittee becomes aware that he or she failed to submit any relevant facts or submitted incorrect information in the Notice of Intent or in any other report to the Director, he or she shall promptly submit such facts or information.

## G. Signatory Requirements

All Notices of Intent, storm water pollution prevention plans, reports, certifications or information either submitted to the Director or the operator of a large or medium municipal separate storm sewer system, or that this permit requires be maintained by the permittee, shall be signed as follows:

1. All Notices of Intent shall be signed as follows:
   a. For a corporation: By a responsible corporate officer. For the purpose of this section, a responsible corporate officer means: (1) A president, secretary, treasurer, or vice-president of the corporation in charge of a principal business function, or any other person who performs similar policy or decision-making functions for the corporation; or (2) the manager of one or more manufacturing, production or operating facilities employing more than 250 persons or having gross annual sales or expenditures exceeding $25,000,000 (in second-quarter 1980 dollars) if authority to sign documents has been assigned or delegated to the manager in accordance with corporate procedures;
   b. For a partnership or sole proprietorship: by a general partner or the proprietor, respectively; or
   c. For a municipality, State, Federal, or other public agency: by either a principal executive officer or ranking elected official. For purposes of this section, a principal executive officer of a Federal agency includes (1) the chief executive officer of the agency, or (2) a senior executive officer having responsibility for the overall

operations of a principal geographic unit of the agency (e.g., Regional Administrators of EPA).

2. All reports required by the permit and other information requested by the Director or authorized representative of the Director shall be signed by a person described above or by a duly authorized representative of that person. A person is a duly authorized representative only if:

   a. The authorization is made in writing by a person described above and submitted to the Director.

   b. The authorization specifies either an individual or a position having responsibility for the overall operation of the regulated facility or activity, such as the position of manager, operator, superintendent, or position of equivalent responsibility or an individual or position having overall responsibility for environmental matters for the company. (A duly authorized representative may thus be either a named individual or any individual occupying a named position).

   c. Changes to authorization. If an authorization under paragraph II.B.3. is no longer accurate because a different operator has responsibility for the overall operation of the construction site, a new notice of intent satisfying the requirements of paragraph II.B must be submitted to the Director prior to or together with any reports, information, or applications to be signed by an authorized representative.

   d. Certification. Any person signing documents under paragraph VI.G shall make the following certification:

   > I certify under penalty of law that this document and all attachments were prepared under my direction or supervision in accordance with a system designed to assure that qualified personnel properly gathered and evaluated the information submitted. Based on my inquiry of the person or persons who manage the system, or those persons directly responsible for gathering the information, the information submitted is, to the best of my knowledge and belief, true, accurate, and complete. I am aware that there are significant penalties for submitting false information, including the possibility of fine and imprisonment for knowing violations.

### H. Penalties for Falsification of Reports

Section 309(c)(4) of the Clean Water Act provides that any person who knowingly makes any false material statement, representation, or certification in any record or other document submitted or required to be maintained under this permit, including reports of compliance or noncompliance shall, upon conviction, be punished by a fine of not more than $10,000, or by imprisonment for not more than 2 years, or by both.

### I. Oil and Hazardous Substance Liability

Nothing in this permit shall be construed to preclude the institution of any legal action or relieve the permittee from any responsibilities, liabilities, or penalties to which the permittee is or may be subject under section 311 of the CWA or section 106 of the Comprehensive Environmental Response, Compensation and Liability Act of 1980 (CERCLA).

### J. Property Rights

The issuance of this permit does not convey any property rights of any sort, nor any exclusive privileges, nor does it authorize any injury to private property nor any invasion of personal rights, nor any infringement of Federal, State of local laws or regulations.

### K. Severability

The provisions of this permit are severable, and if any provision of this permit, or the application of any provision of this permit to any circumstance, is held invalid, the application of such provision to other circumstances, and the remainder of this permit shall not be affected thereby.

### L. Requiring an Individual Permit or an Alternative General Permit

1. The Director may require any person authorized by this permit to apply for and/or obtain either an individual NPDES permit or an alternative NPDES general permit. Any interested person may petition the Director to take action under this paragraph. Where the Director requires a discharger authorized to discharge under this permit to apply for an individual NPDES permit, the Director shall notify the discharger in writing that a permit application is required. This notification shall include a brief statement of the reasons for this decision, an application form, a statement setting a deadline for the discharger to file the application, and a statement that on the effective date of issuance or denial of the individual NPDES permit or the alternative general permit as it applies to the individual permittee, coverage under this general permit shall automatically terminate. Applications shall be submitted to the appropriate Regional Office indicated in Part V.C of this permit. The Director may grant additional time to submit the appli-

cation upon request of the applicant. If a discharger fails to submit in a timely manner an individual NPDES permit application as required by the Director under this paragraph, then the applicability of this permit to the individual NPDES permittee is automatically terminated at the end of the day specified by the Director for application submittal.

2. Any discharger authorized by this permit may request to be excluded from the coverage of this permit by applying for an individual permit. In such cases, the permittee shall submit an individual application in accordance with the requirements of 40 CFR 122.26(c)(1)(ii), with reasons supporting the request, to the Director at the address for the appropriate Regional Office indicated in part V.C of this permit. The request may be granted by issuance of any individual permit or an alternative general if the reasons cited by the permittee are adequate to support the request.

3. When an individual NPDES permit is issued to a discharger otherwise subject to this permit, or the discharger is authorized to discharge under an alternative NPDES general permit, the applicability of this permit to the individual NPDES permittee is automatically terminated on the effective date of the individual permit or the date of authorization of coverage under the alternative general permit, whichever the case may be. When an individual NPDES permit is denied to an owner or operator otherwise subject to this permit, or the owner or operator is denied for coverage under an alternative NPDES general permit, the applicability of this permit to the individual NPDES permittee is automatically terminated on the date of such denial, unless otherwise specified by the Director.

### M. State/Environmental Laws

1. Nothing in this permit shall be construed to preclude the institution of any legal action or relieve the permittee from any responsibilities, liabilities, or penalties established pursuant to any applicable State law or regulation under authority preserved by section 510 of the Act.

2. No condition of this permit shall release the permittee from any responsibility or requirements under other environmental statutes or regulations.

### N. Proper Operation and Maintenance

The permittee shall at all times properly operate and maintain all facilities and systems of treatment and control (and related appurtenances) which are installed or used by the permittee to achieve compliance with the conditions of this permit and with the requirements of storm water pollution prevention plans. Proper operation and maintenance also includes adequate laboratory controls and appropriate quality assurance procedures. Proper operation and maintenance requires the operation of backup or auxiliary facilities or similar systems, installed by a permittee only when necessary to achieve compliance with the conditions of the permit.

### O. Inspection and Entry

The permittee shall allow the Director or an authorized representative of EPA, the State, or, in the case of a construction site which discharges through a municipal separate storm sewer, an authorized representative of the municipal operator or the separate storm sewer receiving the discharge, upon the presentation of credentials and other documents as may be required by law, to:

1. Enter upon the permittee's premises where a regulated facility or activity is located or conducted or where records must be kept under the conditions of this permit;
2. Have access to and copy at reasonable times, any records that must be kept under the conditions of this permit; and
3. Inspect at reasonable times any facilities or equipment (including monitoring and control equipment).

### P. Permit Actions

This permit may be modified, revoked and reissued, or terminated for cause. The filing of a request by the permittee for a permit modification, revocation and reissuance, or termination, or a notification of planned changes or anticipated noncompliance does not stay any permit condition.

### Part VII. REOPENER CLAUSE

A. If there is evidence indicating potential or realized impacts on water quality due to any storm water discharge associated with industrial activity covered by this permit, the discharger may be required to obtain individual permit or an alternative general permit in accordance with Part I.C of this permit or the permit may be modified to include different limitations and/or requirements.

B. Permit modification or revocation will be conducted according to 40 CFR 122.62, 122.63, 122.64 and 124.5.

## Part VIII. TERMINATION OF COVERAGE

### A. Notice of Termination

Where a site has been finally stabilized and all storm water discharges from construction activities that are authorized by this permit are eliminated, or where the operator of all storm water discharges at a facility changes, the operator of the facility may submit a Notice of Termination that is signed in accordance with Part VI.G of this permit. The Notice of Termination shall include the following information:

1. The mailing address of the construction site for which the notification is submitted. Where a mailing address for the site is not available, the location of the approximate center of the site must be described in terms of the latitude and longitude to the nearest 15 seconds, or the section, township and range to the nearest quarter section;
2. The name, address and telephone number of the operator addressed by the Notice of Termination;
3. The NPDES permit number for the storm water discharge identified by the Notice of Termination;
4. An indication of whether the storm water discharges associated with industrial activity have been eliminated or the operator of the discharges has changed; and
5. The following certification signed in accordance with Part VI.G (signatory requirements) of this permit:

> I certify under penalty of law that all storm water discharges associated with industrial activity from the identified facility that are authorized by an NPDES general permit have been eliminated or that I am no longer the operator of the facility or construction site. I understand that by submitting this notice of termination, I am no longer authorized to discharge storm water associated with industrial activity under this general permit, and that discharging pollutants in storm water associated with industrial activity to waters of the United States is unlawful under the Clean Water Act where the discharge is not authorized by a NPDES permit. I also understand that the submittal of this notice of termination does not release an operator from liability for any violations of this permit or the Clean Water Act.

For the purposes of this certification, elimination of storm water discharges associated with industrial activity means that all disturbed soils at the identified facility have been finally stabilized and temporary erosion and sediment control measures have been removed or will be removed at an appropriate time, or that all storm water discharges associated with construction activities from the identified site that are authorized by a NPDES general permit have otherwise been eliminated.

## B. Addresses

All Notices of Termination are to be sent, using the form provided by the Director (or a photocopy thereof), to the following address: Storm Water Notice of Termination, PO Box 1185, Newington, VA 22122.

## Part IX. DEFINITIONS

**Best Management Practices ("BMPs")** means schedules of activities, prohibitions of practices, maintenance procedures, and other management practices to prevent or reduce the pollution of waters of the United States. BMPs also include treatment requirements, operating procedures, and practices to control plant site runoff, spillage or leaks, sludge or waste disposal, or drainage from raw material storage.

**Commencement of Construction**-The initial disturbance of soils associated with clearing, grading, or excavating activities or other construction activities.

**CWA** means the Clean Water Act or the Federal Water Pollution Control Act.

**Dedicated portable asphalt plant**-A portable asphalt plant that is located on or contiguous to a construction site and that provides asphalt only to the construction site that the plant is located on or adjacent to. The term dedicated portable asphalt plant does not include facilities that are subject to the asphalt emulsion effluent limitation guideline at 40 CFR 443.

**Dedicated portable concrete plant**-A portable concrete plant that is located on or contiguous to a construction site and that provides concrete only to the construction site that the plant is located on or adjacent to.

**Director** means the Regional Administrator of the Environmental Protection Agency or an authorized representative.

**Final Stabilization** means that all soil disturbing activities at the site have been completed, and that a uniform perennial vegetative cover with a density of 70% of the cover for unpaved areas and areas not covered by permanent structures has been established or equivalent permanent stabilization measures (such as the use of riprap, gabions, or geotextiles) have been employed.

**Flow-weighted composite sample** means a composite sample consisting of a mixture of aliquots collected at a constant time interval, where the volume of each aliquot is proportional to the flow rate of the discharge.

**Large and Medium municipal separate storm sewer system** means all municipal separate storm sewers that are either: (i) Located in an incorporated place (city) with a population of 100,000 or more as determined by the latest Decennial Census by the Bureau of Census (these cities are listed in Appendices F and G of 40 CFR part 122); or (ii) located in the counties with unincorporated urbanized populations of 100,000 or more, except municipal separate storm sewers that are located in the incorporated places, townships or towns within such counties (these counties are listed in appendices H and I of 40 CFR part 122); or (iii) owned or operated by a municipality other than those described in paragraph (i) or (ii) and that are designated by the Director as part of the large or medium municipal separate storm sewer system.

**NOI** means notice of intent to be covered by this permit (see Part II of this permit.)

**NOT** means notice of termination (see Part VIII of this permit).

**Point Source** means any discernible, confined, and discrete conveyance, including but not limited to, any pipe, ditch, channel, tunnel, conduit, well, discrete fissure, container, rolling stock, concentrated animal feeding operation, landfill leachate collection system, vessel or other floating craft from which pollutants are or may be discharges. This term does not include return flows from irrigated agriculture or agricultural storm water runoff.

**Runoff coefficient** means the fraction of total rainfall that will appear at the conveyance as runoff.

**Storm Water** means storm water runoff, snow melt runoff, and surface runoff and drainage.

**Storm Water Associated with Industrial Activity** means the discharge from any conveyance which is used for collecting and conveying storm water and which is directly related to manufacturing, processing or raw materials storage areas at an industrial plant. The term does not include discharges from facilities or activities excluded from the NPDES program. For the categories of industries identified in paragraphs (i) through (x) of this definition, the term includes, but is not limited to, storm water discharges from industrial plant yards; immediate access roads and rail lines used or traveled by carriers of raw materials, manufactured products, waste material, or by-products used or created by the facility; material handling sites; refuse sites; sites used for the application or disposal of process waste waters (as defined at 40 CFR 401); sites used for the storage and maintenance of material handling equipment; sites used for residual treatment, storage, or disposal; shipping and receiving areas; manufacturing buildings; storage areas (including tank farms) for raw materials, and intermediate and finished products;

and areas where industrial activity has taken place in the past and significant materials remain and are exposed to storm water. For the categories of industries identified in paragraph (xi) of this definition, the term includes only storm water discharges from all areas (except access roads and rail lines) listed in the previous sentence where material handling equipment or activities, raw materials, intermediate products, final products, waste materials, by-products, or industrial machinery are exposed to storm water. For the purposes of this paragraph, material handling activities include the: storage, loading and unloading, transportation, or conveyance of any raw material, intermediate product, finished product, by-product or waste product. The term excludes areas located on plant lands separate from the plant's industrial activities, such as office buildings and accompanying parking lots as long as the drainage from the excluded areas is not mixed with storm water drained from the above described areas. Industrial facilities (including industrial facilities that are Federally, State or municipally owned or operated that meet the description of the facilities listed in this paragraph (i)-(xi) of this definition) include those facilities designated under 122.26(a)(1)(v). The following categories of facilities are considered to be engaging in "industrial activity" for purposes of this subsection:

(i)    Facilities subject to storm water effluent limitations guidelines, new source performance standards, or toxic pollutant effluent standards under 40 CFR subchapter N (except facilities with toxic pollutant effluent standards which are exempted under category (xi) of this definition);

(ii)   Facilities classified as Standard Industrial Classifications 24 (except 2434), 26 (except 265 and 267), 28 (except 283), 29, 311, 32 (except 323), 33, 3441, 373;

(iii)  Facilities classified as Standard Industrial Classifications 10 through 14 (mineral industry) including active or inactive mining operations (except for areas of coal mining operations no longer meeting the definition of a reclamation area under 40 CFR 434.11(1) because the performance bond issued to the facility by the appropriate SMCRA authority has been released, or except for areas of non-coal mining operations which have been released from applicable State or Federal reclamation requirements after December 17, 1990) and oil and gas exploration, production, processing, or treatment operations, or transmission facilities that discharge storm water contaminated by contact with or that has come into contact with, any overburden, raw material, intermediate products, finished products, by-products or waste products located on the site of such operations; inactive mining operations are mining sites that are not being actively mined, but which have an identifiable owner/operator;

(iv)    Hazardous waste treatment, storage, or disposal facilities, including those that are operating under interim status or a permit under Subtitle C of RCRA;

(v)    Landfills, land application sites, and open dumps that have received any industrial wastes (waste that is received from any of the facilities described under this subsection) including those that are subject to regulation under Subtitle D of RCRA;

(vi)    Facilities involved in the recycling of materials, including metal scrap yards, battery reclaimers, salvage yards, and automobile junkyards, including but limited to those classified as Standard Industrial Classification 5015 and 5093;

(vii)    Steam electric power generating facilities, including coal handling sites;

(viii)    Transportation facilities classified as Standard Industrial Classifications 40, 41, 42 (except 4221-25), 43, 44, 45 and 5171 which have vehicle maintenance shops, equipment cleaning operations, or airport deicing operations. Only those portions of the facility that are either involved in vehicle maintenance (including vehicle rehabilitation, mechanical repairs, painting, fueling, and lubrication), equipment cleaning operations, airport deicing operations, or which are otherwise identified under paragraphs (i)-(vii) or (ix)-(xi) of this subsection are associated with industrial activity;

(ix)    Treatment works treating domestic sewage or any other sewage sludge or wastewater treatment device or system, used in the storage treatment, recycling, and reclamation of municipal or domestic sewage, including land dedicated to the disposal of sewage sludge that are located within the confines of the facility, with a design flow of 1.0 mgd or more, or required to have an approved pretreatment program under 40 CFR 403, Not included are farm lands, domestic gardens or lands used for sludge management where sludge is beneficially reused and which are not physically located in the confines of the facility, or areas that are in compliance with 40 CFR 503;

(x)    Construction activity including clearing, grading and excavation activities except: operations that result in the disturbance of less than five acres of total land area which are not part of a larger common plan of development or sale;

(xi)    Facilities under Standard Industrial Classifications 20, 21, 22, 23, 2434, 25, 265, 267, 27, 283, 285, 30, 31 (except 311), 323, 34 (except 3441), 35, 36, 37 (except 373), 38, 39, 4221-25, (and which are not otherwise included within categories (i)-(x))*.

**Waters of the United States** means:

(a) All waters which are currently used, were used in the past, or may be susceptible to use in interstate or foreign commerce, including all waters which are subject to the ebb and flow of the tide;

(b) All interstate waters, including interstate "wetlands";

(c) All other waters such as interstate lakes, rivers, streams (including intermittent streams), mudflats, sandflats, wetlands, sloughs, prairie potholes, wet meadows, playa lakes, or natural ponds the use, degradation, or destruction of which would affect or could affect interstate or foreign commerce including any such waters:

    (1) Which are or could be used by interstate or foreign travelers for recreational or other purposes;

    (2) From which fish or shellfish are or could be taken and sold in interstate or foreign commerce; or

    (3) Which are used or could be used for industrial purposes by industries in interstate commerce.

(d) All impoundments of waters otherwise defined as waters of the United States under this definition;

(e) Tributaries of waters identified in paragraphs (a) through (d) of this definition;

(f) The territorial sea; and

(g) Wetlands adjacent to waters (other than waters that are themselves wetlands) identified in paragraphs (a) through (f) of this definition.

Waste treatment systems, including treatment ponds or lagoons designed to meet the requirements of CWA are not waters of the United States.

## Part X. STATE SPECIFIC CONDITIONS

(See original Federal Register notice.)

---

*On June 4, 1992, the United States Court of Appeals for the Ninth Circuit remanded the exclusion for manufacturing facilities in category (xi) which do not have materials or activities exposed to storm water to the EPA for further rulemaking. (Nos. 90-70671 and 91-70200).

# Example of an SWPPP for an Industrial Site

This storm water pollution prevention plan (SWPPP) deals with the Acme, Inc., school bus maintenance and parking facility on Sawmill Road in southern Montgomery County, Texas.[1] The SWPPP provides information and guidance for employees of the facility in complying with the Environmental Protection Agency's final NPDES general permit for storm water discharges associated with industrial activity, as published in the *Federal Register* on September 9, 1992. It has been prepared by Dodson & Associates, Inc., under contract with Acme, Inc., and in cooperation with employees of the facility.

The certification form shown in Fig. C.1 must be completed before the effective date of the plan.

## Pollution Prevention Team

The following individuals make up the storm water pollution prevention team. They are responsible for developing the SWPPP and implementing the storm water pollution prevention measures identified in the plan:

Each pollution prevention team member has specific responsibilities in maintaining and implementing the SWPPP, as indicated in Table C.1. Note that certain individuals may have more than one responsibility and therefore may be listed at more than one location in this table.

---

[1]Although this is an actual SWPPP, the owner's name has been changed.

CERTIFICATION OF STORM WATER POLLUTION PREVENTION PLAN

This certification must be completed by an authorized signatory before the effective date of the Plan.

I certify under penalty of law that this document and all attachments were prepared under my direction or supervision in accordance with a system designed to assure that qualified personnel properly gathered and evaluated the information submitted. Based on my inquiry of the person or persons who manage the system, or those persons directly responsible for gathering the information, the information submitted is, to the best of my knowledge and belief, true, accurate, and complete. I am aware that there are significant penalties for submitting false information, including the possibility of fine and imprisonment for knowing violations.

Signed:       _____

Name:         _____

Title:        _____

Company:      _____

Address:      _____

Telephone:    _____

Date:         _____

Figure C.1   Certification of SWPPP.

TABLE C.1   Storm Water Pollution Prevention Team

| Responsibility | Name | Phone |
|---|---|---|
| Primary emergency contact | | |
| Secondary emergency contact | | |
| Signatory | | |
| Plan development | | |
| Plan implementation | | |
| Plan revision | | |
| Employee training | | |
| Inspections | | |
| Preventive maintenance | | |
| Spill response | | |

## Potential Pollutant Sources

The following sections describe the existing conditions on the site, including site drainage and topography, existing materials, and operations conducted on the site.

### Storm water drainage

Figures C.2 and C.3 illustrate the western and eastern portions of the site drainage map, respectively, which shows the following:

1. The site topography and pattern of storm water drainage
2. Paved areas
3. Parking areas
4. Fueling areas
5. Earthen areas
6. Vegetated areas
7. Building locations
8. Site boundaries

The facility occupies approximately 4.8 acres of land. The site is roughly rectangular, with the long axis oriented in the east-west direc-

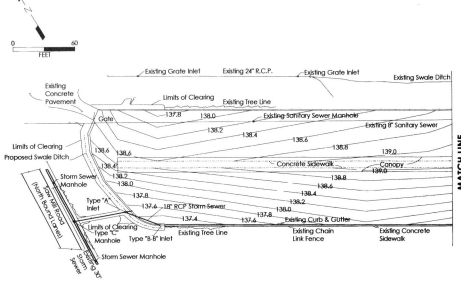

**Figure C.2**  Site map (western portion).

tion. The vehicle maintenance shop and entry gates are located at the east end of the facility. A covered sidewalk starts at the back (west end) of the vehicle maintenance shop and runs almost the entire length of the remainder of the site. The covered sidewalk is located along the center of the east-west axis and serves as a break point for storm runoff, causing the water to flow either north or south. The concrete pavement at the facility also forms a breakpoint near the center of the site along the north-south axis, which causes the runoff to flow east and west. (This is approximately the location of the match line, which divides the two halves of the site drainage map.) Therefore, the four quadrants of the property each drain to separate discharge points.

All four quadrants of the property are within the drainage area of Panther Branch, a tributary of Spring Creek. Spring Creek discharges into Lake Houston on the San Jacinto River. The San Jacinto River system discharges into Galveston Bay on the Gulf of Mexico. The site is not served by a regulated municipal separate storm sewer system.

**Southwest quadrant.**  Storm runoff from the western portion of the facility drains into the Sawmill Road drainage system, which discharges into a tributary of Panther Branch. Storm runoff on the south side of the covered sidewalk in this portion of the facility will flow south until

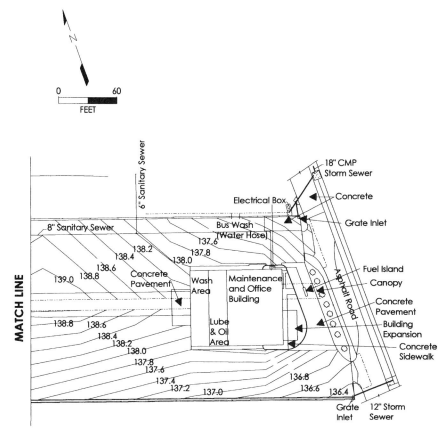

**Figure C.3**  Site map (eastern portion).

it reaches a curb, which runs the entire length of the south side of the site, where it will then be directed into a curb inlet that outfalls into the Sawmill Road drainage system.

**Northwest quadrant.**   Storm runoff on the north side of the covered sidewalk in the western portion of the site will either leave the site through a gate located in the northwest corner of the site or make its way into the wooded area located immediately north of the site. The runoff leaving the site through the gate will flow down a paved drive directly onto Sawmill Road where it will empty into the drainage system via curb inlets. The runoff flowing into the wooded area immediately north of the site either will flow down to Sawmill Road or will eventually drain into a storm sewer inlet located on the north side of the wooded area near Knox Junior High School.

**Southeast quadrant.**   Storm runoff from the eastern portion of the site makes its way eastward to Grogans Mill Road. Runoff from the south side of the maintenance shop and covered sidewalk in this portion of the site will flow south until it reaches the curb that runs along the south side of the facility. The storm runoff will then be directed east toward the access road where it will either empty into a grated storm inlet in the southeast corner of the site or flow through the south entry gate. The flow entering the grated inlet drains into a 12-in storm sewer pipe which crosses beneath the access road and discharges into a drainage ditch located on the east side of the access road. The runoff that leaves the site through the south entry gate will flow over the access road and empty into the same drainage ditch.

**Northeast quadrant.**   Storm runoff from the north side of the maintenance shop and the covered sidewalk in the eastern portion of the site will flow into a drainage ditch located immediately north of the facility, will empty into a grated inlet located in the northeast corner of the site, or will flow through the north entry gate. Storm runoff that flows into the drainage ditch will flow east into a 15-in storm sewer pipe located just outside the northeast corner of the site. Storm runoff that makes its way into the grated inlet will drain into a 15-in storm drain which is connected to the same 15-in storm sewer pipe into which the drainage ditch discharges. The storm drain crosses beneath the access road and discharges into a drop inlet. The runoff will then drain into an 18-in storm drain where it will be directed north toward Campus Road. Runoff leaving the site through the north entry gate will flow across the access road into the drainage ditch located on the east side of the road. The runoff will then flow into the drop inlet where it will intermingle with the runoff being discharged from the 15-in storm sewer drain and then flow north through the 18-inch storm drain. The 18-in storm drain will discharge the runoff into a drop inlet at the northeast corner of the intersection of the access road and Campus Road. The runoff will then drain into a 24-in storm sewer pipe and cross beneath Campus Road. The runoff will then be directed east toward Grogans Mill Road where it will eventually outfall to another tributary of Panther Branch.

### Inventory of Significant Materials

Waste oil from oil changes is stored in a 500-gal waste oil tank located inside the bus maintenance building (see Fig. C.3). The waste oil tank

**TABLE C.2    Significant Materials on Site**

| Significant materials | Storage container | Storage area |
|---|---|---|
| Diesel fuel | Weathertight | Covered |
| Lubricating oils | Weathertight | Covered |
| Antifreeze | Weathertight | Covered |
| Gasoline | Weathertight | Covered |
| Cleaning solvents | Weathertight | Covered |
| Gear lubricant | Weathertight | Covered |
| Grease | Weathertight | Covered |
| Detergent | Weathertight | Covered |
| Spray paint | Weathertight | Covered |
| Transmission fluid | Weathertight | Covered |
| Floor adhesives | Weathertight | Covered |
| Fuel additives | Weathertight | Covered |
| Sealants | Weathertight | Covered |

is located inside the lube/grease pit. The oil is eventually pumped to a truck and is delivered to a recycling facility.

Motor oil is stored in 55-gal drums inside the bus maintenance building (see Fig. C.3).

Unleaded gasoline is stored in a 12,000-gal underground storage tank near the east end of the facility.

Solvents, cleaners, lubricants, and detergents are stored inside the bus maintenance building.

**Materials management procedures.**  Several practices are used at the site to minimize contact between significant materials and precipitation or storm runoff. These are examples of this contact minimization:

1. *Indoor maintenance:* All fluid changes and lubrications are done inside the bus maintenance building to prevent contact between storm runoff or precipitation and any significant materials.

2. *Covered parking:* Buses are parked so that the front of the bus is covered by a metal awning. This practice helps prevent precipitation from coming into contact with any fluids or fuels that may have leaked from the vehicle's engine compartment.

3. *Covered fueling:* An awning over the fueling area prevents rainfall from coming into contact with any accidental drips or spills that may occur.

4. *Cleanup of spills:* Fluids leaked from vehicles are cleaned up immediately to prevent contact with storm runoff and precipitation.

5. *Vehicle maintenance:* Any noticeable leaks from vehicles and equipment are repaired as soon as possible.

6. *Underground storage tank:* Gasoline is stored in an underground storage tank, which prevents the tank from coming into contact with precipitation.

7. *Covered storage:* Lubricating oils, antifreeze, solvents, and cleaners are stored inside the bus maintenance building to prevent exposure to storm runoff and precipitation.

8. *Wash water:* Bus washing is done inside the bus maintenance building. The wash water drains into a sanitary sewer. This procedure eliminates the possibility of contaminants in wash water mixing with storm runoff.

9. *Compressors:* Compressors are located inside the maintenance building to prevent contact with precipitation and storm runoff.

**Existing structural and nonstructural pollution controls.** The existing structural and nonstructural controls used to reduce pollutants in storm runoff include

1. An awning over the fueling station

2. Partially covered bus parking area

3. A fully enclosed bus maintenance building in which all lubricants, fluids, solvents, and cleaners are stored

4. A fully enclosed bus wash

5. Good housekeeping measures, including sweeping and immediate cleanup of spills and leaks

**Existing storm water treatment methods.** The only treatment that storm runoff receives prior to discharge from the site occurs in a vegetated strip located along the east boundary of the site (see Fig. C.2). This strip provides partial vegetative filtration which filters some suspended solids from the storm runoff before the runoff is discharged from the site.

**Significant spills and leaks**

No significant spills or leaks of toxic materials have occurred at the facility within the past 3 years. Several measures have been adopted to prevent spills and leaks at the facility:

1. **Drip pans:** Drip pans are placed beneath all hose connections during transfer of fuels from delivery trucks to the gasoline fuel tank.

2. **Fuel delivery:** Transfers from delivery trucks to the gasoline fuel tank are continuously monitored.

3. **Vehicle fueling:** Completely filling or "topping off" of fuel tanks is discouraged. Topping off often results in overfilling the tank and spilling fuel.

4. **Maintenance:** Leaking or dripping fluids from vehicles, equipment, or piping are collected in drip pans or containers. All leaks are repaired as soon as possible.

5. **Used fluids:** Used fluids are promptly transferred to the proper waste or recycling drums. Full drip pans or other containers are not left lying around.

6. **Daily inspections:** Storage tanks, equipment, and piping are inspected daily to ensure that no leaks have developed.

7. **Battery storage:** Used batteries are stored in a covered, nonleaking secondary container until they are delivered to the recycling facility.

**Non-storm-water discharges**

Outfalls identified on the site layout map were evaluated for the presence of non-storm-water discharges. The methods used to conduct the evaluation included:

1. On-site investigation of storm water management systems

2. Examination of site layout maps, drainage maps, etc.

3. Interviews with plant personnel concerning on-site drainage patterns

Sources of nonstorm water at the site include wastewater from sinks and toilets, bus wash water, shop floor wash water, and engine wash water. These may not be discharged into surface waters under the EPA general permit. Very small amounts of compressor and air-conditioning condensate may also be discharged under certain circumstances. These may be discharged with storm water from the site, if they are referenced in the SWPPP and if appropriate pollution prevention measures are taken, as described later in this plan.

Wastewater from sinks and toilets drains directly into a sanitary sewer. Therefore, these flows are not discharged into surface waters.

Most bus washing takes place in the western end of the maintenance building (see Fig. C.2). The wash water is discharged through a floor drain which is connected to a 4-in sanitary sewer line. The 4-in sewer line is connected to a manhole located in the north-central part of the site which in turn is connected to an 8-in sanitary sewer line. This 8-in sewer line runs west beneath the pavement, eventually connecting to another sanitary sewer line on the west side of Sawmill Road. Therefore, this vehicle wash water is not discharged into surface waters.

A sediment trap and an oil-water separator will be installed in the sanitary sewer line just off the edge of the concrete pavement at the west end of the site. Greases, oils, and fluids washed into the floor drain during bus wash operations will be filtered out before the sewer discharge reaches the main system.

Some bus washing also occurs in the northeast corner of the facility. A water hose, brush, and a 5-gal bucket filled with soapy water are used to clean the buses in this area. Runoff from this bus wash operation drains into the swale located immediately north of the property line.

The wash water from the shop floor cleaning operations drains to either the north or south side of the site in the eastern portion of the facility, depending upon the direction the wash water is sprayed and the direction it is swept out of the building. The wash water either makes its way into the drainage ditch located on the east side of the access road (if enough wash water is discharged from the shop area) or saturates the concrete pavement (which begins just outside the shop doors) and eventually evaporates. Any wash water that happens to discharge into the drainage ditch will eventually outfall into a tributary of Panther Branch.

Engine-cleaning operations take place outside on the south side of the facility just east of the car wash bay. A high-pressure sprayer is used to clean the engines. Runoff from this activity drains into the grated inlet located in the southeast corner of the site, where it crosses beneath the access road via a 12-in storm sewer pipe and discharges into a drainage ditch. Any wash water that does not evaporate or percolate into the ground is eventually discharged into a tributary of Panther Branch.

Some of the non-storm-water discharges listed above (bus wash water, shop cleaning wash water, and engine-cleaning wash water) are not allowable under the EPA general storm water discharge permit and must be eliminated before this SWPPP becomes effective. The bus wash water and engine-cleaning wash water discharges will be eliminated by moving these operations into the existing vehicle maintenance building, so that the wash water is discharged into the floor drains leading to the sanitary sewer system. The certification form shown in Fig. C.4 must be completed by the date required for implementation of this SWPPP. The certification must be signed by the person designated as having signatory authority by the owner.

---

### CERTIFICATION THAT NON-STORM DISCHARGES HAVE BEEN ELIMINATED

This certification is to be completed by an authorized signatory only when all the measures stated in this Plan for eliminating non-storm discharges have been fully carried out. This certification is required before the effective date of the Plan.

---

I certify under penalty of law that this document and all attachments were prepared under my direction or supervision in accordance with a system designed to assure that qualified personnel properly gathered and evaluated the information submitted. Based on my inquiry of the person or persons who manage the system, or those persons directly responsible for gathering the information, the information submitted is, to the best of my knowledge and belief, true, accurate, and complete. I am aware that there are significant penalties for submitting false information, including the possibility of fine and imprisonment for knowing violations.

---

Signed: _____

Name: _____

Title: _____

Company: _____

Address: _____

Telephone: _____

Date: _____

**Figure C.4** Certification form for elimination of nonstorm discharges.

### Sampling Data

No storm water sampling has been performed on this site, and no sampling data are available from other sources. This facility is not a class I or class II facility, according to the designations used in the EPA general permit for storm water discharges. Therefore, no storm water sampling is required for the site.

### Risk identification and summary of potential pollutant sources

The most immediate potential pollutant source at the facility is wash water from outside vehicle washing, engine cleaning, and shop cleaning activities. With the completion of the certification relating to non-storm-water discharges earlier in this plan, however, this potential pollutant source should be eliminated.

A number of processes, activities, and materials at the facility have a reasonable potential to contribute significant amounts of pollutants to storm runoff, unless proper procedures and precautions are taken. Potential contributors include the following:

- *Vehicle maintenance facility:* Many vehicle and equipment maintenance operations use materials or create wastes that have the potential to pollute storm water runoff. Activities that can pollute storm water include parts cleaning; shop cleanup; spilled fuel, oil, or other materials; and replacement of fluids (oil, filters, hydraulic fluids, transmission fluids, and radiator fluids).

- *Rooftops:* Buildings having ventilation systems with discharge vents located on the roof can contribute particulate matter to storm water runoff. These ventilation systems pull dust from inside the buildings and discharge it onto the roof area around the vent. A storm event would wash the dust from the rooftops onto the ground where the dust would mix with storm water runoff.

- *Lubrication and motor oil storage area:* Storage, leaks, drips, and spills of lubrication and/or motor oil in areas exposed to precipitation may increase concentrations of oil and grease in storm water runoff.

- *Bus parking areas:* Drips or leaks of oil, transmission fluid, antifreeze, etc., from buses could potentially have an adverse impact on storm water quality by contributing chemicals such as ethylene glycol to the runoff and by raising oil and grease levels.

- *Bus wash areas:* Washing removes particulate matter from buses, thus increasing the suspended-solids levels. There is also the potential for small amounts of oil and grease or metal fragments to be washed away by high-pressure sprayers at these facilities. Some detergents also contain phosphates, which can cause excessive growth of nuisance plants in water when the phosphates enter lakes or streams in wash water.

- *Fuel pumping stations:* Fuel pumping stations that are exposed to rainfall have the potential to contribute chemicals to storm water pollution through leaks, drips, and spills. These leaks, drips, and spills often occur from small actions such as topping off of fuel tanks, dripping engine fluids, and hosing down of fuel areas.

- *Bus traffic:* Drips or leaks of oil, transmission fluid, antifreeze, etc., from buses could potentially have an adverse impact on storm water quality by elevating oil and grease levels and polluting the storm runoff with chemicals.

- *Engine washing:* Oil, grease, dirt, and metal fragments can be washed from the engine during pressure spraying. These materials could potentially elevate oil and grease levels and suspended-solids levels.

- *Loading and unloading operations:* Materials spilled, leaked, or lost during loading or unloading may collect in the soil or on other surfaces and be carried away by storm runoff or when the area is cleaned. Rainfall may wash off pollutants from machinery used to unload or load materials.

## Consistency with Other Regulations

This site will be operated and maintained in accordance with all applicable laws and regulations of Montgomery County, the state of Texas, and any other agency having jurisdiction over the site.

## Pollution Prevention Measures and Controls

This section describes the measures to be taken to reduce the discharge of pollutants in storm water. Three types of measures are included:

- Pollutant source reduction measures
- Pollutant source control measures
- Storm water recycling and treatment measures

### Pollutant source reduction measures

The most important measures implemented to improve storm runoff will pertain to source reductions which have been addressed previously in the SWPPP. These measures will eliminate or reduce the amount of pollutants generated on the site. Source reductions include

1. Good housekeeping
2. Preventive maintenance
3. Spill prevention
4. Training
5. Materials management practices

**Good housekeeping.**  The following good housekeeping measures are to be conducted at the facility to help keep contaminants out of storm water discharge.

- *Sweeping:* All areas covered with concrete, cement, or asphalt surfaces will be swept regularly. This includes areas located both inside and outside the buildings. All dirt and sediment should be removed from all paved areas on the site. Dust that is allowed to accumulate on the floors of buildings can be tracked outside by vehicle tires or customer and personnel footwear. All matter that is swept from these areas should be disposed of in an area of the site which allows no storm water runoff or should be trucked off site for disposal.

- *Leaks and spills:* Immediately clean up all leaks and spills.

- *Bus Parking:* Limit bus parking to specific areas of the site. Park vehicles under covered areas as much as possible, including the awning designed to cover the front of each bus.

- *Vehicle maintenance:* Conduct all vehicle maintenance in covered areas. If this is not possible, use drip pans and tarpaulins to prevent fluid spills.

- *Pavement washing:* Avoid hosing down work areas which could possibly contain storm water pollutants. Use brooms, shovels, mops, etc., to collect the waste and dispose of it properly.

- *Drip pans:* Keep a drip pan and tarpaulin under vehicles while disconnecting hoses, unscrewing filters, or removing other parts. Use a drip pan under any vehicle that might leak, to keep splatters or drips off the floor or ground.

- *Used fluids:* Promptly transfer used fluids to the proper waste or recycling drums. Do not leave full drip pans or other open containers lying around.

- *Used oil filters:* Crush and recycle used oil filters. Under Texas state law, used oil filters may not be disposed of in sanitary landfills.

- *Waste disposal:* Dispose of trash and debris by putting them into the dumpster or hauling them directly to a landfill. Keep the dumpster lid closed to prevent rainfall from entering the dumpster and washing pollutants out through the drain holes located in the bottom of the container.

- **Employee information:** Post good housekeeping procedures and reminders in appropriate locations around the workplace.

**Materials management.**   The following materials management practices will be used at the facility to protect the quality of storm water discharges.

- **Parts-cleaning agents:** Use noncaustic detergents instead of caustic cleaning agents for parts cleaning.

- **Organic Solvents:** Use detergent-based or water-based cleaning systems in place of organic solvent degreasers.

- **Chlorinated organic solvents:** Replace chlorinated organic solvents (1,1,1- trichloroethane, methylene chloride, etc.) with nonchlorinated solvents. Nonchlorinated solvents such as kerosene or mineral spirits are less toxic and less expensive to dispose of but are by no means harmless themselves. Check the list of active ingredients in each solvent to see whether it contains chlorinated solvents.

- **Recycling cleaning agents:** Choose cleaning agents that can be recycled.

- **Solvents:** Reuse "dirty" solvents. Presoak dirty parts in used solvent before cleaning the parts in fresh solvent.

- **Detergents:** Use phosphate-free biodegradable detergents for vehicle and equipment washing.

- **Recycling waste oil:** Collect waste oil for recycling.

- **Drum storage:** Locate waste and recycling drums in properly controlled areas of the site, preferably in covered areas with a concrete slab and secondary containment.

- **Parts-cleaning procedures:** Clean parts without using liquid cleaners whenever possible to reduce waste. Scrape parts with a wire brush, or use a bake oven if one is available. Do all liquid cleaning at a centralized station so the solvents and residues stay in one area. If parts are dipped in liquid solvents, remove them slowly to avoid spills. Locate drip pans, drain boards, and drying racks so that drips are directed into a sink or fluid holding tank for reuse.

- **Recycling procedures:** Collect old car batteries, used oil, and other fluids, cleaning solutions, and degreasers for transport to a commercial recycling facility. This requires that wastes be separated and stored until they are picked up by the recycling company.

- **Employee information:** Use signs, labels, and color coding to identify problem areas or hazardous materials at the facility. Accurate labeling can help site personnel to quickly identify the type of material released so that they can respond to the spill correctly. Color coding is easily recognized by facility personnel and simply involves painting/coating or applying an adhesive label to the container. Color codes will be consistent throughout the facility, and signs explaining the color codes will be posted.

- **Materials management:** Improve material tracking and inventory practices so that wastes resulting from overstocking and the disposal of outdated materials can be reduced or eliminated.

- **Liquid wastes:** Eliminate intentional disposal of liquid waste into floor drains, sinks, outdoor storm drain inlets, or other storm drains. Signs will be posted at sinks to remind employees, and stencils will be used at drains to tell employees and others not to pour wastes down the drains.

**Preventive maintenance.** A preventive maintenance program which involves regular inspections of storm water management devices and other equipment and systems will be carried out. Systems and equipment to be regularly inspected include:

- **Gutters:** Roof gutters will be inspected quarterly or at the first sign of clogging. Any debris or dust that has collected inside the gutter will be removed and disposed of properly.

- **Fuel pumps:** The fuel pumps will be visually inspected daily. Areas to be inspected include the pump foundations and connections. The pumps will be checked for corrosion, leaks, cracks in hoses, or other physical damage to the system. Should a leak or other threatening condition be found, corrective action will be taken immediately, or else the pump will be shut down until the problem is solved. The pumps will be cleaned only with wet rags or a sponge mop. A water hose will not be used to clean the pumps, in order to avoid washing potential contaminants onto the surrounding pavement where they could potentially enter into storm runoff.

- **Oil storage area:** Oil storage barrels and tanks will be inspected daily for leaks. Should a leak or other threatening condition occur, corrective action will be taken immediately.

- **Record keeping and reporting:** Records and reports of all inspections and maintenance activities will be maintained, as described later in this plan.

**Spill prevention and response procedures.**    Spill prevention and response procedures are a vital part of the SWPPP. Employees should be well trained in material handling procedures, storage requirements, and cleanup procedures that minimize the potential for spills, and, in the case of a spill, how to respond. Containment and diversion equipment also plays an important part in preventing pollutants from entering into storm runoff. Spill prevention and response procedures that will be implemented at the facility include:

- *Plug floor drain:* The floor drain located inside the oil storage area will be plugged to prevent spills from entering into the sanitary sewer.

- *Containment areas:* All petroleum products, solvents, and cleaners will be stored inside a contained area so that all spills or leaks can be controlled.

- *Storage locations:* Containers and drums will be stored away from direct traffic routes to prevent accidental spills.

- *Bulk fuel delivery:* Transfers of gasoline from delivery vehicles to the storage tank will be monitored closely to prevent overfilling and spilling.

- *Spill response:* Mops, rags, or sorbent materials (cat litter, straw, sawdust, etc.) will be used to clean up and contain petroleum or chemical spills. Petroleum spills will not be washed into the storm drain or sanitary sewer.

- *Overflow protection:* Existing overflow protection devices on tank systems will be maintained to warn the operator or to automatically shut down transfer pumps when the tank reaches full capacity.

- *Valve labeling:* Valves will be clearly tagged or labeled to reduce the potential for human error.

- *Inspections:* Visual inspections of the gasoline pump will be conducted on a daily basis. Areas to be inspected include pump foundations and hose connections.

- *Cleaning:* Vacuum and pump systems will be used at the facility to collect both wet and dry materials in material handling areas and work areas.

**Employee training.**    Employee training programs will inform personnel at all levels of responsibility of the components and goals of the SWPPP. Training will address each component of the pollution prevention plan, including how and why tasks are to be implemented.

Topics will include:

- Spill prevention and response
- Good housekeeping
- Material management practices

Spill prevention and response procedures will be discussed in the training program in order to ensure that all plant employees, not just those on the spill response teams, know what to do if a spill occurs. The following measures will be addressed:

- Identifying potential spill areas and drainage routes, including information on past spills and causes
- Posting warning signs in spill areas with emergency contacts and telephone numbers
- Specifying material handling procedures and storage requirements
- Introducing the Spill Response Coordinator and her or his team
- Drilling on spill cleanup procedures
- Posting the locations of spill cleanup equipment and the persons responsible for operating the equipment

On-site contractors and temporary personnel also will be informed of the plant operations and design features in order to help prevent accidental discharges or spills.

Facility personnel will also be taught how to maintain a clean, orderly work environment. These points will be emphasized in the good housekeeping portion of the training program:

- Require regular sweeping.
- Promptly clean up spilled materials to prevent polluted runoff.
- Identify places where brooms, vacuums, sorbents, foams, neutralizing agents, and other good housekeeping and spill response equipment are located.
- Display signs reminding employees of the importance and procedures of good housekeeping.
- Discuss updated procedures, and report on the progress of practicing good housekeeping at every meeting.
- Provide instruction on securing drums and containers and frequently checking for leaks and spills.
- Outline a regular schedule for housekeeping activities to verify that the job is being done.

Personnel will also be trained to handle and organize materials stored on site. This training will help prevent spills and injury to employees as well as reduce wastes due to overstocking. These points will be emphasized in the materials management practices portion of the training program:

- Neatly organize materials for storage.
- Identify all toxic and hazardous substances stored, handled, and produced on site.
- Discuss handling procedures for these materials.
- Tell employees to use the oldest materials first.
- Explain recycling practices.
- Demonstrate how valves are tightly closed and how drums should be sealed.
- Show how to fuel vehicles, and avoid topping off.

Training materials to be included in the facilities training program include the following:

- Employee handbooks
- Films and slide presentations
- Drills
- Routine employee meetings
- Bulletin boards
- Suggestion boxes
- Newsletters
- Environmental excellence awards or other employee incentive programs

Employees at the facility will attend a storm water pollution prevention training course before the effective date of this SWPPP. Refresher courses will be held every 6 months thereafter. Employees hired after the initial storm water pollution prevention course will receive complete training before they begin their new duties at the facility.

**Pollutant source control measures**

**Erosion control.**   The facility is almost completely paved, with small vegetated areas. Erosion is not expected to be a problem.

**Containment and diversion.**   Containment and diversion measures will be implemented at the facility to reduce the amount of pollutants generated. These practices will include:

- *Covering activities:* Used automobile batteries, petroleum products or solvents containers, or any other potential pollutant sources will be stored in covered areas while they wait to be transported off site to recycling facilities or disposal areas.

- *Dust control:* Paved areas of the site will be swept regularly to remove particulate matter that could potentially elevate suspended-solids levels in storm water runoff.

- *Diversion measures:* Engine-cleaning operations will take place inside the bus wash bay so that greases, oils, fluids, and metal fragments will be drained into the sanitary sewer system and then through the oil-water separator and sediment trap before the sewer discharge reaches the main system.

### Storm water recycling and treatment measures

Due to the containment and diversion and exposure minimization practices being implemented at the facility, no storm water treatment practices will be implemented at this time. If future site inspections indicate that additional practices or measures need to be implemented to reduce pollutant loads in storm water runoff, storm water treatment measures may be implemented.

### Record keeping and internal reporting procedures

Keeping records of and reporting events that occur on site are an effective way of tracking the progress of pollution prevention efforts and waste minimization. Analyzing records of past spills, e.g., can provide information useful for developing improved best management practices to prevent future spills of the same kind. Record keeping and internal reporting represent good operating practices because they can increase the efficiency of the facility and the effectiveness of BMPs.

All records will be kept up to date with respect to the following:

- The correct name and address of the facility
- The correct name and location of receiving waters
- The number and location of discharge points

- The number of vehicles maintained and/or stored at the site
- Any other operations performed at the site

Since no storm water sampling is anticipated for this site, records will be retained for 1 year after coverage until the permit expires. If storm water sampling is performed, sampling reports will be retained for 6 years after the date of sampling.

**Public access.**   Despite the fact that the SWPPP and associated reports are not necessarily required to be submitted with the NOI, these documents are considered to be reports according to Section 308(b) of the Clean Water Act, and therefore they are available to the public. The permittee, however, may claim certain parts of the SWPPP as confidential according to regulations in 40 CFR part 2. These regulations state that records which contain trade secrets may be claimed as confidential.

**Spills, leaks, and other discharges.**   A record-keeping system will be established for documenting spills, leaks, and other discharges, including discharges of hazardous substances in reportable quantities. Reports of incidents and follow-up information on the results of inspections and reported spills, leaks, or other discharges will be recorded and maintained.

Records will include the following, as appropriate:

- The date and time of the incident
- Volume spilled
- Weather conditions
- Duration of the incident
- Cause of the incident
- Environmental problems
- Response procedures
- Parties notified
- Recommended revisions of the BMPs program
- Operating procedures
- Equipment needed to prevent recurrence
- Formal written reports (and documentation of all reports called in to the National Response Center in the event of a reportable-quantity discharge)
- A list of the procedures for notifying the appropriate plant personnel and the names and telephone numbers of responsible employees

**Inspections and maintenance activities.**  A log of all inspections and of all maintenance activities, such as the cleaning of oil-water separators or filter systems, will be maintained to allow evaluation of the effectiveness of the program, equipment, and operation. Inspection records will note:

- When inspections were done
- Who conducted the inspection
- What areas were inspected
- What problems were found
- Steps taken to correct any problems, including who has been notified

**Changes to plan.**  This plan will be amended whenever there is a change in design, construction, operation, or maintenance which may impact the potential for pollutants to be discharged or if the SWPPP proves to be ineffective in controlling the discharge of pollutants. The amended plan will be kept at the site along with the original.

### Implementation schedule for pollution measures and controls

All controls or practices identified in this plan will be implemented no later than October 1, 1993, the effective date of this plan.

### Comprehensive Site Compliance Evaluation

A comprehensive site inspection will be conducted annually. The following steps will be completed in connection with the annual inspection:

- *SWPPP review:* Review the SWPPP, and draw up a list of those items which are part of material handling, storage, and transfer areas covered by the plan.
- *Materials review:* Verify the list of equipment and materials in these areas covered in the plan.
- *Operations review:* Review facility operations for the past year to determine if any more areas should be included in the original plan or any existing areas were modified so as to require plan modification. Change the plan as appropriate.
- *Drainage area inspection:* Inspect storm water drainage areas for evidence of pollutants entering the drainage system.

- ***Source reduction measures:*** Evaluate the effectiveness of measures to reduce pollutant loadings, and decide whether additional measures are needed.

- ***Source control measures:*** Observe structural measures, sediment controls, and other storm water BMPs to ensure proper operation.

- ***Equipment review:*** Inspect any equipment needed to implement the plan, such as spill response equipment.

- ***Plan revision:*** Revise the plan as needed within 2 weeks of inspection (potential pollutant source description and description of measures and controls).

- ***Plan implementation:*** Implement any necessary changes in a timely manner, but within 12 weeks of the inspection.

- ***Inspection report*:** Prepare a report summarizing inspection results and follow-up actions, the date of inspection, and personnel who conducted the inspection.

- ***Certification:*** Document all incidents of noncompliance in the inspection report. Where there are no incidents of noncompliance, the inspection report must contain a certification that the facility is in compliance with the plan. Figure C.5 contains a certification form for this purpose.

- ***Record keeping:*** Sign the report and keep it with the plan.

The inspection supervisor and inspection conductor will be responsible for the comprehensive site inspections.

A copy of the Annual Comprehensive Site Compliance Evaluation worksheet will be completed and filed on site. The worksheet will be signed by an authorized signatory authority.

### EPCRA Section 313 Water Priority Chemicals

The EPA general permit has special requirements concerning the storage and handling of water priority chemicals identified under section 313 of the Emergency Planning and Community Right-to-Know Act (EPCRA) of 1986.

#### EPCRA section 313 water priority chemicals on site

EPCRA section 313 water priority chemicals found on site are located inside the bus maintenance shop and in the underground storage tank near the east end of the property. EPCRA section 313 water priority chemicals can be found in the following (p. 399):

---

**ANNUAL CERTIFICATION OF COMPLIANCE**

---

This certification is completed by an authorized signatory after each annual site compliance evaluation. It indicates that the Storm Water Pollution Prevention Plan was evaluated as part of an inspection, is adequate for control of facility storm water discharges, and that the facility is in compliance with the Plan. If changes to the Plan or the site are necessary as a result of the inspection, these changes should be performed before this certification is completed.

---

I certify under penalty of law that this document and all attachments were prepared under my direction or supervision in accordance with a system designed to assure that qualified personnel properly gathered and evaluated the information submitted. Based on my inquiry of the person or persons who manage the system, or those persons directly responsible for gathering the information, the information submitted is, to the best of my knowledge and belief, true, accurate, and complete. I am aware that there are significant penalties for submitting false information, including the possibility of fine and imprisonment for knowing violations.

---

Signed: _____

Name: _____

Title: _____

Company: _____

Address: _____

Telephone: _____

Date: _____

**Figure C.5** Certification of comprehensive site compliance evaluation.

| Unleaded gasoline | Spray lubricants |
|---|---|
| Spray paints | Carburetor cleaner |
| Floor adhesives | Brake cleaner |
| Fuel additives | Welding rods |

Table C.3 lists each EPCRA section 313 water priority chemical, along with the CAS reference number, the substances which contain the chemical, the container used to store each substance, and the reportable quantity (RQ) amount of each chemical.

All substances containing water priority pollutants are stored and used in covered areas, which prevents the substances from being exposed to precipitation and storm runoff.

**Special requirements for EPCRA section 313
water priority chemicals**

Employees and contractor personnel who work in areas where EPCRA section 313 water priority chemicals are used or stored will be trained in the following areas at least once per year:

**TABLE C.3   EPCRA Section 313 Water Priority Chemicals on Site**

| Common name | CAS | Ingredient of: | Container | Reportable quantity, lb |
|---|---|---|---|---|
| Benzene | 71432 | Unleaded gasoline | Underground storage tank (UST) | 10 |
| Toluene | 108883 | Unleaded gasoline<br>Krylon spray paint<br>Silaprene adhesive sealant<br>Reactive polymer adhesive<br>Bumper paint | UST<br>Aerosol cans<br>Tubes<br>1-gal cans<br>Aerosol cans | 1000 |
| Xylene | 1330207 | Unleaded gasoline<br>Diesel fuel additive<br>Krylon spray paint<br>DZL fuel additive<br>Carburetor cleaner | UST<br>55-gal drums<br>Aerosol cans<br>55-gal drums<br>½-gal cans | 1000 |
| 1,1,1-Trichloro-ethane | 71556 | ZEP 45 spray lubricant<br>Safety-Kleen brake cleaner<br>SR-P Rusty E-Z spray | Aerosol cans<br>Aerosol cans<br>Aerosol cans | 1000 |
| Chromium | 7440473 | X-Tract alloy electrode | | 5000 |
| Nickel | 7440020 | X-Tract alloy electrode | | 100 |

- Identification of water priority chemicals used at the site
- Preventive measures, including spill prevention and response techniques
- Pollution control laws and regulations
- The facility's SWPPP
- Features and operations of the facility which are designed to minimize discharges of section 313 water priority chemicals, particularly spill prevention procedures

Spray painting and application of the rust penetrant will be done indoors to prevent overspray from potentially polluting storm runoff.

# D

# Example of an SWPPP
# for a Construction Site

## Project Name and Location

**Name:**      North Wayside Drive Improvements (Ley Road to Tidwell Road)

**Location:**    Northeast side, Houston, Texas

**Latitude:**    29° 50' 28"

**Longitude:**  95° 17' 20"

## Operator Names and Addresses

Table D.1 lists the operators of the project, including the project owner and the general contractor. Figure D.1 illustrates the certification which must be completed by the operators.

TABLE D.1   Operator Names and Addresses

| Owner | General contractor |
| --- | --- |
| City of Houston P.O. Box 1562 Houston, TX 77251 | |

---

*Note:* This is an actual draft plan prepared by Dodson & Associates, Inc., for the city of Houston, Texas.

---

### CERTIFICATION OF STORM WATER POLLUTION PREVENTION PLAN

**Project:  North Wayside Drive Construction, Houston, TX**

This certification must be completed by an authorized signatory of each operator (generally the Owner and the General Contractor) before the effective date of the Plan.

---

I certify under penalty of law that this document and all attachments were prepared under my direction or supervision in accordance with a system designed to assure that qualified personnel properly gathered and evaluated the information submitted. Based on my inquiry of the person or persons who manage the system, or those persons directly responsible for gathering the information, the information submitted is, to the best of my knowledge and belief, true, accurate, and complete. I am aware that there are significant penalties for submitting false information, including the possibility of fine and imprisonment for knowing violations.

---

Signed:      _____

Name:        _____

Title:       _____

Company:     _____

Address:     _____

Telephone:   _____

Date:        _____

**Figure D.1**  Certification of SWPPP.

---

### CONTRACTOR/SUB-CONTRACTOR CERTIFICATION

Project: **North Wayside Drive Construction, Houston, TX**

This certification is to be completed by the general contractor and each sub-contractor involved in any on-site activities related to the construction.

---

I certify under penalty of law that I understand the terms and conditions of the general National Pollutant Discharge Elimination System (NPDES) permit that authorizes the storm water discharges associated with industrial activity from the construction site identified as part of this certification.

---

**Signed:** _____

**Name:** _____

**Title:** _____

**Company:** _____

**Address:** _____

**Telephone:** _____

**Date:** _____

**Figure D.2**   Contractor and subcontractor certification form.

## Contractor Names and Addresses

The following list includes all subcontractors working on the project site at any time. The general contractor and all subcontractors must sign the certification included as Fig. D.2.

Subcontractor: _____

_____

_____

Subcontractor: _____

_____

_____

Subcontractor: _____

_____

_____

Subcontractor: _____

_____

_____

## Project Description

The project consists of roadway improvements to North Wayside Drive and related improvements to underground utilities. North Wayside Drive is a major thoroughfare located on the northeast side of Houston's central business district. The portion of North Wayside Drive included in this project extends from Ley Road to Tidwell Road. The overall length of the roadway to be improved is approximately 6000 lin ft. An additional 4500 lin ft of pavement is included in the project scope for connections to various intersecting streets. Figures D.3 through D.5 illustrate the site layout.[1]

---

[1] In the original SWPPP, Figs. D.3 through D.5 were included on a single sheet of the construction drawings for the project. The construction drawings also contained standard details of sediment and erosion control measures and storm water control measures.

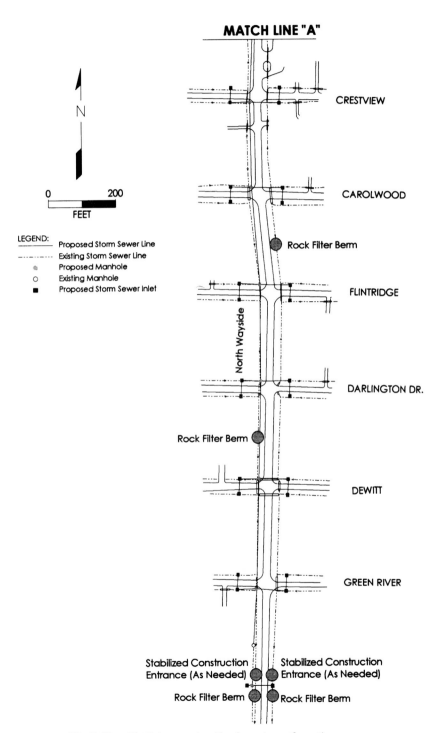

**Figure D.3**  North Wayside Drive construction layout, south section.

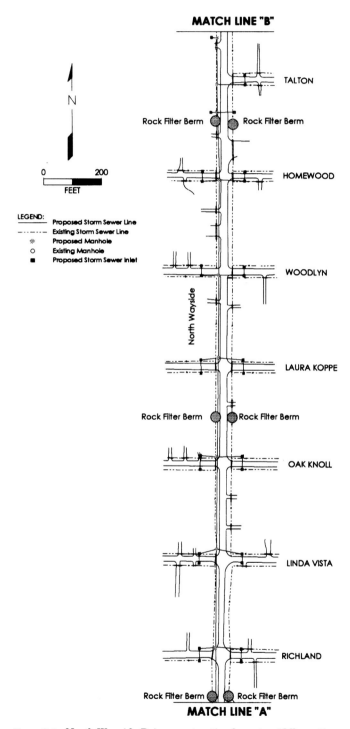

**Figure D.4** North Wayside Drive construction layout, middle section.

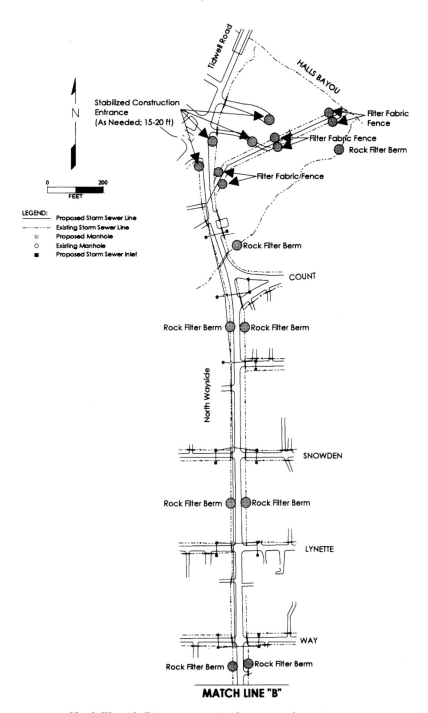

**Figure D.5**  North Wayside Drive construction layout, north section.

The existing roadway in the project area consists of two asphaltic concrete paved lanes running north and south. The following roads either intersect or merge with North Wayside Drive within the project limits:

| | |
|---|---|
| Green River | Laura Koppe |
| Dewitt | Woodlyn |
| Darlington | Homewood |
| Flintridge | Talton |
| Carolwood | Way |
| Crestview | Lynette |
| Richland | Snowden |
| Linda Vista | Record |
| Oak Knoll | Count |

Existing land use in the area is a combination of residential and small business development. Storm water runoff is conveyed through drainage ditches; there are no major storm sewers in the area.

The proposed improvement project calls for reconstruction and widening of the two-lane roadway to a four-lane curb and gutter section with median. The project also includes the establishment of transitions from connecting roadways to the four-lane curb and gutter street and the construction of sidewalks along both sides of the roadway.

In addition to the proposed roadway improvements, a 12-in water main and new storm sewer conduit will be installed along the west side of North Wayside Drive. All construction activities related to these additional projects will be completed before commencement of the roadway improvements.

### Estimated total site area and total disturbed area

The overall area in which the proposed construction activities will take place covers a total of approximately 19 acres. The total disturbed area within the site is estimated to be 19 acres.

### Development

The area along North Wayside Drive between Ley Road and Tidwell Road is mostly developed. The developed areas consist mainly of single-family residences. Small business establishments, such as gas stations, car washes, convenience stores, and lounges, are sparse within the project area.

### Soil description

The soils along the project alignment generally consist of clayey sand or sandy clay to a depth of 2 ft. This is underlaid by a layer of sandy clay to a depth of 12 to 17 ft, which generally contains sand seams and calcareous nodules, ferrous nodules, or ferrous oxide. Below the sandy clay is a silty sand layer that is generally underlaid by a layer of clay.

### Runoff coefficient

The weighted runoff coefficient $C$ for the completed project, including residential and vacant areas, is determined to be 0.70.

### Site map

Figures D.3 through D.5 illustrate the site layout.

### Name of receiving water

The storm water collection system for North Wayside Drive eventually discharges into Halls Bayou, a tributary of Greens Bayou. Greens Bayou discharges into the Houston Ship Channel, which drains into Galveston Bay on the Gulf of Mexico.

### Extent of wetlands

There are no existing wetlands at the site.

## Sequence of Major Activities

The project is scheduled to begin in March 1994. Approximately 10 months will be required to complete the proposed improvements. A copy of the roadway construction phasing plan will be posted at the construction office. The project will be constructed in three major phases:

- Underground utilities and southbound roadway
- Northbound roadway
- Other project details

The following sections describe the sequence of activities in each phase.

## Phase 1: Underground utilities and southbound roadway

- *Construct temporary paving:* Temporary asphalt paving will be constructed at the north and south ends of the project. Two-way traffic will remain on the existing roadway.

- *Relocate existing underground utilities:* Utilities requiring removal, relocation, or adjustments by others will be completed prior to or during this phase.

- *Construct new underground utilities:* New waterline and new sanitary sewer interceptor line including all main lines, laterals, and connections will be installed and in operation prior to construction of the storm sewer main line.

- *Construct storm sewer:* The storm sewer main line and all inlets and laterals will be installed on the west side of the project. Stubouts will be provided for all storm sewer laterals on the east side of the project. Boring and jacking will be required for the main line where it crosses the existing roadway at the north end of the project.

- *Construct southbound roadway:* Southbound roadway pavement will be constructed including alternating intersections. At no time shall the contractor close two adjacent intersections. Temporary shell pavement will be placed to connect new roadway to existing roadway at completed intersections.

- *Complete southbound intersections:* Remaining southbound roadway intersections will be constructed including temporary shell pavement for connection to the existing roadway.

- *Complete temporary striping:* Temporary removable dashed yellow centerline striping will be placed on completed roadway for use in phase 2.

## Phase 2: Northbound roadway

- *Detour traffic to new southbound roadway:* Traffic will be detoured at the north and south ends of the project to provide for two-way traffic on the newly constructed southbound roadway pavement.

- *Complete storm sewer:* The remaining storm sewer inlets and laterals will be installed.

- *Construct northbound roadway:* Northbound roadway pavement and alternating intersections will be constructed. The intersections for the five deadend cross streets cannot be closed and must be constructed in two steps.

- *Complete northbound intersections:* Remaining northbound roadway intersections will be constructed including temporary shell pavement for connection between roadways.
- *Adjust manhole covers:* All existing manhole covers will be adjusted to match the new roadway grade.

### Phase 3: Complete median openings and other details

- *Close inside lanes:* Traffic will be split on the new roadways with the inside lanes closed for phase 3 construction.
- *Complete median openings:* Median openings will be alternately closed to complete construction on the remaining portions of the intersections.
- *Complete other details:* Miscellaneous roadway items such as sidewalks, driveways, pavement markings, signs, seeding, and temporary detour removal will be completed.

## Pollution Controls

### Stabilization practices

Major erosion and sediment controls are shown on Figs. D.3 through D.5. Stabilization practices will include:

- *Vehicle areas:* Stabilization of construction road access, staging, and parking areas using coarse aggregate
- *Mulching:* Mulching of rights-of-way within 14 days if the interim period between construction phases is longer than 21 days
- *Surface roughening:* Texturing of soil surfaces to reduce sheet flow and improve surface water impoundment
- *Sod stabilization:* Stabilizing of disturbed land between the property line and the gutter with sod to minimize erosion and sediment upon completion of pavement sections
- *Permanent vegetation:* Sodding and/or seeding of **all** disturbed areas upon completion of pavement work

### Structural practices

Structural control locations are illustrated in Figs. D.3 through D.5. Structural controls that will be used during construction activities include:

- *Earth stockpiles:* Filter fabric fences or straw bales around temporary earth stockpiles while they are in use.

- *Storm sewer inlets:* Straw bales or filter fabric fence around storm sewer inlets until all disturbed areas surrounding the inlets are stabilized.

- *Trench excavation:* Trench excavation spoils not immediately hauled off will be backfilled into the trenches in a continuous operation. Excavated material required for backfilling will be placed next to the trenches, but no closer than half the depth of the trench, for safety reasons.

### Sequence of major erosion and sediment control activities

The construction will proceed in segments. The stabilized construction access, staging, and parking areas will be constructed first. After construction of the stabilized access, staging, and parking area, the following pollution prevention controls and measures will be implemented:

- *General controls:* Straw bale or rock filter berms will be constructed in predetermined locations (see Figs. D.3 through D.5).

- *Storm sewer inlets:* Straw bales or filter fabric fence will be used around storm sewer inlets until the area surrounding the inlets is stabilized (i.e., paved, sodded, etc.).

- *Earth stockpiles:* Filter fabric fences or straw bales will be placed around earth stockpiles immediately upon creation of each stockpile and will not be removed until the earth stockpile has been completely eliminated.

### Storm water management

Surface roughening will be used for velocity dissipation as a temporary erosion control and storm water management practice. Surface roughening reduces the speed of runoff, increases infiltration, and traps sediment.

Due to site restrictions, detention and retention systems for storm water treatment are not attainable. The vegetated median strips and sodded landscaping strips along walkways will be used to the extent practicable for flow attenuation purposes.

### Other controls

**Off-site vehicle tracking.**   A stabilized construction entrance will be provided to help reduce vehicle tracking of sediments. The paved streets adjacent to the site will be swept or scraped daily to remove any excess mud, dirt, or rock tracked from the construction area. A source of fresh water for washing sediment from trucks, especially during periods of wet weather, may be provided in order to minimize the amount of street sweeping and scraping required. Any wash water resulting from this operation will be directed into a sediment trap.

**Waste materials.**   All trash and construction debris from the site will be hauled to an approved landfill. No construction waste material will be buried on the site. All personnel will receive instructions regarding the correct procedure for waste disposal. Notices describing these practices will be posted in the construction office. The site superintendent will be responsible for seeing that these procedures are followed. Employee waste and other loose materials will be collected so as to prevent the release of floatables during runoff events.

**Hazardous waste.**   No hazardous waste is expected to be generated or encountered in this project. In the event that hazardous waste is encountered, all hazardous waste materials will be disposed of in the manner specified by local or state regulation or by the manufacturer. The site superintendent will be responsible for seeing that these practices are followed.

**Sanitary waste.**   Portable sanitary units will be provided for use by all workers throughout the life of the project. All sanitary waste will be regularly collected from the portable units by a licensed sanitary waste management contractor.

### Demonstration of compliance with state or local plans

The proposed project will be in compliance with applicable state and local waste disposal, sanitary sewer, and paving regulations.

## Maintenance

To maintain the erosion and sediment controls, the following procedures will be performed:

- *Sediment capture devices:* Sediment will be removed from the upstream or upslope side of the filter fabric fences, straw bale barriers, or other devices, when the depth of accumulated sediment reaches about one-third the height of the structure.

- *Storm sewer inlets:* Any sediment in the storm sewer inlets will be removed and disposed of properly.

- *Temporary controls:* All temporary controls will be removed after the disturbed areas have been stabilized.

Sediment that is removed from structural barriers either will be hauled off the site and disposed of properly or will be used as backfill. Sediment temporarily stockpiled on site will be placed in such areas and in such manner as to minimize washoff of sediments back into the local drainage system. Berms, filter fabric fencing, straw bale barriers, and polyethylene or polypropylene covers are measures which may be utilized in minimizing washoff.

### Inspection Procedures

Inspections will be conducted by the responsible person(s) at least once every 7 calendar days and within 24 h after each storm event producing 0.5 in of rainfall or greater. Areas that have been reseeded will be inspected regularly after seed germination to ensure complete coverage of exposed areas.

The contractor will designate a qualified person or persons to perform the following inspections:

- *Stabilization measures:* Disturbed areas and areas used for storage of materials that are exposed to precipitation will be inspected for evidence of, or the potential for, pollutants entering the drainage system. After a portion of the site is finally stabilized, inspections will be conducted at least once every month throughout the life of the project. Figure D.6 shows the inspection form to be used for stabilization measures.

- *Structural controls:* Filter fabric fences, straw bale barriers, and all other erosion and sediment control measures identified in the plan will be inspected regularly for proper positioning, anchoring, and effectiveness in trapping sediments. Sediment will be removed from the upstream or upslope side of the filter fabric. Figure D.7 shows the inspection form to be used for stabilization measures.

- *Discharge points:* Discharge points or locations will be inspected to determine whether erosion control measures are effective in preventing significant amounts of pollutants from entering receiving waters.

- *Construction entrances:* Locations where vehicles enter or exit the site will be inspected for evidence of off-site sediment tracking.

INSPECTION REPORT FORM FOR STABILIZATION MEASURES

INSPECTOR: _____ DATE: _____

DAYS SINCE LAST RAINFALL: _____ AMOUNT OF LAST RAINFALL: _____ INCHES

| AREA | DATE LAST DISTURBED | DATE OF NEXT DISTURBANCE | STABILIZED? | STABILIZED WITH | CONDITION |
|------|---------------------|--------------------------|-------------|-----------------|-----------|
|  |  |  |  |  |  |
|  |  |  |  |  |  |
|  |  |  |  |  |  |
|  |  |  |  |  |  |
|  |  |  |  |  |  |
|  |  |  |  |  |  |
|  |  |  |  |  |  |
|  |  |  |  |  |  |
|  |  |  |  |  |  |
|  |  |  |  |  |  |

STABILIZATION REQUIRED:

_____

_____

_____

_____

_____

_____

_____

TO BE PERFORMED BY:_____ ON OR BEFORE:_____

Figure D.6  Inspection form for stabilization measures.

INSPECTION FORM FOR STRUCTURAL CONTROLS

INSPECTOR: _____ DATE: _____

DAYS SINCE LAST RAINFALL: _____ AMOUNT OF LAST RAINFALL: _____ INCHES

| LOCATION OF CONTROL | IN PLACE? | CONDITION | SEDIMENT DEPTH | WASHED OUT OR OVERTOPPED? |
|---|---|---|---|---|
|  |  |  |  |  |
|  |  |  |  |  |
|  |  |  |  |  |
|  |  |  |  |  |
|  |  |  |  |  |
|  |  |  |  |  |
|  |  |  |  |  |
|  |  |  |  |  |
|  |  |  |  |  |
|  |  |  |  |  |

MAINTENANCE REQUIRED:

_____

_____

_____

_____

_____

_____

_____

TO BE PERFORMED BY:_____ ON OR BEFORE:_____

Figure D.7  Inspection form for structural controls.

### Revisions to the SWPPP

Based on the results of the inspection, the site description and control measures of this pollution prevention plan will be revised as appropriate, but in no case later than 7 calendar days following the inspection. Figure D.8 shows the form to be used to record necessary changes to the SWPPP.

### Inspection report summary

A report summarizing the scope of each inspection, name(s) and qualifications of personnel making the inspection, date(s) of the inspection, major observations relating to the implementation of the SWPPP, and actions taken to revise the plan will be completed and retained as part of the SWPPP for at least 3 years from the date that the site is finally stabilized. Figure D.9 shows the form to be used for certification of the inspection report. The report will be signed by one of the following persons:

- The principal executive officer or ranking elected official of the municipality or agency submitting the SWPPP
- A duly authorized representative of the principal executive officer or ranking elected official

### Non-Storm-Water Discharges

It is expected that the following non-storm-water discharges will occur at the site during the construction period:

- *Dewatering discharges:* Water pumped from the construction area during dewatering operations (this may or may not be storm water)
- *Pressure test water:* Water used to pressure-test the potable water system
- *Disinfectant water:* Water used to disinfect the potable water system

Dewatering discharges will be done in such a manner as to avoid erosion problems and will pass through a portable sediment tank. If they are released to surface waters, pressure-test water and disinfectant water will be impounded for a sufficient period to allow chlorine to aerate out.

REPORT FORM FOR CHANGES IN POLLUTION PREVENTION PLAN

INSPECTOR: _____ DATE: _____

SUMMARY OF REQUIRED CHANGES:

_____

_____

_____

_____

_____

_____

_____

_____

_____

_____

_____

REASON(S) FOR CHANGES:

_____

_____

_____

_____

_____

_____

_____

_____

_____

INSPECTOR'S SIGNATURE: _____ DATE: _____

Figure D.8   Report form for changes in the SWPPP.

INSPECTION CERTIFICATION FORM

Project:  North Wayside Drive, Houston, TX

This certification must be completed after each inspection to sig-
nify that the inspection has been properly completed and the site has
been found to be in compliance with the Storm Water Pollution Prevention
Plan.

I certify under penalty of law that this document and all attachments
were prepared under my direction or supervision in accordance with a
system designed to assure that qualified personnel properly gathered and
evaluated the information submitted. Based on my inquiry of the person
or persons who manage the system, or those persons directly responsible
for gathering the information, the information submitted is, to the best
of my knowledge and belief, true, accurate, and complete. I am aware
that there are significant penalties for submitting false information,
including the possibility of fine and imprisonment for knowing violations.

Signed: _____

Name: _____

Title: _____

Company: _____

Address: _____

Telephone: _____

Date: _____

**Figure D.9**   Inspection certification form.

## Significant-Materials Inventory

Significant materials expected to be found at the construction site include:

- Lime (trucked onto the site for soil stabilization purposes)
- Concrete mix (trucked to the site for roadway construction)
- Steel reinforcing bars and related materials
- Lumber
- Diesel fuel and lubricating oils
- Reinforced-concrete pipe
- Ductile iron pipe
- Steel pipe
- Paints
- Fertilizers

This list of significant materials may be reduced or expanded once a contractor has been chosen and the materials to be used have been specified. If fewer, or additional, materials are required, the SWPPP will be amended to reflect these changes.

## Spill Prevention and Response Procedures

Spill prevention and response include good housekeeping as well as specific practices for certain products and established procedures for responding to spills.

### Good housekeeping

The following good housekeeping practices will be followed on site during the construction project.

- ***Minimize materials:*** An effort will be made to store only enough material required to do the job.
- ***Storage:*** All materials stored on site will be stored in a neat, orderly manner in their appropriate containers in a covered area. If storage in a covered area is not possible, the materials will be covered with polyethylene or polypropylene sheeting to protect them from the elements.
- ***Labeling:*** Products will be kept in their original containers with the original manufacturer's label affixed to each container.

- *Mixing:* Substances will not be mixed with one another unless this is recommended by the manufacturer.

- *Disposal:* Whenever possible, all of a product will be used prior to disposal of the container. Manufacturers' recommendations for proper use and disposal will be followed.

- *Inspections:* The site superintendent will inspect the site daily to ensure proper use and disposal of materials on site.

- *Spoil materials:* Any excavated earth that will not be used for fill material and all demolished pavement will be hauled off site immediately and will be disposed of properly.

### Product-specific practices

**Petroleum products.**    All on-site vehicles will be monitored for leaks and will receive regular preventive maintenance to reduce the chance of leakage. If petroleum products will be present at the site, they will be stored in tightly sealed containers which are clearly labeled. Any asphalt substances used on site will be applied according to the manufacturer's recommendations.

**Concrete trucks.**    Concrete trucks will not be allowed to wash out or discharge surplus concrete or drum wash water at the site.

**Paints.**    All containers will be tightly sealed and stored when not required for use. Excess paint will not be poured into the storm sewer system but will be properly disposed of according to manufacturers' instructions or state and local regulations.

**Fertilizers.**    Fertilizers will be applied only in the minimum amounts recommended by the manufacturer. Once applied, fertilizer will be worked into the soil to limit exposure to storm water. The fertilizer will be stored in a covered area, and any partially used bags will be transferred to a sealable plastic bin to avoid spills.

### Spill control and response practices

A spill prevention and response team will be designated by the owner or the site superintendent. In addition, the following practices will be followed for spill cleanup:

- *Information:* Manufacturers' recommended methods for spill cleanup will be clearly posted, and site personnel will be made aware of the procedures and location of the information and cleanup supplies.

- *Equipment:* Materials and equipment necessary for spill cleanup will be present on the site at all times. Equipment and materials will include but not be limited to brooms, shovels, rags, gloves, goggles, absorbent materials (sand, sawdust, etc.), and plastic or metal trash containers specifically designed for this purpose. The materials and equipment necessary for spill cleanup will be dependent upon the nature and quantity of the material stored on site.

- *Response:* All spills will be cleaned up immediately upon discovery.

- *Safety:* The spill area will be kept well ventilated, and personnel will wear appropriate protective clothing to prevent injury from contact with hazardous substances.

- *Reporting:* Spills of toxic or hazardous material (if present on site) will be reported to the appropriate state or local government agency, regardless of the spill's size.

- *Record keeping:* The spill prevention plan will be modified to include measures to prevent this type of spill from recurring as well as improved methods for cleaning up any future spills. A description of each spill, what caused it, and the cleanup measures used will be kept with the plan.

## Plan Location and Public Access

The SWPPP is not submitted to the EPA for review unless requested. The SWPPP must be available at the construction site from the date of project initiation to the date of final stabilization. The SWPPP and all reports required by the permit must be retained for at least 3 years from the date on which the site is finally stabilized.

Despite the fact that the SWPPP and associated reports are not necessarily required to be submitted with the Notice of Intent, these documents are considered to be reports according to section 308(b) of the Clean Water Act and therefore are available to the public. The permittee, however, may claim certain parts of the SWPPP as confidential according to regulations in 40 CFR part 2. These regulations state that records which contain trade secrets may be claimed as confidential.

# Index

## ABOUT THE AUTHOR

Roy D. Dodson is the president of Dodson & Associates, Inc. in Houston, Texas—a leading supplier of engineering services and computer software for storm water applications. He is a registered professional engineer in the states of Texas and Louisiana, and is a certified professional hydrologist by the American Institute of Hydrology. In addition to his work as a consultant, Mr. Dodson leads training seminars throughout the United States and is the author of several computer programs relating to hydrology and hydraulics.